Scholarly analysis of the relative merits of presidential and parliamentary democracy has emphasized the weaknesses of presidential systems owing to the separation of power between the executive and assembly, which often leads to conflict between the two. Shugart and Carey, by contrast, focus on the potential strengths of presidential systems. They identify a number of alternative ways of balancing constitutional powers between the branches, demonstrating that some forms of presidentialism are more likely than others to generate conflict between the branches.

They also evaluate the role of electoral rules in presidential systems, demonstrating that the ways in which presidents and assemblies are elected play a critical role in determining the shape of the party system, the political agenda, and the prospects for cooperation and conflict between presidents and assemblies.

A typology of presidential systems is developed, including two hybrid forms defined by the authors as premier-presidentialism and president-parliamentarianism, and these various forms are evaluated according to a set of characteristics that determine the efficiency and effectiveness of governance. These characteristics include the manner in which the president is elected, the legislative powers of the president, the authority of the president over the cabinet, the timing of presidential and assembly elections in relation to one another, and the system of representation.

# PRESIDENTS AND ASSEMBLIES

# PRESIDENTS AND ASSEMBLIES

## CONSTITUTIONAL DESIGN AND ELECTORAL DYNAMICS

MATTHEW SOBERG SHUGART
and
JOHN M. CAREY

CAMBRIDGE
UNIVERSITY PRESS

CAMBRIDGE UNIVERSITY PRESS
Cambridge, New York, Melbourne, Madrid, Cape Town, Singapore, São Paulo, Delhi

Cambridge University Press
32 Avenue of the Americas, New York, NY 10013, USA

www.cambridge.org
Information on this title: www.cambridge.org/9780521419628

First published 1992
Reprinted 1994, 1997

A catalogue record for this publication is available from the British Library

Library of Congress Cataloging-in-Publication data

ISBN 978-0-521-41962-8 hardback
ISBN 978-0-521-42990-0 paperback

Transferred to digital printing 2004

To Merry Shugart
and
Mary E. and Robert J. Carey

# Contents

# Tables and figures

# Acknowledgments

The completion of this book was made simpler and more pleasant by the generous help of colleagues who offered their criticisms of all or part of the book. Shugart's involvement with questions of elections and electoral systems in presidential democracies originated in his Ph.D. dissertation, completed in 1988 at the University of California, Irvine. There, Rein Taagepera was the model of what a graduate student's mentor should be. His assistance and encouragement since the completion of the Ph.D. and his comments on this project have been a constant source of inspiration. Arend Lijphart, who also served on Shugart's graduate committee and later on Carey's, has offered cogent analyses and criticisms throughout. Many times we were compelled to rethink an argument as a result of exchanges with him.

Michael Coppedge, Gary Cox, and Scott Mainwaring offered detailed comments and criticisms that helped us sharpen many parts of the book. We also thank Bernard Grofman, Juan Linz, and Mathew McCubbins for comments and intellectual support.

Truly indispensable for both authors was the intellectual atmosphere fostered at the University of California, San Diego, by the faculties and graduate students in both the Graduate School of International Relations and Pacific Studies (IR/PS) and the Department of Political Science. In particular, the students of Shugart's seminar on Politics and Policy in Latin America in 1990 and 1991 deserve thanks both for serving as "guinea pigs" for many of the concepts developed in Chapters 8 and 9 and for proving that one really does learn from one's students! Special recognition is due to a few of them: Richard Rifkin, Michael Thies, and John Warren.

As with any project of this size, there were tasks that the authors were only too happy to delegate to others. Harold Colson of the IR/PS Library graciously handled many anxious requests for hard-to-get data and documents. We are indebted for excellent work in computer graphics, corrections in the text, and bibliographic assistance to several research assistants: Steve Bingham, Dan Nielson, Mary Reiter, Gail Sevrens, and Tony Westerling.

# 1

# Basic choices in democratic regime types

The 1980s were a time of growth in a subfield of political science that has come to be known as the "new institutionalism" (see March and Olsen 1984; Grofman 1987). Often drawing in a matter sometimes more, sometimes less formal, from microeconomic understandings of rational behavior and individual responses to incentive structures, this subfield has placed political, rather than social or economic or cultural, variables at the center of explanation for political outcomes. There is a renewed focus on the importance of political institutions in accounting for the success or failure of democracy. Recent advances of democracy in Central and Eastern Europe and other parts of the globe have given impetus to the study of designing constitutions and the consequences of institutional choice. Old, long unchallenged assumptions about the efficacy of presidentialism in Latin America have been seriously challenged in recent years. Mindful of the spirit of resurgent interest in constitutional design, we have launched this book as a treatise on how various institutional designs for representative democracies affect the ways in which the political process operates.

This book focuses on a set of regimes that, in our assessment, have received too little attention from comparativists. It deals primarily with systems in which there is an elected president. These regimes differ from the common parliamentary type in that there are two agents of the electorate: an assembly and a president. In a parliamentary system, there is only one, the assembly, with the executive being an agent of the assembly,[1] rather than of the voters directly. As this book shows, there are myriad ways to design constitutions that vary the relationship of the voters' two agents to one another, as well as to the electorate. Regimes with elected presidents vary in the ways in which the president may check, cajole,

---

1 For purposes of this book, we do not consider bicameralism to represent two agents of the electorate. In contemporary democracies, both chambers of the assembly are to serve the function of representation, although often the basis of representation differs according to the chamber. In parliamentary systems, ordinarily only the lower house has the power of confidence over the government, and in many cases the lower house may override objections of the upper house on legislation. Lijphart (1984) offers one of the most concise discussions of bicameralism.

confront, or simply submit to the assembly majority. We even find that some systems give the president so little power relative to the assembly that they are effectively parliamentary. We thus do not see a presidential regime as being the polar opposite of parliamentarism, as much of the literature implies; but the development of this point awaits future chapters. While this book is fundamentally about comparing systems with presidents, undertaking such a study requires starting with the dichotomy that most of the literature deals with: presidential versus parliamentary. These two forms are not only the two most discussed in the literature, especially in the polemics regarding the desirability of certain constitutional designs; they are also the two original types of democratic constitution. It was only later that many other regime types or hybrids emerged and gave us the broad range of regime types that we compare in this book.

In a parliamentary system, the executive is chosen by and may be removed by the elected assembly. In a presidential system, the process of forming the executive is institutionally distinct from the process of filling seats in the assembly, as both branches are popularly elected. In each of the other types and hybrids that we assess in this book, there is some combination of presidential and assembly authority over the composition of the executive. As we shall argue and make one of our principal themes, in none of the types is it easy to divorce the process of executive formation from the process of voters' choices for assembly representatives. Typically in parliamentary systems, even though it is only the assembly that comes before the electorate for votes, voters make their choices to a significant degree on the basis of what kinds of policies they want addressed by the executive. In presidential systems, too, there may be "coattails" from the presidential races that affect the vote for the assembly. Where the voting for the two branches is most clearly separated, as in some presidential institutional designs, often the lack of policy agreement between the executive and the assembly majority causes stress in the regime. These are among the principal trade-offs that we shall discuss as the book proceeds.

## THE PRESIDENTIAL–PARLIAMENTARY DICHOTOMY

For us, the authors, a primary factor motivating the decision to undertake this project was our observance of a sharp polemic on the subject of whether presidential or parliamentary democracy is the "better" form of representative government. Most of the scholarly literature on the subject comes out quite squarely behind parliamentarism as the preferred alternative. However, among practicing politicians, the message is getting through slowly, if at all. Nearly all new democracies in the 1970s and 1980s, and in 1990, have had elected presidents with varying degrees of political authority.

Among newer democracies, true parliamentarism remains largely a phenomenon of the former British Empire, as in transitions to democracies in the late 1980s and early 1990s in Pakistan and Nepal. Yet even in the British Commonwealth the appeal of presidentialism among elites has led to the replacement of parliamentary systems with presidential regimes in Guyana, Nigeria, and Zimbabwe, among others.

After the collapse of the Soviet bloc in Central and Eastern Europe, only in Czechoslovakia (and, very briefly, East Germany, before it united with West Germany) did the political elite initially opt for a pure parliamentary system with no popularly elected president. Encouraging for academic partisans of parliamentary democracy, the Hungarian electorate refused to endorse a powerful elected presidency in a referendum.

For the supporters of parliamentarism, the bad news is that no existing presidential system has ever changed to a parliamentary system, while several have made the reverse move. As of this writing, there was at least serious discussion of adopting regime types other than presidential in some Latin American countries, notably Brazil, where, as in Hungary, voters were expected to be given an opportunity to express themselves on the topic.

What we have, then, is a considerable divergence between a virtual academic consensus, on the one hand, and actual political practice, on the other. In the remainder of this introductory chapter, we seek to outline the very basic choices involved in the choice of either the presidential or the parliamentary form as well as sketch briefly the historical origins of these regime types. In so doing we shall be introducing two of the basic themes of the chapters that follow: (1) Especially in regimes with elected presidents, there are many institutional choices that matter besides the choice of what means to employ for the constitution of executive power; and (2) that, even where powers are formally separate, the processes of election to the two branches interact in ways that affect the functioning of democracy.

## *Assemblies and executives: constituting political power*

A major dilemma in democratic regimes concerns a divergence between what representative assemblies do best and what executives must do if democracy itself is to function well. Assemblies, or at least lower houses of assemblies, are intended to be representative of the population.[2] A typical

2 The common generic term "legislature" is often misleading. In many parliamentary regimes, most actual lawmaking takes place within the cabinet. Similarly, as we shall see in later chapters, the executive in presidential systems also has important legislative powers, more in some regimes than in others. Hence, instead of the term "legislature," we shall use the term "assembly" throughout this book. We believe this term more accurately reflects a common feature of democratic regimes: the existence of an institution in which elected representatives assemble for whatever constitutional function they may be granted. In cases in which that function is to sustain confidence in a government, we shall use the term "parliament." For presidential systems, in which executive power is separated from the assembly, we shall use the term "congress." We shall eschew the term "legislature" entirely.

democratic assembly is elected for the purpose of giving voice to the interests of localities or to the diversity of ideological or other partisan divisions
in the polity and society. That is, assemblies are ordinarily expected to be
parochial in nature. Executives, on the other hand, are charged with acting
to address policy questions that affect the broader interests of the nation,
as well as to articulate national goals.

*Geographic representation.* Historically, representative assemblies emerged
for the purpose of offering a link between the central authority and smaller
geographic subdivisions of the state. Typically a locality would elect one,
two, or slightly more members of the assembly by means of some variant of
plurality or majority rule.

  The definition of the basis of representation would change over time in
some systems, particularly those that adopted proportional representation
(PR). For the time being, however, we shall concern ourselves only with
the historical period in which the two basic regime types emerged, and we
emphasize that both did so in a context of assemblies constructed to represent localities.

*Parliamentary confidence.* Over a period of many decades and through a
process that will not directly concern us here, the principle of cabinet
responsibility to parliament developed in Britain. In Chapter 9 we review
this process in more detail. The important point here is that what was
originally the Crown's ministry (and in strictly formal terms remains so),
became a ministry subject to the confidence of a majority of the assembly.
Thus developed what would come to be known as parliamentary democracy, although it must not be forgotten that this system was not originally
"engineered." Rather, it emerged gradually, and to this day no specific
written constitution has been drafted in Britain. Modern parliamentarism
was born as a political system in which an assembly constructed to represent localities coexisted with a ministry that gradually shifted from the
control of the monarch to the control of the assembly itself. We shall return
below to the consequences that parliamentarism holds for the nature of
elections for and representation in the assembly. For now, let us turn to that
other means of constituting executive power that emerged early in the
development of democracy, presidentialism.

*Popular election of the executive.* Where and how did presidentialism
emerge? The answer takes us back to the U.S. Constitutional Convention,
which was the first instance of either type of regime's having been consciously "engineered." The Framers opted for neither the monarchical
form of government that the Revolution had been made against nor the
system of the short-lived Articles of Confederation, under which there was

no national executive. As possible methods of formation of the executive, they considered an executive elected by the Congress and one elected by direct popular vote before settling on the mechanism of the electoral college. They rejected one chosen by Congress on the grounds that corruption would prevail as the executive would owe its very existence in office to another arm of the government.

While the Framers considered an executive *chosen by* the Congress, they did not contemplate an executive *responsible to* the representative assembly. Indeed, such a regime type, which we would now know as parliamentarism, had yet to exist. In Britain, the cabinet was still the responsibility of the monarch, whose authority, of course, did not rest upon any connection, direct or indirect, with the electorate. Once both selection of the executive by the assembly and a monarchy had been rejected, the Framers were in effect replicating the essentials of a form of government that then existed in Britain, an executive with powers separated from the powers of the elected assembly. The crucial difference is that rather quickly the electoral college evolved from being a mere filter for popular preferences into an automatic expression of them. Thus developed the first democratic system in which there are two agents of the electorate.

As voters effectively abandoned the intended practice of simply voting for a delegate who would be entrusted with making the decision of who should be president in favor of making it themselves (by way of electors "pledged" to a particular candidate), the U.S. presidential system took on a new character. By Andrew Jackson's era, the president would be the expression of a popular "mandate," having a special link to the whole national constituency. It is this character of presidentialism that has brought down so much criticism on the regime type, as we shall see. It is ironic that, while the U.S. presidential system was a deliberate response to a problem of how to create a national executive when there was neither a monarch nor any preexisting models besides monarchy, the modern "presidentialism" of a combative partisan political figure often battling the separately legitimated assembly was an unforeseen development.

A second round of creation of presidential systems came with the independence of the Latin American republics. Several of these countries opted for direct popular election of the president, while in others, at least initially, the executive was chosen by the assembly for a fixed term. As in the early U.S. and British democracies, the Latin American systems had assemblies designed to be the expressions of local interests. In some cases, regionalism was by far the most important basis of the polity. We develop in Chapter 9 a theoretical explanation for why a variant of presidentialism with unusually strong presidential powers and weak parties emerged in these settings of preeminent localism.

As in the United States, in Latin America the fixed-term executive was the only available model,[3] yet some early constitutional designers saw their innovations as emulating the British model, only with the "monarch" popularly legitimated. Thus, while the "British model" would later come to refer to parliamentarism, as late as the 1820s when Latin American independence was under way, this model indeed referred to a cabinet responsible only to the head of state and an assembly elected from geographically defined districts. That presidentialism as we know it emerged primarily because there were no other obvious models is borne out by looking into the history of European institutional development.

### Further "engineering": parliamentarism and new regime types in Europe

As in Britain, in all of the other states on the European continent that evolved into constitutional monarchies in the nineteenth century, authority over the cabinet shifted from the hands of the monarch to the parliament. Unlike the cases of the new countries of the New World born of rebellion against monarchies, in Europe the emergence of constitutional regimes did not see the establishment of elected heads of state, since the monarch would serve that role. Even France, which for a while oscillated among republican democracy, dictatorship, and monarchical restoration, parliamentary democracy with no elected president was established under the Third Republic in 1871. Not until Charles de Gaulle's plebiscite under the Fifth Republic in 1962 did popular election of the president become entrenched.[4] By then additional alternative regime types had emerged, so France retained cabinet responsibility to the parliament even while adopting a popularly elected presidency.

A second wave of democratization in Europe led to regime types other than parliamentarism or presidentialism. These regimes emerged after the democratization of Britain, meaning the basic parliamentary feature of cabinet responsibility was a recognized model of constitutional design. However, in the absence of a monarch, the head of state is popularly elected, thus creating a second agent of the electorate. This combination of an elected presidency with a cabinet dependent on the assembly's confidence thus multiplied the number of permutations on constitutional design that we discuss in this book. Some of these regimes constitute a regime type we shall define as *premier-presidential*. Such a regime, sometimes called

---

3 The exception here is Brazil, which originally inherited the monarchy that had been overthrown in Portugal. Later on, the Brazilian monarchy was replaced by a presidential system.
4 Initially, the constitution of the Fifth Republic was simply a "reinforced" variant of parliamentarism. In contrast to the Fourth Republic, the terms under which cabinets could be replaced were changed to favor greater cabinet durability, and the president (still to be elected by an electoral college made up of other elected officials) was granted some emergency provisions.

"semipresidential," ensures that the cabinet depends only on assembly confidence, yet provides certain powers to a popularly elected president. A more detailed definition follows in Chapter 2; in particular, we shall see that many regimes have "confused" control over cabinets, by granting both of the electorate's agents considerable authority in matters of government formation. For now, all we are concerned with is the historical fact that Europe's "second wave" of democratization often took elements of both the British concept of government responsible to parliament and the New World concept of a separately elected president.

This phase of democratization begins with Finland's independence from Russia in 1905 and accelerates after the defeat of the Austro-Hungarian and German empires in World War I and the independence of the remaining dependencies of Western Europe.[5] The nature of presidentialism on the U.S. and Latin American models as defaults chosen in the lack of other models is further underscored when we realize that, while many of these "second wave" states' leaders saw as desirable an elected head of state to replace the monarch, they nonetheless made the cabinet responsible to the parliament. Finland, Weimar Germany, Austria, Ireland, and Iceland all adopted such systems, although they varied widely in the amount of power given to their presidents.

Thus the initial phase of democratization on the European continent was set apart from that of the New World by the existence of monarchies. What set it apart from the process in Britain were two aspects: the prior existence of the "model" of parliamentary confidence, and, later on, the decision to adopt proportional representation for the assembly. In these systems, therefore, a conscious decision was made that the assembly should be elected on the basis of ideological or sectoral, rather than geographical, differences within the society. The later democracies in Europe followed the earlier ones in adopting proportional representation and parliamentary cabinets, but some also adopted elected presidencies.

## ASSEMBLIES AND EXECUTIVES: INTERACTION AND ELECTORAL CONSEQUENCES

A frequent theme of this book is that the means chosen to constitute executive power affect the nature of elections and representation in the assembly as well. In particular the interaction and its consequences manifest themselves as trade-offs between efficiency and representativeness. "Efficiency" refers to the ability of elections to serve as a means for voters to identify and choose among the competing government options available

5 The correlation is not perfect, as some of the new (and short-lived) democracies of Eastern Europe in the early twentieth century chose to have their presidents elected by parliament. One, Estonia, had no head of state, thus being arguably the "purest" of all parliamentary systems.

to them. "Representativeness" refers to the ability of elections to articulate and provide voice in the *assembly* for diverse interests. We argue that parliamentarism virtually requires that a choice be made; either there will be an efficient choice of policy options to be addressed by the executive or there will be a broadly representative assembly, or a compromise must be struck. With only one agent of the electorate, it is not feasible to have both efficient and representative elections in the same system. Having an elected president, on the other hand, at least holds out the promise of serving both ends through elections. The ability of a presidential regime to do so and how it handles the inherent tensions of doing so are the themes of most of the rest of this book. Before looking at how parliamentarism and presidentialism affect efficiency and representativeness, let us elaborate on these terms.

*Efficiency.* It was Walter Bagehot who described the British system as having both "efficient" and "dignified" components. A major message of his famous essay, *The English Constitution,* was to call attention to a then largely unacknowledged transformation that had occurred over time in Britain. The cabinet no longer was under the sway of the monarch; indeed, the portions of the (unwritten) English constitution in which the monarch now had a role were merely ceremonial, hence the term "dignified." The cabinet had fallen under the sway, instead, of the parliament. The cabinet had become the "connecting link" between the "fused" powers of the legislative and the executive authorities. This linkage and its importance in the actual workings of British government made the institution of parliamentary confidence the "efficient" component.

Growing out of this fusion of powers was another form of efficiency and it is in this sense, discussed by Cox (1987) in *The Efficient Secret,* that we use the term in this book. Because governments were made and unmade according to that composition of the majority of parliament, a voters' choice of parliamentary candidate was also a choice of executive. Elections thus came to turn on the voters' preferences for government and, by extension, on policy rather than on more purely local concerns (such as "pork" and patronage). As a result, neither elections nor the legislative process turned on distribution of particularistic goods by means of logrolling across districts. Instead elections offered an "efficient" choice from among competing policy options, and legislation is the domain of the majority party and its cabinet.

An inefficient system, on the other hand, would be one in which elections turn more on the provision of particularistic services to constituents than on policy. Such a legislative process is also likely to be inefficient, as members of congress seek to be able to bring back to their districts projects, jobs, or other services that will help them be reelected.

Efficiency, when centered on elections to the executive, is closely related to identifiability – the ability of voters to identify the choices of competing potential governments that are being presented to them in electoral campaigns. As developed in more detail in Chapter 2, concepts such as efficiency and identifiability relate to models of what Powell (1989) calls "Citizen Control" that provide for governmental accountability and policy mandates. In a highly efficient system like that of the United Kingdom, identifiability is high. The more inefficient an election is, the lower will be its identifiability.

*Representativeness*. Electoral systems may be scaled by the degree to which they represent diversity. That diversity may be expressed in geographic terms as the parochial interests of localities, or it may be expressed sectorally as the narrow interests of groups within the society, whether or not they are geographically concentrated.

If representation takes place on a strictly local basis, it may be associated with a highly inefficient electoral and legislative process, but it need not be so. Local representation can also mean the ability to articulate *policy* concerns that are specific to a region, as, for example, in polities with a geographically concentrated ethnic minority, as in Spain, or significant regional variations in economic standing, as in Canada. Locally defined representation may even be a combination of particularistic services, such as casework and pork barrel, and policy interests of special concern locally, as in the United States.

The articulation of local interests depends on both the electoral system and the constitutional design. Such representation is likely to be maximized under a system of small districts such that each member of the assembly will hail from a clearly defined region. Much of the discussion that follows will consider the relationship between local representation and whether a system is presidential or parliamentary.

If representation is to be based upon group interests, such as clashing ideologies or distinct ethnic or religious segments, it need not be at all local in nature. It must, however, be a form of proportional representation (PR) based on party lists.[6] Indeed, the extreme of such an electoral system would elect all members in a single nationwide district, as is the case in Israel and the Netherlands. Many other countries, including Sweden and Denmark, elect a major part of their assemblies in nationwide districts. Some that have rather small geographic districts nonetheless have a second tier designed to ensure faithfully proportional representation of diverse parties, as in Austria and Germany and, in their first democratic elections, Bulgaria and Hungary.

6 Some PR systems also allow (or require) candidate voting, which often weakens the party-centered nature of elections and may even make elections turn on local particularism. For discussion of one such system, see Ames (1987).

## Parliamentarism

As cabinet responsibility to parliament came to be the basis for constituting executive power in Britain, what happened to the geographic representation in the assembly? And how did the adoption of proportional representation in continental European parliamentary regimes affect the institutions of cabinet responsibility? Efficiency is best served when there are two principal options from which voters may choose, so that one of the options will be certain to hold executive office. Thus efficiency in a parliamentary system would be best served by a low-magnitude electoral system, where magnitude refers to the number of seats elected per district. The reason that low magnitude is tied to efficiency under parliamentarism is that as magnitude is decreased, so ordinarily is the number of parties, while the probability of a "manufactured majority" for a party with less than a majority of seats is increased (Rae 1967; Taagepera and Shugart 1989). Since efficiency as it relates to government formation implies a categoric choice among two contenders, one of whom will gain control over the government, a small number of parties and a majority of seats for one of them are required to maximize efficiency. On the other hand, as district magnitude is decreased, so is the opportunity for the political institutions to articulate minority viewpoints.

*Efficiency.* Owing to the workings of the plurality rule in single-seat districts, one of the British parties usually obtains a majority of parliamentary seats and thus forms the government on its own. Cabinet responsibility led to the emergence of disciplined, programmatic parties. The development of the party system around the institutions of parliamentarism and geographically defined representation led to the basis of election of members ceasing to be primarily local concerns and instead becoming national issues (Cox 1987).

Parties must differentiate themselves on the basis of national policy. Politics in the districts from which members of parliament are elected can no longer focus so much as in the absence of party discipline on the stuff of legislative "logrolling" and compromise – the ability to deliver services to the constituency. Instead it must focus much more on nationally divisive but often not divisible concerns. While this focus on national issues in elections even within locally defined districts is the source of the system's efficiency and is justifiably much admired, the system contains potential problems.

Two principal criticisms of parliamentarism on the British model thus emerge. First, an assembly formally constructed to represent local interests is compromised in that function and instead becomes principally an "electoral college" for determining which party holds executive power. It thus emerges as neither a legislature, as legislative authority is concentrated in the cabinet, nor very representative, at least on the level at which its members are chosen, since the national policy concerns that are expressed by parties capable of winning national power become paramount.

Second, and stemming from the first, where elections are contested almost entirely on the basis of which of two major parties shall receive unchallenged executive power for a prescribed period, electoral contests may become excessively polarized, perhaps raising the stakes of elections so much as to destabilize the system. The collapse of British-style parliamentary regimes in countries as diverse otherwise as Grenada, Nigeria, and Pakistan is an example of potential pitfalls of parliamentary systems.[7]

*Representativeness.* The other model of parliamentarism is more inclusive of broad interests and multiple parties because it employs proportional representation. The extent to which the system will be representative of diversity depends on district magnitude. Previous studies (Rae 1967; Taagepera and Shugart 1989; Lijphart 1990) have shown a compelling relationship between district magnitude ($M$) and the number of parties: the greater $M$ is, the more "relevant" parties there are.[8] Since under PR, multiseat districts must be used, in any district the number of possible winners will be greater than in $M = 1$ systems such as Britain. The result is that, especially as $M$ gets to be very high, representation is defined less by geography and more by ideological or sectoral interests in a multiparty system.

If the dilemma of parliamentarism on the British model is the sharp diminution of local representation, under multiparty parliamentarism there is a different dilemma. With multipartism, coalition or minority governments are likely to prevail. Such a system is thus more representative than the British model, since divergent (parochial) concerns of sectors, classes, or other segments of society may be present at once in the assembly and even in the cabinet. Such constitutional designs are what Powell (1989) called "representational." However, maximizing representativeness through PR almost ensures minimizing cabinet durability, since parliamentary confidence means the cabinet must assuage the interests of diverse parties. In such systems, then, the degree to which voters may assess accountability and confer mandates through elections is limited (Powell 1989). Thus, while this form of parliamentarism enhances representativeness and consequently the

---

7 Even in the United Kingdom, that most venerable of parliamentary systems, the recent decline in the certainty with which cabinets resign upon losing votes that are not explicitly votes of confidence or else major spending bills indicates some dissatisfaction with the strict linkage between MPs' votes and the fate of the national executive. Continuing calls for PR are also a manifestation of this dilemma, as PR and the coalitions that would ensue would enable parties to represent more faithfully sectoral, if not necessarily locally based, constituencies.
8 Further along in the book we shall define terms more precisely, such as "effective magnitude" and "effective number" of parties.

role of the assembly, it limits the possibility that the executive can articulate national policy goals transcending parochial partisan interests. Examples of parliamentary systems that have functioned in this way are the French Fourth Republic, and the current regimes of Belgium and Denmark. In the 1980s, Israel's difficulties in forming governments that had to appease the demands of numerous small parties also manifest the same problem.

*Balancing efficiency and representativeness.* In fairness to those who advocate parliamentary democracy, few today encourage the adoption of either the British model or high-magnitude PR for emerging democracies. Some, such as Linz (1987), specifically refer to PR designed so as not to encourage too fragmented a party system and perhaps with a "constructive vote of no confidence," by which cabinets cannot be replaced by purely negative coalitions but only by a majority coalition in favor of a new alternative cabinet.

Of course, the dilemma of introducing such mechanisms is that they tend to reduce the number of parties and thus the representativeness of the system, compared to one with higher $M$ and lower barriers to changing cabinets. Thus the attempt to balance efficiency and representativeness, like walking a tightrope, is precarious. Indeed, Powell (1989), who considered mostly parliamentary systems, noted that his scores on elements of accountable and decisive (hence efficient) governance were weakly related to his scores on representativeness. Whichever is the formal basis on which the assembly is constituted, geographical representation in low-$M$ districts or ideological representation in higher-$M$ districts, parliamentarism leads to a fundamental conclusion: It is difficult to maximize at once the functions of the two branches. Either the choice of government becomes so important in elections that the more parochial interests of localities or sectors matter little in elections and representation, or else cabinet durability becomes imperiled by an overly representative assembly. The reason that this choice is forced is that only one branch comes directly before the voters for "democratic legitimation" (Linz 1987): the assembly.

## Systems with popularly elected presidents

If parliamentarism makes difficult the maximization of the fulfillment of both executive and assembly roles, what about systems with two agents of the electorate? At first it would seem that systems with presidents would perform extremely well because the choice just described – pursuit of more parochial interests versus supporting the executive – need not be confronted at the level of electoral campaigns. The separate election and possibly independent constitution of executive and assembly powers do not have to compel the essential trade-off between conducting elections on the basis of efficiency or conducting them on the basis of representativeness.

*Efficiency.* In a presidential election, the choice of executive power can be very efficiently presented to voters, provided that the president has real executive powers. If only one of the candidates contesting elections can win the right to fill executive positions or designate who shall perform this function, the ability of voters to identify and choose among options for executive office is quite well achieved when there is an elected president. There are many variations on the presidential role in these matters, but for now the basic point is simply that elections for president tend to be relatively efficient for executive formation to the extent that the executive does not depend entirely upon postelection negotiations, as in multiparty parliamentary systems.

*Representativeness.* An efficient choice for executive under parliamentarism necessarily renders assembly elections less representative than they might be, since the electoral process for executive and assembly is fused. With a presidency, however, the assembly election need not present voters the same narrow range of choices that confronts voters in the executive election. Or, looked at from the opposite angle, even a high-$M$ proportional representation system for the assembly need not compromise the efficiency of executive election or render basic cabinet composition dependent on nonelectoral shifts in party alignments. Thus it is theoretically possible to have representational elections that give voters a wide range of party choices without compromising efficiency in executive formation.

*Balancing assembly and executive power.* Having noted that, in theory, systems with popularly elected presidents do not require the compromising of either branch's electoral connection does not, of course, mean it all works well in practice. Indeed, a reader initiated in the debates about presidential and parliamentary regimes may be surprised to see us pointing to such features as the different composition of assembly and executive powers as a strength. The very benefits we have suggested have also been identified as the regime type's basic flaws, as discussed in Chapter 3.

In setting up the discussion in this way, we are calling attention to the existence of regimes in which the electorate has two agents: one that responds to the desirability of efficiency in executive formation, and the other that responds to the desirability of giving voters choice of parties and policy programs. How these two goals are reached and the degree to which they are achieved – or in less successful designs, the potential for conflict – depends on a number of variations that are discussed in this book. We thus undertake the comparative study of presidencies and their interaction with assemblies from a perspective of "political engineering": the concept that constitutional design matters for the way in which it shapes politicians' pursuit of their interests. Before proceeding with detailed definitions and analysis, we should consider in more detail what we mean by political engineering. In doing so we take as our starting point *The Federalist Papers*.

### CONSTITUTIONAL DESIGN AND POLITICAL INTERESTS: BRINGING THE FEDERALISTS BACK IN

This book fits within the school known as the "new institutionalism" because it is founded on the premise that politicians' "preferences can be understood only in the context of the institutionally generated incentives and institutionally available options that structure choice" (Grofman 1989:1). The new institutionalism draws upon analytic tools from microeconomics, game theory, and social choice as a way to understand how the design of institutions conditions political outcomes. It is appropriate, then, that we begin with *The Federalist Papers*, for the men who drafted and then campaigned for the ratification of the U.S. Constitution well understood that political outcomes could be shaped by the "fine details" of institutions (Schwartz 1989:38).

In seeking to understand better those constitutions that are founded upon the notion that there should be two agents through which the electorate exercises control over the polity, we are drawn into political engineering (Sartori 1968). We agree with Grofman (1989:4) that the Founding Fathers were "the greatest (if not the first) political engineers." In stating our appreciation for the authors of *The Federalist Papers*, however, we are not implying that the Founders had the last word on constitutional design. Rather, we are saying that they provided an essential starting point, as relevant today as in the late eighteenth century, for understanding how institutions shape politics.

Any study that is rooted in the principles of rationality, as is this one, and that employs such tools as principal–agent relations and spatial modeling follows upon the same concerns as *The Federalist Papers:* how the rules of the game can be devised so as to structure incentives in such a way that leads to good government.[9] Madison's underlying assumption is that elected officials will be influenced by the self-interested motive of reelection (Cain and Jones 1989:22). We share that assumption. It was in that vein that the Founders sought to pit "ambition against ambition," in their famous phrase, in order to thwart tyranny. In *The Federalist Papers*, the Founders develop one of the most profound defenses of the promise of political engineering ever written. We would not be undertaking this present study were we not also convinced of the promise of institutional engineering. While we do not proceed mainly with the aim of prescribing "optimal" constitutional designs, we do recognize some as preferable to others. Where we have a clear preference, we shall say so explicitly. Our

---

9 *Federalist* No. 51 defines "Justice" as "the end of government."

main purpose, however, is to consider the implications of the myriad ways in which the powers of presidents and assemblies have been constituted in a wide variety of countries.

Besides their contribution to a theory of constitutional design and rational choice, *The Federalist Papers* are also useful for our purposes because they developed an elaborate constitutional design based on the concept of there being two agents of the electorate: a president and an assembly. Or rather, they set the stage for the development of constitutions with two such agents, even if the product of the Constitutional Convention comprised the ideal of separate agency considerably. As Chappel and Keech (1989:47) observe, *Federalist* No. 51 argued that each department of government was meant to be constituted such that "the members of each should have as little agency as possible in the appointment of the members of the others." A rigorous adherence to this principle would require that all top officeholders "be drawn from the same fountain of authority, the people." Obviously, the original electoral college, which was not dependent on popular elections, was one of several ways in which the original document compromised the ideal of separate agency; but over time the principle came to be more fully realized.

All of the constitutions considered in detail in this book similarly provide for two agents of the electorate. They vary greatly, however, in the extent to which there are also agency relations *among* the electorate's agents, for example by the involvement of the assembly in appointing or dismissing members of the executive. Moreover, as *The Federalist Papers* point out, even a maximum degree of separation in the constitution of authority in the executive and assembly does not preclude overlap in their functions. Here, too, as we shall see, there is enormous room for variation. These variations are the subject of the next chapters.

### PLAN OF THE BOOK

Chapter 2 lays out specific definitions of three types of regime that constitute our primary basis of comparison. We define presidentialism as a regime type based on the ideal of maximum separation of powers and full and exclusive responsibility of the cabinet to the president. We define premier-presidentialism as a type in which the president has certain significant powers, but the cabinet is responsible only to the assembly. The third type is president-parliamentary, a common type with shared – or confused – responsibility over cabinets between president and assembly.

In Chapter 3 we review the criticism of presidentialism as contrasted with parliamentarism. We explore several advantages of presidential over parliamentary democracy and then consider how premier-presidentialism might offset some of the criticisms launched against presidential systems while still retaining the advantages of having two agents of the electorate.

Chapter 4 provides some case studies of premier-presidential and president-parliamentary regimes. We see that the more successful regimes have ensured that the president's powers did not so dominate that the assembly majority could not maintain a cabinet when president and assembly differ. The president-parliamentary regimes have frequently been conflict-ridden, as we shall see.

Chapters 5–8 are studies in the comparative presidency. First, in Chapter 5, we explore the means of constituting chief executive power. We look at cases in which the assembly is involved in choosing the chief executive and consider when such involvement vitiates the ideal of two agents of the electorate and when it does not. The chapter also considers vice-presidencies versus interim elections as means to replace chief executives who cannot fill out their fixed terms. Finally, we discuss a little-known but potentially viable variation on presidentialism: the collegial executive.

Chapter 6 discusses several ways in which powers can be less than separate. Some regimes leave it only to the president to fill and dismiss members of the cabinet, while in others the assembly plays a role in appointments, dismissal, or both. We offer a simple heuristic, based in spatial modeling, that predicts the equilibrium points at which cabinets will rest, depending on the relative symmetry of appointment and dismissal powers. The chapter also considers the powers of dissolution held by some presidents.

In Chapter 7 we look at the legislative powers of presidents, exploring variation on veto and override procedures as well as decree powers. We argue that students of presidential systems have frequently overstated the importance of decree legislation. We distinguish among different forms of decrees and offer a spatial model of conditions under which assemblies are likely to delegate decree powers and with what consequences.

In Chapter 8 we develop a system of scoring presidential powers, with a table of the powers of presidents in forty-four constitutions. We also provide two graphs of the regimes. One graph shows presidential power in two dimensions: legislative and nonlegislative. We find that the most powerful presidencies also have been the most problematic regimes. The second graph locates the regimes according to degree of presidential authority over cabinets and the degree of separation of powers. This graph allows us to see at a glance the most important characteristics of a regime's constitutional design and to what extent each conforms to the types defined in Chapter 2.

In the four subsequent chapters we focus on elections, parties, and electoral rules. Chapter 9 develops theoretical constructs of inefficient and efficient presidentialism, based on the relation between presidential legislative powers and the form of party organization, as shaped by the electoral rules.

Chapter 10 looks at empirical relations between various features of institutional design and the number of parties. Chapter 11 offers a theoretical model for why we observe two-party systems in some cases (despite PR) and multipartism in others. These chapters show the importance of the electoral cycle – the timing of presidential and assembly elections in relation to one another – on party system outcomes.

Chapter 12 takes up the question of designing regimes, focusing on the role of the electoral cycle in shaping the likelihood of compatibility between president and assembly majority. The chapter considers conditions under which such compatibility is desirable as well as when it may be desirable not to have compatibility. We discuss how different constellations of variables can be created to maximize particular political goals. Finally, Chapter 13 offers general conclusions.

# 2

## Defining regimes with elected presidents

Any thorough analysis of presidential systems must first establish clear criteria for what presidentialism is. In this case, the task is especially critical because we shall later examine a number of variations on the institutional arrangements of presidential government, as well as proposals for modifications as yet untested.

The tasks of this chapter, then, are as follows: First, we provide a definition of presidentialism, drawing on the theoretical heritage of *The Federalist* and contrasting ours with other institutional definitions of the regime type. Next, we define premier-presidentialism in contrast to pure presidentialism.[1] We then discuss some hybrid regime types that exhibit combinations of qualities from both the presidential and premier-presidential types. Finally, we introduce a simple typology of regimes based upon two dimensions: (1) the degree of separation of powers, and (2) the nature of the cabinet. We return to this typology in greater detail in Chapter 8.

### PRESIDENTIALISM ACCORDING TO ITS FOUNDERS: SEPARATE ORIGIN AND SURVIVAL

Beginning with *The Federalist,* the central defining characteristic of presidentialism has been the separation of legislative from executive powers. Indeed, this theme predates presidential government. The authors of *The Federalist* based much of their faith in the separation of powers on Montesquieu's arguments for legislative control over a king's ministers. Later, the idea of presidentialism as the separation of powers in a *republican* government is clearly delineated first in *The Federalist,* and this idea will remain central to our definition of presidentialism.

Nevertheless, by itself, the phrase "separation of powers" does not tell us much. Even in the United States, legislative and executive powers are not entirely separate. The presidential veto represents an executive intrusion in the legislative process; and the requirement of Senate ratification of trea-

---

1 Throughout this study, the term "presidential" regime refers to the "pure" type defined in this chapter; we do not use the term to encompass premier-presidentialism or various hybrids.

ties allows for legislative influence in the executive domain of foreign policy. Indeed, without such overlap, it would be difficult to imagine how one branch could check actions of the other. Along with the separation of powers, checks and balances were central to the conception of presidential government elaborated in *The Federalist*.[2]

If we were to define presidentialism as the absolute separation of executive from legislative power, then any veto requiring an extraordinary congressional majority for override would constitute a deviation from presidentialism. We argue that this is not the case. Powers are never entirely separate under presidentialism – nor were they intended to be. In fact, Madison's arguments in *The Federalist* suggest that the rationale for separating the sources of the *origin* and the *survival* of the executive and Congress was to ensure that each branch could impose checks on the other without fear of jeopardizing its own existence. Thus, separation in some respects serves to ensure interdependence – that is, checks – in others.

The critical distinction is between provisions pertaining to the origin and survival of the two branches and provisions pertaining to their actions. Regarding origin and survival, maximum separation is characteristic of presidentialism. But regarding actions, presidentialism seeks to protect mutual checks, which in turn requires that powers overlap considerably.

## CONTEMPORARY DEFINITIONS: INSTITUTIONAL CRITERIA

The definition we use throughout this book when we refer to *presidential* government (or, at times, "pure" presidentialism), is the following:

1. the popular election of the chief executive;
2. the terms of the chief executive and assembly are fixed, and are not contingent on mutual confidence; and
3. the elected executive names and directs the composition of the government.

This three-part definition captures the essence of separate origin and survival of government (executive) and assembly in addition to specifying that the president be elected by voters (or an electoral college chosen by them for that sole purpose). We also identify a fourth criterion that, we maintain, logically follows from the above:

4. the president has some constitutionally granted lawmaking authority.

The latter criterion does not concern the formation and maintenance of powers, but if presidents do not have lawmaking power (such as a veto), then they are chief executives only in the most literal way: they execute laws the creation of which they had no way of influencing. Granting presidents lawmaking powers is a way of ensuring that the popular endorsement of a policy program through a presidential election can be translated into

2 See especially *Federalist* No. 51.

actual policy output. There is only one regime that is fully presidential by
the first three criteria yet fails to meet the fourth: Venezuela.

Having provided a working definition of presidentialism, we now review
briefly some other contemporary definitions, in order to highlight ways in
which our definition differs. In 1959, Douglas Verney offered a list of
*eleven* criteria by which to distinguish presidentialism from parliamentarism, as well as from what he called "assembly government."[3] But Verney's
definition suffers from ambiguity and overlap among his criteria, and from
the fact that he does not establish the primacy of any of them. In his book
*Democracies,* Lijphart (1984:66–71) argues that two criteria are essential
to presidentialism, while a host of others (some of which belong to Verney's
list) are associated with – but not necessary for – presidential government.
Lijphart's two essential criteria are that the chief executive shall:

1. not be dependent on legislative confidence, but rather shall sit for a fixed term;

and

2. be elected by popular vote.[4]

In a recent essay, Lijphart (1989) identifies a third criterion, which he
regards as essential to presidentialism as well:

3. a one-person executive.

3 Verney's conception of assembly (or convention) government is much more like parliamentarism than presidentialism. In effect, it is parliamentarism in which the assembly,
rather than the cabinet, is dominant. His distinction between the two results primarily from
the fact that he regarded the Westminster model as the prototype for parliamentary government, and was therefore forced to define another category for parliamentary forms that
vary significantly from this model. We shall propose a somewhat different definition of the
term "assembly regime" below. Verney's eleven criteria overlap considerably, so we have
distilled Verney's institutional characteristics of presidentialism down to six:
   1. the head of state is also the head of government;
   2. the president appoints the cabinet;
   3. legislative and executive personnel are distinct;
   4. the executive is not dependent on confidence of the assembly;
   5. the president cannot dissolve the assembly; and
   6. the assembly is the supreme branch of government. (Verney 1959: 39–57, 75–7)
4 Students of democratic institutions may object that the formal election of the president by an
electoral college (as in the United States, Argentina, and Finland) violates the principal of
popular election for the president. Nevertheless, the election of members of an electoral
college, who fulfill no other role than casting votes for president, is a vastly different phenomenon from the election of assembly members who also elect a head of government. It would be
a mistake to equate the indirect election of a president, via an electoral college, with the
selection of a head of government by the assembly. For this reason, we reemphasize the
distinction between *popular* election and *direct* election for president. In most presidential
systems, presidents are chosen by direct, popular election. Where an electoral college is
chosen for the sole purpose of naming the president, without conferring or negotiating
compromise candidates, then we still regard the election as popular, but not direct. In
parliamentary and premier-presidential systems, where a prime minister must be approved
by the assembly, the election of the head of government is neither popular nor direct.

Another way of saying this is that the electoral district magnitude – the number of seats elected in a district (Rae 1967) – for the executive equals one ($M = 1$), where the district is the entire nation. Lijphart's primary criticism of presidentialism is that it is inherently majoritarian, providing poor representation for minorities. Where $M = 1$, electoral disproportionality is bound to be high unless one candidate wins virtually all the votes. To *define* presidentialism by virtue of district magnitude, however, and then to argue that presidentialism generates majoritarianism, obscures the issue that majoritarianism is generated by electoral formula, and does not add much explanatory power to the definition of presidentialism. It also requires the classification as wholly distinct regime types systems such as Uruguay (1952–67) and Cyprus (1960–3), which have had popularly elected collegial executives while retaining separation of powers and checks and balances. If a regime has these latter features, we prefer to classify it as presidential, regardless of whether or not its elected executive is unitary or collegial.

In addition, to define presidentialism by the most majoritarian characteristic of most presidential systems seems inherently to contradict the spirit of the first two criteria described by Lijphart. Both of these criteria emphasize the relative independence of the legislative and executive branches. This independence is, as we shall see, essential to protecting the mutual checks in presidential systems – a distinctly antimajoritarian tendency. Thus, aside from the empirical problem of collegial executives, to define presidentialism by its unitary executive seems to be theoretically contradictory.

It could be that the contradiction over the number of persons constituting the elected executive is less a problem of definition than an indication of internal inconsistency in the regime type itself. Indeed, judging from the tensions between Madisonian and Hamiltonian conceptions of democracy evident in papers of *The Federalist,* this point is well taken.[5] We shall explore in the chapters ahead many of the institutional tensions and perhaps contradictions in a wide array of systems generally classified as presidential. For the purposes of definition, however, we seek consistency in addition to generality, and we have chosen to embrace the Madisonian conception of presidentialism over the Hamiltonian.[6] Madison's logic, we believe, generally prevailed over Hamilton's in shaping the first presidential constitution, and better reflects the themes of separation of powers with checks and balances that we deem to be illustrative of presidentialism across all cases.

5 While recognizing the problems of Lijphart's third criterion, we must also acknowledge his point. The overwhelming majority of presidential systems have had unitary executives, and this characteristic *does* generate majoritarianism in the executive. Indeed, because of the preponderance of single-member presidencies, criticisms of majoritarianism are central to the criticisms of presidentialism that we review in Chapter 3.

6 For an example of the contrast between the two, one could examine Madison's *Federalist* No. 51 versus Hamilton's *Federalist* No. 70.

In yet another effort to pin down the institutional nature of presidentialism Giovanni Sartori (1992) suggests as a third criterion that:

the president heads the cabinet, which he or she appoints.

Since the president, rather than the assembly, names the cabinet, this criterion implies that the entire executive is the president's domain, and is responsible to him or her. We regard this as a necessary defining characteristic of presidentialism, as it ensures consistency with the principle that the origin and survival of the executive should be separated from the influence of the assembly.[7]

In fact, the three criteria we have identified entail a complete description, in institutional terms, of this principle. These three criteria, in themselves, however, do not provide a complete definition of presidential government. As we have suggested, the rationale for separating the origin and survival of executive and legislative powers is to ensure the viability of mutual checks. In particular, Madison sought to temper the sweeping legislative authority of assemblies. An independent executive with no real lawmaking power, however, would pose no obstacle to parliamentary sovereignty. Therefore, in defining presidentialism we must add the criterion that the elected executive must have some lawmaking authority. We do not offer a more specific description of this lawmaking authority because, as we shall see, the authorities of the executive vary widely among presidential systems, and there is no single legislative power common to all independent executives. We shall see, moreover, that when the executive and assembly are of different political tendencies, this overlap in lawmaking authority can generate legislative deadlock in presidential systems; and it is where deadlock becomes chronic that presidentialism as a system has been subject to the most severe criticisms.

We prefer the definition of presidentialism given at the start of this section because it clarifies the major point distinguishing presidentialism from other regime types that feature popularly elected presidents, as well as from parliamentarism: the separation of origin and survival. Moreover, it clarifies who is responsible for the executive: the president, hence the term *presidential* government, while in parliamentary regimes, it is parliament that is responsible for the composition of the executive. We now turn to defining the other type that we shall devote considerable attention to in this book, premier-presidentialism.

7 As we discuss in Chapters 5 and 7, there have been a few examples of otherwise presidential systems in which cabinet ministers were directly accountable to the assembly. The dramatically different performance of these regimes from pure presidential systems has prompted many observers to label them parliamentary, notably in the cases of Chile 1891–1924, Brazil 1961–3, and even Cuba in the 1940s. We share the consensus that these regimes were not purely presidential; but we shall consider whether they are most accurately classified as parliamentary, or as hybrid systems.

## PREMIER-PRESIDENTIALISM

A premier-presidential regime is, as its name implies, one in which there is both a premier (prime minister), as in a parliamentary system, and a popularly elected president. The credit (or blame) for first characterizing some regimes as "semipresidential" and describing the constitutional characteristics of these regimes belongs to Maurice Duverger.[8] Duverger's concern is primarily with the nature and performance of the French Fifth Republic. He describes this regime as alternating between presidential and parliamentary phases, according to whether the assembly majority supports the president or not, instead of as an intermediate institutional arrangement somewhere between presidentialism and parliamentarism. Duverger does not characterize the Fifth Republic as purely presidential nor as purely parliamentary in either phase; but he prefers the concept of alternation between phases to that of an intermediate regime type for France. Yet the term "semipresidential" implies a regime type that is located midway along some continuum running from presidential to parliamentary. We find such an implication misleading, owing to the special characteristics such regimes exhibit. For the other European cases he discusses, there appear to be less distinct regime phases, although Duverger does not address this point. As we have stated, we consider such systems neither intermediate nor alternating regime types. Thus, what Duverger refers to as semipresidential, we designate premier-presidential.

Despite our differences with Duverger, we recognize his definition as concise and generalizable. Under premier-presidentialism:

1. the president is elected by popular vote;
2. the president possesses considerable powers; and
3. there also exist a premier and cabinet, subject to assembly confidence, who perform executive functions (Duverger 1980:161).

Our first criterion is the popular election of the chief executive, but, unlike under presidentialism, the president under premier-presidentialism is not necessarily the "chief" executive, but rather must coexist with a premier, who is head of the government. As we shall see, the relative status of each office within the executive may vary both across and within regimes.

Our second criterion is that the president has some political powers. The distinction with presidentialism here is that in premier-presidential systems, presidential powers are not necessarily legislative. There may be authorities such as submitting a bill to the electorate instead of to the assembly or referring legislation for judicial review. The presence of other legislative powers, such as veto or unilateral decree, might well lead the

---

8 The first explicit definition of semipresidentialism published in English, that we are aware of, is Duverger (1980). Nogueira (1986) also provides a theoretical discussion of semipresidentialism.

president into conflict with the rest of the executive itself, which is dependent on assembly confidence. Such powers, however, have existed and do exist in some premier-presidential regimes. More typical – and consistent with the regime type – are powers relating to the formation of governments, such as nominations for ministerial portfolios in addition to the premier, as well as nonministerial appointment powers. Typically, presidents in premier-presidential regimes have the power to dissolve the assembly. The important point here is that premier-presidentialism does not guarantee a legislative check by the president on the cabinet or the assembly. There is, however, one presidential power that moves a regime outside of the category of premier-presidentialism: the power to dismiss ministers unilaterally. Such power would contradict the third criterion of the definition, namely, the dependence of the cabinet on the assembly.

### OTHER REGIME TYPES

We have defined two ideal types of democratic regimes with popularly elected presidents. Real-world regimes come in a variety of shadings and variations on these types. While it would be pointless to identify numerous types in an attempt to encompass all imaginable variations on the criteria of separation of powers and presidential authorities, nonetheless there are significant cases that clearly do not meet the criteria of either definition we have presented. The most common type is one in which both the president and the parliament have authority over the composition of cabinets. If the president both appoints and dismisses cabinet ministers, and if the ministers are subject to parliamentary confidence, we have another distinct type of regime. We designate such regimes, of which there have been several, *president-parliamentary*. Just as the names presidential and parliamentary for common regime types identify what elected institution has authority over the composition of the government, and just as the term "premier-presidential" indicates the primacy of the premier as well as the presence of a president with significant powers, so does the term "president-parliamentary" capture a significant feature of the regime: the primacy of the president, plus the dependence of the cabinet on parliament. Such a regime is defined thus:

1. the popular election of the president;
2. the president appoints and dismisses cabinet ministers;
3. cabinet ministers are subject to parliamentary confidence;
4. the president has the power to dissolve parliament or legislative powers, or both.

The definition captures two senses in which these regimes represent neither of our two ideal types, presidentialism and premier-presidentialism. First, these president-parliamentary regimes provide equal authority to dismiss members of the cabinet, unlike the other types. In either a presidential or a premier-presidential regime, while both president and assembly may play a role in cabinet formation, by nominating or confirming candidates for ministerial positions, only one of the powers may dismiss ministers. The importance of this asymmetry of dismissal powers, alongside possibly shared appointment powers, will become clear in Chapter 6. The second feature captured by this definition is the lack of independent survival of assembly and executive powers, despite the great authority of the president over the cabinet. In a presidential regime, maximum separation of both origin and survival is the norm; under a president-parliamentary system, the ability of the parliament to censure ministers means that the survival of executive power is not separate. This latter point is obviously true in a premier-presidential system as well, but the difference is that under the latter type, it falls to the parliamentary majority to reconstitute the government after a censure, albeit in a process usually initiated by presidential nominations. Under president-parliamentary regimes, presidents themselves reconstitute the government, subject, of course, to the possibility of further censures. Moreover, many of these president-parliamentary regimes provide for the power of dissolution in addition to the powers over cabinets, thus meaning that separation of survival is nonexistent.

In Chapter 8, after we have discussed the various dimensions of presidential power, it will be possible to rate each regime according to the powers of presidents and the degree to which separation of survival characterizes each system. For now, we can provide a schematic that suggests where these regime types would be located in a two-dimensional space (Figure 2.1). There are two axes, one concerning the authority that presidents have over the composition of cabinets, the other concerning the degree to which the survival of assembly and executive are separated. In the upper right, with maximum presidential cabinet authority and maximum separation, we have the ideal-type presidentialism. In the lower left, with a minimum on both dimensions, we have the ideal-type premier-presidentialism, in which the president's powers are restricted to calling new elections to determine the makeup of the parliament that alone determines the composition of the cabinet. Slight deviations from these corner-points do not necessarily render the regime a wholly different regime type. For example, we have already defined a regime in which the president has some leeway in making the initial recommendation for premier or in which her or his powers of dissolution are restricted as premier-presidential. Similarly, a regime that requires assembly confirmation of presidential cabinet appointments would still be presidential.

The more significant deviations are those that would place a regime near the upper left. A regime with minimal separation of survival but maximum presidential authority to name and remove cabinets is a distinct regime type. As we shall see in Chapter 8, many regimes that are encountered in

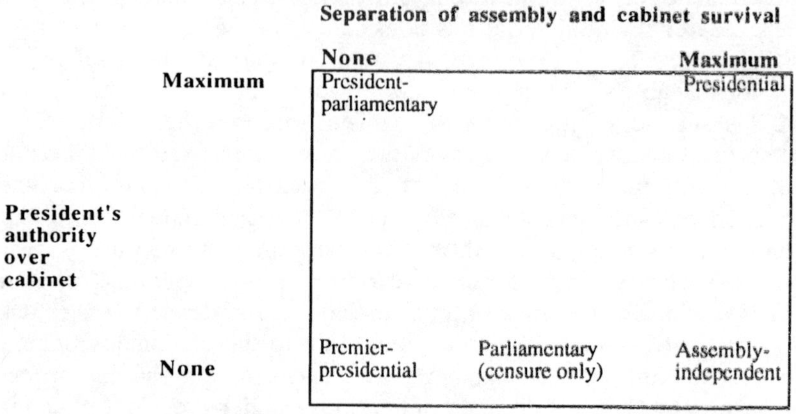

**Separation of assembly and cabinet survival**

| | | None | | Maximum |
|---|---|---|---|---|
| | Maximum | President-parliamentary | | Presidential |
| President's authority over cabinet | | | | |
| | None | Premier-presidential | Parliamentary (censure only) | Assembly-independent |

Figure 2.1. A typology of democratic regimes in two dimensions

this region have experienced serious crises over the authority of presidents and parliaments.

The lower right corner of Figure 2.1 also needs to be addressed, although only briefly. Maximum separation of survival combined with no presidential role in naming or dismissing cabinets would be an approximation of the Swiss regime: an executive chosen by the assembly but not removable by it. The obvious qualifier is that Switzerland has no elected president as head of state, but such a president would have no power over composition of the government anyway, thus (hypothetically) such a regime would be located at that part of the figure. We shall have little to say about this rare combination of powers, except to provide a contrast to presidentialism (see Chapter 5). We propose to call such regimes *assembly-independent,* to indicate the source of executive power, as well as the lack of mutual confidence of assembly and executive.

Even parliamentary regimes are encompassed in these two dimensions. Normally, parliamentary government is contrasted with presidential "separation of powers" systems as an opposite, in which the survival of the assembly and executive are mutually dependent. In parliamentary government, however, there is no president, or at least none with real powers. Thus, there is nobody from whom the assembly might *require* separation, except, of course, the cabinet, which in most but not all parliamentary systems is permitted to dissolve the assembly. The cabinet, however, is a mere agent of the assembly to begin with. So, unlike assembly-independent systems, the survival of the assembly and cabinet between scheduled elections is not inviolate. Yet no institution outside the assembly itself may shorten the mandate of the assembly, as is the case under a typical premier-presidential regime. Thus parliamentary regimes are located at the mid-point of the dimension of separate survival.

## CONCLUSION

We have now provided straightforward definitions for both presidential and premier-presidential government, the two forms with which this book is principally concerned. Our discussion, moreover, has generated a schema for locating these regime types that is generalizable to hybrid systems, as well as to parliamentary government itself. The task of establishing definitions is important so that key terms are clarified early, but we now move on to the more difficult and interesting job of evaluating the performance of different types of regimes.

# 3

# Criticisms of presidentialism and responses

Having defined what presidentialism is, as well as what other types of regimes have popularly elected presidents, we now turn to the scholarly debate about the merits of presidential regimes. In this chapter we concern ourselves primarily with the ideal type of presidentialism that we defined at the beginning of Chapter 2. We address the criticisms of this regime type, then offer responses. Our purpose here is to determine whether it is even worth considering presidentialism as a viable option for democracies, especially new democracies. For, if scholars such as Di Palma (1990) are correct that regimes with elected presidents are "dangerous," especially for new democracies, then there would be little point in considering possible advantages of such regime types. In short, we do not find the criticisms of presidentialism, which have been launched in a nearly one-sided debate thus far, to be unassailable. After responding to these criticisms as they relate directly to pure presidentialism, we turn to the ways in which premier-presidentialism addresses the criticisms, and perhaps offers remedies for some of presidentialism's more dubious qualities.

## THE CASE AGAINST THE PRESIDENT

The myriad criticisms brought against presidentialism have been elaborated in various combinations in a number of recent essays criticizing the system.[1] We understand presidentialism's problems, as described in the current literature, to fall into three broad categories. The fundamental deficiencies of the system are its:

1. temporal rigidity;
2. majoritarian tendencies;
3. dual democratic legitimacies.

### Temporal rigidity

The first group of problems, those of temporal rigidity, refer to the set length of presidential, and congressional, terms. Although most presiden-

---

1 Mainwaring (1989, 1992a) presents the best current synthesis of the arguments in two essays on presidentialism, multiparty systems, and democracy in Latin America.

tial constitutions make provisions for impeachment, they are invariably unwieldy procedures, requiring large extraordinary majorities, which formally can be used only when there is evidence of malfeasance or disregard for constitutional procedure on the part of the chief executive. In sum, presidents are elected for a fixed period, from four to six years, and cannot be removed for political reasons. While constitution builders promoted such a provision as generating stability in the executive, critics of the system argue that is is politically crippling – and the critics have a strong case.

The principal dilemma presented by the set presidential term is what to do with a highly unpopular chief executive; or even one who may enjoy some popularity but who faces stiff majority opposition in congress (Mainwaring 1992a; see also Linz 1987). Such presidents are unlikely to be able to initiate and pursue effectively their legislative programs. They may be at constant loggerheads with the majority of members of the assembly, who are attempting to pursue a rival legislative program. These presidents may even be widely repudiated by the majority of citizens. But they are heads of government (as well as heads of state) until their fixed terms expire, barring impeachment or extra-constitutional removal. Without the option of a no-confidence vote, presidential systems have no institutionalized means of removing an unpopular – and possibly feckless – chief executive.

The opposite manifestation of the same problem occurs when a highly popular and competent president must step down at the end of a fixed term. Where constitutions forbid reelection (at least immediate reelection), as in most of Latin America, the country is faced with the ironic problem of deciding between losing an effective government and tampering with the constitution. Most presidential systems – and even each party that hopes to compete at the highest level – must generate a viable national leader every four or five years (Linz 1987:31). Critics of presidentialism point out that this is a substantial, and unnecessary, burden to place on the system.

The problem of temporal rigidity in presidentialism is not restricted to the executive's term. Assemblies, too, are elected for fixed terms, and as with presidents their terms cannot be shortened for political reasons. The problem just described of a weak president can alternatively be described as one of an intransigent congress. Unlike many parliamentary systems, presidential systems do not afford the head of state the alternative of dissolving congress and calling new congressional elections, even in cases in which a new president with strong popular support is elected to face a hostile congress elected at an earlier date.

The inabilities of the assembly to remove the executive and of the executive to remove the assembly prevent either branch from resolving political crises based on fundamental mutual opposition. In systems where presidents cannot be reelected, moreover, they are effectively lame ducks immediately on taking office (Mainwaring 1992a). The date of their demise – while it may be years away – is known. And for a legislator disinclined to compromise with the executive on legislation, the certainty of this date might be enough to turn stubbornness to intransigence.

## Majoritarianism

Another group of problems associated with presidentialism is caused by the majoritarian tendencies within most presidential systems. The various manifestations of this presidential majoritarianism have been most central in analyses of Lijphart (1989), Lijphart and Rogowski (1991), and Linz (1987).

The majoritarian critique seems odd at first glance, in light the Madisonian rationale for presidentialism as a system that offers the best protection against the tyranny of factions – be they of the minority or of the majority.[2] The critics of presidential majoritarianism, for their part, are concerned with the effects of electoral disproportionality – both in the executive and in the assembly – which distort the accuracy of representation in the system and can contribute to political extremism. Even majoritarianism may be an insufficient description of the extent to which presidentialism distorts the proportional representation of voters' choices in the executive, where $M = 1$. Adherents of PR will point out that no presidential election – even the biggest landslide – begins to approximate a proportional representation of voter preferences. Since the winner by definition wins 100% of the seats when only one seat is at stake, deviation from proportionality (Loosemore and Hanby 1971) is 100% minus whatever share of votes the victor received. If the presidential election is a multicandidate affair, deviation may be 60% or even higher. Even in a two-candidate race, deviation is seldom lower than 40%. Then the result is that the head of state and of government may accurately represent only a minority of voters.

Not only is the balance of voter preferences distorted in the person of the presidents themselves, but the composition of the cabinet will likely reinforce the effect, rather than temper it. Unlike parliamentarism (and premier-presidentialism), which encourages compromise among parties in the construction of executive coalitions,[3] presidentialism does neither. Within the cabinet, the president is by no means first among equals, as the prime minister ostensibly is (Lijphart 1989:4). Even in those few cases where cabinet members are subject to congressional approval for appointment, they can be dismissed only by the president. They are generally members of her party, or nonpartisan experts, but less often are opposition

---

2 See especially *Federalist* No. 10.

3 In parliamentary executives, deviation from proportionality is thus unlikely to be as high as in presidential systems. However, given that cabinets are small compared to assemblies and that many parties may be shut out of the cabinet, deviation is still higher than the corresponding figure for parliament as a whole.

partisans. In most presidential systems, they cannot be members of the assembly, thus reducing the potential for the congressional opposition to participate in shaping the executive agenda.

Finally, as Lijphart and Rogowski (1991) have convincingly argued, minority representation in presidential cabinets is characterized by tokenism, or "descriptive representation." Blacks, Hispanics, and women in U.S. cabinets, for example, have tended not to be aggressive supporters of the political agenda promoted by the minority groups to which they belong. Rather they have generally been moderate and acquiescent to the programs of their presidents.[4] Because of the dominance of presidents over the rest of the cabinet, and the paucity of constraints on their ability to choose ministers, minority representation is more symbolic and less meaningful in presidential than in parliamentary systems.

Lijphart contends that this lack of meaningful representation in cabinets hinders the ability of presidential systems to resolve conflicts based on multiple or deep political cleavages – those divisions that mark plural societies. Below, we examine the obstacles to consensus politics *between* the assembly and executive in presidential systems. At any rate, Lijphart's argument is that the disproportionality of representation within the executive makes politics based on consensus *within* that branch less likely in presidential than in parliamentary systems. It is important to note, however, that at the core of the majoritarian criticism of presidentialism is the presupposition that $M = 1$ for the executive. This point is viable for the vast majority of presidential systems, but, as argued above, it is not essential to the nature of presidentialism.

Because of the exclusive nature of the unitary executive, the importance of capturing the presidency becomes paramount, dwarfing all other electoral goals for parties in presidential systems. This is what Linz (1987:13–15) describes as the "winner-take-all" nature of presidentialism. The high stakes, and the certainty that control of the executive will not be open to question again for a set period, raise the tension of electoral politics. In the wake of presidential elections, moreover, the winners have no reason to try to make amends with the losers. The ultimate prize has been secured, and those who contributed to the victory are clamoring for compensation, perhaps patronage or cabinet positions. The losers, moreover, have no reason to try to cooperate with the new incumbent. There is little to be gained, given the exclusive nature of presidential executives.

In addition to these manifestations of majoritarianism in the executive, the representation in the assembly of parties not winning the presidency

4 Polsby (1983) has argued that American party and electoral reforms of the late 1960s and 1970s have increased the feasibility and the incentives for presidents to rely on "descriptive representation" of minorities in their cabinets; and for cabinet members in general to act more as personal ambassadors of the president than as representatives of distinct group interests. See also Pitkin (1967).

can be dampened when assembly and presidential elections occur concurrently or in fairly close succession. The effects of electoral cycles will be developed fully in Chapters 10 and 11. For now, the point is that the relative timing of presidential and assembly elections can benefit the president's party in congress considerably. This phenomenon reinforces Linz's argument regarding the urgency of presidential elections. Evidently, the winner takes all of the executive, and depending on the timing of congressional elections, can expect to take more than her share of congress as well.

We do not universally condemn the pull of presidentialism on assembly elections. In countries with multiple, factional, and personalized parties, the impetus to coalesce for presidential competition may counteract the tendency toward fragmentation. The point for now is that those who concur with Lijphart on the desirability of consensual over majoritarian democracy have lodged serious complaints against presidentialism. To the extent that certain institutional designs in presidentialism may generate a congress dominated by the president's party, it is majoritarian. Even where the timing of congressional elections prevents this effect, the unitary executive in most presidential systems is highly majoritarian.

Moreover, in addition to distorting representation, this phenomenon can inspire a false sense of popular mandate (Blondel and Suárez 1981:63–5; Suárez 1982:137). Although presidents may be elected with a mere plurality of the votes – and even a small one, as Salvador Allende was in Chile in 1970 – those who are personally dominant over a homogeneous cabinet are likely to develop an inflated notion of the support for a presidential program and the inevitability of its implementation. This is both a function of and a contributor to presidentialism's majoritarian problems. The nature of elections and of the executive branch generates the false sense of mandate, and the misperception in turn inhibits cooperation and consensus-building between president and opposition, both within the government and without, according to these critics.

### Dual democratic legitimacy

The remainder of the criticisms against presidentialism share common roots in the existence of the separate and competing claims to democratic legitmacy made by assembly and executive. These claims are based on the first two defining criteria of presidentialism. Because both the assembly and executive are popularly elected, both can claim a unique popular mandate. Moreover, because the tenure of members of each branch is unaffected by relations with the other, the need for cooperation between president and the congress is not urgent. This category of criticisms is the most central in that the problems generated by temporal rigidity and majoritarianism become practically irresolvable when presented to institutions that lack built-in incentives to achieve compromise (Mainwaring 1989).

In the first place, presidents in multiparty systems who do not have majority party support in congress have far less incentive to seek and maintain lasting coalitions in congress than do parliamentary executives. The success of any given piece of legislation may depend on putting together a majority coalition, but the survival of the executive does not. For this reason, coalition building in many presidential regimes tends to be piecemeal, and the incentives for cooperation offered to congresspersons particularistic (Stockman 1985; Birnbaum and Murray 1987; Kaminsky 1989; Jacobson 1990; Mainwaring 1992a). Since the need for presidents to cultivate support in the assembly is not as pressing as for prime ministers, presidents tend to be less receptive to dissatisfaction with the executive than prime ministers do, thus increasing the chance of political crisis.

A complicating factor here is that the electoral process in presidential systems facilitates the selection of "political outsiders" as chief executives. While this is particularly dramatic in the United States, where primary elections determine party nominees, it is true as well where parties are less subject to grass roots pressures. Direct election of the executive dictates first and foremost that candidates have widespread popular appeal, even at the expense of political experience. Moreover, presidential aspirants who are well known independent of any leadership position in party or government can run for highest office with the support of parties formed expressly for the purpose of conducting presidential campaigns. As a result, we can expect presidents to have less political experience than prime ministers.[5]

Data presented by Suárez (1982) supports this proposition, at least as regards Latin America. Examining aggregate data on heads of state and government around the world between 1940 and 1976, Suárez found that Latin American presidents had on average far less ministerial experience than leaders in the Atlantic democracies. Adherents of parliamentarism regard this as a disadvantage, in part because of the lack of experience, but also because political outsiders are likely to be less disposed than "insiders" to coalition building in the assembly.

In addition to producing leaders who are unable or unwilling to cooperate with congress, the system's dual democratic legitimacies generate no incentives for members of the assembly to seek rapprochement with the executive, according to the critics. For representatives of parties other than the president's the logic of opposition is clear, and no different from that of opposition members in parliamentary systems: There is nothing to gain

5 The 1990 presidential election in Peru is perhaps the most striking manifestation of this tendency ever. The novelist Mario Vargas Llosa exemplifies the phenomenon of a nationally known figure who assembles a party that is purely a personal vehicle to achieve the election of an individual to the presidency. Even more remarkable, however, was the rise of the eventual winner, Alberto Fujimori, whose "party" was no less personalistic, and whose platform was even more dramatically defined by its single-minded opposition to, and contrast with, traditional Peruvian politics.

from cooperation with the executive. Even for congresspersons from the president's own party, however, the separation of powers weakens incentives to support the president, and can create incentives to oppose him.

Valenzuela (1989b) argues that presidentialism fostered polarization of the Chilean party system in congress. His logic is that even members of congress from the president's own party have less to gain than to lose through unconditional loyalty to the president. This is especially true in systems where the president cannot be immediately reelected. Although members of congress have an interest in their own party retaining the presidency, the success of the incumbent does not guarantee this; nor does his or her failure preclude it. Congresspersons from the president's own party, then, do not have an overwhelming incentive to support a lame duck. On the other hand, while the president may not have an election pending, the congressperson does. Dips in presidential popularity, in particular, prompt congresspersons to distance themselves as much as possible from the chief executive. The result, according to Valenzuela, is polarization in the assembly, both among parties, as opposition congresspersons attack the president, and within parties, as the president's own party members try to stake out some space far enough from the president that they can divorce their political fates from hers or his.[6]

This is an argument that presidential systems generate weak – or at least vulnerable – executives. Still, the case is not incompatible with Lijphart's charges of presidential majoritarianism. The paradox of presidentialism is that, while its majoritarian characteristics create great expectations for the potency of the executive, the competing incentives within the system prevent these expectations from being realized (Moe 1987; Lijphart 1990a:76–7; Mainwaring 1992a).

In a further argument that combines the themes of temporal rigidity and separate democratic legitimacies, Linz suggests that presidentialism suffers, in effect, from too much electoral accountability. Because it is so difficult to build support coalitions for the executive after presidential elections, he points out, these coalitions must be presented before the election, offering to the voters the choice of providing the president with a congressional majority. But once the electoral decision is made, according to Linz, political leaders are left with less room to maneuver, to make "deals difficult to defend in public but that might be necessary" (Linz 1987:33).

Linz wants to allow room for coalition building away from the public spotlight. But the same process can equally be described as private dealmaking by political elites. The argument is less than compelling in that it implies a proclivity toward elitist politics and dismisses the principle of

6 The literature on midterm elections in the United States examines at length the proposition that voters cast congressional ballots based on presidential performance, and that congressional candidates position themselves accordingly. See Campbell et al. (1964); Kernell (1977); Erikson (1988).

accountability. Furthermore, the critics of presidentialism take aim primarily at systems in which reelection is prohibited. Proponents of such a rule argue that the lame duck president should not be constrained by short-term electoral considerations in pursuing the national interest. Indeed, we see no reason to believe that parliamentary leaders should be any more willing to take action that is "difficult to defend, but necessary" than should a president barred from reelection.

At any rate, the critics of presidentialism rightly point out that the difficulties of building and sustaining support for the president's legislative agenda pose a serious problem for effective government. The principle of separating legislative from executive powers as a check against the abuse of either can go awry when neither branch is able to exercise power effectively. This dilemma prompts the question of whether a president lacking congressional support would pose a problem if legislative initiative rested primarily in congress. If coalition building is not primarily an action taken by the executive to coordinate the congress, then the disincentives to cooperation between the two branches should not present a problem. The evidence from the United States seems to support this proposition. The U.S. Congress has functioned most of the time since World War II with opposition majorities. It is not the most decisive and effective legislative body imaginable, but it has avoided chronic deadlock with the executive. Further, the Chilean Congress was, for much of the twentieth century, one of the most independent and activist of Latin America's assemblies. Although minority presidents were a regular phenomenon in Chile, immobilism and deadlock did not reach crisis levels until the 1970s.[7] The evidence is not conclusive; but it is suggestive that the critics of presidentialism might qualify their attack on the separation of powers, to direct it at those systems in which congresses are primarily reactive, rather than initiative (Mainwaring 1992a). Such a qualification would then direct attention to the question of whether the problem of presidential immobilism could be alleviated by strengthening congresses, a topic to which we devote considerable attention in Chapters 5, 7, 8, and 9. However, where multiple parties exhibit substantial ideological differences, confrontations between congress and a president who perforce represents only one political tendency may be chronic.

The last criticism of presidentialism we shall address holds that chronic legislative–executive conflict presents dangers far greater than that of deadlock; it invites rule by executive decree (Mainwaring 1992a) and regime instability – even military coups.

---

7 Indeed, one could argue that, had the Eduardo Frei government not obtained a constitutional weakening of the Chilean Congress, the center-right opposition in the early 1970s might have curbed Allende's program, and possibly even prevented the crisis of 1973 from escalating to the point where the military was able to seize power with substantial civilian support. These points are addressed in Chapter 9.

The case that immobilism invites rule by decree is straightforward and is supported by the example of Colombia in the years during and after the National Front (Hartlyn 1989:16–18). Intense factionalism in a congress with limited powers of legislative initiative made coalition building virtually impossible, even though both major parties nominally supported the Front's common presidential candidate at election time. Owing to their inability to secure support in the congress for their legislative programs, Colombian presidents ruled by decree under the State of Emergency as a matter of course throughout the 1960s and 1970s (Vásquez 1979).

Some authors have extended the criticism of presidential immobilism to conclude that the executive's inability to maintain consistent support has directly caused regime instability and encouraged military coups. Scott (1973:290) argued that civilian political elites would encourage and welcome military intervention in the face of congressional–presidential immobilism. Furthermore, using worldwide data from 1940 through the 1970s, Suárez (1982) demonstrates that Latin American governments have endured for less time on average than those in other parts of the developing world, and that these presidencies have had an inordinate proportion of unconstitutional transitions of power. He goes on to argue that in at least three cases – the overthrows of Presidents Fernando Belaunde in Peru, João Goulart in Brazil, and Salvador Allende in Chile – congressional–presidential deadlock was the primary factor triggering the military coups. Valenzuela's (1978) account of polarization and crisis in Chile under Allende certainly supports Suárez's thesis.

### PRESIDENTIALISM AND AUTHORITARIANISM

The suggestion that presidential democracy is prone to breakdown, leading to authoritarian government, is the most troubling of all the criticisms leveled by adherents of parliamentarism. Before offering a defense of presidentialism, then, we suggest reconsidering the logic by which presidentialism is tied to authoritarianism. Two points, in particular, need to be addressed:

1. the difference between presidential constitutions that are formally democratic but fail, and those in which formal presidential dominance over other actors precludes workable checks and balances to begin with; and
2. the question of whether parliamentary democracy has in fact performed as well relative to presidential democracy as parliamentarism's adherents have claimed.

One key criticism of presidentialism stems from a failure to differentiate presidential constitutions developed in an authoritarian context from those in which power is less concentrated in the executive. A fundamental criticism of presidential systems concerns the extent of presidential powers and the independence of presidents from party and assembly. Lijphart (1989) is especially clear on this point when he argues that parliamentary cabinets are necessarily more collegial than presidential cabinets. Even a prime minister who appears to exercise dominant power over his or her colleagues, as did Margaret Thatcher in Britain, is ultimately responsible to the party. The Conservative Party's removal of Thatcher from office in November 1990 after some of her erstwhile cabinet colleagues publicly criticized her policies only underscores the point. Under a presidential system, on the other hand, the cabinet, and especially the head of government, is not responsible to other elected officials for survival.

Even in an authoritarian context, a formally parliamentary constitution may allow the party to retain significant political power over the authoritarian head of government. Thus, where a party organization matters, formal parliamentary rules may be expected. Indeed, the Communist systems of Eastern Europe and the Soviet Union before 1990 were generally parliamentary in form. That this feature from time to time worked is shown by the replacement of such leaders as Nikita Krushchev and Edward Gierek by their own parties.

More personalized authoritarian systems where party either does not exist or is less developed, such as those of Chile under Augusto Pinochet and Paraguay under Alfredo Stroessner, have tended to be presidential. In Mexico, where the official party is not a mass party in the Leninist model but rather was created as a means of circulating the top leadership among several competing caudillos (Craig and Cornelius 1991), a presidential system was adopted. And, tellingly, when Mikhail Gorbachev sought a way to protect his political power from elements of the party that he feared might want to replace him, he opted for a presidential constitution. In each case just mentioned, not only was executive power protected from party and assembly by means of presidentialism, it was also given significant powers over legislation.

This latter point, the extent of legislative powers in the hands of the president, affects the policy content of a presidential system's legislative process more than the degree to which executives are responsible to their own parties. Additionally, the more the president is given substantial legislative authority, the more the outcome of conflicts between the assembly and executive is skewed in favor of the latter. Further, many presidential democracies have inherited constitutions from an authoritarian period and those constitutions were developed at the service of a dictator. This has also been the case in some transitions where new constitutions have not been written.[8] Wherever such resulting democratic regimes prove troublesome, we have further evidence for our proposition that it is the balance of presidential–congressional powers, more than presidentialism per se, that

---

8 See Geddes (1990) for a discussion of transitions in Latin America in which new constitutions were written versus those in which an existing or prior constitution was retained.

has hampered democratization in many countries. In Chapters 7 and 8, we undertake a systematic analysis of the many possible ways of arranging the relative powers of presidents and assemblies, and the implications of such arrangements for the balance of powers.

From this postulated affinity of dictators and constitutions with strong presidential powers, then, flow some of the exaggerated criticisms of presidential political powers in the *democratic* context. Precisely because a presidential constitution allows the head of government to be sheltered even from his own party and can be – *but need not be* – designed as well to give superior legislative powers to the president, authoritarianism and presidentialism have tended to go together. However, the category denoted by the term presidential *democracy* includes wide variation in the extent to which presidents have legislative powers. No criticism of authoritarian tendencies in presidential democracy is adequate without reference to authoritarian legacies that remain in many presidential constitutions in the form of superior legislative powers accorded the executive.

### IS PRESIDENTIALISM ESPECIALLY PRONE TO BREAKDOWN?

The criticisms of presidential democracy that we have reviewed are more than simply arguments about the quality of democracy. Indeed, even Linz, perhaps the harshest of the current critics of presidentialism, concedes that direct election of the executive is highly democratic. So does Lijphart (1984). Rather, as we have noted, the critics tend to express their arguments in terms of the likelihood of stable democracy. Parliamentary democracy, because it does not suffer from maladies such as temporal rigidity and competing claims to legitimacy and because it has the vote of confidence to resolve interbranch conflicts, is more conducive to stable democracy, the critics say. Interbranch conflicts under presidentialism are likely to be resolved through coups or other nondemocratic measures. Thus, according to critics, presidential systems are especially prone to breakdown.

Mainwaring (1992a) provides a list of stable democracies, where stability is defined in terms of longevity, that appears to be a clear vindication of the argument that presidential systems are inimical to the continued functioning of democracy. He lists thirty-two democracies that, as of 1991, had been democratic for at least twenty-five years. Of those countries, twenty-three (72%) are parliamentary. But is this the final word on the relationship between regime type and democratic longevity? We should like to try a different approach. Rather than take a "snapshot" of democracies as of a specific date, we shall look at democratic failures throughout the twentieth century.

Why should our method be a more reliable measure of the proclivity (or lack thereof) of different democratic regime types to break down? There are two basic reasons, both of which stem from historical observations. The first historical reason is that there have been two waves of breakdowns of democracy in this century, one between World War I and World War II and the other in the 1960s. The first wave claimed mostly parliamentary regimes (and no true presidential regimes). The second claimed mostly, but not exclusively, presidential systems. Of the three paperback volumes containing case studies on *The Breakdown of Democratic Regimes* (Linz and Stepan 1978) that were originally published, only the volume on Europe between the wars was out of print by 1990. Apparently there is not as much of a market for studies of failures in an earlier period – when the failed regimes happened to have governments based on parliamentary confidence – as there is for the contemporary period, when several Latin American presidential systems broke down.

The second historical reason that our method of counting breakdowns is more valid than counting twenty-five-year-old (or older) democracies as of one point in time is that there have been three waves of democratization in this century (cf. Huntington 1991). The first was in the aftermath of World War I. The second occurred after decolonization in the post–World War II period (and extended up to the early 1960s). The third began in the 1980s and continues into the 1990s. Of these, only the third wave has given birth mostly to presidential (and some premier-presidential) democracies. Thus the method of counting successes, as Mainwaring does, cannot take account of new presidential democracies that, for all we know, might prove to be long-term successes, any more than it can account for failures (whether presidential or parliamentary) in earlier periods.

We have, in Table 3.1 compiled a list of democratic failures. We define a failure as a breakdown that led to a *replacement* of the regime by a nondemocratic regime. We thus do not count cases in which there was a brief lapse of democratic authority that was followed by either a new democratic constitution or a renewal of the former one. Such cases are not regime failures and replacements, but rather what Linz (1978) calls "cases of reequilibration." Cases of reequilibration include both presidential and parliamentary systems that suffered crises: Chile in 1925 and 1933, France in 1958, and India in 1972. In the Chilean cases and in France, democratic authority was restored in less than a year. And in India, where an election led to the ruling party's defeat despite emergency rule, there was never a break in the constitutional order. Indeed, in these cases arguably democracy (of whatever institutional form) reemerged stronger from the crisis. Another criterion we have used is to count only those cases in which at least two consecutive general elections were held before the breakdown. In so doing we avoid ambiguous cases in which one election was held under the watchful eye of a departing colonial power or as a mere "demonstration" for foreign consumption (Herman and Brodhead 1984). If such an election was followed by another and only subsequently by a breakdown, we count it.

Table 3.1. Breakdowns of democratic regimes in the twentieth century by regime type

| Parliamentary systems | Presidential systems | Other types |
|---|---|---|
| *Burma 1962 | *Argentina 1930 | Austria 1933 (premier-presidential) |
| Estonia 1934 | *Bolivia 1964 | *Ecuador 1962 (president- |
| *Fiji 1988 | *Brazil 1964 | parliamentary) |
| Greece 1936 | *Chile 1973 | Germany 1933 (pres.-parl.) |
| Greece 1967 | *Colombia 1953 | *Korea 1961 (pres.-parl.) |
| *Guyana 1978 | *Cuba 1954 | *Peru 1968 (pres.-parl.) |
| Italy 1922 | *Guatemala 1954 | *Sri Lanka 1982 (pres.-parl.) |
| *Kenya 1969 | *Korea 1972 | |
| Latvia 1934 | *Nigeria 1983 | |
| Lithuania 1926 | *Panama 1968 | |
| *Nigeria 1966 | *Philippines 1972 | |
| *Pakistan 1954 | *Uruguay 1973 | |
| *Pakistan 1977 | | |
| Portugal 1926 | | |
| *Sierra Leone 1967 | | |
| *Singapore 1972 | | |
| *Somalia 1969 | | |
| Spain 1936 | | |
| *Surinam 1982 | | |
| *Thailand 1976 | | |
| *Turkey 1980 | | |

*Third World cases

We have identified twelve presidential regimes and twenty-one parliamentary regimes that have broken down in the twentieth century. Additionally, we identify six other types that have broken down. Except for the premier-presidential regime of interwar Austria, these six "other" breakdowns were all president-parliamentary regimes.

Our greater number of parliamentary failures than presidential failures is hardly what one would expect from reading most of the comparative literature. Perhaps parliamentary regimes have received more credit than they are due as means to resolve political conflicts. Some refinement of the sample needs to be made, however. For example, if parliamentary regimes were far more common, especially in the Third World where the success of any type of democracy has been minimal, then our simple counting of breakdowns might obscure a greater *rate* of presidential breakdowns.

Table 3.2 shows democratic regimes that have not broken down in the twentieth century or, for newer regimes, that have passed the threshold of two elections that we referred to above. Included are only those countries with at least 200,000 population, to avoid microstates. The table lists twelve presidential systems, twenty-seven parliamentary, and eight other types,

Table 3.2. Countries that have held at least two democratic elections without break-down, as of 1991

| Parliamentary systems | Presidential systems | Other types |
| --- | --- | --- |
| Australia | *Argentina | Austria (premier-presidential) |
| *Bahamas | *Brazil | *Bolivia (assembly-independent) |
| *Barbados | *Colombia | *Ecuador (president-parliamentary) |
| Belgium | *Costa Rica | Finland (premier-presidential) |
| *Botswana | *Dominican Republic | France (premier-presidential) |
| Canada | *El Salvador | Iceland (premier-presidential) |
| Denmark | *Guatemala | *Peru (president-parliamentary) |
| Germany | *Honduras | Portugal (premier-presidential) |
| Greece | *Senegal | Switzerland (assembly-independent) |
| Ireland | United States | |
| Israel | *Uruguay | |
| Italy | *Venezuela | |
| *Jamaica | | |
| Japan | | |
| Luxembourg | | |
| *Malaysia | | |
| Malta | | |
| Netherlands | | |
| New Zealand | | |
| Norway | | |
| *Papua New Guinea | | |
| *Solomon Islands | | |
| Spain | | |
| Sweden | | |
| *Trinidad and Tobago | | |
| *Turkey | | |
| United Kingdom | | |

*Third World cases

indicating that parliamentary regimes are more common. The breakdown rate is higher for presidential regimes, 50.0%, compared to 43.8% for parliamentary regimes.

When we consider only Third World cases, however, we find that just over half (52.2%) of the presidential regimes in the less developed countries have broken down, while a higher percentage (59.1%) of the parliamentary regimes have. A remarkable fact revealed by the tables is the extent to which presidentialism is a Third World phenomenon, as only the United States is a developed nation with a presidential regime. Also striking is that most of the presidential failures from Table 3.1 reappear as democracies subsequently in Table 3.2. Among the parliamentary failures in the Third World, on the other hand, only Turkey reappears. While we shall not attempt to provide a theoretical justification for this observation, which could simply be spurious, it does indicate that the parliamentary failures in the Third World have tended to be irreversible, at least as of

1991. More importantly, parliamentarism has not fared any better in the Third World than has presidentialism; arguably, it has fared worse.

Indeed, we find no justification for the claim of Linz and others that presidentialism is inherently more prone to crises that lead to breakdown. Nor is it our purpose to stand that argument on its head and argue that parliamentarism is inherently prone to breakdown. On the other hand, these caveats about the link between regime type and regime breakdown does not mean that institutional choice does not matter; some presidential democracies that broke down might have survived had they been parliamentary (Chile in 1973, perhaps). It is also possible that some failed parliamentary democracies might have survived had they been presidential instead (the first republics of Nigeria and Pakistan, perhaps). Some crises may be so severe that no constitutional system could endure (perhaps the Weimar Republic).[9] Our central point here is that the argument against presidentialism has often been expressed universalistically, as if presidentialism *as a regime type* were prone to breakdown, while parliamentarism contained conflict-regulating mechanisms that would ordinarily shield it from breakdown. The historical evidence presented in Tables 3.1 and 3.2 suggests that the critics of presidential systems should rethink their case.

The presence of so many young democracies in our list of failed parliamentary systems might appear to be stacking the deck against that regime type. Ironically, however, much of the criticism of presidentialism and support for parliamentarism centers around the superior appropriateness of a parliamentary system for new democracies (Di Palma 1990; Mainwaring 1992a). So a list that includes young democracies is hardly inconsistent with the critics' means of conceptualizing the problems and choices at hand. There is also a theoretical reason for not excluding new democracies, as long as they have survived long enough to hold a second general election. Conceptually we agree with Di Palma that a lengthy period of "habituation" (Rustow 1970) is not necessary to prove the "consolidation" and "legitimacy" of a democracy. Once a transition to a democratic regime is complete, the new institutions either obtain what Di Palma calls "behavioral compliance" or they do not. Among new democracies, cases of both regime types have failed to obtain the behavioral compliance of political elites. Indeed, some of the new presidential democracies established since around 1980 have already outlived several of the young parliamentary systems that failed in the 1960s or earlier.

The critics of presidentialism might counter that the failures of parliamentarism in the 1920s and 1930s were concentrated in one region and resulted from international circumstances, such as economic disaster and the imposed peace of the Treaty of Versailles. However, as we foreshad-

---

9 However, Adolf Hitler three times ran for the presidency and lost. He was ultimately appointed chancellor because only a cabinet headed by him could count on parliamentary confidence, which the Weimar constitution required.

owed above, a similar argument resting upon regional concentration of breakdowns and international determinants can be made for Latin America in the 1960s (Therborn 1979). Besides, the proponents of parliamentarism have not framed their case in terms of anything other than the domestic political process and the ability of the regime to handle pressures, whatever the source of those pressures.

To be fair, Linz (1987) has stated his defense of parliamentary democracy in terms of other institutional choices besides the basic choice of parliamentarism or presidentialism that can affect the chances for stable democracy. Specifically, he cites the adoption of electoral systems less conducive to party system fragmentation and the constructive vote of no-confidence when comparing the interwar German and Spanish regimes to those countries' current systems. We wholeheartedly agree that other choices besides the basic regime type matter. We simply argue that, to be fair to presidential democracy, the critics should recognize that choices within presidential democracy as well can make a difference. Neither parliamentary nor presidential democracy is a unified regime type. Nor, as we have argued, do these commonly recognized types constitute an exhaustive typology. Indeed, that is one of the principal points of this book. Before going on to discuss institutional choices within presidential democracy that may be more or less conducive to democratic success, let us first address the question of why one might favor *any* variant of a presidential system.

### IN THE PRESIDENT'S DEFENSE

The criticisms of presidentialism have been discussed at length and refined in a number of recent analyses. Defenses of presidentialism, on the other hand, have been few and far between.[10] We should reemphasize that our defense of presidentialism is not meant to imply that we regard presidentialism in all cases to be a superior regime type to parliamentarism. Indeed, we acknowledge most of the criticisms of presidentialism reviewed above as penetrating. Nor do we reject the common empirical assertion that presidential institutions, as they have been realized, have often performed poorly. Much of our project in the chapters ahead will consist of discussing the variations in institutional arrangements found within the presidential-regime type, as well as premier-presidentialism and other forms. In some cases, we shall suggest alternative arrangements that might mitigate problems of less successful systems. At any rate, for now our discussion remains abstract; the only qualities of the presidentialism we discuss here are those outlined at the beginning of this chapter. We suggest four areas in which

10 Hartlyn (1989) offers intermittent and strictly qualified praise of Colombia's National Front as a consociational adaptation of presidentialism. Rather than a defense of presidentialism, however, Hartlyn's response to the system's critics is that even parliamentarism would not have prevented the conflicts that made the National Front necessary.

presidentialism offers at least potential advantages over parliamentary democracy. In some respects, these advantages can be understood to reflect merely the flip side of presidentialism's deficiencies. For example, vetoes built into the legislative process can be defended as protection against the capricious use of state power, rather than attacked as the roots of immobilism. Broadly, then, in response to the advocates of parliamentarism we offer the following ideal-type advantages of presidentialism. What presidentialism provides, to a degree that parliamentarism does not, is:

1. accountability;
2. identifiability;
3. mutual checks; and
4. an arbiter.

### Accountability

Accountability describes the degree and means by which elected policymakers are responsible to citizens. The more straightforward the connection between the choices made by the electorate at the ballot box and the expectations to which policymakers are held, the greater accountability. Accountability is closely related to concepts such as retrospective voting (Fiorina 1981), or "throwing the rascals out." Under these conceptions of electoral connection between constituents and government, voters need not be able to assess prospectively the policy directions with which they wish to endow a mandate on the government (Riker 1982a). Rather, voters need only have the opportunity to impose sanctions on elected officials at the next election. Officials can be expected to anticipate such sanctions if they stray too far from voters' wishes between elections (Eulau and Prewitt 1973; Pennock 1979). As Powell (1989) has observed, this form of accountability is weakened if governments tend to change between elections, and especially if the government changes shortly before an election, as happens frequently in parliamentary systems.[11] Under such circumstances, the responsibility for policy in the interelection period is less clear, making it difficult for voters to know whom to hold accountable on election day.

On the principle of maximizing direct accountability between voters and elected officials, presidentialism is clearly superior to parliamentarism, since voters vote directly for an executive that cannot be removed by shifting coalitions in the assembly. However, the principle itself is not universally accepted. Linz's argument regarding the inflexibility of political alliances in presidential systems and the advantage for members of congress to be able to make deals that are difficult to defend before the electorate is a direct contradiction of the principle of accountability. As we have stated, we are not convinced of Linz's case. Without wandering

11 Strom (1990:75) notes that only 49% of the governments in his sample of parliamentary regimes were formed near elections.

into an extended analysis of whether the electorate – or any particular electorate – is capable of exercising the kind of citizen control implied here, we simply suggest that the principle of maximized opportunity for accountability is complementary with the principles of representative democracy. The debate between presidentialism and parliamentarism is over the most effective institutional means of maintaining representative democracy. Therefore, the direct election of the executive by the electorate, and the accountability of the president to the public that this entails, will be considered an advantage of presidentialism.

In addition to its direct relationship to executive accountability, presidentialism clarifies the motivations behind the votes of individual legislators on important issues.[12] Where legislative voting does not have implications for government survival, a legislator or a party leadership can be held directly accountable for votes on legislation.

### *Identifiability*

An aspect of the connection between voters and the electoral outcomes that is related to accountability is the degree to which voters can identify before the election the likely alternative governments that may emerge after the election. The concept of identifiability is closely linked to theories of democratic government that call on voters to be able to provide a policy mandate for their elected representatives (Ranney 1962). Unlike accountability, which requires only that voters be afforded clear governmental responsibility in order to punish or reward their representatives retrospectively, maximizing identifiability requires that voters have an opportunity to make a clear prospective choice.

Strom (1990) has developed an indicator of "identifiability" for his sample of stable parliamentary democracies. The indicator can run from 0 to 1, with 1 indicating that in 100% of a given regime post–World War II elections the resulting government was identifiable as a likely result of the election at the time voters went to the polls. The average of all Strom's sample is .39, meaning that far more than half the time voters could *not* know what government they were voting for. Yet, under a parliamentary regime, voting for MP or party list is the only way voters can influence the choice of executive.

Among parliamentary systems there is a great range of identifiability scores (Strom 1990:75). Not surprisingly, systems with only two major parties, such as Canada and Britain, have scores of 1.00. Those with a clear left–right divide, such as Sweden (1.00), Norway (.83), or Ireland (.83)

---

12 Of course, under list PR systems, the relationship between voter and representative will always be less than clear. This is a function not of presidentialism or parliamentarism but of ballot structure and electoral formula. The point remains, however, that where accountability *is* possible under presidentialism, it becomes more difficult under parliamentarism.

also score high. But multiparty systems without a two-bloc format tend to be far lower, with extremely low figures for some, such as Belgium (.10), Israel (.14), and Italy (.12).

In presidential systems, identifiability is bound to approach 1.00 in most cases. As we shall see in Chapters 10 and 11, even in multiparty systems, if the president is elected by plurality rule, ordinarily only two "serious" presidential candidates compete in the election for chief executive.[13] Thus, if we value the ability of voters to be able to know which alternative executives are likely to emerge out of an election, presidentialism appears superior to most variants of parliamentarism.

To this argument one might respond that while voters in a typical two-candidate presidential race know what their alternatives are, their range of choice is sharply restricted. A vote for a minority viewpoint is effectively "wasted" in the vote for executive in a presidential system, while in a parliamentary system, a minor party may be able to play a role in cabinet formation. On the other hand, such a party may be shut out entirely due to the preferences of leaders of major parties. We could sum up this trade-off by indicating that, given multiparty competition for the assembly, a parliamentary system is good at allowing voters, with their range of partisan options, to know what they are asking for, but presidentialism makes it clearer what they are getting. We do not wish to claim that voters are universally able to make use of prospective voting, but we suggest that democratic constitutions ought to give voters the opportunity to do so.

Later, we discuss some institutional variations on regimes with popularly elected executives – specifically, premier-presidentialism, collegial presidencies, and modifications to the electoral cycle – which are potential ways to enhance both the advantages of accountability and identifiability, on the one hand, and the ability to make a vote for a minor party that is meaningful from the standpoint of policy output.

### Mutual checks

In much the same way that it clarifies the relationship between representative and constituent, presidentialism clarifies the stakes between legislator and the executive on any given issue. Following the logic above, members of the assembly freed from the threat of a vote of confidence can ratify or check executive initiatives based on the merit of the legislation itself rather than on the survival of the government. Of course, it is precisely this independence of the assembly that generates the problem of immobilism. Is legislative independence an advantage or a flaw? The critics of presidentialism unanimously see it as a drawback, although Mainwaring (1992a) qualifies this position somewhat in his argument that presidentialism is

13 In Chapter 10 we propose an electoral method, the "double complement rule," which safeguards plurality rule against the possibility of very narrowly endorsed victors.

particularly inappropriate in multiparty democracy, where minority presidents are the rule. Still, the flip side of immobilism is rule by consensus in the sense that one party is prevented from ruling alone; where a president lacks a majority in congress, consensus may be favored, provided the balance of powers is conducive to compromising.

If, on the other hand, the president's party, or a stable coalition supporting him or her, has a majority in congress, assembly independence may be a distinct advantage of presidentialism. Under such conditions, we do not expect immobilism. Moreover, it is under such conditions that parliamentary systems exhibit quasi-majoritarian characteristics. The incentive not to jeopardize the survival of the government pressures members of parliament whose parties hold executive office not to buck cabinet directives. The opposition will unlikely be able to solicit any defectors from among the majority to oppose the cabinet. The ability to coerce parliamentary majorities, then, can render the bloc of opposition votes in parliament meaningless. On the other hand, if the ability of parties to influence legislation from outside the cabinet is high (e.g., as in Belgium and Italy), we tend to find lower scores of identifiability and the most unstable executives (Strom 1990:73). Either condition – the impotence of the opposition, or cabinet instability – can be regarded as a drawback to parliamentary democracy.

In contrast, by reducing the coercive capacity of the executive over members of the assembly majority, presidentialism preserves the viability of the opposition, without necessarily endangering stability – provided the executive can solicit some defections on particular votes. Insofar as we share Lijphart's preference for consensual government over majoritarianism, we regard this characteristic as an advantage of presidentialism. At the same time, Mainwaring's point is well taken. Presidentialism without a presidential majority can be problematic. The question becomes, Is it possible to preserve the congressional check under majority conditions, while providing for the resolution of deadlock in the absence of a majority?[14] This is a question to which we turn later in the chapter.

On the subject of mutual checks, it is worth pointing out that presidentialism fortifies the executive check over the assembly as well as the reverse. Where legislative initiative lies predominantly in the executive, this is not so much an issue. However, in systems where assemblies are dynamic, such as the United States and Chile until the reforms of the late 1960s, this check can be critical. The logic is straightforward, as follows.

14 Requiring a constructive vote of no-confidence may well free up legislators from the parties in cabinet to oppose cabinet initiatives occasionally – provided they are confident that no alternative cabinet can be offered to defeat the current government. However, in two cases that use this format, West Germany and Spain, the cabinet has the authority to make any proposal before the parliament an ordinary vote of confidence, thus making the whip as effective as it can be in any parliamentary system. Only votes of no-confidence initiated in the assembly must be "constructive."

Where executive survival is based on assembly confidence, the executive is in no position to resist assembly initiative. In those parliamentary systems in which there are fragmented party systems and considerable initiative in parliament, the potential for coercion of the executive by the assembly is clear and is the key reason for frequent cabinet crises. Under presidentialism, on the other hand, use of the veto to resist assembly majorities does not jeopardize the executive's tenure. In sum, under conditions in which mutual checks do not threaten presidentialism with immobilism, they act to prevent majoritarianism, and should be regarded as advantages of the system.

### Arbiter

Turning on its head the criticism that presidents have no means of enforcing discipline on members of congress, some authors have suggested that the president might serve as an above-partisan arbiter of political conflict.[15] In a sense, this approach seeks a silver lining in the fact that the executive cannot threaten legislators with a crisis of government stability in order to secure support, as a prime minister can by declaring a given measure before parliament to be a matter of confidence.

The arbiter president resembles Neustadt's (1960) ad hoc bargainer, or cajoler. It is precisely the distance from congressional alliances which the separation of powers ensures that allows the president to act as a moderator of dispute in order to secure a legislative agreement. This distance, taken to its extreme, implies both a lack of influence, and perhaps as result, a lack of fetter. Because presidents serve a fixed term and often are not eligible for reelection, they will allegedly not be averse to making concessions even on issues central to the party platform, especially if the alternative is no compromise, and ultimate deadlock.

There are two primary problems with this view. The first is that to expect presidents to act in a nonpartisan manner under any circumstances is not entirely realistic. It is true that presidents are less bound by partisan constraints than are prime ministers, but their independence is not complete. Most are, after all, the leaders of major – if not majority – congressional parties. The second problem is that the case for the president as arbiter is, in effect, a celebration of presidential weakness and, at the extreme, compromises accountability. Weakness over legislation itself is not necessarily a bad thing. The Madisonian perspective, for example, prefers a weak president. The problem is that arbitration will be most needed under pure presidentialism at times of regime crisis, when support for and stature of the presidency is lowest (Valenzuela 1989a:15).

Basically, the scenarios are as follows: When the president has majority

---

15  See Karl (1986:213) and Valenzuela (1989a:19); also Neustadt (1960).

support, there should be no need for an arbiter. Congressional support for executive initiatives should be regular, although the congressional check remains viable. When the president has no majority, the arbiter is the role of last recourse. A president's separation from entanglement in assembly alliances should make her or him a better arbiter than would be a minority prime minister.[16] If the president may stand for reelection, accountability can still be preserved.

To this point, we have established a working definition of presidentialism, reviewed the central criticisms leveled against presidential systems, and outlined some tentative advantages of such systems over parliamentarism. We stress once more that the criticisms of presidentialism are not directed entirely against what we regard as the criteria that define presidential government, but rather against many of its associated characteristics, such as the unitary executive, the tendency to generate presidents who face hostile congressional majorities, or the ineligibility of the president for reelection. At the same time, we acknowledge that many of the criticisms directly address the core elements of presidentialism. Therefore, let us consider another regime type – premier-presidentialism – that retains some of the advantages of presidentialism, while showing the potential to diminish some of presidentialism's defects.

### HOW PREMIER-PRESIDENTIALISM ADDRESSES THE CRITICISMS OF PRESIDENTIALISM

In order to assess the potential advantages of premier-presidentialism, we return to the framework constructed to review the criticisms and defenses of presidentialism. We consider in turn the issues of temporal rigidity, majoritarianism, dual legitimacies, mutual checks, and the viability of the president as arbiter and as head of state.[17] Using both the criticisms and the defense of presidentialism as points of contrast, we hope to illustrate the potential virtues as well as the ambiguities of premier-presidentialism. In the following chapter, we shall undertake brief case studies of the performance of premier-presidential government in five countries. We suggest there that

16 Ultimately, the case for the president's potential as arbiter is far more compelling under premier-presidential systems. In such systems, the president without majority support enjoys at least equal distance from involvement in partisan alliances as under pure presidentialism; yet the provision for the formation of a government in opposition to the president establishes a safety valve short of regime breakdown by which political crisis can be quelled.

17 It seems straightforward that the accountability of the president to the electorate should be equal in premier-presidential systems to that in presidential systems. For this reason, we will not review the accountability argument separately in this section. The question of the incentives for legislative support of the president is considered in the section on mutual checks.

the performance of premier-presidential systems has been largely attributable to the institutional arrangements unique to each system.

### Temporal rigidity

Presidential terms under premier-presidentialism are generally fixed, as
under presidentialism.[18] The problem of a president facing an opposition
assembly, however, is not defined by the same temporal rigidity as under
pure presidentialism, for two reasons. In the first place, the president is not
necessarily the head of government. When an assembly will not support a
government of the president's party or coalition, the president must name a
prime minister to form an opposition government, as François Mitterrand
acceded to Jacques Chirac in France in 1986. Moreover, it is not required
that the president should dominate the prime minister – and so, indirectly,
the cabinet – under premier-presidentialism, even when he or she enjoys a
legislative majority. If the prime minister rather than the president is the
leader of the principal governing party, for example, then the president's
fixed term of office does not imply the potential for crises of temporal
rigidity. But even if presidents do dominate the executive, a potential
midterm loss of legislative support will not portend crisis if they name an
opposition cabinet that enjoys assembly support, and they are capable of
exercising the constitutional powers of the presidency while ceding control
over the cabinet to an opposition prime minister.

The second means of avoiding the problems of fixed terms in several
systems is to provide the president the authority to dissolve parliament and
call new elections. This provides the chief executive the opportunity to
appeal to the voters for a sympathetic assembly, and may be particularly
appropriate when a new president faces an opposition assembly elected at
an earlier date.[19]

### Majoritarianism

The problem of majoritarianism in presidential systems is mitigated under
premier-presidentialism primarily by the nature of the premier-presidential

18  In Austria and Iceland, extraordinary assembly majorities of two-thirds and three-fourths,
    respectively, can call for plebiscites on the continuation in office of the president (Iceland,
    Art. 11; Austria, Art. 6, Sec. 6). We know of no cases in which these provisions have been
    exercised. In addition, in some premier-presidential systems (France, for example) presi-
    dents may resign and call for presidential elections before their term is complete. Neverthe-
    less, while these provisions could mitigate the problem of temporal rigidity found in pure
    presidential systems, the more important characteristic of premier-presidentialism in this
    respect is the provision for assembly confidence in the cabinet.
19  Of course, as Chapters 11 and 12 illustrate, this particular scenario can be avoided by
    synchronizing assembly and executive terms.

cabinet. Because the cabinet is subject to parliamentary confidence,[20] it will not be as narrowly representative of the president's interests as will a presidential cabinet – unless of course, there is majority support in parliament for the president's narrow interests. But under such conditions, we would expect cabinets in parliamentary regimes to be highly majoritarian as well. Thus, if we can expect a given party to enjoy dominance in a parliamentary cabinet, we can also expect it to enjoy dominance in a premier-presidential cabinet.

### Dual legitimacies

Premier-presidentialism replaces the problem of competing legitimacies between the assembly and the executive with the potential problem of competing legitimacies within the executive itself (Pierce 1990). We address this dilemma in later chapters as we discuss the dangers of cohabitation. For now we consider the advantage of premier-presidentialism in providing an institutionalized means of resolving legislative deadlock between the president and assembly. The replacement of the president as head of government with a prime minister with legislative confidence has been discussed already. Only a couple more points have to be made on this subject.

First, it is worth noting that even a majority president will have a greater incentive under premier-presidentialism than under pure presidentialism to anticipate and accommodate the demands of his or her coalition, since a president's status within the executive depends so directly on the coalition's cohesiveness (Suleiman 1981:98–103). This consideration may temper the danger of an exaggerated sense of mandate, for which presidentialism has been criticized.

Second, while political outsiders can still be elected president under premier-presidentialism, the prime minister enjoys constitutional protection from dominance by the president. Thus, when the president is not the leader of the prime minister's party, we expect the prime minister to be able to act relatively independently. Provided that the responsibilities accorded the heads of state and of government are clearly distinguished, an outsider in the presidency should not present the problems associated with such scenarios under presidentialism. The strict separation of powers is reduced under premier-presidentialism by the requirement of parliamen-

---

20 Of course, cabinet nominees in the United States are subject to Senate approval as well. Cabinets in premier-presidential systems are inarguably more subordinate to assembly preferences than are those in the United States, since they are subject to collective rejection, which can be imposed ex-post as well as ex-ante and because the U.S. president retains the right to dismiss ministers. See our discussion in Chapter 6.

tary confidence for the government. Among other things, this requirement ensures that the head of government's level of political expertise will be sufficient to satisfy the political insiders in parliament.

### Mutual checks

If presidents were provided a veto, then their check against a legislative majority would be no different under premier-presidentialism than under presidentialism. However, as already noted, most premier-presidential regimes do not provide for a veto that requires an extraordinary majority to override. The relationship between premier-presidentialism and the legislative check on the executive, however, is less clear. Certainly, the requirement of parliamentary confidence in the government implies a check of some sort. But we have noted that the same requirement constrains, rather than fosters, legislative independence from the executive under pure parliamentarism. Do we have reason to expect that the majority of legislators who support a government under premier-presidentialism will be any more likely to vote their consciences to oppose cabinet initiatives?

The answer must be a qualified no. No, because the logic of parliamentary voting still applies under premier-presidentialism. Legislators in the majority coalition still face a disincentive to jeopardize cabinet stability. We qualify the answer because the disincentive may not be so great under premier-presidentialism as under parliamentarism. If the president dominates the prime minister, then the vote of no-confidence threatens this position, but not the president's continuance as head of state. To the extent that significant political authority is retained even by a minority president, then independent opposition by legislators to government initiative does not connote such high stakes as under parliamentary regimes.

Despite this conjecture, there is little evidence that legislators under premier-presidentialism actually demonstrate more independence than their parliamentary counterparts. During the first years of the Fifth Republic, de Gaulle relied on shifting majorities to build support for various legislative proposals (Wood 1968:103–4; Pierce 1990). But by the mid-1960s, as partisan divisions under the new regime became clear, so too did discipline improve – at least among the main party in a given majority coalition. Similarly, Kaminsky (1989:28–9) finds that Mitterrand relied on shifting majorities on budget legislation in his second term, but the support of Socialists was dependable. On the other hand, Suleiman (1980:103–4) points out that Giscard d'Estang was abandoned by the Gaullists in 1976 when he attempted to pass a major reform of capital gains tax laws over their objections. Legislators of parties peripheral to the majority coalition, then, seem to be more inclined to vote independently. This is often true as well under pure parliamentarism.

## Arbiters

When presidents dominate a premier-presidential system, it is because they enjoy majority support in the assembly. Under these conditions, it would seem, the need for an arbiter to cultivate legislative support for executive proposals ought to be minimal. Nevertheless, students of premier-presidentialism have observed that when the president dominates the executive, the prime minister becomes something of arbiter, or as Duverger (1980:184) describes it, chief of staff. Provided that the president and prime minister share a similar political agenda, then the prime minister acts as the executive liaison to the assembly. Suleiman (1981:121) points out that the prime minister may also serve at times to shield the president from political harm. If the executive's economic policies fail, for example, the president can sacrifice the prime minister, provided the president can credibly stick the PM with the blame.

While the prime minister may play the arbiter's role when the president enjoys an assembly majority, the president can serve as arbiter of partisan conflicts under divided government. When presidents face an opposition government, or when they are not the party leader, they are necessarily removed somewhat from the partisan politics of legislative coalition-building. It is precisely this distance that can allow the president to arbitrate partisan disputes (Lijphart and Rogowski 1991).

First, and perhaps most important, the president has the prerogative of naming the prime minister who will form a cabinet. The president-as-arbiter can use his or her discretion in choosing among whichever candidates could form viable governments to seek concessions from the future prime minister, and possibly to ensure a broad representation of interests in the cabinet.[21] In the second place, minority presidents can rely on whatever formal powers are granted them constitutionally to influence the outcomes of legislative struggle, including (in some systems) referring government legislation to judicial review or referendum. Finally, where presidents are accorded the authority to dissolve the assembly, they may use this leverage to pressure prime ministers to accept compromise with coalition partners or face the electorate. As we shall see in the next chapter, this means of presidential arbitration has been used effectively in premier-presidential systems such as Finland and Portugal, but destructively in president-parliamentary systems such as the Weimar Republic.

## CONCLUSION

This chapter has weighed theoretically the advantages and disadvantages of presidentialism and premier-presidentialism, based on their institutional

21 See Duverger (1980:169–70) on the role of Austrian Socialist presidents in cabinet formation during the 1950s and 1960s.

characteristics. In particular, we have reviewed the central criticisms of presidentialism made by proponents of parliamentarism, and have offered a series of responses suggesting that the basic principles of presidential government may be worth preserving. We argue that presidentialism offers the advantage of allowing the clearest possible choice to voters as to the constitution of the executive. The checks and balances inherent in presidentialism are also desirable when majoritarian rule is opposed.

We have provided some arguments for why both presidentialism and premier-presidentialism might be desirable as a format for representative democracy, but we have yet to explore empirically the performance of these regime types. This is the project we begin in Chapter 4, briefly considering the performance of premier-presidential institutions in a number of countries, and contrasting these regimes with president-parliamentary regimes.

# 4

## The premier-presidential and president-parliamentary experiences

### INTRODUCTION

Before proceeding with our analysis of the relationship between presidents and assemblies more generally, we now consider the performance of premier-presidential government as well as a few systems that we deem president-parliamentary. Such a task is necessary in order to illustrate more clearly the nature of the regime types, and their distinction from both presidentialism and parliamentarism. This is so particularly because premier-presidentialism and president-parliamentarism have been discussed infrequently in the comparative literature, and may be unfamiliar to many readers. When students of democratic institutions have spoken of premier-presidentialism (what others have called "semipresidentialism"), they have rarely shared a specific, common idea of its institutional structure. And, of course, regimes that we define as president-parliamentary have been described a number of ways: as presidential, semi-presidential, parliamentary, and as hybrids. In Chapter 2, we provided definitions that we believe are exhaustive and generalizable for all these regime types. We begin here with a general discussion of the thorniest institutional problem that is, in effect, built into premier-presidential government – the possibility of a divided executive.

Where the president and the cabinet are of opposing parties or blocs, premier-presidential government faces a challenge somewhat similar to that of presidentialism under divided government. The specific tensions among political adversaries, the dangers to regime stability, and the potential means of resolving those threats, however, are all different under premier-presidential and president-parliamentary as opposed to presidential systems. The theoretical discussion of divided executives will be followed by examinations of premier-presidential and president-parliamentary regime performance. We begin by discussing some of the more well-known cases of these regime types: France under the Fifth Republic, Finland, and Portugal, as well as Sri Lanka since 1979 and Weimar Germany. As we shall see, although the latter two cases have been identified as premier-presidentialism (semipresidentialism) elsewhere, a careful examination of the formal bal-

ance of powers, and the performance of some of these regimes, suggests that
they more closely approximate our definition of president-parliamentary. In
the case of Sri Lanka, this is so despite the influence of France's system on
the designers of the Sri Lankan constitution.

We then proceed to consider other cases in which independently elected
presidents coexist with cabinets dependent on assembly confidence. We
shall see that such an arrangement does not necessarily produce the direction of the cabinet by the assembly. Finally, we consider some new premier-
presidential regimes, and a new proposal for premier-presidential government, in which the performance of the institutions cannot yet be assessed.

Many of these brief case studies underscore the danger of institutional
arrangements that do not provide clear mechanisms for the resolution of
conflict between presidents and opposition assemblies. But the cases also
illustrate the potential advantages of premier-presidential systems in some
of the areas in which we have suggested the regime type might differ from
both presidentialism and parliamentarism.

### THE PERILS OF COHABITATION

For any of the potential advantages of premier-presidentialism to hold, two
assumptions must hold: first, that the system will provide for a clear division of presidential from prime ministerial responsibilities; and second,
that this division will be respected on both sides, instead of producing
competitive dyarchy. That the second condition should be met is by no
means self-evident, even where the constitution is textually clear on executive responsibilities and the division is clear and mutually exclusive. Unfortunately, the ambiguity of some constitutions has been a common stum-
bling block to cooperation within the executive. Judging from three
president-parliamentary regimes that have been less than satisfactory –
those in Portugal, Sri Lanka, and the Weimar Republic – it appears that a
primary challenge of constitutional design must be to establish a clear
division between the authorities of head of state and head of government,
and to make clear within the constitution that the formal distinction between the two roles will be recognized upon the loss of the presidential
majority in the assembly. In the case studies that follow, we shall see more
clearly the problems that constitutional ambiguity, or disproportionate constitutional powers, can cause.

Before examining the cases, however, we must consider the question of
whether constitutional divisions of authority will be respected when a president and prime minister are of opposing political tendencies – a scenario
dubbed "cohabitation" to describe the French experience of 1986–8. The
fundamental problem of the "executive divided against itself" (Pierce 1990)
would parallel the problem of dual legitimacies under pure presidentialism,
as described in Chapter 3. In premier-presidentialism, the executive could

be divided into opposing segments – the president on the one hand, and a cabinet with assembly support on the other – elected with separate mandates by distinct constituencies. Where either or both segments fail to recognize the claims to executive authority made by the other, cohabitation could generate regime crisis. As we shall see, the risk is especially great in president-parliamentary systems.

We can imagine two potential scenarios of conflict under cohabitation. First, the cabinet may refuse to accept the legislative powers of a president, despite the fact that the president may be provided such powers in the constitution.[1] Second, a president may refuse to acknowledge the claims to executive leadership made by an opposition assembly majority. If this is the case, the president might use her authority over government formation to deny the prime ministership, or even cabinet membership, to a key party or parties. Or she might simply ignore cabinet and assembly opposition and attempt to legislate over the head of the assembly, if constitutional means exist to do so.[2]

Pierce (1990) has argued convincingly that where a president and an assembly majority each have sufficient constitutional authority to challenge the other's direction of the executive, neither can be expected to defer to the other in the absence of quite unusual circumstances. Regarding the French experience of 1986–8, Pierce points both to consensus between President Mitterrand and Prime Minister Chirac on important policy dimensions, and to the short prospective time horizon for cohabitation and the electoral incentives of both sides. We believe that Pierce's second point is generalizable; that is, that the relative timing of presidential and assembly elections is a critical determinant not only of whether presidents and assembly majorities will have incentives to make the concessions necessary to co-inhabit the executive, but also whether the conditions of cohabitation are realized to begin with.

Because of the requirement of confidence in the cabinet, assembly elections in premier-presidential systems will always be contested at least partially as judgments on executive performance. Therefore, if either the assembly or the president can claim a more recent electoral mandate, that

1 This scenario may be especially likely where the president is not a leader of any major party in the assembly, and so cannot provide support in the form of votes for any cabinet or legislative program. This was the situation in Germany during Paul von Hindenburg's final year as president, and in Portugal under the constitution of 1976, before the curtailment of presidential powers in 1982. Indeed, we shall see below that the conflict between President Ramalho Eanes and a series of opposition prime ministers fueled assembly support for the constitutional changes.

2 Again, we are thinking of here of Weimar, but in the years preceding Hitler's rise to the chancellorship. Also relevant, while less ominous, are President de Gaulle's uses of referenda in the 1960s on proposals for which he lacked assembly support. As we shall see below, de Gaulle's extra-constitutional actions could well have prompted regime crises had he been challenged, or had he failed to resign upon the rejection of his last referendum.

mandate may be interpreted as a valid claim to exclusive control of the executive.[3] This being the case, the scenarios for crises of cohabitation described above will be most likely either where:

1. a new assembly is elected with a majority in opposition to the incumbent president; or
2. a newly elected president faces a sitting cabinet composed of the president's principal opposition.

In the second instance, if the presidents are allowed to dissolve the assembly, they can do so as a means of petitioning the electorate for assembly support. In the first case, assembly elections must be interpreted as a repudiation of cabinet performance. To the extent that the president exercises influence over the cabinet (as leader of the previous majority party, for instance), then, it is a repudiation of this leadership.

The potential scenarios for crises of cohabitation just described will be most likely when elections for one branch regularly occur in the midst of the other branch's term. That is, where presidential and assembly elections are concurrent or held within a short time of each other, we expect the assembly majority to be compatible with (or at least not diametrically opposed to) the president; but the likelihood of compatibility declines and the likelihood of sharp division increases with midterm elections. We elaborate on electoral cycles under premier-presidentialism in Chapter 12. For now, the following points are in order. First, cohabitation presents distinct dangers for premier-presidential regimes. Second, the most likely source of cohabitation crisis is the claim by either the president or the assembly majority that a recent election imparts a more legitimate mandate for exclusive control of the executive than that of the opposing actor. Third, although cohabitation is possible under any electoral cycle, it is more likely under some formats than others.

THE CASES

*France*

In the French case, the two phenomena we consider – the use of referenda on legislation, and the successful experience of cohabitation – demonstrate a certain irony. One of the principal dangers associated with premier-presidential government is that any constitutional ambiguities are likely to foster conflicting claims to executive leadership when presidents and assembly majorities oppose each other. Regarding the referendum, the letter of the constitution is quite clear, but was disregarded by French presidents. On the question of the division of responsibilities under cohabitation, on

---

3 The same claim could not be made under pure presidentialism, where elections in one branch do not directly affect the composition of the other.

the other hand, some ambiguity exists, yet the two-year period produced no crises or dangerous confrontations.

We have already suggested that where presidents do not recognize the claim to executive leadership of the assembly majority, they may attempt to avoid conceding leadership of the executive by exercising extraordinary legislative authorities. Where presidents have the authority to call referenda, this would be a means of bypassing assembly opposition. Even a minority president might use the device selectively, putting together single-issue majorities on issues that cross-cut partisan cleavages, to retain some control over the legislative agenda.

Of course, the power to call referenda provided the French president in Article 11 of the constitution is not unilateral. The referendum must be proposed as well by the government or by a joint motion of the two assembly chambers. Moreover, the issues which may be subject to referenda are limited to those which will affect the organization and functioning of existing political institutions.[4] However, the referendum has been used in the Fifth Republic without reference to these checks and limitations. President Charles de Gaulle, who refused to recognize the assemblies as the president's equal in legitimacy as representative of the nation, first invoked the referendum in his direct appeal to the people, without assembly or cabinet approval, for the authority to set up a provisional executive in Algeria in 1961. The Constitutional Council did not challenge the move. De Gaulle used the referendum five more times in the next eight years, and it was the rejection of his sixth attempt by the electorate that prompted him to resign in 1969. Following de Gaulle's precedent, President Georges Pompidou also used the referendum unilaterally in 1972, to propose British membership in the Common Market. The referendum barely passed, and the reaction to Pompidou's use of the device without cabinet or assembly authorization was lukewarm at best. He did not use the referendum again (Wilson 1979).

The ability of de Gaulle and Pompidou to ignore the letter of the French constitution underscores the limitations of formal institutional arrangements as solutions to political conflict. Rather than being interpreted as evidence that the formal rules of political contestation are meaningless, however, these cases ought to remind us of the bounds of this type of study. It remains true that politicians opposed to the president's actions could have used constitutional means to challenge them, had they anticipated political advantage to doing so. The experience of cohabitation, on the other hand, reinforces the potential of institutional analysis. Where conditions were favorable, even a somewhat ambiguous set of constitutional provisions for the division of executive powers served to guide President Mitterrand and Prime Minister Chirac through two years of cohabitation

4 Constitution of the Fifth Republic, Title II, Article 11.

without incident, until compatibility within the executive was restored in 1988.

For the first three decades of the Fifth Republic, there was some skepticism that the system could adapt to cohabitation without competitive dyarchy and possibly regime crisis as a result. The 1986–8 period produced no great crisis within the executive, however, even while Mitterrand retained leadership over substantive policy areas. Article 5 of the constitution states that the president "shall be the guarantor of national independence, of the integrity of the territory, and of respect for Community agreements and treaties," while Article 20 determines that "the Government shall determine and direct the policy of the nation." These two provisions have generally been interpreted as reserving the domain of foreign and security policy initiative for the president, although it is by no means inconceivable that an opposition prime minister with a recent mandate would challenge the president's authority to determine policy of any kind. During cohabitation, it was to this interpretation of the division of responsibilities that Mitterrand and Chirac referred when each made claims for the scope of his authority. We acknowledge Pierce's (1990) point that a general consensus on security issues, as well as the electoral cycle, created incentives for each man to make concessions to the other. Yet it is important to recognize that even a less than perfect constitutional division of authorities provided a point of reference on which a mutually acceptable interpretation was agreed.

The annual summits of the seven major industrialized democracies present good examples of how the constitutional division of responsibilities was implemented, since the summit agenda include both trade and security issues. According to the interpretation just described, we should expect the president to represent the country's interests alone on international security, while the division of authority on trade will not be as clear. Trade issues, it seems, could be classified as both foreign and domestic policy. The arrangement adhered to by Mitterrand and Chirac at the summits fits precisely with this complex schema.

At the 1986 Tokyo summit, Mitterrand arrived a day before Chirac, to attend the formal opening dinner – the symbolic head of state representing France. Without Chirac, he also attended meetings the following morning on terrorism and security. The prime minister's arrival was carefully choreographed so that he could join the meetings by Mitterrand's side just as they turned to trade matters.[5] Likewise, the following year at Venice, Chirac deferred on the symbolic and security portions of the summit, but participated in the trade negotiations.[6] In the trade negotiations themselves, of course, the unified position of the president and prime minister

5 "French Power-Sharing Alters Summit Protocol," *International Herald Tribune*, May 5, 1986, p. 6.
6 Cover photo, *International Herald Tribune*, June 10, p. 1; June 12, p. 4.

had to be carefully negotiated before the summits began. Nevertheless, the two men succeeded in speaking for France "with one voice, but through two mouths."[7]

The example of French cohabitation does not furnish conclusive proof that a minority president with a significant reserve domain of powers will necessarily function effectively with an opposition government. But it does demonstrate that such an arrangement is feasible under premier-presidentialism, and that the constitutional division of responsibilities within the executive can provide a salient point of reference for politicians who acknowledge the rules of the game (see Schelling, 1960). Where such divisions have been less clear than in France – and especially in the president-parliamentary systems – regime performance has been much more problematic. We shall see this more clearly with Portugal, Sri Lanka, and Weimar Germany. Before proceeding to those cases, however, it will be worthwhile to examine another successful premier-presidential system: Finland.

### Finland

Nousiainen (1988:232–3) has argued that the Finnish constitution does not make entirely clear the division of authority between the president and the government (Council of State). This assessment is most likely because Finnish presidents have consistently played an arbiter's role, rather than directing the cabinet through the prime minister, regardless of the cabinet's partisan composition.[8] Actually, the interaction between the president and the Council of State is not entirely clear-cut. The president does indeed chair weekly council meetings, but the only subjects discussed at those meetings are those which fall under his reserve domain. He does not attend the cabinet meetings chaired by the prime minister, in which most legislative and administrative matters are handled. As Arter (1985:480–1) describes it, "The Prime Minister leads the government and there has been no attempt at a 'divide and rule' strategy, with the President cutting out the Prime Minister by sending messages to ministers." The lack of clarity Nousiainen notes in the division of responsibilities, then, has not generated crises in the actual functioning of the Finnish system. This is due in large part to the clarity with which the president's reserve domains – in foreign policy and the formation of governments – are established, and the relative importance of these reserve domains to Finnish politics.

Article 33 of the Finnish constitution establishes unequivocally that "the President shall determine the relations of Finland with foreign powers." While treaties and declarations of war must be approved by parliament, foreign policy initiative clearly rests with the president. Moreover, students

---

7 "Two French Leaders Take Delicate Duet to Tokyo," *New York Times,* May 5, 1986, p. A7.
8 Finnish constitution, see Articles 2, 39.

and participants in Finnish politics agree that the overwhelming importance of foreign affairs in postwar Finland – in particular, of sustaining
amicable relations with the Soviet Union while retaining as much independence as possible – has produced a system in which the president's role is
enormously important, even apart from the workings of the parliamentary
government (see Arter 1981:221; Arter 1985; Nousiainen 1988). As ex-
President J. K. Paasikivi (1946–55) said, on being asked what his job entailed, "I sit, read and ponder over how to keep this nation independent . . . one mistake might well prove fatal" (Arter 1981:222).

The centrality of foreign affairs to Finnish politics is one reason why
parties have delegated to the president, especially during crises, the ability
to act outside his reserve powers. The party-based electoral college (see
Chapter 10) is another reason; we also discuss the implications of the
method of presidential election in Finland further in Chapter 12. Examples
of presidential actions beyond those specifically authorized in the constitution include President Urho Kekkonen's intervention in 1970 in income
policy negotiations, which had bogged down between the government and
the nation's largest labor federation. When talks collapsed, the president
presented his own alternative settlement in a speech broadcast on televi-
sion and radio. His intervention prompted renewal of the negotiations, and
an eventual settlement. In another instance, Kekkonen applied pressure on
successive governments deadlocked on farm incomes policy and pensions
policy to overcome intracoalitional divisions, or resign. Following the
back-to-back resignations, Kekkonen then explicitly demanded concessions on the part of the Centre Party, stating that its future claims to govern
would otherwise be jeopardized (Arter 1981). In this instance, Kekkonen
was extending his constitutional power to appoint the members of the
Council of State[9] to influence policymaking outside the realm of presidential authority. It was Kekkonen's ability to take such actions without
prompting serious resistance that induced Arter (1981) to describe the
Finnish system as "president-dominant and president-reliant" in times of
consensualism in crisis.

Studies of the postwar Finnish presidency have until recently been tantamount to studies of the Kekkonen presidency, 1955–81. The most vocal
critics of Kekkonen's exercise of powers beyond constitutional limits under-
standably were members of the Conservative Party, which Kekkonen excluded from every government he named after 1966. But both Arter (1985)
and Nogueira (1986a) argue that in a multipolar party system such as
Finland's, presidential prerogative as builder of governments will necessarily be greater than in a more bipolar system, such as France's.

Finally, while Kekkonen wielded power to steer even specific domestic
policies under certain conditions, the end he consistently pursued was the

9 Finnish constitution, Article 36.

maintenance of relatively broad coalitions in government – which is, after all, well within the realm of the president-as-arbiter described above. While his exclusion of the Conservatives shows that Kekkonen was not strictly a nonpartisan arbiter, his role in arbitration among a wide spectrum of parties is consistent with his having been regularly endorsed by broad multiparty coalitions in the Finnish electoral college. He pursued his government-building actions without demonstrating outright bias toward the party (Agrarian, later renamed Centre) for which he ran. His manipulation of presidential prerogative as government builder aimed at maintaining the Red–Green alliance between the urban left and center-left, and rural interests, in Finnish coalition governments to the greatest degree possible (Arter 1981:231; Anckar 1984:135; Arter 1985:480). In Chapter 12, we say more about the role of the Finnish electoral college in relations between parties and the president.

### Portugal

Although it was regularly described as premier-presidential (semipresidential) (Duverger 1980; Opello 1985; Bruneau and Macleod 1986; Nogueira 1986a), Portugal's 1976 constitution suffered from precisely the lack of clarity between presidential and prime ministerial responsibilities described in Chapter 2 as president-parliamentary. Competitive dyarchy within the executive was exacerbated, moreover, by the existence of an "outsider" president.

Portugal has historically had a somewhat confused balance of power between head of state and head of government. While the constitution of the Estado Novo vested the nation's president with broad authority, Premier Antonio de Oliveira Salazar in fact wielded authoritarian power from 1930 to 1968 (Bruneau and Macleod 1986:128). But the nondemocratic Estado Novo is not of too much interest here. Portugal's experimentation with democratically elected presidents began with the constitution promulgated in 1976.

Under this constitution, a popularly elected president would serve alongside a prime minister, named by the president and subject to both presidential and parliamentary confidence, who directed the government. In addition to his powers to form and dismiss governments and dissolve the assembly, the president was given control over national defense, through his chairmanship of the Council of the Revolution; and he was given a de facto pocket veto over all legislation, since his signature was required for promulgation of any law and could not be impelled by the government or parliament. At the same time, the president was not given authority to preside over the cabinet (Opello 1985:149). And while his chair on the Council of Revolution assured him control over defense policy, the constitution reserved initiative on all nonmilitary foreign affairs for the government.[10] This arrangement seems to ensure that control over the executive would not be secured by either the president or the prime minister, a point supported by a theoretical discussion to be presented in Chapter 6. Moreover, the specific mixture of authorities does not suggest any clear division of authority, either by type of power or by policy area.

The ambiguous position of the president was exaggerated by his nonpartisan status during Portugal's early years under the new democracy. Portugal's first president under the 1976 constitution was General Ramalho Eanes, who had been instrumental in thwarting a leftist military coup during the transition from the Estado Novo to the new constitution. Although Eanes enjoyed widespread popularity, he had been elected without party affiliation.[11] His relationship to the government, then, could be defined solely in institutional terms – by the constitution.

With an outsider president, a cross-partisan alliance among parliamentarians opposed to presidential influence over the policy process seems natural. After all, the common interests were institutionally defined: to reduce the powers of the president and increase those of the government, made up of assembly members and supported by an assembly majority. At the same time, Eanes had no partisan defenders in the assembly. Thus, when the center parties began to call for constitutional reform because of objections to the socialist economic goals elaborated in the 1976 constitution, they were able to enlist the support of the Socialist Party by making presidential power the central issue (Bruneau and Macleod 1986:121–2).

With a two-thirds majority in the assembly supporting the revision, President Eanes was unable to block the adoption of a new constitution in 1982. As promised, a number of presidential powers were severely curtailed, including the president's power to dismiss cabinets or ministers, thus moving the current Portuguese system down along the vertical axis in Figure 2.1, into the premier-presidential area in the lower left quadrant. While parliament can still remove the government for political reasons, the president can do so only when the functioning of the nation's democratic institutions is threatened.[12] This restriction permits the president to invent "threats" to democracy, but it forces the president to provide extraordinary justification, which was not required under the 1976 constitution or in other cases that we identify as president-parliamentary. Given the existence of a Constitutional Court, a president's use of this power in dubious circumstances could be challenged and possibly overturned. The new constitution also restricts the

10 Constitution of 1976, Article 138.
11 Portugal's only requirement for inclusion on the presidential ballot is the submission of between 7,500 and 15,000 signatures to the Constitutional Court at least a month before the national election (Art. 127). This minimal requirement, it would seem, should encourage the "political outsiders" described by Blondel and Suárez (1981) to throw their hats in the ring.
12 Constitution of 1982, Article 198.

president's power to dissolve parliament: not within six months of its election, nor within six months of the end of the presidential term. Furthermore the document suspends the president's pocket veto. It now requires promulgation or veto within twenty days of passage, but the veto may be overridden by an absolute majority of parliament except for foreign policy and defense legislation and laws pertaining to the Constitutional Court or elections. Vetoes to the latter types of bills require a two-thirds vote to override (Opello 1985:155). Moreover, the Council of the Revolution is eliminated, and the president is given chairmanship of the Council of State. But the new council is a purely advisory body; and the authority over defense policy that had been vested in the Council of the Revolution is transferred to the government and the new Superior Council for National Defense. Finally, the power to suspend regional governments is also transferred from the president to the government.

Eanes complained that the new document not only reduced his powers but also made it more difficult to tell who was responsible for what (Bruneau and Macleod 1986:129). In fact, while Eanes's dissatisfaction is understandable, the 1982 constitution is more clear than that of 1976 on the relative powers of president and cabinet. It unequivocally reduces the powers of the president – virtually eliminating legislative powers – and correspondingly increases those of the cabinet. This is not to suggest that the new presidency is completely ineffectual. For example, even in 1985, Eanes was able to use a threat to dissolve parliament to compel Prime Minister Mario Soares to refrain from perpetual cabinet shuffling, and make concessions to the members of his coalition government (Bruneau and Macleod 1986:141).

Nevertheless, the powers of the Portuguese president are significantly less than they were previously. The difference since 1982 is reduced lawmaking power and the denial of a reserve domain in policy initiative. The change should not have been surprising, given the combination of a confusing division of responsibilities under the 1976 constitution, and an outsider president.

### Sri Lanka

If Portugal from 1976 to 1982 does not fit our definition of premier-presidentialism, the Sri Lankan system fits even less. The reason is not dyarchy, however, but complete presidential dominance over the rest of the executive, guaranteed in the constitution itself.

Article 30 states unambiguously that the president is the head of state, of the executive, and of the government, without qualification. Moreover, in Article 44, the presidents are given unlimited power to appoint all ministers and make their assignments; and presidents may retain personal control over any ministry or ministries, as they see fit. As a result, even a vote of no-confidence against the government in parliament would not affect the president's standing in the executive (Zafrullah 1981:39). The government would be removed, and the president would be required to name a prime minister who enjoys parliamentary confidence, but even within an opposition government the prime minister would remain entirely subordinate to the president.

Because of the presidential dominance inherent in the fundamental rules of the game, there is no confidence among students of Sri Lankan politics that the system could respond without a serious crisis to the election of a legislative majority hostile to the president (see Warnapala, 1980; Wilson 1980, chs. 4, 5; and Warnapala and Hewagama, 1983). Three scenarios are possible. First, the president might acquiesce completely to the parliamentary opposition, naming an acceptable prime minister, consulting and deferring to the prime minister on other ministry appointments, and directing the government according to the demands of the opposition. Given that the president has clear and viable alternatives to acquiescence, there is no reason to expect such a result. The second scenario would be a hostile confrontation with parliament, with the president retaining a minority cabinet. In the event that such a confrontation escalates to a crisis point, the president can unilaterally declare a state of emergency (Perera 1979:37). But the state of emergency must be approved by parliament after fourteen days, so we can imagine that this scenario would ultimately yield a severe crisis of legitimacies. In the third scenario, the president would name an opposition prime minister, and possibly a cabinet with substantial opposition representation, but he would proceed to legislate in direct competition with the government and parliament through the use of referenda.

The authority to invoke referenda granted to the president by the Sri Lankan constitution is far broader than that in the Fifth Republic of France. The president may submit at her or his discretion *any* bill that has been rejected by parliament.[13] Coupled with the president's authority to initiate legislation, it is clear that the power of the referendum can allow even a minority president to bypass parliament on legislation of any type. A wily chief executive will be able to appeal directly to the people on any issue for which he or she can engineer one-time popular support. The effect is to put in the hands of a majoritarian official the most majoritarian of policymaking devices – at the expense of parliament's role in legislation, and of the control of the government of the assembly.

President J. R. Jayewardene's use of the referendum to extend the life of parliament in 1982 presents a fascinating case that illustrates at once the president's fear of a hostile parliament and the danger of his unrestrained recourse to direct democracy. The sequence of events is somewhat complex. In the first place, the Sri Lankan parliament is elected for a full six years, both under the constitution of 1972–7 and under the current constitu-

13 Constitution of Sri Lanka, Section 85(3).

tion of 1978. Thus, the parliament elected in 1977, which had approved the new constitution and had originally named Jayewardene president before the days of popular presidential elections, remained in place in 1982.

Moreover, Jayewardene's party, the United National Party (UNP) held more than 80% of the seats in parliament despite having gained little more than 50% of the aggregate 1977 vote, owing to the distortions inherent in Sri Lanka's former one-seat district plurality electoral formula. The old plurality formula had historically caused enormous swings in parliamentary representation, and as part of the constitutional revision, the UNP had implemented a proportional representation system. The party leadership evidently believed that its broad support would ensure it a majority, or near majority, consistently under PR; whereas under plurality, even minor fluctuations in support could have drastic repercussions in terms of seats.

But in 1982, the UNP did not want to subject its majority to a test. In the country's first presidential elections under its new constitution in October of that very year, Jayewardene had won a full six-year term. But judging from Jayewardene's mandate, the UNP did not expect to receive a two-thirds parliamentary majority in PR elections. The president would likely be constrained in pursuing his agenda of further amendments to the new constitution. The near total domination the UNP had enjoyed since 1977 seemed preferable. So Jayewardene simply presented a referendum to the people in December 1982, proposing the extension of the 1977 parliament for another full term, beginning in 1983, when its current term ended. As expected, the referendum received bare majority support, and Jayewardene retained a docile parliament (see Warnapala and Hewagama 1983, esp. p. xiv and ch. 7).

Sri Lanka's dramatic ethnic violence during the late 1980s and early 1990s has overshadowed the less than satisfactory performance of its government institutions in mediating political contestation. Nevertheless, given the disincentives to compromise built into the institutions, and Jayewardene's ability to avoid coalition building, it seems likely that the 1979 constitution has contributed to the transfer of conflict from the institutions to the countryside. As with the Portuguese case before 1982, however, it is important to recognize the ways in which the constitutive rules of the game have been contradictory from the outset. Where an assembly majority supports the president, the president will dominate the executive, much as in France. But where an assembly majority opposes the president, the president's constitutional authorities both allow and encourage him or her to ignore the assembly. One of the principal means by which the president can end-run, or even overrun, potential assembly opposition is through the exercise of unrestrained referendum power. The dominance of the Sri Lankan president, based on formal powers, precludes the system from meeting the description of premier-presidentialism established in Chapter 2.

## The Weimar Republic

No review of the performance of premier-presidential regimes would be complete without consideration of Germany's Weimar Republic of 1919–33, although a close examination of the Weimar experience demonstrates that it, too, is a case of president-parliamentarism rather than premier-presidentialism. The failure of the Weimar regime, of course, carried profound implications. The specific regime type may be insufficient to account for the totalitarian regime and world war that followed it. And we do not claim that some other type of regime, such as true premier-presidentialism, would necessarily have prevented the rise of Nazism, although the frequent cabinet crises, dissolutions, and use of presidential emergency powers set the stage for the appointment of Adolf Hitler as chancellor (premier) even though he had failed three times in bids for the presidency. Our purpose here is simply to examine the Weimar institutions and their relationship to the destruction of democracy in Germany in the 1930s.

The Weimar president retained considerable legislative powers and the right to dismiss cabinet ministers in such a way as to thwart the possibility that ultimate authority over the direction of the government could rest with the assembly majority. Thus, the principal problem with the Weimar constitution, as we see it, was not so much any ambiguity over the relative status of the president and chancellor (as in Portugal, and perhaps Finland) as the constitutional dominance of the president, despite the requirement for parliamentary confidence in ministers. This dominance rendered the Reichstag helpless to control the government, and ultimately made the government and chancellor mere instruments of the president.[14]

The Weimar president was elected for a term of seven years, by a two-round majority-plurality system. In lieu of a first round majority, a runoff was held among the top *three* candidates, at which a plurality would suffice. The president alone named and removed the chancellor, and on the chancellor's advice named the government. It was not required that the chancellor be a member of the Reichstag. The Reichstag could remove the government, or any minister, by a vote of no-confidence, although no vote of investiture was necessary for the president to form a government. More important, the president had virtually unrestrained authority to dissolve the Reichstag.

The above provisions stacked the constitutional powers of both legislation and government formation heavily in the president's favor. Although the

14 This description, of course, does not fit the situation after Adolf Hitler's appointment as chancellor in January of 1933. But by that point, the entire political order in Germany was rapidly disintegrating. We are concerned here with the function (or dysfunction) of the Weimar regime leading up to the breakdown of formal democratic procedure. Hitler's final destruction of the Weimar Republic is beyond the scope of this institutional analysis.

Reichstag could reject his ministers and whole governments, the president needed no parliamentary approval to replace censured cabinet positions. Moreover, a troublesome Reichstag could simply be dissolved, subject to the weak limitation that it not be dissolved more than once "for any one reason" (Art. 25). Only the most unimaginative president could not conjure up unlimited "reasons" for dissolution. Indeed, as conflict grew more intense and chronic between president and Reichstag in the 1920s and early 1930s, President Paul von Hindenburg relied repeatedly on dissolution.

In addition, the Weimar president had the authority to refer any law passed by the Reichstag to popular referendum. While there was no presidential veto, then, this provision prevented the assembly from securing sovereignty over legislation, and made the president the gatekeeper over such sovereignty. Finally, the president could issue decrees with the force of law "in states of emergency to restore order, with the endorsement of the chancellor" (Lepsius 1978). The endorsement of the chancellor really provided little constraint, given the chancellor's responsibility to the president. And given the power of dissolution, even the Reichstag's formal authority to revoke decree laws proved ineffective. The events of the early 1930s demonstrated the dominance of the president in the Weimar system, and the disincentives for compromise and coalition-building that this dominance implied.

It is worthwhile to note here the theoretical foundations on which the Weimar constitution was based. The document was written, during the transition to elected government in 1918, by the legal and political theorist Hugo Preuss, on the counsel of two other eminent social scientists: Robert Redslob and Max Weber. Preuss accepted Weber's proposals for the appropriate term, means of election, and powers of the presidency, and Redslob's theory of the proper balance of powers between assembly and executive. Redslob sought to ensure that the Weimar system was not dominated by the assembly, as he felt the French Third Republic was, and so wanted to vest in the independent executive the ability to dissolve the Reichstag. His search for "balance" of power between the branches, however, failed to reckon with the absolute lack of reciprocal responsibility on the part of the president before the Reichstag.[15]

In the first years of the Weimar Republic, Presidents Friedrich Ebert and Paul von Hindenburg tried to form governments with parliamentary support. The limitations on the use of presidential decree powers, however, were never entirely clear, despite the constitutional provision that they be used to "restore order" (Art. 48). Ebert used the decree both in the face of revolts against the new government and to implement economic policies (Lespius 1978:47). In the latter years of Weimar, however, the use of

15 For more background on the Weimar constitution, see Neumann, 1942; Needler, 1959; Weber, 1968; Kircheimer, 1969.

decrees expanded tremendously, and efforts to base government formation on parliamentary support ended.

The fragmentation of the Weimar party system made forming and sustaining parliamentary coalitions exceedingly difficult. In the first place, the Reichstag was elected by proportional representation out of a single, nationwide district (see Taagepera and Shugart, 1989). Such an arrangement, coupled with the ease of admission to the assembly, generated a proliferation of tiny, special-interest parties, and decreased incentives for coalition building. In addition, the majority runoff system of electing the president failed to provide any incentive for coalition building around the competition for control of the presidency. Together, these two institutional characteristics complicated considerably the project of maintaining a government with support in the Reichstag.

As the economic crisis escalated in Germany with the onset of the Great Depression, and the threat to the political system grew from antidemocratic movements – primarily the Nazis – President Hindenburg began to rely more heavily on his formal powers to create governments, and to forgo efforts at building parliamentary support. On numerous occasions, he preempted or responded to opposition in the Reichstag by exercising his power of dissolution. Beginning in March 1930, Hindenburg named Heinrich Bruning to head a "presidial" cabinet – one based only on the support of the president. Hindenburg proceeded in July of that year to decree the national budget. When the budget decree was revoked in the Reichstag, the Reichstag was dissolved. This event was a benchmark in executive–assembly relations during the Weimar era. Lepsius (1978) provides the following data on the explosion of presidential decree activity, and the corresponding decline of assembly activity in the years 1930–2:

|      | Laws passed by parliament | Presidential decrees | Days in session, Reichstag |
|------|---------------------------|----------------------|----------------------------|
| 1930 | 98                        | 5                    | 94                         |
| 1931 | 34                        | 44                   | 41                         |
| 1932 | 5                         | 66                   | 13                         |

While such figures are by nature impressionistic, and do not illustrate the content of the various laws, the pattern is nevertheless impressive.

By 1932, the Nazis had become the largest political party in Germany, and the threat to institutional stability had grown correspondingly. In an effort to capture support from Hitler on the authoritarian right, Hindenburg named a new government headed by Franz von Papen in June. To preempt a certain parliamentary vote of no-confidence, the president immediately dissolved the Reichstag (Lepsius 1978:48). The new Reichstag elected at the end of July was also subsequently dissolved in September. Following the November election of yet another Reichstag, Hindenburg proceeded to form a new government in December, this headed by yet another non-Nazi authoritarian, General Kurt von Schleicher. Finally, confronted with the prospect of civil war and the explosive growth of Nazi protest and activism, Hindenburg named Hitler chancellor in January 1933. Two days later, the Reichstag was dissolved again, to preempt an expected no-confidence vote. In the elections that followed in March, the Nazis secured 44% of the vote, and in coalition with an antidemocratic partner, put together a 52% parliamentary majority for Hitler's chancellorship. The Reichstag subsequently suspended the constitution to allow Hitler absolute authority to impose his program.

Of course, this account of the institutional maneuverings of Hindenburg and Hitler cannot provide a full explanation for why Weimar could not survive. But it should be clear from these events and from the institutional qualities of the system, that the formal political rules in Weimar encouraged polarization and political conflict, rather than compromise. Even at a time when the Nazi rise to power was far from inevitable, and while politics conducted within the constitutional framework was predominant, the position of the Weimar president rendered the Reichstag ineffectual. Needler points out that it was formal powers, not the existence of procedural "loopholes" in the Weimar constitution, that "allowed men of ill will to fashion presidial cabinets" (Needler 1959:697). What is more, the chronic instability of the early 1930s provided Hitler the perfect opportunity to blame the current system for Germany's economic and political problems, and substantiated his claims that only through outright rejection of the democratic process, and under his leadership, could Germany prosper. The Sri Lankan and Weimar cases both demonstrate the important point that the formal characteristic of government responsibility to the assembly must not be rendered ineffectual in practice by the dominance of the president.

### Other cases

Although we do not undertake further detailed case studies here, it is worth noting that both Duverger and Nogueira identified three additional countries as semipresidential: Austria, Ireland, and Iceland.[16] The most notable characteristic common to these three is the failure of their presidents to exercise political influence – either in the legislative process or as arbiters among parties. In the case of Ireland, as we shall see, this is not surprising, given that the president has no constitutional powers. In the Austrian and especially Icelandic cases, however, the evident passivity of the president is an enigma.

For the Austrian case, Nogueira offers a plausible explanation. The leverage of the president as arbiter rests primarily upon the power to name

16 Neither identified Sri Lanka as a semipresidential system. Thus, each identified a total of six extant cases of the regime type.

prime ministers, but where a party system is dominated by two main parties or blocs, one of which generally secures a majority in parliament, the arbiter power of the president will likely be mitigated. The leaders of the principal Austrian parties have not run for president, but have remained in the assembly to compete for the prime ministership. Moreover, the use of grand coalitions in Austria for much of the postwar period, reduced the potential for presidential discretion even further.

The Icelandic case seems to challenge Nogueira's logic. Here, we have both a multiparty system and strong formal presidential powers over legislation and government formation. Yet not only are Icelandic presidents uniformly acquiescent to government directives, the presidency is not even sought by partisan candidates. The constitutional provisions may be in part attributable to borrowing of the formal powers of the Danish monarch and applying them to the Icelandic head of state at the time of Iceland's independence from Denmark. Just as the Danish monarch's powers are never exercised in the era of a constitutional monarchy, neither are those of the Icelandic presidents. Still, the provision of popular election would seem to imply that partisan candidates would compete for the office. Perhaps the main reason that no such candidate has emerged is the ease with which the constitution could be amended by parties that would oppose such a president. Lijphart (1984:189) shows no premier-presidential system besides Iceland in which the constitution may be reformed by "pure majority rule" within parliament. Thus the presidency (like a monarchy) could be simply amended away or have its powers curtailed, as happened in Portugal, should a threatening president ever emerge.[17]

In addition to the cases identified by Duverger and Nogueira, and those discussed above, we shall discuss briefly two new regimes, those of Haiti and Namibia, as well as one officially endorsed proposal. In Argentina, there has been a proposal for premier-presidential government by the Comisión por la Consolidación de la Democracia established during the Alfonsin administration. The Argentine proposal for a new form of government was a response to the standard criticisms of presidentialism outlined in Chapter 3. The members of the *comisión* outlined a premier-presidential alternative for Argentina, but the proposal has not been formally considered by the Argentine Congress or a constitutional convention. For the purposes of comparison, we include the relevant elements of the reform purposal presented by the *comisión*'s report in our analysis in Chapter 8 of presidential powers.

The new Haitian constitution of 1987 stands out for at least three reasons. First, Haiti's was the first new democratic constitution of all those

---

17 Although the provision requires a three-fourths majority to carry forward, the Icelandic parliament may call for a plebiscite on the president's removal from office, providing a further check on presidents' exercise of powers that might threaten the institutional independence of the assembly.

enacted in the Western Hemisphere in the 1980s in which the cabinet relies exclusively on parliamentary confidence. Second, the constitution attempts to avoid crises over appointment of the premier and relations between the premier and president. The president must, according to Article 137 of the constitution, propose as premier a member of the majority party in the assembly. In the event that there is no such party, the president must first "consult" with the presidents of both chambers of the assembly. While the precise meaning of "consult" is left unclear, the intention is obviously to make sure that whenever there is no majority party, the assembly retains primacy in determining the makeup of the government. In this sense, the Haitian president would seem to be virtually, if not completely, powerless, as is the Irish president. The final noteworthy aspect of the Haitian constitution, and one that could be a source of friction, is its requirement for simultaneous confidence in the cabinet by both chambers. Since the chambers are constituted differently, it is possible that their majorities might differ at times.[18] As Lijphart (1984) observed with respect to Australia, such bicameral confidence can hold the potential for a constitutional crisis. Indeed, the requirement of confidence before a bicameral assembly could be construed as a form of dual democratic legitimacy, a factor that critics of presidentialism attribute uniquely to that regime type.[19]

Namibia under the constitution of 1989 is another president-parliamentary regime, but with an unusual variation that may provide a "safety valve" for conflicts between president and assembly, although it is still too early to tell. The president has the power to name the entire cabinet and may dismiss it in whole or in part, provisions that on the surface imply presidential dominance akin to that in Weimar and Sri Lanka. But Namibia may have retained a means of ensuring that the president cedes at least some authority to the assembly (or, more directly, to its agent, the prime minister) over the direction of the cabinet by requiring that a president who dissolves the assembly stand for reelection concurrently with new assembly elections. That is, if the Namibian assembly repeatedly censures cabinets, presidents have the alternative of calling for new elections, but only if they are willing to face the electorate themselves. Rather than risk such a confrontation in which they could be removed from office, we might expect Namibian presi-

18 The electoral system used for both chambers is majority runoff, diminishing somewhat the likelihood of different majorities. On the other hand, the upper house is to be elected on staggered six-year terms, with one-third of the seats at stake every two years, while the lower house is to be renewed in full every four years.

19 It is indeed possible, that with the "arbiter" in cases of noncompatible majorities in the two assemblies being a popularly elected president instead of an appointed governor-general (as in Australia), the potential for conflict might be less. On the other hand, the Haitian head of state lacks the authority to dissolve either chamber as a possible means of resolving deadlock, as happened in Australia in 1975. If the president were from one party or an "outsider" and each assembly were controlled by different coalitions, there could be "*triple* democratic legitimacy"!

dents to be willing to accept independent direction of the cabinet by the prime minister. At this point, with the first Namibian President Sam Nujoma enjoying a secure majority of SWAPO partisans in the assembly, the system's performance under other conditions is undetermined.

Finally, Chile's so-called parliamentary republic (1896–1925) and the current regime in Peru have been described both as parliamentary and as effectively premier-presidential, on account of the existence and frequent use of the no-confidence vote for cabinet members (Needler 1965; Heise 1974). Here too, however, we maintain that it is more apt to classify these systems as president-parliamentary regimes, owning to the dual responsibilities of the cabinet to both the president and assembly, as well as the fact that while the assembly could reject cabinets, it had no say in how to reconstitute the government. Although the effectiveness of censure in each case significantly weakened the president's control over the cabinet, censure did not ensure cabinet responsiveness to the assembly majority.[20]

Our definition of premier-presidentialism requires that a prime minister direct the cabinet, which in turn requires that the cabinet depend only on the confidence of the assembly. Those who would label Chile and Peru premier-presidential would argue that the assembly (without a prime minister as agent in Chile's case) effectively directed the cabinet. But when the president and congress were fundamentally at odds on the direction of the cabinet, both Chile and Peru experienced chronic cabinet turnover – effectively, cabinets with no clear direction at all. We reiterate that just as Chile and Peru do not meet our requirements for premier-presidential government, neither does Portugal from 1976 to 1982, nor Sri Lanka, nor Namibia. In the Sri Lankan case, the assembly clearly has little recourse to ensure that the prime minister can direct the cabinet. Indeed, given the inordinate formal powers of the president, it is difficult to understand how the existence of a prime minister and the requirement of cabinet responsibility to the assembly can moderate presidential dominance at all, short of triggering some sort of constitutional crisis. For all these systems, we shall be able to see more clearly why they fail to be genuine cases of premier-presidentialism (or, for that matter, presidentialism) when we consider powers of presidents more systematically in Chapter 8. For now, we simply point out one of that chapter's conclusions, which already has been foreshadowed in the discussion here: Those regimes with dual responsibility of the cabinet to both the assembly and the president have tended to be unsatisfactory in their performance.

## CONCLUSION

Part of the problem in assessing the viability of premier-presidentialism has resulted from confusion over what the regime type is. In Chapter 2, we

20 The same observation is likely to prove true for the new constitution of Colombia.

proposed a number of characteristics that we understand to be essential to the regime type originally described by Duverger. In this chapter we have suggested that the performance of premier-presidential regimes, particularly during the periods of cohabitation that are most likely to threaten regime stability, will depend on the clarity of the division of executive responsibilities between president and cabinet. The specific combinations of responsibilities can vary. One key point is that ambiguity will increase the danger that either a president or an opposition assembly majority will reject the claims to executive authority of the other. This has proven especially true in the cases we have identified as president-parliamentary. We suggest that, to minimize conflicts between premier and president, a "residual powers" clause should grant any unspecified or unclear powers to the premier. Another matter that should be recognized by constitution designers is that placing sufficient powers in the hands of the president that he or she can ignore pressures from the assembly altogether is a dangerous formula, and one that we would not recommend. Finally, as we shall develop more fully in Chapter 12, the relative timing of presidential and assembly elections will largely determine the likelihood both of compatibility within the executive and that claims to executive authority will be challenged. We now turn to a more systematic examination of the constitutional balance of powers between presidents and assemblies. We shall begin by reviewing the means by which executives and assemblies are elected or selected, proceed to examine their mutual dependence or independence for survival, and finally consider their relative legislative powers.

# 5

# The constitutional origins of chief executives

## INTRODUCTION

As defined in Chapter 2, a principal aspect in which presidential regimes are distinct from parliamentary, premier-presidential, and various hybrid regime types is in the separate origin and survival of executive and assembly. Recall that a requirement for presidentialism is that the chief executive be elected by popular vote. However, in a number of regimes that have generally been considered presidential or hybrid systems, the chief executive has been constituted according to various means, which sometimes modify and sometimes preclude the criterion of popular election. In this chapter, we shall examine in detail various means of constituting chief executive power in presidential and hybrid systems, reviewing a number of case studies to illustrate the possible variations. We undertake this exercise for two main reasons. First, we demonstrate that there are any number of ways to constitute executive power in regimes that are neither presidential nor premier-presidential, nor parliamentary. Second, and more important, the cases highlight the impact that various rules guiding the origin of the executive have on the incentives that drive political behavior. As we shall see, the nature of the party system and of coalition building, as well as the means of replacing the chief executive, all depend largely on the constitutional means by which the executive originates. In this chapter, we shall discuss in turn:

1. selection of the chief executive by the assembly (instead of the electorate);
2. variations on presidential eligibility for reelection;
3. the existence and role of the vice-presidency; and
4. the prospect of a collegial presidency.

## SELECTION OF THE CHIEF EXECUTIVE BY THE ASSEMBLY

Of the variations we shall discuss, the selection of the executive by the assembly is one of those most likely to constitute a serious breach of the presidential principle that the origin of assembly power should be distinct from the origin of executive power. Indeed, only if assembly selection of the executive is in practice no more than ratification of the popular electoral plurality would we consider the regime presidential. Chile from 1925 until 1973 was such a case. In other cases, where selection of the executive involves the formation of coalitions among parties within the assembly, we cannot call the regime presidential, even if there is an initial round of voting for executive by the electorate.

In the United States, the so-called Virginia plan at the Constitutional Convention would have provided for selection of the president by congress instead of the separately elected electoral college that was adopted (see Ketchman 1986). In the U.S. Constitution there is, nonetheless, a provision for congressional selection in the event that the electoral college does not produce a majority for one contender. In such cases, the House of Representatives selects the chief executive from among the three (originally five) top candidates (Art. II, Sec. 1). Of course, the conditions for congressional selection have proven truly extraordinary; it has happened only twice, and not since the 1824 election.

Interestingly, the provision for congressional selection even under extraordinary circumstances contradicts Alexander Hamilton's argument in favor of an electoral college as offering the best combination of directness and prudence in selecting an executive. Hamilton writes:

[The authors of the constitution] have not made the appointment of the President to depend on any pre-existing bodies of men who might be tampered with beforehand to prostitute their votes; but they have referred it in the first instance to an immediate act of the people of America, to be exerted in the choice of persons for the temporary and sole purpose of making the selection. And they have excluded from eligibility to this trust all those who from situation might be suspected of too great devotion to the President in office. No senator, representative, or other person holding a place of trust or profit under the United States can be of the number of the electors.

And elsewhere, "Nothing was more to be desired than that every practicable obstacle should be opposed to cabal, intrigue, and corruption" (Hamilton, *Federalist* No. 68).

It may be that Hamilton was able to reconcile his determined opposition to congressional selection with its existence in the constitution because it seemed such an unlikely turn of events. At any rate, his is perhaps the most eloquent rebuttal to current arguments in favor of backroom parliamentary negotiations to select an executive.[1] Still, as we shall see, a regime with congressional selection of the executive can offer certain conditional advantages over either presidentialism or parliamentarism, especially for societies with deep divisions.

1 See Linz (1987), as well as the discussion of his argument in Chapter 2.

*Congressional selection: not parliamentary, but
assembly-independent regimes*

Where the executive emerges out of coalitions in the assembly, the regime
takes on a key feature of parliamentarism. However, if the assembly cannot pass a resolution of no-confidence and replace the executive with a new
one before the end of the constitutional term of office (other than by an
extraordinary procedure, such as impeachment), the regime is not parliamentary. In Chapter 2, we offered a general typology of regime types in
which we label such a hybrid an assembly-independent regime, and we
shall offer a more extensive discussion of this typology in Chapter 8. In this
hybrid regime, the origin of executive power is not separate from assembly
power, but the survival of the two branches remains independent.

The oldest current case of this type of hybrid regime is the Swiss system.
In Switzerland, a collegial executive is chosen for a fixed term by the
bicameral elected assembly. The Swiss experience suggests what might be a
more general lesson of this regime type: Unlike the assemblies of many
parliamentary regimes, the Swiss assembly remains an important source of
legislation. Lijphart (1984) reports that, measured by the degree to which
the assembly makes both general laws and more specific rule-making (regulations), the Swiss assembly is the second most powerful legislature in his
sample of twenty-two democracies. We partially disagree, however, with
his assessment of the reason. Lijphart attributes the power of the Swiss
assembly as a legislature to its being "the second clear case of separation of
powers" (Lijphart 1984:79) in addition to the United States, which Lijphart
reports as having had the most active legislature.

It is only partly accurate to refer to Switzerland as having a separation of
powers. The separation of survival of powers – owing to the lack of a vote
of no-confidence (or dissolution) – no doubt accounts for the activism of
the assembly. However, the origin of executive power in the assembly
means that, to be selected in the first place, the members of the executive
must be in general agreement with the policy wishes of their parties in the
assembly. They do not have separate accountability before the electorate,
as does a presidential executive. On the other hand, the assembly can
engage in active lawmaking without risking bringing down the government
if some proposal deviates from the principles upon which the government
was originally formed. In parliamentary systems, allowing the assembly to
remain activist in lawmaking may entail a cost: executive instability.

In order to see if there is such a connection between assembly activism in
legislation and short-lived cabinets, we have prepared a simple table to
capture a sample of parliamentary democracies in these two dimensions
(Table 5.1). We rely on Strom's (1990) scores of "opposition influence" and
Powell's (1989) scores of "government domination" in legislative committees to measure the extent to which the assembly initiates legislation of its

Table 5.1. *Opposition influence and cabinet durability in parliamentary democracies*

|  |  | Cabinet durability | | |
|---|---|---|---|---|
|  |  | High (over 48 months) | Low (less than 48 months) | |
| Opposition influence | High | Austria Canada Norway Sweden | Belgium Denmark France IV Finland Germany | Greece Iceland Italy Spain |
|  | Low | Australia France V Ireland New Zealand U.K. | Israel Netherlands | |

*Source*: For cabinet durability, Lijphart (1984:83); for opposition influence, Strom (1990:73) and Powell (1989).

own or amends legislation presented by the cabinet. Lijphart (1984) supplies the data on cabinet durability, which we have broken down into two categories: greater or less than four years, which is the typical term of parliaments, discounting early dissolutions. We should expect that active assemblies and short-lived cabinets would tend to go together. As legislation is made by shifting coalitions, given a high degree of opposition influence, some of these coalitions would form for a larger purpose: replacing the government.

Indeed, nine cases are located in the cell identified by high opposition influence and short-lived cabinets. Israel and the Netherlands stand out as exceptional, but given their very large district magnitudes and associated extreme multipartism, their cabinets would be expected to be unstable regardless of the degree of opposition influence. Dutch and Israeli cabinets would probably be even shorter-lived if opposition influence were high, since minority governments might then be more common and such cabinets are typically short-lived (Lijphart 1984:81).[2] At the other corner of the

2 According to Strom (1990), minority governments are most common when opposition influence is high. The reason is that, given opportunities for parties not in the cabinet to be effective legislatively, the costs of being in opposition are not great. This may appear to contradict our argument regarding a tendency of parties in active assemblies to initiate votes of no confidence. However, our observation is independent of the frequency of minority governments: the cost of being out of government is indeed low if one can influence legislation from outside government, but is also low if one expects that changes in government are relatively easy and will occur relatively frequently. Lijphart's data on the short life of minority cabinets support this assessment.

table, we find Canada, which because it uses single-member districts usually has single-party (and therefore long-lived) cabinets. Likewise, Austria has a two-party system that makes long-lived cabinets the norm. Sweden's presence there is harder to account for, although even its minority cabinets have often consisted of one party that was near a majority, making it (and Norway, too) a case of a two-bloc (government–opposition) party system (Strom 1990). Generally, then, there is a trade-off under parliamentarism between having an assembly that is active in legislation and having cabinets that endure in office long enough to provide a program of policy options for the polity. Powell's (1989) findings of a low correlation between "representational" constitutional designs and governmental accountability and a negative correlation between majoritarian constitutional design and his "representative delegates" model of citizen control offer confirming evidence for our assertions.

Because the Swiss hybrid regime provides for fused origin and separate survival, executive stability can be assured while maintaining an assembly independent enough to allow the enactment of legislation by shifting multiparty coalitions. We should expect such a regime format to be especially favorable for divided societies. Indeed, Switzerland, with its multiple cleavages and assembly-selected collegial executive, is Lijphart's clearest case of a consensus democracy (Lijphart 1984).

*Lebanon.* A regime similar to that of Switzerland has existed in Lebanon. While Lebanese democracy broke down in the mid 1970s, as Lijphart (1977) observes, nearly all proposals for dealing with the Lebanese situation start from the same basic assumptions about power sharing that lay behind the original creation of the Swiss and Lebanese constitutions. In 1989, a proposal known as the Taif Accord called for reinstituting a power-sharing executive in which the Christian president would continue to be selected by the parliament for a fixed term. Under the Taif Accord, however, the Muslim premier, who is responsible to parliament, would be given nearly coequal powers (personal communication with Lijphart). Given that part of the Lebanese executive has been dependent on parliamentary confidence, the regime is of a different type than Switzerland. Still, with a fixed-term president selected by the assembly and possessing political powers, the regime is not parliamentary. See Chapter 8 for a further characterization of this and similar regimes.

*El Salvador.* Three Latin American systems are also noteworthy for their use of assembly selection of the president. One, El Salvador, used this method only as a transitional device before the writing of a new constitution which provided for the direct election of the president. The brief (1982–84) regime must be considered a success, given the extremely difficult circumstances under which it was implemented. A presidential election at that time would surely have pitted Roberto D'Aubuisson, the leader of the extreme (perhaps one could say fascist) right, against the left-of-center Christian Democratic leader, José Napoleón Duarte. The powers of the office they were contesting would not yet have been determined. Such an election thus would have confirmed Linz's worst fears about winner-take-all presidential elections. Instead, those two parties and several others participated in an assembly election in the midst of a heated guerrilla war. The assembly, in which the Christian Democratic party won a plurality but various right-wing parties combined had a majority of the seats, selected a Christian Democrat other than Duarte to be interim president. It also created three vice-presidencies (each held by a different party) and a power-sharing cabinet, thus resembling the Swiss model. By 1984, a new presidential constitution had been produced that gave only limited powers to the president, thus preserving the assembly as an arena of compromise while still creating a popularly accountable chief executive.

Bolivia and Chile are the two other instances of congressional selection of the president. However, the operation of these systems presents a stark contrast, in which the Bolivian president has been selected out of assembly bargaining, while in Chile, the electorate's plurality choice was consistently simply ratified by congress. After discussing each case in turn, we shall consider some reasons why Bolivia and Chile differed even though both have had the same formal provision for the selection of the president in the assembly in the event that the popular election does not produce a majority winner.

*Bolivia.* The Bolivian case is different from the others so far discussed in that there are presidential as well as assembly elections, although voters must vote the same party ticket for both assembly and executive. If one candidate obtains a majority of votes, that candidate becomes president. In the event of no majority of popular votes, the assembly chooses the president from the top three contenders.[3] As we shall see, the prevailing situation has been for presidents not to have been the choice of a plurality of the electorate.

Given its seemingly endless history of political turmoil, it is difficult to distinguish the exceptions from the rules in Bolivia. The presidency has

3 We are leaving aside here what Malloy and Gamarra (1987) call the *salida* option. By the *salida*, Congress, in an unconstitutional procedure, selects a compromise candidate who had not contested the popular election and is inoffensive to any of the competing parties. During the tumultuous year 1979, as Bolivia began its halting transition back to civilian government after fifteen years of military rule, Congress opted for the *salida* twice. Bolivia's *salida* presidents have proven ineffectual vis-à-vis the legislature (and vis-à-vis the military as well); but of course, this was most likely the result intended by Congress in selecting them. The *salida* represents an attempt to buy time, maintaining civilian control over the executive while a stronger mandate can be sought, either through another election or through further elite bargaining. See Gamarra (1987) for details.

been seized by extra-constitutional means more frequently than by election in the last half-century.[4] Still, of those presidents selected by constitutional means since the implementation of the 1967 constitution, congressional selection by parliamentary-style negotiations has been the rule. What's more, plurality winners in the general election have fared remarkably poorly in the congressional selection process.[5]

In 1982, two years after he had won a plurality in the June 1980 election, Hernán Siles Suazo of the Nationalist Revolutionary Movement (MNR) was awarded the presidency as the military returned to the barracks. But Siles's ascendance to office was negotiated between party leaders and the outgoing generals rather than in congress. When elections were next held, in 1985, Víctor Paz Estenssoro (Paz E.), one of the original leaders of the MNR, finished second in the popular vote. Former military dictator Hugo Banzer, heading the Democratic and Nationalist Action Party (ADN), led by less than 2%. In the congress, Banzer was unable to secure majority support. The MNR and ADN voted together to support the accession to the presidency by Paz E. His government proceeded to enact a major economic restructuring or "shock" to stanch hyperinflation (Gamarra 1990). Banzer ran again in 1989, and finished second with 22.6% to the MNR's 23.0%. This time, in congress, Banzer threw his support behind the candidate of the center-left Movement of the Revolutionary Left (MIR), Jaime Paz Zamora (Paz Z., Paz E.'s nephew), who had finished third with just under 20% of the vote. Like his uncle and predecessor, Paz Z. has governed with a coalition cabinet composed largely of members of Banzer's ADN and continued with the program of structural adjustment.

The legislative effectiveness of the coalition governments led by Paz E. and Paz Z. since 1985 has been noteworthy. For better or worse, they have succeeded in implementing and maintaining a harsh package of austerity measures. Bolivia's public sector has been cut considerably and its currency has stabilized, making Bolivia a showcase for neoliberal development economics (Gamarra 1990). In these governments, the conservatives have formed the largest consistent support block in congress. The center and center-left, on the other hand, have been awarded the presidency in exchange for acquiescence to the right's economic program. As long as centrist or leftist presidents are willing to trade control over policy for congressional support, the coalition can survive. Ironically, the very success

4 By our estimation of Bolivia's often complicated transitions and interim periods between 1952 and 1989, the presidency has been secured by overtly unconstitutional means eleven times, and by either direct election or congressional selection eight times.

5 Since 1967, the president has been selected by Congress five times. Only in 1982, when Hernán Siles Suazo was named president based on aborted 1980 election results, has the plurality winner actually assumed office. Two times in 1979, members of congress who were not presidential candidates at all were selected in extra-constitutional procedures. In 1985, the second-place presidential contender was named; and in 1989 the third-place finisher became president.

of these administrations may be attributable to the dependence of their presidents on congressional coalitions. Stronger presidents – perhaps plurality winners – may have been less prone to compromise with and even acquiesce to coalition partners. And it is this compromise that is essential to breaking congressional deadlock.

Thus, the system appears to be executive-dominated, leading Conaghan, Malloy, and Abugattas (1990) to argue that the Bolivian Congress was reduced to nothing more than legitimating or ratifying, as Gamarra (1987:411) puts it, policies designed by a small circle of technocrats insulated within the executive. Gamarra (1987:412) goes so far as to brand Bolivia an "authoritarian democracy." We maintain that the process is subtler than that. As the products of congressional bargaining, these apparently dominant executives actually represent a rough equilibrium between parties in congress and the executive (see Ordeshook 1986; Rasmussen 1989). However, there may be severe losses when authority is delegated without a specific means of retracting it. Despite the origin of executive authority in the assembly, the assembly cannot vote no confidence and thus enforce its will on the executive, as in a parliamentary system. This explains why Bolivian coalition governments have functioned in what appears to have been a majoritarian, if not downright authoritarian, manner. Governments have achieved considerable insulation from political pressures, but their own origin has depended on the willingness of the assembly to delegate the authority in the first place. Even where no specific retraction of delegated authority is available immediately, we should expect to see attempts by the parties to equilibrate the situation subsequently, given the means of executive selection in Bolivia.

This is, in fact, what we see in the case of intracoalition conflicts during the Paz Estenssoro government, which prevented the coalition from holding to a prior agreement, signed by the ADN and MNR in May 1988, to present Banzer as a common candidate in 1989 (Gamarra 1992). Gamarra indicates that, while MNR militants complained about the domination of Paz E.'s government by the ADN and the ADN did not trust the MNR's promises of support for Banzer, weekly meetings between the ADN and MNR leadership were instituted to hold the coalition together. When the MNR indeed failed to endorse Banzer, the path was again paved for a new postelection coalition after the 1989 election. Banzer, in effect, was thus denied the presidency because of the MNR's loss of "confidence" in a government that had become overdependent on the ADN for its policies and support.

Had the parties stayed together and presented a common candidacy in 1989, the role of postelection negotiations within the assembly might have been reduced. Even if the Banzer coalition candidacy had failed to win a majority of popular votes, the combined votes of the ADN and MNR could have put it in such a commanding position that the opposition in congress would have found it nearly impossible to put together an alternative to Banzer after the election. As it turned out, the parties ran separate candidacies, so a bargain afterward was necessary again. Now the MNR paid the price for having broken the agreement with the ADN, which voted for the MIR candidate. The implication is that any one of the three largest parties needs at least one of the other two to win: It needs either for the other not to present a candidate or for the other to vote for it after the election. This basic fact of the Bolivian "game" should enforce considerable compromise between parties – even when they may complain about executive dominance – and thus helps account for early success in implementing the difficult and politically risky austerity program.[6]

A parliamentary system, on the other hand, could have been a victim of considerable executive instability,[7] given the large number of players and the difficult policy choices needed. A pure presidential system would not have been as capable of holding together or reconstituting coalitions as has Bolivia's hybrid (assembly-independent) system, since executive power would then be independent of cross-party bargaining in the assembly. The Bolivian system combines the coalitions of multiparty parliamentarism and the executive stability of single-party parliamentarism or (true) presidentialism. While we would not be inclined to endorse the Bolivian system as a model, its performance under difficult conditions and, even more notably, in a country with a history of repeated coups earns it considerable respect in our view.

One final set of observations about Bolivia concerns the comparison with Switzerland, with which we started this section on assembly selection of a fixed-term executive. Despite the similarity between Bolivia and Switzerland in the method of executive selection, obviously the Bolivian Congress has not been an active legislature in the same sense that the Swiss assembly has been. While we have argued that this does not mean that the Bolivian Congress and the parties represented therein have been rendered meaningless or mere "rubber stamps," neither has Bolivian legislation been initiated and debated in the congress to a great extent. Partly this is a result of an executive in Bolivia that, unlike the Swiss, possesses a veto on legislation (subject to a two-thirds assembly override). Thus it takes a large coalition to legislate over the president's head. The fact that some of the legislation has been carried out under a state of siege, which requires a two-thirds vote of congress to sustain (Gamarra 1992), has made it even more unlikely that we would see legislative activism. Thus a very large coalition was required to enable the implementation of policies suppressing labor,

6 We do not mean to endorse the austerity program itself; indeed, according to Gamarra (1990), it dealt "a heavy blow to labor" and has caused considerable hardship. What we regard as instructive is that other countries' governments found it considerably more difficult to implement similar programs, while Bolivia was able to hold to the program.

7 See Gamarra (1992) for a discussion of this point.

for example, in the first place. Finally, the Swiss executive is collegial, unlike Bolivia's, meaning that there is no single "program" of government in Switzerland against which to compare legislation passed in the assembly.

In Bolivia, in a context of severe economic hardship, the congress has delegated wide responsibility to the executive. The selection of the executive in congress has been crucial to the early (compared to some other Latin America countries) success of the stabilization program. A lesson of the Bolivian case, then, is that mechanisms that give incentives for cross-party coalitions can make for effective policymaking even in as difficult an environment as that afforded by Bolivia.

### Congressional ratification: Chile

Before its interruption by the military coup in 1973, Chile's line of democratically elected presidents led back to the early 1930s, when a populist and reformist junta ruled briefly. Beyond that, Chilean presidents had been chosen by legitimate elections (albeit with restricted suffrage) back into the mid-nineteenth century. Until the promulgation of the most recent constitution in 1989, the Chilean constitution of 1925 had provided for the selection of the president by the Chamber of Deputies in the absence of a majority winner in the popular election. However, throughout the 1925–73 period, presidential elections operated under a de facto plurality rule. That is, when no candidate won 50% or more of the vote, the chamber named as president the candidate who had won the plurality, almost always without rearranging party coalitions or striking cloakroom deals for the formation of an executive.

Before the adoption of the constitutional provision for congressional selection in 1925, there had been one case in which a Chilean president was appointed by means other than direct vote. In this instance, the plurality winner was bypassed for the second-place candidate, Arturo Alessandri Palma, who finished second by 1% of the popular vote. The constitution of 1891, which was in effect until 1925, did not call for congressional selection, but because of disputes over election results, congress appointed a tribunal of legislators to select the new chief executive (Drake 1978). At the time, Alessandri was a political outsider whose platform called for redistributive policies. The tribunal awarded him the presidency to quell protests by his working-class supporters, but the plan was to block any attempts at socioeconomic reform in the conservative-dominated congress (Drake 1978). Alessandri broke Chilean presidential tradition, however, by campaigning hard for reformist candidates for congress in midterm elections, successfully strengthening his parliamentary support base. His reformist efforts paid off, as in 1925 Chile ratified the new constitution which, among other changes, strengthened the president's control over cabinets.

The Chilean Chamber of Deputies proceeded to name the pluraity winner to the presidency without exception in every successive election in which there was no majority winner: in 1946, 1952, 1958, and 1970. So while the practice of congressional selection in mid-century Chile was nonpresidential by strict constitutional standards, the system functioned essentially as presidential. Given the regularity with which the chamber named the plurality winner president, in fact, the Chilean case actually illustrates the implications of plurality elections better than of congressional selection.

### Accounting for different practice in Bolivia and Chile

Before the Chilean coup, congressional and presidential executive elections were never concurrent. We suggest that this difference in the electoral cycle can account for why Bolivian parties regularly did not coalesce before presidential elections, while Chilean parties usually did. Additional factors include ballot format and, crucially, the number of contenders from which congress may choose.

At the time of presidential elections, the electoral mandate of the Chilean Congress was always at least one year old. In contrast, in 1985 and 1989, the Bolivian Congress has been elected concurrently with the direct balloting for president. The timing of elections affects both the knowledge parties have of their strengths before the selection of the president and the actual bargaining power that they will have in postelection negotiations. Owing to concurrent elections, Bolivian parties have no congressional election before the presidential election to provide them knowledge of what their congressional bargaining power will be in the postelection congressional negotiations that lead up to the vote on presidential selection. Therefore, it is rational for each of the three major parties to present its own candidate to establish bargaining power rather than risk being in a lesser coalition and thus squandering bargaining power.[8] Moreover, the separation of presidential and congressional power in Bolivia is weakened by the ballot structure. Elections for president and congress are "fused," meaning there are no split ballots. Thus, unlike Chile's elections, which are separated by date as well as by ballot, Bolivia's elections are indeed more like parliamentary elections: one voting result determines the electoral resources of the parties. If, as we have suggested, the very weakness of these Bolivian presidents has been the source of congressional–executive cooperation since 1985, it is likely that the electoral format has contributed to this effect.

In Chile, on the other hand, the congress that would have the ultimate choice in the absence of a popular majority would be the same one that was already sitting at the time that the presidential election would take place. An

8 Bolivian parties do have midterm *municipal* elections, which provide one element of the information puzzle, tracking voter loyalties, but this information tells them far less about bargaining resources than would a congressional election.

election would already have taken place shortly before the presidential election to track any possible trends in voter support. Other parties than the strongest would find it rational to join either with the party that looked likely to win or with an opponent that might be able to block the rising party. Because parties would know the bargaining power they would have in congress should a vote there be necessary, they could anticipate both the likely electoral rewards of any preelection coalition and the ability to structure a new postelection coalition, if necessary. For this reason, some parties generally had forged a coalition before the presidential election that either obtained a majority or was sufficiently close to a majority that no new coalition could be easily formed in congress to undo the preelection coalition.

One final matter needs to be addressed with regard to the Chilean case: What about those cases when the candidate who received a plurality did so very narrowly? Why, when Jorge Alessandri won only 31% in 1958 and, even more significantly, when the Socialist Salvador Allende won only 36% in 1970, did the parties in congress not make use of their formal power to select a contender other than the plurality winner? In 1958 the answer is obvious enough, since the congress had to select from among the top two contenders. The runner-up, Allende, was certainly less desirable to a majority than was Alessandri. In 1973, the congress faced the same choice, except that this time Alessandri was the runner-up. Why opt for Allende, the plurality winner? The key was in the Christian Democrats' preferences. The incumbent president, a Christian Democrat, had been elected in 1964 by a majority because he received the conservative parties' endorsement. Because Alessandri's candidacy in 1970 represented a break with the center-right coalition and the conservatives and Christian Democrats had been fighting for hegemony over the nonsocialist electorate, ironically, the vote to Allende may have appeared politically less risky. Allowing Alessandri to become president would have been to risk conceding hegemony over the nonsocialist forces to the Christian Democrats' convervative rivals. Thus the restriction on congressional choice to the top *two* candidates was as important as the electoral cycle: Unable to bargain for the selection of the third candidate, as happens in Bolivia, the Christian Democrats, whose candidate had placed third but who held the largest share of seats in the previously elected congress, punished their erstwhile allies and voted for the plurality winner.

## VARIATIONS ON PRESIDENTIAL REELECTION

The modal rule among presidential systems prohibits immediate reelection. In many, reelection is forbidden outright; in a number of others, a president can be reelected after one interim term; and in Venezuela, two terms must elapse before a former president may be reelected. In the United States, which many scholars have assessed as the presidential archetype (an

Table 5.2. Reelection of presidents

| No Reelection | Two interim terms | One interim term | Two-term limit | No limit |
|---|---|---|---|---|
| Colombia 1991 | Venezuela | Argentina | Bulgaria | Dominican |
| Costa Rica | | *Bolivia | Namibia | Republic |
| Ecuador | | Colombia pre- | Portugal | Finland |
| El Salvador | | 1991 | Romania | France |
| Guatemala | | Panama | United States | Nicaragua |
| Honduras | | Peru | | Paraguay |
| Mexico | | | | Philippines |
| Sri Lanka | | | | |

*Although Bolivian presidents are usually elected by the assembly, the process begins with a popular election. The term limit applies regardless of whether the president is ultimately chosen in the assembly or by the electorate.

assessment that seems to have been based mostly on provincialism, and one that we do not share), the Twenty-second Amendment to the constitution imposes a two term limit where there had been none. And in a handful of countries, there remains no limit at all. Table 5.2 groups systems with elected presidencies according to their rules on reelection.

What may account for these variations among systems on provisions for presidential reelection? Bans or restrictions on reelection are typically perceived as a check on presidential power, or, more specifically as a safeguard against an executive's self-perpetuation in office. A second concern has been articulated clearly by supporters of the Twenty-second Amendment to the U.S. Constitution, who feared that the executive branch, which had grown enormously during the thirteen years of President Franklin Roosevelt's administration, could grow uniquely responsive to a multiple-term president. This point is applicable to other countries as well, where presidents have occasionally served even longer than Roosevelt. We might expect that variations would reflect the nature of those elites whose acceptance was necessary to put into effect the constitution.

In Mexico, "effective suffrage, no reelection" was a battle cry of the revolution against the dictatorship of Porfirio Díaz. Given that no cohesive party emerged out of the early revolutionary struggles, the adoption of absolute no reelection not only signified the codification of revolutionary rhetoric but also served the interest of the many competing factions within the new leadership. The chances that all of them could one day take turns in the presidential office would be enhanced by a provision that ensured that any one *caudillo*'s term in office would be his last.

Similarly, another source of absolute no reelection might be a situation of fragmentation, in which several parties expected to have a chance at the presidency but wanted to ensure that one would not, by virtue of winning one election, be able to assume a dominant role.[9] Ecuador and Guatemala fit this scenario.

At the other extreme are systems with no restrictions on reelection. Any leader who by himself could prevail on the question of whether or not to incorporate in a new constitution a provision on reelection would be expected to prefer constitutional silence on the issue. Thus, if one *caudillo* dominates the process of forming the new regime, reelection may be permitted with no restrictions. In the Dominican Republic, the dominant force at the time of the constitution writing in 1962 was the Dominican Revolutionary Party, a tightly organized quasi-Leninist party headed by a *caudillo*, Juan Bosch. Bosch's dominance at the time may explain the lack of restrictions on reelection in the Dominican constitution. If so, this is highly ironic, as it is another *caudillo*, Joaquín Balaguer, a onetime figurehead president under the dictatorship that Bosch fought against, who has benefited from the ability to be elected again and again. Balaguer has been elected five times since 1966.

Nicaragua's constitution of 1986 also provides no restrictions on the number of terms a president may serve. Perhaps this case is also explicable by the dominance of one leader within a party. While the Sandinista Front was sometimes portrayed as having had a collegial leadership, the leading role of Daniel Ortega (as "Coordinator" of the revolutionary junta) had been established even before a formally presidential system was put in place. A collegial party would be expected, as in Mexico, to opt for no reelection, while Ortega's dominance since 1979 explains why other party leaders would accept a constitution which would theoretically permit Ortega to remain president for many terms.

There are cases of Leninist or otherwise tightly organized parties not imposing constitutions allowing perpetual reelection. In Venezuela, the Acción Democrática (AD) by 1961 had accepted consensus among parties as critical to the maintenance of democracy (Levine 1973); thus it did not insist on a constitution that would permit long-run rule by its maximum leader, Rómulo Betancourt, but would have allowed him to serve again after two terms had elapsed, had he lived long enough. Compare the current Venezuelan constitution with that of 1947. The earlier constitution, adopted when AD was hegemonic, allowed reelection only after a single intervening term, rather than two terms, as in the 1961 document. The reason for the difference may be found in AD's choice of a nonpartisan and famous novelist as its candidate in the first democratic presidential election, in 1945. Preventing this president, Rómulo Gallegos, from running for immediate reelection would have made Betancourt the easy choice for AD in 1950 (and perhaps 1960) had a military coup not intervened. By 1961, with Betancourt already having been elected in 1958, a rule requiring two intervening terms must

9 We are indebted to Barbara Geddes for spurring us to think of these issues.

have been desirable, not only to other parties but also to younger AD activists who had fought the dictatorship at home while the older leadership, including Betancourt, had been in exile (Levine 1973).

In Namibia, the majority party in elections to a constituent assembly in 1989 was a former guerrilla movement, the South-West Africa People's Organization. SWAPO would be expected to be in the same category as the Sandinistas and the Dominican Revolutionary Party, having tight central leadership. It would thus be expected to opt for no provision prohibiting re-election. However, the UN-imposed rules under which the constitution was drafted required a two-thirds vote in the constituent assembly to approve the constitution (Shugart 1992b). SWAPO lacked such a large majority, and thus had to defer to other parties, which feared SWAPO leader San Nujoma's potential for perpetuating his rule. Thus Namibia has a two-term limit.

Limitations on reelection, however, have effects on presidential government beyond simply forcing turnover in the executive. First, a no-reelection rule prevents the electorate from returning to office a popular president. This in itself is a loss for the public interest because an equally competent successor may not always be available. Moreover, by removing the possibility that the president will face judgment at the hands of the voters, prohibitions on reelection eliminate the only link by which the executive in a competitive political system is directly accountable to the electorate. Voters may make the initial decision as to who leads the executive – and in this sense their impact on the nature of the branch will likely be greater than in most parliamentary systems – but presidents barred from reelection know they will not answer to the voters at the end of their term.

A final effect of the no-reelection rule relates not to the president's relationship with the electorate, but to that with congress. As many critics have pointed out, presidentialism offers scarce incentives for congresspersons – even those of the president's party – to support the executive. A president who is immediately a lame duck can offer no coattails to potential supporters in congress, and so will likely have even greater difficulties soliciting cooperation among congresspersons than one who can be reelected. This difficulty may exacerbate the problem of immobilism that leads to criticisms of presidentialism (Coppedge 1988).

None of the arrangements regulating reelection violate the essential criteria for presidentialism we have established. Prohibitions on reelection do not prevent the executive from being shaped by popular vote, and certainly do not threaten the independence of the executive from the congress for its survival. Nevertheless, in our opinion, placing no limit on reelection is most in keeping with the principles of presidentialism. Presidentialism requires that the chief executive be elected by popular vote. A logical corollary of this statement would be that there should be as few restrictions as possible on the will to be expressed in that vote. In addition, we have already argued that a contingent advantage of presidential democracy is the increased accountability it provides of the executive to the electorate. To prohibit reelection erases that characteristic of presidential government and the advantage it provides. Finally, the concern about incumbent presidents' misusing the office to electoral advantage – while often valid – is diminished to the extent that a system has competitive elections. Although fraud and intimidation are still serious problems during elections in some presidential systems, in recent years, many more than ever before have reliably neutral, multiparty agencies to conduct elections. Where electoral fairness is less well institutionalized the presence of international observer groups, United Nations oversight, and the computerization of ballot counts have all contributed tremendously to deterring or exposing fraud by incumbents. Without implying that presidential elections are uniformly beyond reproach, we only suggest that elections are more likely to become progressively more fair rather than more corrupt. Thus, prohibiting reelection to prevent fraud may be an unnecessarily large sacrifice.

### THE VICE-PRESIDENCY, OR NOT

The question of whether or not to have a vice-presidency, and if so, how to fill the post, is important to the question of the origin of chief executive power in the event of a vacancy in the presidential office. The office of the vice-presidency is subject to perpetual criticism – in the United States at least – for a couple of reasons. In the first place, pundits claim to struggle in vain to discern exactly what it is that vice-presidents do, once in office. Second, vice-presidential candidates are widely thought to be chosen as presidential running mates for reasons unrelated to their most important function: serving as president if the office is vacated before the end of the term. Certainly a presidential contender chooses his or her running mate (or, in some cases, running mates) to maximize the ticket's strength at the polls, and the value of a vice-president in this regard does not necessarily correspond to qualifications to serve as president.

Nevertheless, our project here is to demonstrate that the office of vice-president, and the means of filling vacated presidencies more generally, can be arranged in various ways. What problems, if any, a vacated presidency causes depends on the path to succession. In addition, the vice-presidency may be organized in such a way as to encourage compromise among contenders for control of the executive, to allow presidential contenders to signal to the electorate their political inclinations, or to ensure electoral legitimacy for any presidential replacement. Other systems simply have opted not to have a vice-presidency at all – in the event of a vacancy, a new presidential election is held, in most cases.

The first decision in organizing the path to succession is simply whether the vice-presidency should exist or not. When there is a prime minister, the nearly unanimous choice is no, although the 1991 constitution of Bulgaria provides for both a (constitutionally powerless) president and a vice-president. Peru likewise has all three posts. Some strictly presidential systems, including Venezuela, Mexico, Paraguay, and the Chilean constitutions of 1925 and 1989, also do not provide for the office. The absence of the vice-presidency obviously means that voters electing a president can have no idea of who will fill that office if it is vacated during the regular constitutional term. However, holding a new election means that, in the event of a vacancy, voters again enjoy the advantages of choice and identifiability inherent in any presidential election. Ironically, in a few cases that are otherwise presidential the path to succession is often more parliamentary (or, more accurately, akin to the assembly-independent regimes discussed earlier), in that voters are excluded from influencing the choice of the interim chief executive, who is chosen by the congress.

In Mexico, if more than four years remain in the presidential term when the office is vacated, then an interim is chosen by a joint session of congress to serve for fourteen to eighteen months, at which time a popular election is held to elect a president to serve the rest of the original term. If less than four years remains when the office is vacated, however, the interim chosen by congress serves out the remainder of the term, and no special election is held. Colombia's constitution of 1886–1991 had a similar provision.[10] Likewise in Paraguay, if more than half of the original term remains, new elections are held; but if less than half remains, congress selects the successor. In Chile 1989, the successor is chosen by the senate to fill out the remainder of the term, regardless of when the presidency is vacated. In Venezuela, a similar choice is made by a joint session of congress. And in unicameral Sri Lanka, the assembly chooses the successor as well.[11]

Among the systems without vice-presidents, all currently provide that newly elected or appointed presidents shall serve only the remainder of the original term – not a full new term. However, the 1925 constitution of Chile provided that the replacement serve a new six-year term. We regard as a desirable characteristic the provision for simply filling out the original term in order not to disrupt the electoral cycles of the systems. We discuss the importance of electoral cycles at length in Chapter 11. For now it suffices to say that even though a successor elected to fill a vacated presi-

---

10 In Colombia, the Congress selected a *designado,* or designated successor, every two years, while the presidential term was four years. This unusual arrangement allowed the choice of successor to respond to shifting congressional coalitions, although not as readily as if the *designado* were chosen after the presidency is vacated. On the other hand, the Colombian system provided that there would be a successor prepared to fill the presidency immediately, if need be.

11 Finally, there is the consistently unique Bolivian formula, in which presidential and vice-presidential candidates run on a team ticket during the popular election, but where none receives a majority the offices are filled separately by Congress from among the top three candidates for each. Thus, the Congress may mix and match from among the tickets, so as to construct a coalition executive.

dency might win a strong mandate at the polls, such a successor should serve no longer than the duration of the original term.

If the office of vice-president is to exist, the next decision is whether it should be filled jointly with the presidency or separately. Most systems elect both president and vice-president on a joint ticket; voters cast one vote for a team of candidates. Where this is the case, and where the president chooses her or his running mate, the choice can serve as a signal to voters as to the political inclinations of the candidate for chief executive. Voters can assess both the sagacity and the coalitional instincts of the presidential candidate by his or her choice for vice-president. On the other hand, separate election of the vice-president provides for maximum influence of the electorate over the line of succession to the presidency, and so prevents the possibility of a successor who cannot claim electoral legitimacy. This is currently the case in Peru and was so in the Brazilian constitution of 1946 and the Philippine constitution of 1935.

If the elections for president and vice-president are on separate ballots, it is possible (perhaps likely) that the two officials will be of different parties, perhaps even one the other's opposition. Such a situation occurred most prominently in Brazil in 1960 when Jânio Quadros was elected president, while the far more radical João Goulart was elected vice-president. When Goulart succeeded Quadros in 1962, a regime crisis resulted that ultimately led to the 1964 coup. Despite that experience, is there any reason why the president and vice-president must be politically compatible? As long as the vice-president assumes no executive functions until the *permanent* absence of the president, the answer is no. Providing separate elections at least allows voters directly to choose not only the president but also the president-in-waiting, should a successor be necessary.[12] The primary advantage of using a fused ticket for president and vice-president is in multiparty systems, in which parties can form coalitions for two offices more easily than for one. The ticket arrangement does, however, lessen somewhat the connection between voter choice and chief executive in the event that the vice-president must assume the presidency. Perhaps the best solution is no vice-presidency at all, with a special election being held to fill the remainder of the term when there is a vacancy.

### DIVIDED POLITIES AND COLLEGIAL PRESIDENCIES

Chapter 3 noted that one of the criticisms of presidential systems has been their tendency toward majoritarianism in the executive. While the most

12 Going a step further, the elections need not even occur at the same time. Colombia's constitution of 1832 provided for nonsynchronized terms, with the vice-president elected at the president's midterm (Gibson 1948). This arrangement does strike us as undesirable, as it is preferable for the two executive-level offices at least to emerge out of a common campaign and common voter concerns.

majoritarian democratic political system model is surely a form of parliamentarism – the Westminister model in which one party ordinarily captures a majority of seats and thus forms its own government – in polities using proportional representation, the divide between parliamentarism and presidentialism is more stark. With PR, most parliamentary executives will be coalitions, or else minority cabinets dependent on support of other parties in parliament. However, even with PR and in the absence of a majority party in the assembly, most presidential executives are composed only of those ministers whom the president chooses. In many cases this means members of only the president's party or closely associated parties. For this reason presidentialism is criticized as majoritarian, despite varying degrees of institutional checks placed on presidents and their cabinets. Of course, the greater the checks, the more the risk of executive–assembly stalemates or even crisis and the less the chance that the popularly endorsed executive program will be enacted.

In the last two chapters we have discussed one type of constitutional design, premier-presidentialism, that seeks to address the problems of (pure) presidentialism while still maintaining the perceived advantages of a directly elected president to serve the various roles of head of state[13] and arbiter, and as an expression of the broader electorate in a plural political context. However, what if a political system is so divided that placing a presidency in the hands of any one political tendency might itself be destabilizing? The assembly-independent regime is one solution, but one that does not allow direct voter choice of the executive. If the response is to design either a weak presidency or an electoral format that minimizes the chances of a presidential majority in the assembly, we risk losing one of our conditional advantages of having a directly elected presidency in the first place, which was to allow voters to identify alternative possible governments, and then choose one and hold it accountable. Can these goals be maintained without risking a majoritarian executive? We think that the answer is yes, as a variant of presidentialism can be designed that makes for an executive both collegial and accountable.

### The collegial executive under presidentialism

As we discussed in Chapter 2, some definitions of presidentialism exclude the possibility of a multi-person presidency. The question may be framed in terms of whether or not it might be contradictory to have a system based on checks and balances but having a unitary executive. Lijphart (1989) suggests that it is contradictory, but that this internal contradiction

---

13 Of course, a system could be a pure presidential regime, by our definition, even if the directly elected head of government were not also the head of state. It is almost inconceivable, however, that a premier-presidential regime would have some figure other than the elected president as head of state.

of majoritarianism versus consensualism is inherent in presidentialism. By this logic, a collegial "presidency" must be an entirely separate type of regime. Aside from the taxonomical debate, our idea that a regime can incorporate both separation of powers and a multi-person executive is most forcefully challenged by Alexander Hamilton. Thus we now turn to Hamilton's words expressed in the debate over ratification of the U.S. Constitution.

In *Federalist* No. 70, we see quite clearly the tension between Hamiltonian and Madisonian democratic theory – a tension manifest in this instance in the issue of whether a plural executive is compatible with presidential government. Hamilton's answer is an emphatic no. He makes the case that the principle of checks and balances should not apply within the executive branch. Hamilton thus distinguishes the internal organization of the executive from that of Congress – with its bicameral structure and multiple opportunities for minority vetoes – and of the federal system as a whole. He justifies this distinction arguing that while caution is desirable in the legislative process, the execution of the laws requires singlemindedness and an "energy" that can only be supplied by a unitary presidency (*The Federalist Papers* 1961:423–35).

This distinction between the executive and the rest of the American constitutional structure is based, ultimately, on the presumption that the power of the executive in shaping policy is small relative to that of Congress – that the executive is an executor of laws with little discretion over their content. Insofar as the executive is a mere executor, Hamilton's logic is compelling. To the extent that the executive role transcends this limited sphere, however, the logic of checks and balances would seem to apply to the executive equally as it applies to Congress. In practice, the executive in some presidential systems is accorded powers of decree, at least for purposes of rule making (see Chapter 7) – and almost universally is active in drafting and initiating actual legislation. Given the uniformity with which presidential executives exceed the role as mere executor of legislation, however – even while remaining well within their constitutional powers – Hamilton's vision of the presidential executive is somewhat limited. In the context of modern presidencies it is not at all clear that Hamilton's argument for the unitary executive agrees with the larger principles of presidentialism elaborated elsewhere in *The Federalist*.

There is a second area in which Hamilton's condemnation of the plural executive seems unfounded. He argues that such an arrangement would "split the community into the most violent and irreconcilable factions, adhering differently to the different individuals who composed the magistry" (*The Federalist Papers* 1961:426). The logic here runs counter to the consociational argument that a plural executive can be created to guarantee the representation in that branch of minority groups which would be excluded by a majoritarian executive. The consociational logic holds that a plural executive can foster compromise and cooperation (Lijphart 1977), bridging cleavages rather than fostering them.

Before dismissing Hamilton, we want to acknowledge his most persuasive argument in favor of the unitary executive: the case for accountability. We argued earlier that the popular election of the executive provides superior accountability of the elected to the electors in presidential over parliamentary systems, although this accountability is undercut if a president is constitutionally barred from reelection. Hamilton's point extends our argument considerably – in a way that is valid under some conditions but not under others. Hamilton contends that when responsibility is shared, it is more difficult to determine where the credit or blame for executive action lies. By this logic, even where popular election may enhance accountability, a plural executive might undermine it. But we can imagine cases in which power sharing is desirable in the executive, where multiple or deep political cleavages in a society mean that a unitary presidency will necessarily be unrepresentative of a large proportion of the population. These are the conditions Lijphart identifies as requiring consociational government, although Lijphart concludes that the collegial executive is viable only under parliamentarism. We, on the other hand, maintain that, where power sharing is desirable, a collegial presidency need not be so constructed as to reduce accountability. Indeed, where a unitary but highly unrepresentative executive can win office, its accountability must also be suspect.

In sum, there may be presidentialism with a plural executive. Such an executive maximizes checks and balances, and may provide superior representation to minority groups in deeply divided societies. The level of accountability to which the plural executive can be held will depend on the cleavage structure of the society. Collegial executives may make the attribution of credit and blame more complicated, but where a unitary executive is not representative of its society, neither can it be held accountable. Finally, where checks internal to the executive are unrestrained, the plural executive may increase a system's tendency toward immobilism. We shall return to this problem after considering the performance of some experiments with collegial presidencies.

### Actual popularly elected collegial executives

Perhaps the most famous example of a collegial executive is the Swiss Federal Council, which was discussed at the beginning of this chapter. The Swiss system is not, however, presidential, since the executive is chosen by the assembly. Two countries have used popuarly elected collegial executives: Uruguay from 1952 to 1966, and Cyprus from 1960 to 1963. The Uruguayan experience was specifically inspired by the Swiss example, even though the origin of executive power in the Uruguayan case and its "model" differ fundamentally.

Our first step in this section is to provide a brief overview of the Uruguayan and Cypriot collegial presidencies. We wish to indicate at the outset, however, that our reason for discussing these systems is not that we consider them to be models to be applied elsewhere. In fact, in many ways they represent models of what is to be avoided in designing collegial presidencies. After reviewing the Uruguayan and Cypriot experiences, we shall discuss alternative ways of constituting plural executives under presidentialism that will stand in contrast to the institutional designs employed in those two countries.

*Uruguay.* Uruguay's experiment with its *colegiado* was the belated result of the José Batlle y Ordoñez's long effort in the early twentieth century to establish a collegial executive based on the Swiss formula, which he admired. Troubled by the personalistic and *caudillo* nature of Uruguayan politics, Batlle's idea was to let all the *caudillos* be president at the same time (Taylor 1960:153), in much the same manner that the Swiss formula ensures that none of the major players is shut out of the executive at any time. The 1918–33 Uruguayan constitution provided for a dual executive, with a unitary presidency existing beside a nine-member National Administrative Council. This was the closest Batlle was able to come to achieving a *colegiado* in his lifetime. But even this arrangement was not a truly plural presidency, since executive responsibilities were sharply divided between the two arms of the executive, rather than shared (Gillespie 1989:5–6).

In the early 1950s, however, debate over the collegial executive once again dominated Uruguayan politics. This time, the idea was championed by José Batlle's sons, Lorenzo and César, leading a faction of the Colorado Party known as List 14. In the 1950 election, List 14 finished behind Colorado List 15, headed by Luís Batlle Berres, who assumed the single-person presidency. José Batlle's sons turned to Blanco Party leader Luís Alberto de Herrera for support. Herrera had made his sixth unsuccessful run at the presidency in 1950, and had won ninety-two thousand more votes than Luís Batlle Berres, but lost the office under Uruguay's electoral rules because his party did not win a plurality. In an effort to prevent Batlle Berres from controlling a powerful presidency, Herrera threw his support behind the efforts of Colorado List 14 to establish a fully collegial executive. A special constitutional convention ratified the new arrangement in 1951, the following year forming a popularly elected executive consisting of six members of the party winning the presidential election and three members of the second-place party. For the heirs of José Batlle y Ordoñez, the *colegiado* represented an effort to fulfill the vision of their father, who distrusted *caudillo* rule. But the *colegiado* could not have been established without the support of Herrera and the Blancos, who originally opposed it (Marotta 1985:36). For them, the plural executive was an opportunity to reduce the power of Batlle Berres and to lay claim to a guaranteed share of executive power.[14]

If the conditions under which the *colegiado* was established were complex, so must be any assessment of its performance. Early in its tenure, the *colegiado* seemed to be serving the goal of fostering interparty cooperation. At the end of 1952, Dr. Andrés Martínez Trueba, a Colorado member of the executive and former President of Uruguay, praised the *colegiado* as more efficient than the single-member presidency. In particular, Martínez pointed out that the opposition's presence in the executive prevented it from attacking all executive actions in order to make political capital from any controversial decisions. Martínez contended that the *colegiado* had been able to "act firmly" in the face of illegal strikes by government employees "keeping control in the hands of the Government where the unions were unreasonable" – all without prompting accusations of dictatorial tendencies from a disenfranchised opposition.[15] Because the secondary party was not represented with parity in the executive, it could, of course, have been outvoted by the majority party. Therefore its participation in an executive council in which one party held a majority of seats could not guarantee that its views would be taken into consideration. On the other hand, the ability of the secondary party to distance itself publicly from the majority party is diminished by its being part – even a junior part – of the executive. Notice that in Martínez's account, he praises the collegial executive not for having moderated the actions of the majority party, but rather for having restrained the criticisms of the minority. This feature of the Uruguayan system is not one we should want to endorse – to be truly a power-sharing presidency, no one party should hold a majority of the seats – but Martínez's comments certainly contradict the argument that a plural executive must necessarily be indecisive, or "feeble" in Hamiltonian terms. By Martínez's account, energy in the executive and interparty compromise are not at all incompatible.

Other accounts with the advantage of greater hindsight, however, have concluded that the nine-person executive committee was unwieldly. In 1960, Taylor intended an unflatterinng comparison when he likened the *colegiado* to a third legislative chamber, where extended debate slowed down decision making, ultimately impeding the administration of government programs (Taylor:103–4). While one similarly could call any unitary presidency that possesses a veto a "third legislative chamber" that impedes

14 The static 6-to-3 division of seats in the *colegiado* was insisted on by the Blancos. This plan was a move away from proportional representation in the executive, as it made rigid the distribution of partisan power regardless of who controlled the majority of seats, and excluded all but the top two parties from any share of executive power. This latter condition came under attack from the leftist segment of the electorate that was growing in the 1960s.
15 "Uruguay's System of Ruling Praised," *New York Times,* December 18, 1952.

(or immobilizes) the governing process, Taylor's comments provide an echo of Hamilton's warnings: Applying checks and balances within the executive might sap the energy of day-to-day administration. More specifically, Needler pointed out that the difficulty in reaching decisions within the plural executive forced Uruguay twice in the early 1960s to send delegations to inter-American conferences uninstructed on national policy (Needler 1965:156).

In addition to these political difficulties, Uruguay suffered an extended economic decline beginning in the 1950s. By the mid-1960s, both the need for government austerity and the inability of the now Blanco-dominated executive to adhere to its economic program were attributed at least in part to the country's unorthodox executive design, although such claims appear to be more a result of scapegoating than of careful analysis. The List 15 Colorados remained determined opponents of the *colegiado,* and they were joined by the Blancos whose support had earlier been essential to its adoption. By 1966, a constitutional reform that included the return to a unitary executive was on the national ballot and was supported by 62% of the Uruguayan electorate (Gillespie 1989:5–6).

*Cyprus.* Cyprus's experiment with a plural executive was even more ephemeral, and considerably less successful, than Uruguay's. On the other hand, the problems that Cyprus's dual presidency sought to resolve were far more daunting. Cyprus gained independence from British colonial rule in 1960, under a constitution that sought to guarantee shared political power between the Greek majority composing 78% of the population, and the Turkish minority composing 18%. The 1960 constitution established a dual executive structure with a Greek president and a Turkish vice-president, holding almost equal powers and elected separately by the Greek and Turkish Cypriot communities. Similarly, in the cabinet and the national assembly, seats were to be divided on a 7:3 Greek–Turkish ratio, as was membership in the police, army, and civil service. Further, the constitution established separate assembly chambers by which the two ethnic groups could govern religious, educational, cultural, and personal status matters. Finally, both the president and vice-president had ultimate veto power over all legislation concerning foreign affairs, defense, or security; and any tax legislation required concurrent majorities of both the Greek and Turkish caucuses in the assembly (Kyriakides 1968).[16] In short, the 1960 constitution implemented a host of consociational measures in addition to the plural executive, including disproportionally high representation of minority Turks in government offices, communal autonomy, and minority veto (Lijphart 1977:158).

16 For a detailed description of the provisions of the 1960 constitution, see Kyriakides (1968), ch. 3.

The Cypriot dual presidency and the other consociational features of the constitution, however, failed to accommodate the level of political conflict between the island's ethnic adversaries. Lijphart suggests a number of reasons why this was so. In the first place, consociational arrangements with extensive power-sharing and minority vetoes are most feasible where no single group constitutes a clear majority of the population. Such a majority is likely to see consociationalism as unnecessary and discriminatory, according minorities excessive negative powers. This attitude was prevalent among Greek Cypriots, and the status of the Turkish vice-president as coequal to the president was a particular target of criticism (Polyviou 1980:20). Second, Lijphart notes that the Greek and Turkish populations were homogeneously interspersed among Cyprus's six districts, complicating the construction of any federal structure that might have allowed for more complete self-rule according to geographic divisions. Third, there existed at the time of indepdendence virtually no conception of or loyalty to Cypriot national identity; instead, Greek Cypriots understood themselves to be Greek, and Turkish Cypriots saw themselves as Turkish (Lijphart 1977:159–60).

A final point is that the conditions for Cypriot independence were negotiated not primarily by Cypriot leaders themselves but by the Greek, Turkish, and British governments, during talks in London and Zurich in 1959. Thus the legal frameowrk of the new republic was constructed by outside forces, and presented to the Cypriot leaders, who accepted it as a package in 1960 (Polyviou 1980:13). This process did nothing to instill a commitment to the institutional arrangements among Cypriot leaders. And in fact, the consociational spirit of the 1960 constitution was never reflected in the political process itself. The Turkish minority in government used its veto on legislation to press demands outside the legislative arena (Lijphart 1977:160). And the Greek president, for his part, had presented by November 1963 a set of thirteen constitutional amendments that would have eliminated outright most of the consociational provisions protecting the Turkish minority (Ertekun 1984:11). Civil war broke out on the island within days, destroying the Cypriot experiment with consociationalism and a dual presidency.

The experiences of Uruguay and Cyprus are not especially encouraging if one wanted to make a case for a collegial presidency. However, the specific institutions employed in these cases may have been well short of optimal, and the conditions they were expected to deal with may have overwhelmed any system, at least in Cyprus. The failure in Cyprus can be attributed less to its effect on assembly–executive relations (although its performance here was by no means satisfactory) than with vehement opposition by ethnic groups to an entire government system arranged primarily by outside forces. In Uruguay, the *colegiado* was blamed for stalemate in both the legislative and administrative process. However, chronic standoff between Colorados, Blancos, and leftist parties was a problem in the late 1960s, even after the abandonment of the *colegiado;* so it is difficult to see how this institutional arrangement was uniquely responsible. Next, let us consider some problems of collegial presidencies that are suggested by the Uruguayan and Cypriot cases.

### Pitfalls of actual collegial presidencies

Having reviewed the actual experiences of two countries with plural presidencies, we now turn to alternative arrangements. We identify two pitfalls of these collegial executives:

1. restricted access, in the case of Uruguay; and
2. deficiencies in accountability and identifiability, in both cases.

*Restricted access.* In Uruguay, even though there were nine seats available, access to the executive was restricted to the two largest parties. This restriction became an issue as a third party gained in strength in the 1960s. Ironically, the method chosen to redress this issue was not to open up access to the third party, but rather to abolish the council altogether in favor of a unitary executive elected by plurality.[17] In this manner, the two largest parties ensured that executive power would remain in their own hands.

The restriction on access to the collegial presidency runs counter to the ostensible consociational design of the system. It would be preferable to have access restricted only by the threshold set by the magnitude of the district and the formula employed, as with assembly elections in democracies. For instance, with $M = 9$, in a hypothetical distribution of vote shares of 40–35–15–10, the four parties would split the nine seats 4–3–1–1 if the common procedure of simple quota and largest remainders were used,[18] instead of Uruguay's 6–3–0–0.

Besides shutting out all parties other than the leading two, having a fixed ratio of seats in the council, regardless of the votes, meant that representation in the council could not be reflective of shifts in the support of the two parties (except when one surpassed the other), any more than it could reflect the growing support of a third party (again, unless that party supplanted one of the others).[19] This deficiency gets us to the next set of concerns, those of accountability and identifiability.

17 More precisely, the presidency was once again elected by double simultaneous vote.
18 And, of course, the possibility of such small parties as in the example being in the executive could be avoided, if desired, by simply lowering the magnitude.
19 Had the latter occurred, we suspect that the two traditional parties would have had considerably greater interest in opening up representation on the council to parties other than the two largest.

*Deficiencies in accountability and identifiability.* Both elected collegial executives suffered from deficient accountability and identifiability. Voters in Uruguay could not easily express any policy direction in their executive, partly because of the fixed ratio of representation. To make matters worse, the electoral rules used allowed internal factions of a party to be the real competitors. The large spoils available to each party (6 seats to the larger and 3 to the smaller) virtually guaranteed fragmentation while making turnover difficult.

In Cyprus, the president and vice-president were effectively co-presidents, as noted. Even though each had almost equal powers, each was accountable to only a portion of the electorate. Greeks and Turks formed separate electoral rolls and separate constituencies for the election of an executive with powers over all citizens. While it might be desirable, according to the theory of consociational democracy, to ensure that only Greeks could designate the Greek member of the executive and only Turks the Turk, this format also made it difficult for voters to express any other policy preference for the nation as a whole, other than protection of their ethnic identity.

We do not agree with Hamilton that collegial executives necessarily encourage divisiveness in the polity. However, by enhancing ethnicity as the source of electoral support for "co-presidents" elected in virtual isolation from one another, the Cypriot format may indeed have encouraged divisiveness. From the standpoint of diminishing the salience of this cleavage in the national election for the executive (as distinct from assembly elections), as well as for the sake of accountability, it would be preferable to require the prospective Greek and Turk co-presidents to stand together before the whole electorate.

### Alternative designs

The deficiencies of the Uruguayan and Cypriot cases suggest that, where a collegial presidency is desirable as a conflict-regulative device, there might be alternative designs that would function better.

*PR in the executive.* If we want to ensure minority representation in the executive, one method is simply to use proportional representation to elect the multi-seat council. This possibility was suggested in the context of our discussion of the problem of restricted access in Uruguay. There are empirical examples of such collegial presidencies, although at the national level there never have been any that we are aware of. The actual cases are in some of the Swiss cantons. All Swiss cantons have collegial executives, but, modifying the Executive Council that exists at the federal level, some cantons directly elect their executives. Thus, unlike Switzerland as a whole, they have, by our definition, presidential systems.

While the use of PR in the executive redresses the problem of excluding minorities, it does so at a cost: undercutting accountability and, especially, identifiability. As we have made a theme of this book, one purpose of an executive is to articulate policy alternatives for the nation as a whole. If this executive role is desirable, then an executive elected by PR will most likely be undesirable.

*Co-presidential tickets.* A possibility that we prefer over the use of PR in the executive is to create a co-presidency, as in Cyprus, but to have both (or perhaps three) co-presidents elected on a common ticket by the whole electorate. If a ticket of co-presidential candidates were elected by a method that encourages the formation of broad preelectoral coalitions (see Chapter 10), there would be a powerful incentive for parties to seek tickets that spanned across the blocs that divide the party system. Since the prospective co-presidents would have to stand or fall electorally as a ticket, it would be feasible for them to present a program before the electorate. On the other hand, using an electoral formula whereby the winners would be the two or three most-voted-for candidates (or slates), running independently, would make the task of presenting such a program inherently more difficult. A format without tickets would also run the risk of having a co-presidency made up of leaders of the more extreme parties, rather than a coalition tending toward moderation.

An objection might be that the format we propose would not be faithfully representative. Critics might make such a claim on the grounds that if an extreme is one of the two or three most popular options, it should win one of the two or three executive seats. Our response is that we seek to preserve the advantages of presidentialism stemming from the regime type's ability to give voters a choice between alternative executives and then give that executive ability to lead (subject, of course, to whatever institutional checks might also be part of the constitutional design). This proposed form of collegial presidency is meant to make the coalitions that tend to emerge under plurality rule (and its variants) explicit. To illustrate the point let us consider the example of Chile's 1964 election.

In Chile in 1964 the Christian Democrat Eduardo Frei was elected president with 56% of the vote. Frei interpreted his victory as a mandate for Christian Democracy, pursuing a single party administration despite the fact that Chile's was a deeply divided political system the customary practices of which were coalition rule. More to the point, Frei's own victory had been made possible only because the right-wing parties had sought to protect themselves against what had nearly happened in 1958: a victory in a three-way race by a socialist. Thus the right endorsed Frei rather than present its own candidate.

Had Chile been using a co-presidential system at the time, the center-right coalition would have been explicit. Frei and a conservative (assuming a two-person presidency) would both have been running together and a single-party cabinet and its policies would not have occurred. It is true that this design might not have allowed voters a center-left coalitional possibility, since there would probably not have been any nonleftist forming a ticket with the socialist Salvador Allende; but then, neither did the actual unitary presidential election of 1964 offer a center-left option to Chilean voters. In either format, voters would have been offered a choice between a Socialist-Communist coalition or a center-right coalition. The difference with the co-presidency is that this executive would have been more likely to continue functioning like the (preelection) coalition it really was.

Besides preventing one party from assuming full executive power despite a preelectoral coalition, a co-presidential format would make far less likely the three-way races that preceded and followed the 1964 Chilean election. With the winner-take-all stakes reduced, coalitions might well have been a more attractive option in those campaigns. Indeed, by 1970, Chile's center had been fully taken over by the Christian Democrats and the declining Radicals moved leftward. With the different coalition-building incentives of a co-presidency rather than a unitary presidency, a center-left alternative ticket versus a continuing center-right co-presidency might have been offered voters.

*Size of the co-presidency.* We mentioned earlier in this chapter that defining an optimal size for a co-presidency was not a clear-cut task. We did, however, stress that a *colegiado* as large as that in Uruguay (nine) did not seem desirable and that it should be as small as possible. A two-member executive eliminates – within the context of a collegial presidency – the problem of unwieldiness that dogged Uruguay's experiment.

A two-member presidency does, of course, raise the potential for deadlock on some issues. The co-presidential option could be therefore modified to consist of a three-person rather than a two-person executive. With three, presumably the executives would still seek consensus whenever possible, but in the event they could not achieve it, a 2-to-1 vote would prevent deadlock. However, it should be stressed, in a system of great interparty polarization, deadlock is not inherently bad. Without periodic deadlock, there would be no incentive to make compromises. One other potential plus for a three-person presidency is that it opens up more room for coalition building, as a clearly stronger party would not have to make a smaller party an absolutely equal partner. We shall not take a stand on which size is best, but simply say that we suspect a collegial presidency with more than three members would not ordinarily be desirable.

As we have suggested, a collegial presidency might be applicable to societies divided by deep partisan or ideological divisions as well as societies that conform more generally to what are denoted by the term "plural societies," those with ethnic or other subcultural divisions. For some multiethnic societies there may remain an appeal of electing a unitary president, but using a method that guarantees the election of a moderate (see Chapter 10).

## CONCLUSION

In this chapter, we have considered a series of variations on the means of constituting chief executive power. Our survey has examined diverse methods of choosing executives, as well as variations on the structure of the executive itself; and we have spanned both pure presidential and hybrid regimes. Many of the cases represent deviations from the principle of separation of the origin of assembly and executive powers, in particular those in which selection of the chief executive is left to negotiation in the assembly.

We have argued that fixed-term executives who are selected by assemblies sacrifice the ability of the electorate to determine directly the nature of the executive; but nevertheless we acknowledge that such an arrangement can reduce the dangers of winner-take-all presidential elections, and foster coalition building under difficult political conditions. We have reviewed variations on eligibility for reelection among presidencies, concluding that to place no restrictions on reelection is most in keeping with the principles of presidentialism that the electorate should choose its executive free of constraint, and that the executive should in turn be accountable to the electorate. We have also reviewed diverse means of organizing the office of the vice-presidency, or, in its absence, paths to succession to a vacated presidency. Here we pointed out the trade-offs between providing for a successor at the outset of a presidential term versus waiting until the presidency is vacated by some unforeseen event. Finally, we undertook a more extensive analysis of collegial executives under presidential government. Differing from other students of democratic institutions, and basing our case on our understanding of *The Federalist*, we maintain that the collegial presidency is not incompatible with the principles of presidentialism. Indeed, we suggest that under certain conditions, collegial presidentialism may offer the best possibiity for resolving conflicts peacefully in deeply divided societies.

# 6

# Constitutional limits on separate origin and survival

We turn now exclusively to regimes with single-person, separately elected presidencies. While separation of the origin and survival of the executive from the legislative branch was seen by the authors of *The Federalist* as imperative, the notion of checks and balances implied to them some overlap of functions, even to the extent that the Federalists did not see Senate "advice and consent" in the president's cabinet appointments as a violation of the principle of separate powers. Among presidential systems, however, this provision is rare: Complete separation of the origin of executive office from the assembly is the norm. There are many other regimes, such as the president-parliamentary systems, however, in which the principle of separate survival is obviated.

In this chapter, we shall consider three means by which separation of origin and survival has been limited in some systems:

1. assembly involvement in the appointment of cabinet ministers,
2. censure of cabinet ministers by the assembly, and
3. dissolution of the assembly by the president.

The latter two attributes, in particular, can entail sharp deviations from the Madisonian ideal that each branch, secure in its independence, will without hesitation check the other in the lawmaking process. Yet it can be argued that the possibility of both censure and dissolution encourages cooperation between branches, as each anticipates the likely reaction of the other to its actions. We shall see that whether censure or dissolution produce such cooperation and anticipation depends largely on the specific rules by which each authority is exercised, and the incentives these rules create for politicians. In particular, incorporating a theme from the preceding chapter, we shall demonstrate that the impact of assembly censure authority on the nature and stability of cabinets hinges on the process by which cabinet members are originally appointed.

## ASSEMBLY INVOLVEMENT IN THE APPOINTMENT OF CABINET MEMBERS

In archetypal presidentialism, the origin of the entire executive is divorced from congressional influence. In a few presidential systems, nevertheless, although the president is chosen by popular election, appointees to cabinet positions are subject to congressional approval. Congressional involvement in the appointment of cabinet ministers appears at first to represent a threat to the separation-of-powers principle as we have defined it. If an assembly were in fact to make cabinet nominations, then we would no longer consider the system presidential. In the cases we shall consider, however, congressional powers in the appointment process are strictly negative. That is, they are powers of approval or disapproval, but do not give the assembly power of initiative in cabinet formation. Because the assemblies we discuss cannot actively name the members of the executive, we do not regard these cases as violations of the third criterion, and so as departures from presidentialism. On the other hand, a requirement of advice and consent clearly imposes some congressional influence on the construction of the executive. It is worth reiterating that the modal arrangement of presidential systems does not include congressional approval. In the vast majority of such systems, presidents appoint their cabinets with no congressional input. In this regard, Korea 1987, Nigeria, the Philippines, and the United States deviate from the presidential norm.

The power of initiative in the "appointment game" gives presidents a definite advantage over congressional opposition in filling cabinet positions with nominees who are acceptable to them. From observation of the appointment process in the United States one might easily induce that the advantage is manifest simply in the fact that so few cabinet nominees are actually rejected. We contend that the dynamic of congressional appointment is more subtle than that.

Consider the "appointment game" represented by Figure 6.1, in which we posit that the preferences of the president and the assembly (in the United States, the Senate) for candidates for positions as cabinet ministers (secretaries) can be mapped in one dimension. Point $P$ represents the president's ideal candidate for a given post, while point $S$ represents the Senate's ideal. At point $I_P$, the president is indifferent between filling the post and leaving it vacant. The same is true for the Senate at point $I_S$. That is, the president would rather leave the position vacant and accept whatever political repercussions there are than to fill the post with a nominee further from her ideal point, $P$, that is $I_P$. And the same is true of the Senate for any nominee beyond $I_S$. If point $I_S$ lies to the left of point $I_P$, as depicted in Figure 6.1, by definition, there would then be no section of the line segment $S-P$ along which a nominee could be acceptable to both players. The president would never nominate a candidate acceptable to the Senate, and the Senate would never accept a nominee chosen by the president. The post would remain unfilled.

Now consider Figure 6.2, in which point $I_P$ lies to the left of $I_S$. All of the points along line segment $I_P-I_S$ represent potentially acceptable nominees. The president's goal is to nominate a candidate as close to her or his ideal point as possible and still acceptable to the Senate. That candidate would

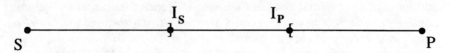

Figure 6.1. Hypothetical indifference points for senate (*S*) and president (*P*): no overlap, thus position would remain unfilled

Figure 6.2. Hypothetical indifference points for senate (*S*) and president (*P*): president nominates candidate at point $I_S$

be located at the point $I_S$. The Senate's goal, of course, is to secure an appointment at point $I_P$. The president's advantage lies in the fact that the power of initiative is the power to make a take-it-or-leave-it offer.[1] To the extent that the president has accurate information about the location of the Senate's indifference point, he or she will be able to nominate a candidate approaching point $I_S$. The Senate is powerless to secure a nomination at $I_P$ unless it can convince the president that $I_P$ is the same as $I_S$.

Despite the just-described power of initiative in the hands of the chief executive, one might feel that the assembly still has both the right and the ability to reject several nominees until the president finds one more in turn with the preferences of the assembly majority. Why should the assembly (Senate in the U.S. case) settle for a nominee who is merely not objectionable? The question becomes all the more important when we consider those premier-presidential systems in which the president also names a prime minister, who must be approved by the assembly. The appointment game in those regimes suggests a critical contrast with the appointment game in the United States. For example, there is the case of the French Fifth Republic in 1986, when President François Mitterrand faced a just-elected assembly in which his Socialist Party had lost its majority.

The French constitution gives the president the power to initiate a nomination to the post of prime minister. Mitterrand appointed the leader of the major opposition party, Jacques Chirac, as prime minister, who was, of course, confirmed by the assembly. Why did Mitterrand appoint his principal opponent, when, given his powers of initiative in this matter, he could have demanded that the assembly accept a moderate prime minister more to the president's liking? Or, asked from the other perspective, why do Republican presidents facing Democrat-controlled Senates in the United

1 For more on the importance of initiative in policy games between president and congress, see Kiewiet and McCubbins (1985).

States not act as Mitterrand did, nominating cabinet officials whose preferences conform to those of the assembly majority? The answer to this question rests in the next phase of the game: Who has power of *dismissal*. After discussing censure in a number of cases, we shall see, in a section on building and maintaining cabinets, that presidential initiative in the appointment game is merely a necessary, but not a sufficient, condition for the president's ability to obtain ministers generally in accord with her or his preferences. First, however, it will be helpful to consider the appointment process in some *presidential* systems in more detail.

### Experience in the United States

Clearly, the figures above are only heuristics; appointments cannot be mapped neatly on two dimensions, and candidates would not be available at every conceivable point on the plane even if they could be. But the figures demonstrate nicely the strategic advantage that the power of initiative provides the president in the appointment game, and the degree to which incomplete or inaccurate information about the other player's preferences limits this advantage. Moreover, the figures demonstrate that there is more than one possible explanation for why cabinet nominees in the United States are rejected so infrequently. It has been suggested that the U.S. Senate has forgotten or abandoned its power of "advice and consent" (Hess 1988; Moe 1987, 1989).[2] We see no reason to believe that the Senate would willingly abandon this formidable power and adopt a norm of consent for appointment votes. Moreover, the periodic rejection of a cabinet nominee indicates that senators have not forgotten their authority altogether. To us, it is more plausible that the regularity with which nominees are accepted merely demonstrates that U.S. presidents generally have pretty good information regarding Senate indifference, or else generally are cautious in naming candidates closer to the Senate's ideal point than to its indifference point, in order to avoid political battles.

Nevertheless, there is some evidence that reforms in the nomination process for presidential candidates – most notably the dominance of primaries and the corresponding reduction of influence for party leaders – have forced acknowledgment (in words, if not by vote) of a president's prerogative in assembling a cabinet that is his personal political resource (see Polsby 1983, ch. 3). Here, the tension is quite apparent between the presidential ideal of separation of powers and the involvement of congresspersons in the construction of the executive. To the extent that Senators acknowledge the president's right to fill cabinet positions with candidates politically compatible with the president, the only room left in public dis-

2 This theme is by no means new among students of the United States. Ford (1898) proposed the same idea of an acquiescent Senate in the nineteenth century.

course for Senate objections is for objections based on personality and character (as opposed to political) deficiencies.

President George Bush's nomination of John Tower for the position of Defense Secretary in 1989 illustrates this point nicely. Tower was unacceptable to many senators for political reasons; he was far more hawkish than the Senate median. Yet scores of senators who certainly found Tower politically objectionable justified their nay vote on the nomination according to Tower's alleged social excesses, drinking and womanizing. These are hardly habits that ordinarily raise eyebrows around Capitol Hill. Tower's case contrasts sharply with the Senate's rejection of Robert Bork as a Supreme Court nominee less than a year before. Objections to Bork were purely political, and they were justified as so publicly.

The difference in Senate discourse between the two cases seems particularly odd given that Tower's cabinet post was an explicitly political position, while Bork's seat was ostensibly nonpolitical. But the difference highlights an important quality of appointments in presidential systems. The cabinet is understood to be the political resource of the president alone, especially so because the president alone may dismiss a member of the cabinet (while neither the president nor the Senate may dismiss a Justice of the Supreme Court). Although the Senate can reject candidates – and does in fact reject them for political reasons on occasion – rejection on political grounds is difficult to defend and often not worth the trouble, since a president could always dismiss a cabinet member whom he or she found to be too receptive to Senate preferences. For the occasional rejection, then, other justifications are sought, perhaps fabricated. The difficulty for senators in objecting to cabinet nominees should contribute to an explanation of why only nine cabinet nominees have been rejected in U.S. history, compared with twenty-eight Supreme Court nominations. We have more to say about this comparison of cabinet appointments to Supreme Court appointments in a later section of this chapter.

### Other cases

Apart from the United States, only Korea, Nigeria, and the Philippines require any form of congressional approval for presidential nominees to the cabinet. The Korean and Nigerian experiences are short as of this writing, so we cannot offer discussions of actual performance. What we can do is consider the processes themselves, and how they might resemble or differ from the experience in the United States. Korea's requirement for confirmation dates only to 1987 and is more restricted than in the other cases considered here anyway. Only the prime minister is subject to confirmation by the unicameral assembly. Subsequently the prime minister appoints the other cabinet ministers. Neither the prime minister nor any other members of the cabinet are subject to ongoing confidence of the assembly; thus, as is so by definition in presidential (but not premier-presidential) systems, only the president may remove members of the cabinet. In the Korean context, the ability of the president to get cabinet ministers acceptable to him or her depends entirely upon how good an agent the prime minister proves to be. If presidents are forced by the assembly to compromise considerably in the choice of this official, then they could endure significant agency loss in the composition of "their" entire cabinet. However, since the process of filling the prime minister's seat is identical to the appointment game of Figure 6.2, we should expect Korean cabinets to reflect closely the preferences of the president, although not necessarily the president's ideal.

In Nigeria, only two presidents have been elected under the constitution of 1979, which was suspended in a military coup in 1983 but was scheduled to be reestablished in 1992. Article 135 of the constitution restricts the president's appointments to ministries in two ways. First, as in the United States, Senate confirmation is required. Second, there must be at least one minister native to each state. Both provisions are attempts to ensure representation of as many of Nigeria's diverse ethnic groups as possible, as state boundaries were based on ethnic communities and each state is accorded equal Senate representation.

Cabinet nominations in the Philippines are subject to approval by the congressional Commission on Appointments, consisting of the president of the Senate as well as twelve senators and twelve representatives. The commission is selected according to the proportional representation of parties in each chamber.[3] The president of the Senate presides over the commission, but only casts a vote on appointments in the case of a tie. The provision for a form of congressional approval of cabinet nominations in the Filipino constitution of 1935 may represent an emulation of one of the unusual characteristics of United States presidentialism. A number of discussions of Filipino political history note that congressional challenges to presidential dominance in policymaking grew more frequent in the 1950s and early 1960s than they had been in the 1930s and late 1940s (Veloso and Guzman 1969; Stauffer 1975), and that congressional challenges to presidential discretion affected the appointment process. The Commission on Appointments exercised its authority to reject nominees during the 1960s to the extent that it drew criticisms that it was harassing the president (Stauffer 1970).

### CENSURE OF CABINET MEMBERS

As with congressional selection of the executive, provision for the censure of cabinet members by the assembly can entail a dramatic break from separation of powers, provided that censure entails meaningful ministerial responsibility before the assembly: the right of the assembly majority to

3 Philippine constitution, Article VI, Section 18, and Article VII, Section 16.

dismiss individual ministers or the entire cabinet. In some systems, censure has not always implied the automatic dismissal of a minister or cabinet, as the term implies under parliamentary government. In some presidential systems, censure is an official political rebuke of a member of the executive by congress, but the decision of whether or not to retain the censured official is ultimately the president's. When censure (sometimes called "interpellation") is nonbinding, we might refer to it as "toothless." Next, there are cases where the actual practice of censure has been rare or simply not politically threatening to the executive, despite its provision in the constitution. Among the cases in this group, we shall consider the specific conditions that reduce the frequency or effectiveness of the practice. Where the term "censure" is meaningful and may be equated with parliamentary confidence is where assemblies have relied on censure as a potent and standard means of exerting pressure on a presidential executive by requiring the dismissal of censured ministers. Here, of course, the impact of censure on the balance of power between the executive and assembly has been most profound: A regime with such a provision is *not* presidential.

### *Potent censure: Peru, the Chilean "parliamentary republic," and Ecuador*

Two Latin American cases deserve special attention because their *potent* censure has represented such a contrast to the norm of pure presidentialism in the region. These two cases are Peru and Chile (before 1925). A third case, Ecuador, has also employed censure, but there are troubling ambiguities in the constitutional language that may exacerbate interbranch confrontations.

In both Peru and Chile, presidents have remained the formal heads of government (even if ineffective) despite cabinet turnover. Nevertheless, in both cases, the dispatch with which majority congressional oppositions have disciplined cabinets has meant that ministers have been both directly answerable to congress for their actions and dependent on congress for their survival.

Although congressional censure was included in the Peruvian constitution of 1933, the provision was exercised only six times in the next thirty years (Needler 1965:158). During much of this time, of course, Peru was ruled by governments that could not be called democratic. During the first administration of President Fernando Belaunde Terry (1963–8), the American Popular Revolutionary Alliance, (APRA), in opposition to the president, wielded the censure weapon freely. As APRA party leader Raúl Haya de la Torre explained, "We did not win control of the [presidential] Palace, but we did win Congress, and from there we have begun to teach the conception of a new democracy, to endow Parliament with true institutional hierarchy. It is Parliament which makes the laws that are the norms and the base of an organized democracy" (McCoy 1971:352). The first Belaunde cabinet was censured within six months of inauguration. Blaming cabinet responsibility in part for the instability that preceded Peru's 1968 coup, McCoy wrote that "cabinet instability was primarily due to pressure from Congress" and that "many ministers and even entire cabinets resigned under threat of censure" (McCoy 1971:351–2). By 1968, the *New York Times* reported that during his five year term, President Belaunde Terry named 178 cabinet ministers.[4]

Peru's current constitution of 1979 retains the provision for parliamentary censure (Art. 226). Under the first two administrations following redemocratization in 1980, Presidents Belaunde Terry and Alán García each enjoyed congressional majorities (a reliable coalition in the former case, a single-party majority in the latter). With the election of Alberto Fujimori to the presidency in 1990, however, the Peruvian system once again confronts the problem of a president lacking a stable majority in congress. Moreover, in this instance, the president is a self-proclaimed outsider to partisan politics. While it is early to assess the performance of the system under these conditions, we are circumspect that the provision for censure, combined with absolute presidential authority to fill vacated cabinet posts, can be a recipe for extreme cabinet instability, and possible standoff between president and congress. We discuss the theoretical problems with such a formula further in Chapter 8. For now, let us consider the performance of another such regime: Chile's so-called Parliamentary Republic.

*Chile.* In his two-volume history of Chile through 1925, Julio Heise González (1974) argues that the country was far more parliamentary (and conversely, less presidential) than has been generally acknowledged by political scientists and historians, even before what is commonly called the "Parliamentary Republic" of 1891–1925 (Heise 1974, 1:61–3). One of the key factors noted by Heise as contributing to the parliamentary quality of the system was congressional censure of cabinet ministers. Provision for censure existed as far back as Chile's constitution of 1833, although it was not invoked until 1849. Throughout the latter half of the nineteenth century, censure was the standard means by which congressional majorities enforced political compliance on the executive. Censure – either of an individual minister or of an entire cabinet – was voted many times between 1862 and 1864, and in 1870, 1875, 1878, 1881, and 1890. In addition, many more ministerial changes in the 1880s were prompted by the threat of censure. Throughout this period, censure votes were defended by congressmen on the basis that the removed ministers "merely represented the policy of the President," and that their maintenance in office contradicted the fundamentals of a parliamentary republic (Heise 1974, 1:63–7).

4 *New York Times,* October 6, 1968, p. 4E.

Opposition to the principle of cabinet responsibility was central to President José Manuel Balmaceda's objections to the current political system in 1890. With Balmaceda's defeat and the promulgation of the constitution of 1891, however, Heise contends that commitment to the principle of responsibility was virtually unanimous among the leaders of Chile's significant political parties (Heise 1974, 1:121). Finally, although he presents no comprehensive data, Heise argues that censure was commonplace during the 1891–1925 period, providing an "escape valve" for the relief of political tension between the branches. Moreover, he contends that the control the legislature exerted over the ministries created a situation in which the president was not necessarily even head of government. Rather, the cabinet reflected the will of the parliamentary majority, while the president "played the role of regulator between government and opposition" (Heise 1974, 2:118–19). Although the system Heise describes seems a bit more unwieldy than pure parliamentarism, its provision for censure, like Peru's, clearly violated the principles of presidentialism.

*Ecuador.* Ecuador's 1929 constitution allowed for a congressional "vote of confidence" on cabinet ministers. The constitutions of 1945, 1946, 1967, and 1978, however, have allowed instead for votes of "censure." Although students of parliamentary procedure may not recognize a distinction between the two, and we have used them interchangeably, the difference in Ecuador often has been between dismissal and symbolic rebuke. Censure has been treated as no more than a recommendation of dismissal from congress, with the president making the ultimate decision on whether to retain the minister. The practice has, however, been of some political significance. Pinoargote argues that motions of censure have been used by the Ecuadorian Congress to extract concessions from the executive since the nineteenth century. Although he provides no comprehensive list of censures, Pinoargote (1982:41–2) points to specific cases in 1961, 1970, and 1979 in which the procedure has been used to challenge the legitimacy of the cabinet. Yet the 1978 constitution remains ambiguous.

The most troublesome aspect of Ecuador's censure mechanism for students of political institutions is that the constitution of 1978 itself is unclear on whether censure is meant to be implemented for political reasons, or only in cases of criminal wrongdoing, as with impeachment. As Pinoargote points out, Article 59, Section (f) authorizes congress to make "political judgment" on members of the executive "for infractions committed in the exercise of official functions." The implication is that censure can be a legal procedure, like impeachment. Moreover, the constitution uses different language with reference to censure of different officials. For example, the president may be censured, but only for taking bribes, treason, or the like. No such restrictions are placed upon censure of cabinet ministers. We have entered into this discussion of censure in Ecuador not to attempt to resolve the question of whether or not censure has been effective in the particular case in making cabinets approximate the will of the assembly majority, but to indicate that provisions for censure should be explicit as to whether they are intended to be used for political reasons or not. Ecuador's constitution is fraught with ambiguity that only serves to heighten the pitch of confrontation when the president and assembly majority are of different political tendencies.

### Restricted censure: Uruguay, Guatemala, and Cuba

In another group of systems with constitutional provision for censure, the mechanism has likewise not proven a threat to the independence of the executive. It is not that censure in these systems is toothless, however, but rather that it has been implemented so infrequently or ineffectively. The reasons lie in constitutional provisions that are worth brief consideration.

*Uruguay.* In Uruguay, the congress can invoke censure only at the risk of beginning a process under which the president can dissolve the assembly itself.[5] Between 1934 and 1952, moreover, if congressional censure had led to dissolution, the next step for the assembly that was returned could have been removal of the president. This process is discussed later, in a separate section on dissolution. Under any of these conditions, then, for the two houses of congress, acting jointly as the General Assembly, to invoke censure has been to begin a game of political chicken with the president. Because of this deterrent, the Uruguayan assembly has barely made use of its power to remove cabinet ministers. In 1969, the assembly censured one of President Pacheco's ministers, but by less than a two-thirds majority. The constitution permitted the president in such cases to veto the censure, which Pacheco did. Then members of Senator Jorge Batlle Bere's faction of Pacheco's own Colorado Party defected to uphold the censure and ensure that the president could not invoke dissolution (Gillespie 1989:22; González 1989:5–6). In doing so, Batlle Bere's faction stated explicitly that the defection represented only a political maneuver and not a defense of the principle of cabinet responsibility. This is the only case of censure in Uruguay outside the period of the plural executive, or *colegiado*. But even under the conditions of the *colegiado*, censure did not carry the political implications it does under a unitary executive. The heads of ministries who were subject to censure were primarily administrators, whereas members of the Executive Council – the collegial presidency that was the *colegiado*'s approximation of a cabinet – could not be removed by the assembly.

Censure is a potentially powerful provision in Uruguay's institutional arrangement. But for the assembly to invoke it risks a lopsided version of

5 This was not the case during the period of the *colegiado* (1952–66), nor is it when the censure vote passes by a majority greater than two-thirds.

mutual assured destruction. This deterrent has created a sometimes uneasy standoff between congress and executive, preventing censure from being used to enforce cabinet responsibility.

*Guatemala.* The Guatemalan constitution also provides for congressional interpellation and censure of ministers. A majority of deputies in the unicameral congress can vote no-confidence in up to four ministers at a time. The president, however, can veto the censure, which requires a two-thirds majority for override.[6] Thus censure cannot be used to invoke cabinet responsibility to the legislative majority. We know of no cases when the process has even been initiated (García Laguardia and Vásquez Martínez 1984:76–7).[7]

*Cuba.* The Cuban political system in the 1940s has been called "semi-parliamentary," primarily because the constitution of 1940 provided for political responsibility of cabinet members to Congress (Stokes 1949). By our estimation the system still functioned essentially as presidential. Presidents were elected directly, and for absolutely fixed terms. Moreover, as Stokes himself points out, the Cuban president remained the effective head of government even while the new constitution created the post of prime minister (Stokes 1949:342–3). Nevertheless, the vote of censure during this period remains worthy of attention, largely because a principal intention of the framers of the 1940 constitution was to create cabinet responsibility.

In this intent they were only minimally successful, mainly because there were some procedural impediments to the enforcement of responsibility. A new cabinet member could not be censured for six months after assuming the post, and no motions of censure were allowed in the last six months of a president's term. Both Presidents Fulgencio Batista and Ramón Grau San Martín named their ministers without regard for the partisan balance in the congress, even though both originally faced majority opposition in Congress.

In May 1942, Congress interpellated the entire cabinet for questioning to assess the need for a congressional committee on executive oversight. Although Congress voted confidence in the entire cabinet, every member proceeded to tender resignations to President Batista, who accepted all but one (Stokes 1949:348–9). The congressional challenge to Batista's administration certainly appears to have prompted this turnover, although the provision for censure was not specifically invoked.

A second incident demonstrates how particular constitutional provisions for censure in what otherwise would be a presidential system may encourage

6 Constitution of Guatemala, Articles 166–7.
7 Moreover, given Guatemala's extended periods of nondemocratic rule, with close ties between the military and the presidency, it is doubtful that Congress has been in a strong enough position vis-à-vis the executive to challenge cabinet ministers.

presidents to seek to circumvent the intended congressional confidence. In October 1945, congress voted to censure the minister of commerce, Dr. Inocente Alvarez, but did so on charges of fraud, not for acknowledged political motives. More importantly, President Grau responded to the censure of his long-time friend by immediately naming Alvarez as prime minister (Stokes 1949:360–1). Grau's move was clearly intended as provocation, but congress failed to respond to the challenge. So while the formal measure of censure was not disputed, the principle of cabinet responsibility was defeated. It was defeated within the limits of the constitution, however. Presidents (as in the several president-parliamentary regimes) were not required to obtain prior approval to appoint a cabinet minister. Thus, although congress could respond with another censure, no provision exists in such regimes to prevent this minister from initially assuming his post upon nomination by the president. Further complicating matters in Cuba, once appointed, a minister could not be censured for six months. Thus presidents were afforded considerable leeway in filling cabinet posts or shuffling their cabinets, despite the formal provision for censure.[8]

### Censure and the appointment game

We have seen that in both Peru in the 1960s and the Chilean so-called Parliamentary Republic, cabinet responsibility to the assembly coexisted with directly elected presidencies. In this sense, both appear to have foreshadowed the regime type we have identifed as premier-presidential. However, we should like to make clear here why we regard these two cases as having been president-parliamentary rather than premier-presidential (for reasons more profound than simply the lack of a post of premier in the Chilean case), and why the difference between these two regime types is important to the prospects for democratic success.

In the previous discussion of assembly involvement in the appointment of cabinet members, we saw that initiative matters a great deal in structuring the appointment game. Because they make the initial appointment, and because the cabinet is recognized as the personal domain of the president, U.S. presidents are able to obtain cabinet members that accord well with their policy preferences, even when the Senate is controlled by the opposition. Additionally, U.S. presidents, and not the Senate, have the power to remove a cabinet member at will. In France, on the other hand, the president cannot remove a cabinet member or the premier, but the assembly can; thus, the French president facing an opposition-controlled National Assembly is weaker in the appointment game than is his U.S. counterpart.

In France, the asymmetry in powers of removal compensates for the asymmetry in nomination: While the president retains initiative in propos-

8 In October 1947, Grau's minister of education was censured for explicitly political reasons, and promptly resigned. We know of no other cases of censure under that constitution.

ing a premier, the assembly has the initiative in removing him or her. A president who did not want to nominate someone who would be approved and retained by the assembly would have to be willing to leave the post unfilled. Such a threat is rarely credible. In the United States, asymmetry works in favor of the president only: An assembly unwilling to accept any nominee would have to be willing to leave the post unfilled, which can be politically costly, especially at the cabinet level. The president, on the other hand, does not bear the political costs of leaving posts unfilled, as long as she or he is at least willing to submit nominations to the Senate.[9]

How does the appointment game look in cases such as Chile before 1925, and Peru? In neither case is it required that a president's nominee be confirmed by the assembly. While the assembly can censure and remove cabinet members, as in premier-presidential systems, so too can the president remove cabinet members at will. The structure of the game by no means compels the president to retain a cabinet acceptable to the assembly. When the assembly exercises censure, the president can simply continue to fill cabinet posts apace. In Chile and Peru, then, there is symmetry in the game after appointment in that either president or assembly may remove the cabinet or members of it. But because only the president can propose appointees, the assembly lacks the ability to make its own preferences stick. Thus censure becomes a strictly negative power, one with which to harass the president, but not a power with which to reconstitute the government. As we saw in Chapter 4, symmetry in removal powers contributed to interbranch conflict in Portugal (1976–82), and to chronic cabinet instability in Germany's Weimar Republic as well. We maintain that giving the assembly the power to censure but effectively depriving it of the ability to construct a new government by letting the president both propose appointees and remove sitting members of the cabinet is a dangerous prescription for conflict and instability, of the sort that led to the coup in Peru in 1968.

### BUILDING AND MAINTAINING CABINETS

Our point is more clearly illustrated in Table 6.1, which situates all of the regimes discussed in this book according to how cabinet positions are filled, and how ministers or entire cabinets are removed. In the rows of the table, regimes are grouped according to who has the authority to fill cabinet positions: the president, the assembly, or both working in consensus.[10] In

---

9 Of course, in some cases, and especially at the lower levels of the appointed bureaucracy, even the task of submitting nominations for the hundreds of executive posts to be filled can overwhelm an administration – as it did that of George Bush for the first two years.

10 The regimes are located in this figure according to the scores given for cabinet formation and cabinet dissolution in Table 8.2, below. Even in Chapter 8, our scoring system is intended to approximate and to order presidential powers, not to quantify them. Moreover, for Table 6.1, we have collapsed some scores further, to provide a broad, but rough, illustration of the origin and survival of cabinets. For example, those presidential systems

Table 6.1. *Filling and dismissing cabinets*

|  |  | **Dismiss** | | |
| --- | --- | --- | --- | --- |
|  |  | President | Assembly | Either |
|  | President | Presidential (e.g. Costa Rica, Venezuela) | Finland Iceland (premier-presidential) | President-parliamentary (e.g. Chile pre-1925, Namibia, Peru, Sri Lanka) |
| **Fill** | Assembly |  | Parliamentary systems |  |
|  | Both | Other presidential systems: Korea 1987 Nigeria Philippines United States | Most premier-presidential systems (e.g. France, Portugal 1982) | Portugal 1976 |

the columns, regimes are grouped according to who possesses the power to dismiss ministers: the president, the assembly, or either on its own. Two of the nine boxes in the figure are empty. We know of no regimes in which the assembly alone fills cabinet positions, but in which a president – either exclusively or in addition to the assembly – has the power to remove ministers. The other boxes all contain at least one existing or historical regime.

At the top left lie most of the systems that we have identified as pure presidentialism, where the cabinet is literally the personal domain of the president. At the bottom left are systems that we also regard as presidential, but in which the president's dominance over the cabinet is compromised slightly by the requirement that the assembly (or some delegation thereof) approve of cabinet nominations. In our discussion and modeling of the appointment game, we suggested that the president's initiative in appointments, and the ability to make take-it-or-leave-it offers provides him or her with a distinct advantage over the assembly in securing desired appointments.

In the middle column of the figure are the pure parliamentary regimes and the more successful premier-presidential systems. The differences among these regimes (on the question of government formation and dismissal powers) are over who names the cabinet. Simply put, if a popularly elected president has any substantive authority to fill cabinet posts, the regime can be premier-presidential. If the cabinet is filled through assem-

in which presidents name all cabinet members, subject to assembly approval, are grouped with those premier-presidential systems in which the president names the premier, who subsequently names the ministers. Despite the differences, we argue that in all these regimes, "both" the president and the assembly have significant powers in filling the cabinet. For the purposes of Table 6.1, these differences are ignored.

bly initiative, or by parties in the assembly, then the regime is closer to parliamentary – even if a ceremonial head of state *formally* appoints a premier.[11] The premier-presidential systems shown differ over the particulars of how cabinets are named. In Finland and Iceland, the president names all the cabinet positions, which are, of course, subsequently subject to parliamentary censure. In France and Portugal, the president names only the premier, who proceeds to fill cabinet posts after being confirmed by the assembly. Under both formats, however, the president makes the critical first move in cabinet formation, after which the cabinet is dependent exclusively on the assembly for its survival.

As suggested, this format encourages negotiation and compromise between president and assembly over the appointment of cabinet members at the outset of the appointment game. The president's resource is his or her initiative in the game, and the ability to make the assembly bear a disproportionate political cost for leaving the cabinet unfilled if it rejects all nominees. The assembly's primary resource is its exclusive ability to dismiss the cabinet; although it may also be able to impose a political cost on a president whose nominees it routinely rejects, if the president is perceived as making unreasonable nominations. Thus, presidents have an incentive to name the acceptable candidate with whom they are most politically compatible. The assembly's incentive is to accept the first nominee for whom the political costs of rejection (and thus, leaving the cabinet empty) are greater than the costs of confirmation.

Moving to the right in Table 6.1, we encounter the more problematic regimes among those in which either the president or the assembly may remove cabinet ministers. We suggested above that the interaction of censure and the appointment game becomes more complex, and potentially dangerous, when there are both asymmetry in appointment and symmetry in dismissal. If this is true, then Portugal (1976–82), while unique, might not have proven problematic, because although either president or assembly could remove ministers, both were also required to construct a cabinet. Indeed, the conflict between governmental branches that produced the constitutional reform of 1982 was based more on differences between a nonpartisan president versus parties in the assembly, and did not threaten to generate regime crisis or political disorder. We do not, then, see such an arrangement as necessarily unworkable, since the same incentives for compromise exist here as under other systems in which presidential nominations require the consent of the assembly. Nevertheless, the responsibility of cabinet members to both the president and the assembly can generate a "confusion" of loyalties in the executive, as we shall see below. In short, the Portugal 1976 formula is somewhat more clumsy than the premier-presidential regimes in the center column of Table 6.1, but certainly supe-

---

11 It could still be premier-presidential, if the president holds the powers of dissolution.

rior to the other president-parliamentary regimes in the upper-right-hand box.

The problematic systems, then, are those in which the president alone fills cabinet posts, but in which either the president or the assembly can dismiss ministers. These regimes might be labeled "confused," in that the responsibility of cabinet members is unclear and quite possibly contradictory. They can also be characterized as "asymmetrical," since the president alone makes appointments while either branch can disassemble the cabinet. The problem here is that there is no incentive for negotiation and compromise on the part of any player, neither at the stage of filling cabinet posts, nor in dismissing ministers. The president fills positions without constraint. Thus, the assembly's only means of affecting the constitution of the cabinet is to dismiss it. But this is a purely destructive tool, which provides no manner of ensuring that the cabinet or portfolio that follows the dismissal will be acceptable. Because cabinet positions need not remain indefinitely vacant, moreover, neither the president nor the assembly can be held directly responsible for a prolonged standoff. Instead, the dominant strategy for each player is to make the next move, creating an appointment–dismissal game in which there is no stable equilibrium.[12] Thus, when the president and assembly are at odds, the arrangement encourages the unstable pattern of appointment and dismissal that we see in Weimar, Cuba, Peru, and Chile before 1925. Two newer systems, Colombia 1991 and Namibia, may be expected to encounter similar difficulties.

### THE APPOINTMENT – DISMISSAL GAME

Having discussed the processes of building and maintaining cabinets under various institutional formats and their potential for compromise or conflict, we return now to spatial reasoning. The appointment game we have just presented can now be expanded to accommodate not only the initial play – nomination – but also the next move, taking into account who has the authority to dismiss an appointee.

Table 6.2 represents the importance of the power of initiative in the appointment–dismissal game. Where a party has initiative, either by making a nomination or by dismissing an officeholder, we give a value of two points. Since we wish to place the players (president and assembly) at opposite ends of a unidimensional scale in order to map preferences and predict outcomes in a two-player game, the president's nomination or dismissal is a +2, while the assembly's dismissal (via censure) is a −2, from the standpoint of its effect on the president's ability to retain ideal appointees. Assembly confirmation, being a power that is reactive, rather than initiative, we score as −1 from the president's perspective; the president

12 For an extensive theoretical discussion of dominant strategies, see Ordeshook (1986), ch. 3.

Table 6.2. *A schematization of presidential powers in the appointment–dismissal game*

| President | | Assembly | | | |
|---|---|---|---|---|---|
| Nominate | Dismiss | Confirm | Dismiss | Total | Examples |
| 2 | 2 | 0 | 0 | 4 | Most pres. systems |
| 2 | 2 | -1 | 0 | 3 | U.S., Philippines |
| 2 | 2 | 0 | -2 | 3 | Peru, Weimar |
| 2 | 2 | -1 | -2 | 1 | Portugal 1976 |
| 2 | 0 | -1 | 0 | 1 | U.S. Supreme Ct. |
| 2 | 0 | 0 | -2 | 0 | Finland, Iceland |
| 2 | 0 | -1 | -2 | -1 | France |

loses power relative to the assembly when the latter must confirm her or his nominations. If the assembly, or an agent thereof, could initiate appointments by presenting a nominee, it would gain two points, meaning a −2 on presidential power. The scale that results is depicted in Figure 6.3 and runs from −4 (which represents the assembly's ideal appointee) to +4 (which represents the president's ideal point). We should caution that these scores do not represent specific quantification; rather, this exercise is a heuristic in which the scores represent relative placement in a unidimensional spatial model. The several institutional arrangements are displayed in Table 6.2 in numerical order, but we deal with them in the text below in a different order, proceeding by regime type, as in previous discussions. The discussion that follows allows us to refer back to Figure 6.3 and see how different institutional arrangements affect likely outcomes in the appointment–dismissal game.

The spatial model suggests that the U.S. or Philippine cabinet members would be at about point 3 in Figure 6.3. They would thus be close to, but somewhat removed from, the president's ideal point. U.S. presidents could hold out for a 4, but to do so they would have to be willing to risk an empty seat, for they do not have the unrestricted appointment power of presidents in most other presidential systems, such as Costa Rica or Venezuela. For the assembly (the Senate in the United States), it must prefer either an empty seat or constant turnover *not* to confirm a nomination at 3, since the president can always dismiss a minister who is too far from presidential preferences. In other words, as we saw in Figure 6.2, the indifference curves overlap closer to the ideal point of the president than to that of the assembly, assuming that there is a divergence between the preferences of the president and the majority of the assembly.

If the president initiates the appointment process, subject to confirmation by the assembly, but *neither* may dismiss, we have a case such as the U.S. Supreme Court. The score, according to the method of Table 6.2, is thus +1. The model thus implies that presidents typically would have to

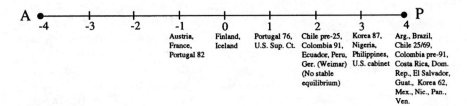

Figure 6.3. Schematized outcomes of equilibria in appointment–dismissal game, relative to ideal points of president (*P*) and assembly (*A*)

settle for appointees who are less close to their ideal than is the case for cabinets, but still closer to presidential than to assembly preferences. This turns out to be another way of saying that because these appointees are not subject to having their career advancement curtailed if they deviate from presidential (or assembly) preferences, they are relatively free of political constraints. Knowing this, Senate majorities in the United States should be more capable of demanding appointees who are farther from the president's ideal (at the time of appointment) than is the case for cabinet positions. The frequency of rejection, relative to cabinet positions, bears this out, as do the occasional occurrence of "mistakes," justices who prove in office to deviate from the preferences of the presidents who nominated them. Still, the president retains the initiative in the appointment game, thereby encouraging the Senate to be cautious in rejecting a nominee, realizing that, in the event of rejection, a replacement nominee may be no better for them, and could be worse.[13]

Now let us consider the case of cabinet appointments in a premier-presidential system that has the appointment–dismissal game characteristic of France: The president nominates the premier, subject to confirmation, but only the assembly may dismiss. The model predicts an equilibrium at $-1$. In other words, we find that the post of premier, and, by extension, other cabinet seats, should be filled by someone closer to the assembly majority's ideal point than to the president's ideal point, but that the assembly would not obtain its ideal. So what about the French case in 1986, when President François Mitterrand nominated as premier the leader of the assembly majority coalition, Jacques Chirac, thus representing the assembly's ideal point ($-4$ in the graph)? Why did he not try to fill the post with some other rightist who was not as unpalatable to him as Chirac, his principal political opponent? The answer, again, lies in the dismissal phase

13 There are some presidential constitutions (El Salvador, for example) in which only the assembly fills Supreme Court vacancies. This sort of arrangement leads to a prediction of appointees at $-2$ (the score for assembly nomination, not subject to confirmation or dismissal), or responsive to the assembly more than to the president, but straying from the assembly's ideal. Systematic research on court decisions in cases with this sort of appointment process would be worthwhile.

of the game, as well as in Mitterrand's lack of interest in provoking confrontation (see Chapter 4 and also Pierce 1990). If the president in such a system would prefer cabinet instability or empty cabinet posts to accepting a −4, she or he can appoint a −1, despite knowing that the assembly has the next move and can topple the government. If the president prefers an assuredly stable cabinet (−4) to the marginal utility to be gained by a −1 (who, after all, would still be from across the partisan divide in a bipolar party system like that of France), he or she might as well appoint a −4. This is a fair characterization of the calculation that Mitterrand made in nominating Chirac. However, the potential for a president to risk cabinet crises by refusing to appoint at or very near the assembly's ideal point is real and, as indicated in Chapter 4, the French experience from 1986 until 1988 by no means proves that cohabitation must go as smoothly as it did in that one example.[14]

Even if the appointment–dismissal game is exactly as in France, outcomes might be different if there is a multipolar party system. In such a case, with parties divided across several dimensions and therefore no clear, stable majority, the president's initiative might permit a −1, since precisely what candidate would represent the theoretical ideal point of the assembly would be less clear. Presidents could exploit this uncertainty with their power of initiative. They are even freer to do so if they have the power to appoint all members of the cabinet, rather than just the premier, without a formal vote of confirmation (usually called investiture in the parliamentary context). In such a case, the model predicts appointments at 0. Thus, theoretically, presidents operating in this kind of an institutional environment should be able to get appointees closer to their ideal than they might in systems structured like France. However, the ability of the assembly to invoke censure again, as in France, implies that presidents would have to be willing to tolerate considerable turnover in cabinets in order to maximize the proximity of cabinets to their ideal point. They might opt instead for appointments at points farther left in Figure 6.3.

This modeling of the game just described allows us to make some informed speculation about Finland and Iceland, two premier-presidential systems in which the president appoints all cabinet members. The frequent portrayal of Finnish presidents as playing a stronger-than-legal role in cabinet formation (e.g., Duverger 1980) as well as the extremely high turnover in cabinets (Strom 1990) both can be accounted for by our model. If Finnish presidents (or at least the long-reigning Urho Kekkonen) have regularly sought appointees at the midpoint of the scale, frequent censure would be the predicted result. On the other hand, in Iceland, where presidents are observed not to have exercised powers they are entitled to exer-

---

14 See Chapter 12 for further discussion of cohabitation and ways to design premier-presidential constitutions so that it is less likely or less problematic.

cise (Duverger 1980) and where turnover of cabinets is much lower, despite a multiparty system (Lijphart 1984), it is arguably because presidents have regularly avoided provoking censure by making appointments closer to the assembly's ideal point.

Next we must consider instances in which the president makes appointments wihout needing confirmation, but either the president or the assembly may dismiss ministers. Such regimes, which we have dubbed "president-parliamentary," have been found in the German Weimar Republic, Peru, and other cases we have identified. The scheme of Table 6.2 suggests an equilibrium around 2, implying a consensus on cabinet appointments only slightly farther from the president's ideal than in the presidential systems that require confirmation. However, as indicated earlier, the dominant strategy for each player in this game is likely often to be to make its move rather than to negotiate a compromise. Presidents can appoint a 4 and dare the assembly to censure. Presidents can appoint an official more acceptable to the assembly, confident that they also can remove this official at any time. Chronic cabinet instability is the likely result under this design when president and assembly are of opposing political tendencies.

Perhaps somewhat less conflictual, as already discussed, is a game like that of Portugal's 1976 constitution, in which both the appointment and dismissal phases of the game involve shared powers. This design may thus be the one most likely to generate consensus cabinets and thus true joint confidence. The reason is that the president cannot make an appointment at 4 and simply dare a censure as in cases like the Weimar Republic. Moreover, as in the United States or the Philippines, any attempt to obtain a 4 against the wishes of the assembly would require a willingness on the part of the president to leave the post vacant, which is presumably worse than turnover. This design builds the mutual confidence into the appointment phase, a clear improvement over designs such as those of the Weimar Republic and Peru. However, we still caution against such an arrangement, in part because its very limited use does not allow for meaningful empirical assessments. Besides, the problem remains of a lack of ultimate authority (and therefore of ultimate accountability before the electorate) for the actions of the cabinet. Either presidential or premier-presidential systems give one or the other player in the game ultimate authority through exercise of asymmetrical dismissal powers.

The arrangements most conducive to clear accountability in cabinets are those that provide for asymmetry in the authority to dismiss governments or ministers. Where only the president may dismiss, cabinets will tend to approximate the president's preferences. Where only the assembly may dismiss, the assembly majority's preferences will be approximated. When the branch that has sole authority to dismiss is not alone free to fill the posts, as is the case variously in France and the United States, there is a potentially desirable check by one branch on the preferences of the other, compared to either the pure presidential cases (Costa Rica, for example) or straight parliamentarism. However, when powers overlap to the extent that the dismissal game is symmetrical – and especially if the appointment phase of the game is asymmetrical – conflict and instability are severe risks.

## DISSOLUTION OF THE ASSEMBLY

Dissolution of the assembly by the president is a significant break with the principle of separation of powers and the final one we shall discuss. However, in the first two systems considered here, dissolution has been confined to extraordinary situations; in the third, the provision for dissolution is brand-new and unused. Another, Paraguay, has no record of democratic government before 1990 on which to base any assessment.[15] Paraguay and the 1989 constitution of Chile are the only cases that we know of in which the president had both the power to direct the cabinet and the power to dissolve the assembly purely on her or his own initiative.[16] In both the Uruguayan and Peruvian cases, dissolution can be invoked only after congress has censured cabinet ministers – or even the entire cabinet – for political reasons.

The provision for dissolution would seem to provide an institutional resource to resolve the problem of congressional deadlock decried by the critics of presidentialism. Indeed, in a parliamentary context, dissolution does just that. On the one hand, the parliamentary executive can use the threat of dissolution as leverage to secure legislative support for cabinet proposals. On the other hand, dissolution is not without risks for the parliamentary executive and therefore cannot be used indiscriminately; the voters may very well return a parliament which will replace the current government. Where the authority exercising the power of dissolution is one who stands outside of parliament, as with a president, there is thereby an external check on parliament and its cabinets. Indeed, a hypothetical form of premier-presidentialism would be one in which the power of dissolution is the only political power that the president wields. If dissolution resulted in the voters' returning parliamentary majorities more to the president's liking, the president would be able to obtain a cabinet (and therefore policy) likewise closer to his preferences. If, however, the voters return parliaments opposed to him, he must accept a cabinet not to his liking. Where dissolution takes on a very different characteristic is where cabinets are either jointly responsible to president and parliament, or where they are presidential cabinets. In the first instance, often dissolution is allowed only after the censure of ministers. The president then cannot use the threat of dissolution

15 At the time of writing, a constituent assembly was planned to revise the constitution.
16 The current Chilean provision for dissolution of the Chamber of Deputies, which, of course, remains as yet untested, is described below.

selectively as leverage to secure majorities for government policies. In the case of presidential cabinets, the president remains head of government even if a hostile congress is returned after dissolution. In such a situation, the problem of deadlock is likely to remain or even to be antagonized.

Let us now turn to some systems that are not premier-presidential according to our definition, but in which some constitutional provision for dissolution nonetheless has been made.

### Uruguay

During the periods of Uruguay's history in which dissolution has been allowed (1934–52, 1967–73, and 1983–present), it has always been contingent on the censure of cabinet ministers by the assembly. Under the constitutions of 1934 and 1942, the two houses of congress, acting together as the General Assembly, could censure cabinet ministers. Provided that the censure passed by less than a two-thirds majority, the president then had the right to dissolve congress and call new elections. However, if the new General Assembly upheld the original censure, the entire government, including the president, would fall (González 1989:4). During the period of the collegial executive (1952–66), congress retained the right to censure ministers, but not members of the Executive Council. In turn, the executive did not have the authority to dissolve the legislature (Gillespie 1989:12). Under the 1967 constitution, with the return to the unitary executive, the president was once again accorded the right to dissolve congress, although under somewhat more restrictive conditions. If a censure vote in the General Assembly passed by less than a two-thirds majority the president could refuse to dismiss the minister in question. The vote then had to be repeated, and the president could dissolve congress only if less than 60% of legislators upheld the censure. What's more, the president could do this only once during his term, and not during the last year of an assembly's term. The 1967 constitution has been retained largely intact since the return to democracy in 1983, including the provisions for dissolution.

Despite the many and extended periods in which dissolution has been possible in Uruguay, it has never been invoked. For the 1934–52 period, González (1989) attributes this to consistent Colorado control of the executive and sufficient congressional support. Even since 1967, however, when the provision for dissolution was reinstituted, the process has never been carried out, and has only been initiated once. In the incident in 1969 that we discussed in the section on censure, the legislators were able to protect themselves from the threat to their positions that the dissolution provision implies by a politically calculated defection of members of the president's party. Since the return to democracy, no movement toward dissolution has progressed as far. At one point, with his minister of the interior embattled during a controversy over police brutality, President Julio Sanguinetti threatened dissolution, successfully preempting a censure vote (Gillespie 1989:36).

The variations in Uruguay's rules and the episodes related illustrate many of the points we wish to make regarding dissolution. First, although dissolution was never invoked during that period, the 1934 and 1942 constitutions allowed for the possibility of a congressional vote of no-confidence in the executive following any dissolution of congress. Although the process could only be initiated following a censure vote, the requirement of mutual confidence was a distinctly nonpresidential characteristic of those constitutions. Second, the fact that the president cannot be removed as head of government under the current arrangement regardless of the results of new congressional elections suggests that deadlock is likely even after dissolution, should it occur. Third, the provision for dissolution only after censure does not significantly strengthen the president vis-à-vis congress, since dissolution cannot be used as an executive initiative. A president can invoke dissolution only when under attack, to save an embattled cabinet. The fact that dissolution has not been invoked despite conditions of immobilism underscores this point. Finally, a president might possibly try to provoke the censure of ministers in order to prompt the conditions for dissolution. This strategy would require extraordinary political loyalty on the part of "kamikaze" ministers, however, and would be inordinately risky, given the potential for antagonizing congress. We suggest, then, that dissolution under Uruguayan conditions will most likely remain a defensive weapon, if it is used at all.

### Peru

According to the Peruvian constitution of 1979, there is the possibility of dissolution in response to censure of the cabinet, but the conditions are more restrictive than in Uruguay. The Peruvian government has a pseudo-parliamentary structure in that the directly elected president names a prime minister to head the cabinet. The president and prime minister then concurrently name the cabinet members.[17] We refer to the arrangement as pseudo-parliamentary, however, since the president remains head of government throughout, while the prime minister effectively serves as chief of staff. The cabinet is subject to the confidence of the Chamber of Deputies. The chamber can censure an individual minister, or the entire cabinet, by a simple majority vote.[18] Only after the chamber has voted no-confidence in three cabinets, however, can the president dissolve the chamber – and even then may do so only once per term, and not during the last year of a term.[19]

17 Peruvian constitution (Art. 216).
18 Ibid. (Art. 226).
19 Ibid. (Arts. 227, 228, 229).

We know of no instance in which dissolution has been invoked in Peru, or even when the sufficient condition of three no-confidence votes has been established. Under these conditions, even more than in Uruguay, it seems that dissolution will remain the recourse of an embattled and highly confrontational president, and probably not much of a threat to the congress.

### Chile: presidential cabinets, yet dissolution

In its provision for dissolution, the Chilean constitution of 1989 marks a dramatically greater departure from the principle of separation of powers than either Uruguay or Peru. In the latter two, the conditions for dissolution must be created (and can be avoided, as we have seen) by congressional action. In Chile, this is not the cse. The Chilean president may dissolve the Chamber of Deputies once during a term, and not in the last year of the term; but there are no other conditions stipulated.[20] The lack of preconditions seems to entail an enormous shift in power toward the executive in Chile relative to the pre-1973 congressional–executive balance. Indeed, the power of the Chilean president to dissolve the chamber may be even more significant than the power of a parliamentary executive to dissolve the assembly, since for the Chilean executive to do so entails no risk to its own survival.

At this point, it is difficult to determine to what degree this institutional arrangement will actually alter the traditional balance; the dissolution power, of course, has not yet been used. Nevertheless, the degree to which it compromises the principle of separation of powers is sufficient that Chile should not be considered a true presidential regime by our criteria. Indeed, it might be more appropriate to call the regime "super-presidential." On the other hand, neither Uruguay nor Peru would be regarded as nonpresidential due to dissolution alone (Peru's potent censure, however, does make the regime nonpresidential). In neither case has dissolution been invoked, of course; but more importantly, in neither case may executives take the initiative to dissolve congress except under a set of extraordinary conditions in which cabinets appointed by the president have been censured by congress either excessively, or by less than overwhelming majorities.

#### CONCLUSION

This chapter has emphasized three central points. First, we have further evidence for the argument, made at the outset of the book, that there is a huge variety of institutional arrangements for assembly–executive relations in systems generally grouped together as presidential. To students of political institutions, this statement should seem self-evident. Nevertheless, it is

20 Chilean constitution (Art. 32, Sec. 5).

worth emphasizing the point, particularly since much of the current literature critical of presidentialism leans heavily on blanket portrayals of
assembly–executive relations. Among its critics, presidentialism tends to
be dismissed as a monolithic regime type. We intend here to emphasize the
very diversity of institutional arrangements in presidential, and premier-
presidential systems, so that we may better understand what specific provisions generate conflict between the branches, and whether these provisions
can be modified, short of eliminating the popularly elected chief executive
altogether.

Second, much of our discussion here has highlighted the ambiguities in
the concept of the separation of powers. We have suggested that merely a
provision for censure or for dissolution does not necessarily represent a
jump to a parliamentary executive. So when the authority to threaten the
survival of the other branch is contingent on that other branch's actions,
there are serious constraints on the use and impact of censure or dissolution. For example, dissolution power does not strengthen presidents who
can use the authority only when their cabinet (or successive cabinets) has
been dismissed nearly so much as dissolution power that may be used at
will. The array of arrangements, and sometimes contingent combinations,
of the powers reviewed here suggest that many of the regimes widely
considered presidential (or parliamentary, like Chile 1891–1925 or Cuba in
the 1940s) were in fact hybrids.

Third, we regard as important the point that "confusion" over to whom
the cabinet is responsible is a recipe for dangerous cabinet instability. This
is especially true where one branch alone names the cabinet to begin with.
We know of no regime in which the assembly alone names a cabinet that
can be removed by either president or assembly. But we have discussed a
number of problematic cases in which presidents alone fill cabinets, which
are then responsible to both the president and the assembly. We have
reviewed the incentives for each player (president and assembly) in a
"game" of appointment and dismissal, and have concluded that asymmetry
of power in such a game is disadvantageous for cabinet – and, quite possibly, regime – stability.

We have now completed our review of the constitutional origin and
survival of assembly and executive in presidential and premier-presidential
systems. We have provided an overview of how executives are constructed
and how they coexist with assemblies that may represent a different aggre-
gation of interests from their own. Our focus has been on the role and
strength of popularly elected presidents in these areas. We shall move in
Chapter 7 to discuss the legislative powers of presidents, particularly veto
and decree powers.

# 7

# Legislative powers of presidents

## INTRODUCTION

Regarding the subject of presidential power in the legislative process, we are interested in two main themes: the extent of constitutional (entrenched) presidential power, and the extent of legislative power delegated to the president by congress. These two types of legislative power are not unrelated. In particular, we argue that the presence of the former may encourage the delegation of the latter, suggesting also that students of presidential systems have regularly mistaken delegated authority for the usurpation of political power by presidents. We recognize that any delegation of authority implies the potential for agency loss but intend to demonstrate that the conditions under which delegation takes place can greatly constrain presidents from defying congressional will.

The chapter begins with a brief discussion of the distinction between entrenched and delegated legislative powers in parliamentary and presidential systems. We then proceed to examine the scope and configurations of presidential powers among systems with elected presidencies, focusing on the veto, the authority to introduce legislation, decree power, and emergency powers. It is in the areas of decree and emergency powers that the question of delegation versus entrenched authority is most pertinent. Where relevant, we include in the discussion the legislative powers of presidents in premier-presidential systems. However, most such presidents are accorded no such constitutional powers, and where delegation of legislative authority takes place in such systems, it generally involves delegation from the assembly to the premier or the cabinet. Therefore, the premier-presidential systems are not prominent in this discussion.

## DELEGATION VERSUS CONSTITUTIONAL POWERS

As noted in Chapter 2, one of the defining criteria of presidentialism is that the president possesses some legislative power. While the executive in any parliamentary system also possesses legislative power, there are two important distinctions between parliamentary and presidential systems in this respect. First, a parliamentary executive holds only those legislative powers that have been delegated to it by the assembly, while a presidential executive typically has entrenched legislative powers in addition to powers delegated by the assembly. The second distinction is that because some legislative powers are constitutionally given to the president, there is wide variation among presidential systems in terms of how much legislative power their executives hold.

The importance of delegation in distinguishing parliamentary from presidential executives (and some presidential executives from others) can hardly be overstated. A parliamentary executive with a secure basis of support among a majority in the assembly can legislate in a virtually unimpeded manner. That is, nearly all proposed laws may be initiated by the cabinet and supported without amendment after their official reading before parliament. It would be folly, however, to infer from this situation that the parliament is powerless and that the regime is therefore a "facade democracy." Yet such assumptions are regularly made with regard to presidential systems where a congress is observed not to play a significant role in legislating and rather appears to be bypassed or, at best, acting as a rubber stamp.[1]

What is going on in such situations? In the hypothetical majority-party parliamentary case just sketched, a clear equilibrium stems from the constitutional balance of powers between executive and assembly. To the extent that the majority party can come to agreement internally on policy matters, cabinet proposals will reflect the general position of the party at large. When the cabinet is a minority or coalition government, finding such a basic agreement may be more complicated and the scope of agreement more limited, but still whatever powers the cabinet has to make and implement law reflect a delegation by the parliament to the executive. In having been selected as the executive agents of the parliamentary majority, members of the cabinet have been charged with the authority to carry out the will of that majority.

From time to time, almost inevitably, the executive may deviate from the intended policy direction of the mainstream of the party or parties that constitute the assembly majority. In the language of principal–agent approaches, the principals – in this case, the party holding the parliamentary majority – are said to be suffering agency losses. What happens if these agency losses become severe but the agent – here, the cabinet – does not change its ways? The requirement of parliamentary confidence means that the principals can wield their ultimate sanction, voting for censure and thereby bringing the downfall of the government.

In a presidential system, it may be more difficult to see what represents delegation of authority and what represents an executive simply circumventing the assembly while the assembly abdicates its own authority. Much literature on the U.S. system argues that the Congress has abdicated its

1 For a typical example, see Conaghan, Malloy, and Abugattas (1990).

formal powers to make law, which is instead made by executive regulatory agencies (Lowi 1979; Fiorina 1982; Moe 1987). Yet, as is argued in McCubbins and Schwartz (1984), and Kiewiet and McCubbins (1991), Congress retains a number of means for minimizing its agency losses.

In many Latin American presidential systems, the emission of decrees plays an important role in policymaking. The widespread use of decrees raises question about the extent to which congresses in such systems maintain a role in the legislative process. Unfortunately, in our view, too little research has been done on the legislative processes of individual presidential democracies other than the United States. All too often, studies of particular countries have argued that congresses are rubber stamps or regularly have their powers usurped by the executive (Taylor 1960; Scott 1973; Levine 1973; Kelley 1977; Vázquez Carrizosa 1979; Suárez 1982; Linz 1987; Archer and Chernick 1988). We argue, however, that, as in the United States, many of these powers have been delegated by congress. As such, they can also be revoked.

There is another element to presidents' legislative powers beyond delegation: presidents' constitutional powers over legislation vary quite widely among presidential democracies. In Chapter 8 we present a ranking of presidential constitutions on the basis of how much legislative authority their presidents are constitutionally granted. If a given executive is constitutionally powerful relative to the assembly in the legislative process, then we have a case in which more than delegation is taking place, but not a case of circumvention, since presidents in such cases are acting within their constitutional authority.

With regard to the question of presidential usurpation – or congressional abdication – of legislative powers, we intend to make the following points in this chapter. First, delegation of power from the assembly to the executive is neither usurpation nor abdication if authority is delegated carefully, such that agency losses can be detected and authority easily revoked. Second, to the extent that the constitution grants presidents wide powers, it is inaccurate to speak of congressional abdication or presidential usurpation. That is, congress cannot abdicate what it does not have and the executive cannot usurp what it legally has. Third it is important to examine the legislative powers that are constitutionally granted to presidents, both to appreciate the vast differences in the powers of the office across systems, and to determine whether some configurations of legislative power are less conducive to smooth assembly–executive relations, and perhaps even more prone to regime crises.

## COMPARING LEGISLATIVE POWERS OF PRESIDENCIES

We now consider basic legislative powers that presidents may be constitutionally allocated. First is the veto, but there are many variations on this power. Override provisions vary, as do provisions such as whether the president may veto parts of a bill (a partial veto) or must accept or veto the entire bill (a package veto). If an executive wields a partial veto, this is a powerful weapon against congress and can render the congress much less effective in passing, for example, patronage-type legislation than if the president has only a package veto. There is also considerable variation among presidential systems in the extent to which lawmaking and rule making may be undertaken via decrees or under states of emergency.

## VARIATIONS ON THE VETO

Across the range of presidential systems, the veto is the president's most consistent and direct connection with the legislative process. Theoretically, it is considered the primary check of the president on congressional power. Nevertheless, the nature of the veto power provided in presidential constitutions varies enormously. Highly constrained, the veto can allow the president no more than an opportunity to express disapproval for a law, with no ability to block it. At the other end of the spectrum, it may endow the president with effective power to designate the specifics of large legislative packages. Or, of course, the effective power of the veto can fall anywhere between these extremes. Clearly, variations on the veto can tip the balance of power between congress and the executive strongly toward one or the other, and can do so without affecting the principle central to presidentialism that the origin and survival of the two branches remain independent.

In assessing the impacts of alternate veto formats, it will be helpful to break the variations into three categories, which we shall address in order:

1. partial vetoes;
2. pocket vetoes;
3. condition for override.

### Partial veto

Partial vetoes (also known as item vetoes) increase presidential power dramatically. With a partial veto, congress cannot present large legislative packages to the president, which effectively force the latter to accept pork projects or other objectionable amendments or "riders" in order to pass desired legislation. The partial veto allows the president to target specific elements of legislation for veto while promulgating the rest. While it is still technically a negative power, the partial veto allows the president to pull legislation apart and so to craft final packages that are more acceptable to the executive. As a result, presidential power becomes more flexible and potent than is possible with the cumbersome package veto. Conversely, one of congress's primary bargaining chips – and the ability to "logroll" – is lost or weakened.

Partial vetoes are common in Latin American presidential systems. Brazil, Chile, Colombia, and Ecuador are among the countries that have had for long periods of time constitutions granting the president a partial veto. In the Philippines, as in several U.S. states, the partial veto applies only to the budget or appropriations legislation, while in many other countries it applies to any legislation to which the president objects in part.

As with package vetoes, the conditions for override vary somewhat across systems. Overrides of vetoes are discussed below.

### Pocket veto

In all presidential systems, the president is required to take some action on legislation passed by congress – either to promulgate or to veto it – within a prescribed time period. The period is generally ten or fourteen days, but in some instances can be shortened to five days by a congressional decree that action is "urgent." The pocket veto, then, is never unrestricted in the sense that a president could simply refuse to promulgate legislation, without vetoing it, and thereby kill it without risking override. If a bill is passed within the last week of a congress, however, the president might wait until the recess period before vetoing. If the president alone is authorized to call special sessions of congress, then any action on an override will necessarily be delayed until the next congress. The pocket veto considerably strengthens the president relative to congress by denying congress the last move in the legislative process – its opportunity to respond to the veto.

More than simply a negative power, the pocket veto is a passive power. Restrictions are placed on its use in strikingly few presidential systems, perhaps because the imperative to regulate an official's prerogative to do nothing is less compelling than the need to regulate presidential actions. Nevertheless, in both Guatemala and Honduras, the pocket veto is explicitly prohibited in the constitution.[2] Congress does not recess until the president has either promulgated or vetoed all pending bills, and congress has had the opportunity to override.

### Conditions for override

Among presidential systems, the modal requirement for congressional override of a veto is a two-thirds majority in both chambers for bicameral systems, or in the single chamber for unicameral assemblies. It is also important to point out that among premier-presidential systems, effective vetoes (those requiring an extraordinary majority for override) are almost entirely absent. The ubiquity of the two-thirds rule among presidential constitutions may be testament to the influence of the U.S. Constitution on

---

2 Guatemala, Article 178; Honduras, Article 217.

later framers of presidential systems. Or perhaps it would be less parochial to suggest that this cutoff for extraordinary majorities has become a Schelling-esque focal point for constitution builders (Schelling, 1960). At any rate, the point is that there is no logic inherent to presidential government requiring the two-thirds cutoff. The president's power could be reduced or increased by setting the cutoff at three-fifths or three-quarters, respectively, while maintaining a similar executive check on congress. It has been rare for overrides to require more than two-thirds, but overrides of less than two-thirds are quite common.

In considering cases with lower thresholds for overrides, we must distinguish *absolute* from *simple* majority. An absolute majority is 50 percent plus one of the membership of the assembly (or of each chamber, where applicable), while a simple majority is 50 percent plus one of a quorum. Because legislation passes in nearly all systems by a simple majority and frequently the full membership is not present or some members or parties abstain, raising the requirement for a veto override to an absolute majority implies that some legislation may fail to clear this hurdle when vetoed by the president. In Venezuela, the president may veto a bill, and immediate override requires a two-thirds majority. A *simple* majority, however, can return the bill to the president's desk. The president again may veto the bill, but the second time around a simple majority in congress can promulgate it (Art. 173). In such a case, the president's "veto" does not ultimately require any greater a majority to override the president's objections than to pass the bill in the first place. Although the constitution may refer to the review process as a veto, then, the process does not constitute an effective executive veto as it is commonly understood. Rather, it constitutes a formal process by which presidents can "go public" (Kernell 1986) with their objections to particular legislation, forcing congress to reemphasize its support for a bill. But a persistent assembly in the end is sovereign on legislation. This type of "veto" is found as well in many premier-presidential systems, including France.

The executive check entailed in an effective veto is most important when the president faces an opposition majority in congress. Where party discipline is tight, therefore, and the requirement for override is a simple majority, congress's immunity from such a check is underscored. This indeed is the case in Venezuela, where the closed-list ballot structure ensures nearly airtight party discipline. Coppedge (1992) has furnished examples, from several administrations, where minority presidents in Venezuela have been powerless to prevent narrow congressional majorities from legislating "over their heads." According to Coppedge, since the Venezuelan president can be circumvented by congress in the legislative process, there is the danger that such a president will simply fail to execute laws which are passed by narrow majorities over executive objections.

In Brazil and Nicaragua, both the package and partial vetoes require only an absolute, rather than extraordinary majority to override. At first blush, the fact that override requires only an absolute majority may seem to indicate that the provision for a partial veto would be minimal. Even so restrained, however, the partial veto could be a powerful tool for these presidents. Consider the classical legislative logroll, in which assembly members bundle diverse pork barrel spending items together, attaching the items to legislation which the president regards as critical. Each individual pork item may benefit a minority of assembly members – perhaps only one – and could not survive an up or down vote on its own. Through the logroll, however, assembly members agree to support each other's items in order to secure a majority for their own. If presidents with only a package veto find the rest of the legislation more desirable than the pork is objectionable, they will sign it. Now consider the response of a president with a partial veto, even with a *simple* majority override. If an override vote must be held on each vetoed part of the bill, the logroll strategy falls apart. Item by item, the pork is unpopular across all districts or parties.

In addition to these examples of low thresholds for override, there are instances when the requirement of an extraordinary majority for override is required or relaxed only for specific types of legislation. In Colombia before 1991, override of a veto on appropriations legislation required two-thirds majorities, whereas override for all other legislation required only an absolute majority (Art. 88). Although the Colombian budget process was complicated by other institutional arrangements besides the veto, this arrangement strengthens the president's hand in budget matters relative to nonfiscal issues. In Paraguay, where the actual experience with nonauthoritarian government has been minimal, the constitution requires a two-thirds majority for override of a package veto, but only a simple majority to override a partial veto (Art. 158, 159). In Ecuador, on the other hand, a partial veto can be overridden by two-thirds majority, whereas congress by itself cannot override a package veto at all. Congress can, however, submit vetoed legislation to a referendum (Art. 69, 70). In Ecuador, the president is thus faced with a subtle calculation in deciding whether to exercise the partial veto. The partial veto can be overridden by a two-thirds vote, while a package veto cannot be directly overridden by congress at all. However, Congress can move to have legislation vetoed as a package submitted to a referendum. Therefore, use of the partial veto may reduce the obstacles to override on that particular point, since a referendum is not necessary; but it also could preempt congress from going "over the president's head" to the people to pass the entire package.

Bolivia's constitution requires a two-thirds majority in a joint session of congress for override (Art. 77). If the veto were to take place in the two chambers separately, the power of the less populated departments would be amplified in the senate, as is usual on all legislative matters in bicameral systems where representation in the upper house is geographically determined. Because the vote takes place in joint session, the power of the less populous departments is dampened somewhat during direct confrontations between congress and the president. Brazil's votes on overrides similarly take place in joint session.

As we noted above, the power of the president in premier-presidential systems usually is relegated to the sphere of government formation and possibly dissolution of the assembly. As the principle of separation of powers is compromised, the primary check that Madison saw as being protected by separate branches is generally absent; premier-presidential constitutions rarely provide the president an effective veto. The proposed Argentine premier-presidential model would be an exception, requiring a two-thirds override. Poland's transitional premier-presidential arrangement after 1989 similarly provides for such a veto. The 1976 Portuguese constitution provided an absolute veto for the president, by stipulating that no legislation could become law without the president's signature. This provision, however, was scrapped in the constitution reform of 1982, leaving the current president with weak veto power on legislation on most matters other than foreign policy (where there is a veto and a two-thirds override). In addition, a number of president-parliamentary regimes have provided for a two-thirds override on vetoes. These cases included Chile's "Parliamentary Republic," Cuba in the 1940s, and Namibia.

Of the areas we have identified in which presidential systems vary, the veto formats offer the greatest range for potential manipulation. The other types of variation we review can have tremendous impact on congressional-executive relations, but the diverse blueprints for the exercise of the veto can be adapted to adjust the relative strengths of the branches, in large or small increments, and for specifiable situations and types of legislation.

### OTHER LEGISLATIVE POWERS OF PRESIDENTS

We now move on to the other legislative powers of presidents, including special authority to introduce legislation, decree powers, and emergency powers, of executives in presidential and premier-presidential systems. The preceding section illustrates that across the range of presidential systems the veto is the most prevalent, flexible, and routine tool by which presidents can affect the lawmaking process. We also saw, however, that some chief executives in presidential systems, and most in premier-presidential regimes, do not have an effective veto. Where this is the case, and where the president faces an opposition majority in congress, we might expect that an independently elected president should be irrelevant to policy outcomes. Congress cannot terminate such an executive as under parliamentary government, but even a bare majority can legislate "over the president's head," as we saw in the Venezuelan case.

The first question that arises, then, is: Does a president without a veto necessarily imply outright congressional sovereignty? We shall see that an array of non-veto legislative powers exists in various combinations among regimes with elected presidents. All constitute real lawmaking power. In most presidential systems, moreover, at least one of these powers exists in addition to an effective veto. The second question, then, is: In what ways do non-veto lawmaking powers strengthen presidents relative to assemblies?

### Legislative introduction and budgetary powers

The most common non-veto presidential power is the authority to introduce legislation in congress. Most presidents have the authority to introduce legislative proposals, but even where they do not, there is no meaningful restriction on presidential power. Surely any president can find some member of the assembly to introduce a desired bill. Where provisions relating to the introduction of legislation become important is in those cases in which *only* the president may introduce certain types of legislative proposals. In particular, many constitutions grant powers of initiative to the president in budgetary matters.

The importance of legislative introduction, especially where it is the exclusive power of the executive, is fourfold. In the first place, it takes presidents out of the position in which they can respond only to take-it-or-leave-it legislative offerings from congress. In the discussion of congressional approval for presidential appointments in Chapter 6, we used a simple spatial model to demonstrate the advantage that such asymmetric initiative power provides to the president. Thus, any president with the authority to introduce legislation has the potential to counter unsatisfactory legislative offerings from congress by attempting to engineer a congressional majority for alternative legislation more to his or her liking.

Second, the advantage of initiative is increased when the president is provided *exclusive* authority to introduce certain legislation. Where the executive is given exclusive authority to initiate legislation in certain key policy areas, as in Brazil, Chile, Colombia, and Uruguay, the president necessarily becomes the most important legislative actor in those domains. Even if presidential legislation can be amended in congress, congresspersons are limited to a reactive position, able only to modify. If the president wants no action, then no action can be taken. The bottom line is that when presidents, or ministers who are exclusively accountable to presidents, are allowed to initiate legislation on their own, they are generally among the primary forces in the legislative process.

Third, legislative power is greater still when the president can make take-it-or-leave-it proposals – those that cannot be amended. Although such restrictions on amendment are rare, they exist in Uruguay, where congress cannot increase tax exemptions proposed by the president or lower proposed maximum prices. Similar restraints existed in Chile before 1973. Congress could not increase the president's proposed ceiling for spending on particular items without simultaneously creating new appropriations or reducing other items. The current Chilean constitution goes a step farther: The president's budget bill imposes a spending cap that cannot be amended (Art. 64), meaning that congress can shift the allocation of appropriations but only within a fixed budget. Some other constitutions have gone farther still in granting initiative to the president in budgetary matters. For example, in the Korean constitutions of 1962 and 1987, the congress may not even move expenditures around from item to item, let alone increase items of expenditure; it may only reduce amounts proposed for given items.

Fourth, presidents are commonly able to influence the legislative agenda by combining introduction power with dramatic advantages in information. The centralized nature of executives provides them an advantage over assemblies in collecting and managing information. Much of the most important information for putting together viable legislative packages is available primarily in the ministries and bureaucracy of the executive branch. In many presidential countries, moreover, congress is notoriously poorly funded and understaffed. Where presidents have extraordinary powers in the budget process, they may even be able to cultivate this informational advantage by keeping congress underfunded.

### Decree powers

Presidential decree power is related to the power to introduce legislation in that it reverses the standard relationship by which congress proposes actions while the president serves as a veto gate. But it goes farther. A bill introduced by the executive still must pass through the ordinary legislative process in congress and then be submitted back to the president for approval or, if congress has modified beyond what the president will accept, veto. A decree law is not merely a bill introduced by the executive, but rather a law or regulation issued by the executive. In some cases, congress must specifically act to accept or "veto" a decree. In other cases, a decree stands unless specifically rejected by congress. In still others, and more significantly for the balance of powers, a decree is simply law made by the executive and not subject to congressional review.

We distinguish between two variants of decree authority granted to presidents. The first is the constitutional authority to legislate by decree in specified policy areas, whereby the decree is law unless it is overturned by congress. The second is the ability to have the authority to legislate by decree delegated by congress to president.

The first form, constitutional decree authority, is found, currently with various limitations and permutations, in a few countries, including Brazil, Chile, and Iceland.[3] Under Brazil's constitution of 1988, the president may

---

3 Historically, the president in Weimar Germany had extensive decree powers, as discussed in Chapter 4.

decree "urgent" laws that are immediately effective; but if they are not passed by congress within forty-five days, they lose effect. Since the president may decree the same matter once again, effectively this "urgency" clause grants the president decree power that is not subject to rescission. In Chile under the 1989 constitution, the president, with the consent of the cabinet, may decree expenditures that cannot be ignored without "causing serious detriment to the country" (Art. 32, Sec. 22). In Iceland as well, the president may issue decrees with the force of law when parliament is not in session. Such laws are, however, subject to approval or rejection as soon as parliament reconvenes, which it may do under its own initiative at any time.

This first type of decree power allows the president to dominate the agenda by which applicable legislation is considered. However, it would be misleading to argue that any of these presidents – assuming competitive electoral processes – are able to use their decree powers rampantly and without any congressional checks. In each case, decree powers are embedded within a constitutional structure that imposes many restraints on presidents in other aspects of the legislative process. For example, although the Brazilian president theoretically may declare a matter urgent, wait for congress to vote to rescind it, then re-decree it repeatedly, such a determined president might find many obstacles placed in his or her path by congress. Foremost among these would be the ability of the congress to override with relative ease (an absolute, as opposed to a two-thirds majority) any presidential veto. Additionally, of course, the congress can use its budgetary powers, even though they are somewhat restricted, to cut appropriations desired by the president. Thus the urgency powers give the president considerable leeway to shape the legislative agenda, but an all-out confrontation is one that the president could not win, given the considerable legislative weapons retained by the congress.

In Colombia before 1991 the president with the consent of all cabinet ministers could declare a State of Siege or a State of Economic Emergency without congressional sanction and could issue decrees with the force of law. Given this authority, and the existence of one or the other form of state of exception for almost three-fourths of the time since 1958 (Archer and Chernick 1988), the Colombian president may be said to have had significant powers to enact laws on his own. On a careful reading of the constitution, however, what at first appears as a virtual absence of institutional constraint on these supposedly exceptional powers reveals itself as institutionalized delegation. In a 1968 amendment, Congress assumed the power to reject or amend a State of Emergency declaration, although not a State of Siege. The constitution itself could be amended by absolute majorities in successive congresses, so one can imagine that even the president's constitutional decree power could be relatively easily revoked if it were abused to the point where it no longer served congressional interests.[4] As evidence that this is so, consider that the constitution provided that any laws issued during such periods lapse when the period of exception ends. That many of these laws were subsequently converted into ordinary legislation by congress (Archer and Chernick 1988) simply suggests that the "emergency" decrees passed by the president did not deviate substantially from congressional majority preferences. If so, then the Colombian legislative process, often portrayed as having been abdicated by the congress, was in equilibrium after all, albeit an equilibrium based in an institutional context that was skewed in the short term toward an executive that can always call yet another state of exception.[5] As such, the Colombian president's "extraordinary" and "temporary" decree powers were de facto ordinary legislative powers that served to overcome the slowness and logrolling that characterize ordinary congressional legislation, but not to run roughshod over congressional preferences and prerogatives.

In most constitutions that permit presidential decree legislation, there are countervailing powers in the hands of the assembly. In Brazil and Colombia, the relative ease of veto overrides is one such countervailing power. In France, the German Weimar Republic, Iceland, in the Korean constitution of 1948 and the new Colombian constitution (as well as in Brazil after a constitution amendment in 1961), the assembly holds the power of censure over cabinet ministers. In all cases, the assembly holds at least restricted powers over the budget. That assemblies retain means to keep presidents from using their decree authority rampantly, however, does not imply that these powers do not grant presidents a formidable advantage in the legislative process. While a president must consider costs that may be incurred when a decree is issued that goes beyond known congressional majority sentiment, the existence of the authority allows presidents to bring legislative outcomes closer to their ideal point than would be feasible if only congressionally sanctioned measures could become law. We return to this later on in the form of a spatial model when we consider decree powers delegated by congress.

4 In addition, and as a more short-term and piecemeal solution, Archer and Chernick (1988) report that the Supreme Court of Colombia has increasingly reviewed, and in some cases overturned, legislation issued during states of exception. Under the 1991 constitution, the emergency powers are restricted in time, subject to senate approval before extension, and more closely guarded by congress owing to cabinet members' dependence on the confidence of the chambers.
5 That this latter observation about the ever present threat of a new state of exception is not the full explanation of congressional acceptance of these decrees is suggested by the discussion in Archer and Chernick (1988). They indicate that presidents cannot hope to undertake any fundamental reform under states of exception, presumably because the congress would not convert such decrees into ordinary legislation. This, then, is an argument that congress accepts only those that are not much at variance with its own preferences.

### Distinguishing decree legislation from rule making

Any student of Latin American politics will immediately recognize that "decrees" are issued far more commonly and in far more countries than is indicated here. Are we therefore overlooking some factor of presidential power that cannot be explained by reference to "formal" constitutional powers? The problem is largely semantic. In Latin America the term *decreto* (decree) is used more widely than we use it in this book. Almost any executive act, from a regulatory decision through a pardon to constitutionally sanctioned lawmaking, is called a decree. We use the term more narrowly; only those laws which the president can initiate and which maintain the force of law unless specifically rescinded (vetoed) by congress are meaningfully called decree laws. Although one might not realize it by reading the literature on Latin America, few systems grant this form of decree authority. Moreover, most allow it only in constitutionally specified policy areas, as already discussed, and embed the authority within constitutional rules that significantly restrict presidential legislative powers in other ways.

Most other cases of decrees in Latin America or elsewhere are regulatory matters rather than new legislation. As such, the range of options that may be "decreed" by the president (or, in some cases, a minister) is limited by legislation already passed by congress and, where necessary, approved by the president through ordinary legislative procedures. These regulatory decrees are thus not much different from the rule-making authority granted to independent agencies in the United States, where the term "decree" is never used. If the parameters within which the executives of some systems issue regulations are much more vaguely circumscribed than in the United States, one reason is the greater legislative powers of such presidents in the ordinary legislative process compared to the United States. For example, where the president may veto part of any bill, congressional ability to fine-tune legislation is sharply limited and delegation of specific authority to the executive is an obvious solution.

### Distinguishing decree legislative authority from emergency powers

Decree legislation, as we have defined it, must be distinguished not only from regulatory decrees (rule making) but also from states of emergency. In nearly all presidential systems other than the United States, and in some premier-presidential systems as well, emergency powers allow the president to suspend civil liberties and take direct command of local agencies in times of unrest. Constitutions differ in the degree to which congressional ratification or oversight of states of exception is required. In Costa Rica and Namibia, for example, a state of emergency may be declared only with the consent of two-thirds of the assembly. Several require congressional action, but only a vote of a simple majority to continue the state of emergency. Article 16 of the French constitution provides broad and rather vaguely defined authority to the president when the "independence" or "integrity" of the nation is threatened. Requiring only consultation with the premier, the presidents of the two chambers of the assembly, and the Constitutional Council, the French provision offers potentially the most extensive emergency powers of any presidency. If the premier is of a different party or coalition from the president, the requirement of "consultation" with the premier may imply a check on the president. However, it is potentially significant that the constitutional language is not stronger, perhaps requiring the "consent" of the premier and the assembly, rather than mere consultation. Emergency powers are untested in France in situations in which the president and premier are politically divided. We can say only that language such as that in the French constitution carries the potential for a constitutional crisis.

All things considered, only in very few regimes does a state of emergency imply legislative powers. The case of Colombia has already been addressed. In El Salvador, the president may authorize the disbursement of unappropriated funds to meet needs created by the emergency. And in Ecuador and Bolivia, presidents may advance the collection of taxes and other revenues ahead of schedule (but not authorize any new ones), in order to meet the budgetary needs generated by the emergency. In Chile before 1973 the president was allowed an amount equivalent to 2 percent of the budget to meet "emergency" needs, at his discretion. Other than these examples, presidents do not enjoy special legislative decree powers under states of siege or emergency.

### Delegation of decree powers

Under another variant, decree power may be delegated to the president by congress for a specified time and in certain policy areas. The constitutions of Chile, Colombia, Peru, and Venezuela specifically allow for such delegations, although we expect that unless such delegations are explicitly prohibited, they remain an option for congress. Because this power may be retracted prematurely by statute, the effects of delegating such authority depend on the requirement for veto overrides. Interestingly, in Peru and Venezuela, the congress can retract a delegation of decree authority by simple majority, even over a presidential objection, since in both cases there is no requirement for an extraordinary majority to override a veto. In some other cases including Colombia before 1991, an absolute majority is required. Where one party holds a majority of all members, but less than two-thirds, a veto requiring no more than an absolute majority to override makes the delegation of decree powers far less costly than if a

Figure 7.1. Presidential (*P*) and congressional (*C*) ideal points on hypothetical policy: indifference point for simple majority ($I_{C^{1}/_{2}}$) and two-thirds majority ($I_{C^{2}/_{3}}$)

greater majority is required to retract such power. In these countries, then, the actual effect of delegating decree authority is merely to transfer the powers of legislative initiative to the president for the duration of the decree period. If the president were to decree legislation objectionable to a majority in congress, we expect the decree power to be promptly retracted. Under the new Chilean constitution, on the other hand, once decree power is delegated, it cannot be prematurely retracted unless either the president capitulates, or congress overrides the presidential veto by a two-thirds vote of each chamber. Under these conditions, unless one party or stable coalition holds at least two-thirds of the seats (a relatively rare occurrence), delegation would entail an abdication of legislative authority to the president.

The situation is modeled in Figure 7.1. For a given issue on which the president might issue a decree, point *P* is the president's ideal policy and point *C* is congress's. $I_{C^{1}/_{2}}$ represents the point at which a majority of congress is indifferent between the status quo and new legislation which lies closer to the president's ideal than to congress's. This point is not necessarily the same as point C, since the power of initiative now belongs to the president. Theories of social choice (Arrow 1951; McKelvey 1976) show us that congressional majorities will rarely be unique to any given policy point,[6] so we expect that congress's ideal point and its indifferent point should not be exactly the same. but $I_{C^{2}/_{3}}$, much farther from point *C,* is the point at which two-thirds of members are indifferent between a presidential initiative and the status quo. Put another way, $I_{C^{1}/_{2}}$ is the point beyond which any presidential decree would be revoked by a majority, but $I_{C^{2}/_{3}}$ is the point beyond which a presidential decree would have to go in order for congress to override the veto that would be likely if it attempted to revoke decree power. What Figure 7.1 shows is the area, in "policy space," on any given issue that a congress abdicates if it delegates decree power to a

6 With either strong party discipline (for example, with closed-list electoral systems) or bicameralism (see Miller and Hammond 1989) or both, an assembly may approximate a unique majority position more closely than most models of social choice instability assume. Even if so, the relevance of distinct "ideal" and "indifference" points in understanding delegation remains. Over time, the ideal legislative point of even a disciplined majority of bicameral legislature may shift from where it was when the delegation was made, while the agent's preferences might not shift, or might shift in a different way. Thus the model that we develop here should be applicable, to varying degrees, to any situation in which an assembly delegates decree powers.

president that can only be revoked with legislation requiring an extraordinary majority. In this model, the amount of abdication is the space between points $I_{C^{1/2}}$ and $I_{C^{2/3}}$. The space between $I_{C^{1/2}}$ and $C$, in turn, is the amount of abdication entailed by delegating decree power that can be revoked by a simple majority.

Where delegation does not entail abdication, we might expect congress to rely on delegation as a means of overcoming coordination problems in the legislative process. The incentive to delegate, of course, would depend on the ability of congress to minimize agency loss to the president (see Kiewiet and McCubbins 1991), and the extent of its own coordination problems. The evidence on this count is suggestive. Archer and Chernick (1988) report that Colombian presidents held some decree powers 75 percent of the time between 1958 and 1988, not necessarily because of threats to the political order but because legislative coalitions were so fragile. Unfortunately, Archer and Chernick do not distinguish between decree powers delegated by congress and "economic emergency" powers declared by the president. In Venezuela, decree authority has been granted only to presidents with majority support in congress – three Acción Democrática presidents have requested and received decree powers since the current constitution was promulgated in 1961. In no case was the authority overturned prematurely. During his first presidency, however, Carlos Andrés Pérez issued the staggering total of 830 decrees and established fifty-one government commissions on a broad range of policy areas in the space of twelve months. Coppedge (1988) reports that in the one subsequent case of delegation that he studied, the party in congress was cautious in limiting the extent of decree powers it authorized.

While the specific conditions surrounding decree powers are diverse, they are a common form of non-veto legislative authority for presidents. In some cases, decree powers surpass the veto as the prime source of presidential power in the legislative process. This is most clear in Peru and Venezuela, where vetoes are ineffective. It is also true in Colombia, where decree power in the economic sphere can be seized by the president without a clear congressional check. In Chile, the prospect of delegated decree power is formidable, but it remains to be seen whether congress would ever delegate such authority to a president, given the difficulty to retract it.

## CONCLUSION

This chapter began by noting the distinction between entrenched, constitutional legislative power and delegated presidential power. We have discussed the extent of each type across systems with elected presidencies. Regarding the first type, we concluded that although the veto is the most common legislative power of presidents, it is neither uniformly configured across systems, nor the only significant entrenched power. Our examination of vetoes demonstrates that a number of factors determine its impact on presidential strength, including the conditions for override, the ability to target specific items for veto, restrictions on what kinds of legislation may be vetoed, and the presence or prohibition of pocket vetoes. Moreover, we have demonstrated that the authority of the president to introduce legislation makes him or her a central player in the legislative process from the outset, and a privileged one if the president is accorded exclusive authority to introduce certain types of legislation, or if restrictions are placed on congressional amendments. We have noted that those emergency powers granted to presidents that do not require case by case approval by congress, with a few exceptions, do not include legislative authority. And we have argued that where other, nonemergency decree power exists, it also is exercised based on delegation from congress more often than has been recognized by students of presidential government.

On this subject, we stress that congresses that appear to be passive, reactive players in the legislative process might well be those that have delegated legislative authority to the president. But, we argue, it would be to commit a fallacy of equilibrium to declare these congresses ineffectual without examining the terms on which authority is delegated. As we have discovered, in most systems where decree authority can be delegated, for instance, it can also be retracted easily by congress.

We have noted that among students of Latin American politics (who, for geographical reasons, most frequently encounter presidencies), the assessment that decree power is more pervasive and broad than it actually is may be based in part on a semantic misinterpretation. That is, the Spanish term *decreto* is used to describe what we call in English regular rule-making authority, as well as to demark real legislative decree power. However, we suggest that real decree power is most likely to be delegated to presidents where certain conditions hold. One is that the president already possesses strong entrenched powers such as a partial veto or the exclusive right of legislative introduction, and so is able to fine-tune legislation regardless of congressional will. Another condition is the fragility of congressional majority coalitions, perhaps in multiparty systems, which may encourage the delegation of decree authority to break congressional deadlock. Ultimately, we have seen that the legislative powers – entrenched as well as delegated – of presidents greatly vary across systems. This should no longer be surprising, as we have drawn similar conclusions in Chapters 5 and 6, on the comparative presidency. In the following chapter, we turn to the task of systematically assessing the scope and configurations of all presidential powers – legislative and governmental – and drawing conclusions regarding the relationship between presidential power and regime performance.

# 8

# Assessing the powers of the presidency

In this chapter we undertake a process of assessing just how powerful a president is in constitutional terms. We identify two basic dimensions of presidential power: one concerning power over legislation, the other encompassing nonlegislative powers, including authority over the cabinet and calling of early elections for congress. Additionally, because the latter powers are directly related to the question of separation of powers, we provide a comparison of presidential powers over the composition of cabinets to separation of executive from assembly. There are two main, related lessons we shall be able to draw from this exercise. First, systems that score high on presidential powers, and in particular those that are extreme on presidential legislative powers, are often those systems that have exhibited the greatest trouble with sustaining stable democracy. Second, systems that give the president considerable powers over the composition of the cabinet but also are low on separation of survival of assembly and executive powers likewise tend to be among the "troubled" cases. There are thus left two basic clusters that, we argue, are "safer" for the success of democracy: (1) those with high separation of survival of powers but low presidential legislative powers; and (2) those with low separation of survival but also low presidential authority over the cabinet. These categories happen to be those approximating the (more or less "ideal") types we have discussed in previous chapters: presidential and premier-presidential, respectively. The more troubled regimes prove to be hybrids.

## POWERS OF THE PRESIDENCY: LEGISLATIVE POWERS

To assess presidential powers, it is possible to devise a simple interval scoring method on each of several aspects in which systems with elected presidencies vary. The first set of aspects entail legislative powers constitutionally granted to the president. These aspects are the veto, the partial veto, presidential authority to legislate by decree, exclusive right to initiate certain legislative proposals, budgetary initiative, and power to propose referenda. Aspects of presidential power apart from the legislative domain include cabinet formation, cabinet dismissal, lack of assembly censure, and dissolution of the assembly. The scores on each aspect of each dimension can then be summed to arrive at an overall indicator of presidential powers on the respective dimension. This is not a perfect method – for instance, it might be justifiable to weight some dimensions more than others – but it is preferable to a purely nonquantitative, impressionistic ranking or to no assessment of comparative presidential powers at all.

*Package veto/override.* As discussed in Chapter 7, if presidents are to have any authority to shape the legislative output of the congress, they must be provided with a veto over legislation. However, if this veto were absolute, no piece of legislation objected to by the president could ever pass, hence the president would be extremely powerful. The latter scenario existed in Chile in the mid-nineteenth century. Something similar, but not quite as strong, exists today on nonbudgetary legislation in Ecuador. A veto cannot be overridden by congress alone, but the congressional majority can submit the vetoed bill to a binding referendum, thereby potentially weakening the absolute nature of the veto. In most other cases, as in the United States, a veto may be overridden by a two-thirds majority of the congress. As seen in Table 8.1, we have given a score of 4 to a veto that may not be overridden, 2 to one requiring a two-thirds override, and 0 to one that can be overridden by the exact same majority that passed the original bill. Intermediate cases are also possible.[1] If the majority required is more difficult for congress to obtain than a two-thirds majority, but the veto is nonetheless not absolute, we score it a 3. We include Ecuador as a 3, because the provision for a referendum means that the president's veto is not final, but it is costly for congress to seek overrides with great frequency. At the other end of the scale, we score at 1 any case in which the veto override requires more than a simple majority but less than two-thirds. Included here are the several cases in which the majority is 50 percent plus one of the whole membership (as in Nicaragua), rather than half plus one of a quorum (as in Venezuela).

*Partial veto.* As discussed in Chapter 7, some presidential systems allow the president to veto part of a bill rather than simply being required to accept or veto the entire package. The majority needed to override a partial (item) veto varies, as does the override majority for package vetoes. Usually the majority is the same for both types of vetoes (Ecuador is an

---

1 We have not considered separately those cases in which an override is voted in a joint session of both chambers of a bicameral assembly (Bolivia, Brazil), rather than by both chambers voting separately. Whether such a provision strengthens or weakens presidential power is contingent on other factors, including how the two houses are constituted and whether the president would be more likely to find favor in the upper house (the power of which is diluted in a joint session with a typically larger lower house). At any rate, the difference in scoring for these systems would be marginal.

Table 8.1. Powers of popularly elected presidents

## LEGISLATIVE POWERS

**Package Veto/Override**
4 Veto with no override
3 Veto with override requiring majority greater than 2/3 (of quorum)
2 Veto with override requiring 2/3
1 Veto with override requiring absolute majority of assembly or extraordinary majority less than 2/3
0 No veto; or veto requires only simple majority override

**Partial Veto/Override**
4 No override
3 Override by extraordinary majority
2 Override by absolute majority of whole membership
1 Override by simple majority of quorum
0 No partial veto

**Decree**
4 Reserved powers, no rescission
2 President has temporary decree authority with few restrictions
1 Authority to enact decrees limited
0 No decree powers; or only as delegated by assembly

**Exclusive Introduction of Legislation (Reserved Policy Areas)**
4 No amendment by assembly
2 Restricted amendment by assembly
1 Unrestricted amendment by assembly
0 No exclusive powers

**Budgetary Powers**
4 President prepares budget; no amendment permitted
3 Assembly may reduce but not increase amount of budgetary items
2 President sets upper limit on total spending, within which assembly may amend
1 Assembly may increase expenditures only if it designates new revenues
0 Unrestricted authority of assembly to prepare or amend budget

**Proposal of Referenda**
4 Unrestricted
2 Restricted
0 No presidential authority to propose referenda

## NONLEGISLATIVE POWERS

**Cabinet Formation**
4 President names cabinet without need for confirmation or investiture
3 President names cabinet ministers subject to confirmation or investiture by assembly
1 President names premier, subject to investiture, who then names other ministers
0 President canot name ministers except upon recommendation of assembly

**Cabinet Dismissal**
4 President dismisses cabinet ministers at will
2 Restricted powers of dismissal
1 President may dismiss only upon acceptance by assembly of alternative minister or cabinet
0 Cabinet or ministers may be censured and removed by assembly

**Censure**
4 Assembly may not censure and remove cabinet or ministers
2 Assembly may censure, but president may respond by dissolving assembly
1 "Constructive" vote of no confidence (assembly majority must present alternative cabinet)
0 Unrestricted censure

**Dissolution of Assembly**
4 Unrestricted
3 Restricted by frequency or point within term
2 Requires new presidential election
1 Restricted: only as response to censures
0 No provision

exception). The power of the partial veto when it requires a two-thirds override is so formidable a weapon in the hands of the president that we have scored such a power as a 3. (An absolute partial veto would, of course, be a 4.) Where a majority of the whole membership is required to override (an absolute majority), we give it a 2, while a simple majority of a quorum is a 1. The reason that a simple majority override of a partial veto is not scored as 0 is that a part of a bill that was passed because of a logroll may not pass when sent back to congress after a veto, as the whole package most surely would. As suggested in Chapter 7, members of congress who voted for an amendment only to gain assent to other parts of the bill no longer have incentive to pass the amendment when the president already has promulgated the other parts of the bill.

*Decree.* We refer here to the ability of the president to make law. Such power should be distinguished from decrees that are of a regulatory or "rule-making" nature, as we saw in Chapter 7. "Decree" here refers to the authority to make new laws or suspend old ones without the power of decree first having been delegated through enabling legislation. The most severe form of presidential lawmaking power is found in Brazil, where the president may declare a matter "urgent." These matters have the force of law upon such a declaration and remain law unless congress explicitly votes to rescind within forty-five days. Since the president is not prevented from simply redeclaring the same measure upon such congressional action, a determined president can simply make law over the head of the congress. Rescission in this case is ineffective and we score this a 4. Colombia before 1991 is an example of the second most powerful decree authority, for reasons detailed in Chapter 7. Unanimity of president and cabinet was required, but because the president alone appointed and dismissed ministers, this was a minimal restraint. We score such cases a 2. Cases such as Colombia 1991, in which the president and a cabinet that does not depend exclusively on assembly confidence can impose a state of "emergency" and legislate with little or no involvement by the assembly, are scored as 1. Also at 1 are provisions granting the president discretionary spending not to exceed a constitutionally specified share of the budget in the event of executive-declared "emergencies."

*Exclusive introduction of legislation.* Where the assembly is barred from considering legislation in certain policy areas unless the president first introduces a bill, the president possesses a powerful agenda-setting power: If she or he does not want a matter discussed, it will not be discussed. The greatest power would be if the president could require a strict up or down vote, not subject to amendment by the congress. Such a power exists nowhere, but could be provided for. If it existed, we would score it a 4. Considerably weaker, but still significant, is any restriction on amendment, which would be scored a 2. The actual powers in most systems that grant exclusive power of legislative introduction to the president are weaker still: Just as with any bill, congress may amend it or reject it outright, so we give these countries only a 1 on this power.

*Budgetary initiative*. Several constitutions stipulate that it is the president who initiates the annual budget bill. However, this alone would not be a formidable power. There will be a budget, whether or not the congress may initiate one, so giving the right of initiative to the president means little unless there are restrictions on congressional amending ability. If the president's budget could only be approved or rejected, while congress obviously would be far from powerless, its ability to attend to specific political needs via the budget would be sharply curtailed. It would be like the presidential package veto already discussed: a blunt instrument, merely requiring that the initiating agency (here, the executive) make the whole package minimally acceptable to the majority of legislators. Such a power would be scored a 4. Variations on restrictions on amendment exist elsewhere, from prohibition on congressional increase in the amounts allocated to any item or the creation of new items (scored a 3) to a ceiling on overall spending, within which the congress may move funds around (scored a 2), to a requirement simply that congress must designate the revenue source of new expenditures not proposed by the president (scored a 1).

*Proposal of referenda*. In some systems, the president is granted the power to propose referenda, usually on matters that have been previously rejected by the assembly. If this power is unrestricted, we score it a 4. In some cases, there are various restrictions on the president's power to submit legislative proposals to referenda. For example, in France the constitution requires that a proposal be made jointly with the cabinet or else by a concurrent resolution of the two houses of the assembly. In Guatemala the president may submit any matter of "special importance" to a referendum, but so may the congress. If only the president had this power, as is the case in Ecuador (except on vetoed bills, as just discussed), it obviously would be a 4. In such a case, the ability of congress to give consideration to amendments to a proposed bill would be blunted by the realization that the president could always submit the matter to a plebiscite, in which case the president's preferred text is voted up or down. However, uniquely in Guatemala, the congress also has the power to submit matters to referendum, thus bypassing a possible presidential veto. This symmetry to the process of initiating a referendum justifies a "restricted" score (2) on the president's power.

### NONLEGISLATIVE POWERS

In the realm of nonlegislative powers are presidential authority over the cabinet and the power to dissolve the assembly and call new elections.

*Cabinet formation*. In some systems the process of cabinet formation depends entirely on the president's choices. If the president names members of the cabinet without any need for confirmation of appointees by the assembly, we score this a 4. Where the assembly (or a special committee elected by it, as in the Philippines) must approve nominations made by the president, the president's ability to get "ideal" ministers is weakened, thus we score such cases a 3. Considerably weaker are instances in which the president first nominates a premier, needing parliamentary confirmation (or investiture), and the premier then nominates the rest of the cabinet (with or without presidential involvement). Such cases are scored a 1. The weakest of all, and thus scored a 0, is any case in which the president is barred from nominating anyone to a cabinet post, including premier, except upon the prior recommendation of the assembly, or an agent thereof, such as a speaker of the house.

*Cabinet dismissal.* Many presidents have the right to dismiss members of the cabinet (or the entire cabinet) at will. Such cases are scored a 4. In other cases, the president has no such power, giving the president a 0. We have a few instance in which the president may dismiss ministers, but the power is restricted. In Portugal since 1982, for example, the president may take such action only when he or she can justify it as a response to a threat to the democratic institutions themselves. While presidents need not be very creative to find a "threat" to democracy when they dislike the policies of some ministry that enjoys the confidence of the assembly, such a move in times of no obvious threat to the country could be subject to judicial review and may entail political costs. Thus the power is weaker than if the president may simply dismiss a minister or cabinet without even being required to give a justification. There could also be a stronger restriction requiring the president to propose an alternative minister or government that would need assembly approval before the incumbent minister or cabinet could be replaced. Such a "constructive" dismissal would be scored a 1.

*Censure.* The power of censure is actually, of course, not a presidential but an assembly power. However, it directly concerns the authority of the president over the cabinet and is clearly separate from cabinet formation and dismissal. Accordingly, when there is no censure, meaning that only the president may remove ministers, the president's authority is strongest, hence the score 4. When censure is unrestricted, the president's score is 0. There are some intermediate cases – for example, Cuba, in which a minister could not be censured in his or her first six months in a given post – that are scored 3 because the restriction limited the extent to which ministers were genuinely subject to assembly confidence. If a vote of censure is tied to a process that leads to dissolution of the assembly, the score is 2. When a censure must be "constructive," requiring the assembly majority to propose a new minister or cabinet at the time of censure, the score is 1.

*Dissolution of the assembly.* Some presidents are permitted to dissolve the assembly at any time, a power that is scored a 4. Others have dissolution powers but with restrictions. If the restriction is defined either in terms of frequency – once a year, for example, as in France – or in terms of time point within the term – not in the last six months of the president's term, as in Portugal – we score it a 3. Another restriction that renders the power of dissolution more symmetrical with regard to the assembly's powers is where the president, too, must stand for reelection along with the assembly after a dissolution (as in Namibia). Hence we score such situations as 2. Weaker still (scored as 1) is where dissolution may be invoked only after censure or a certain number of censures by the assembly (as in Peru and Uruguay).

Table 8.2 shows the scores on our two dimensions of presidential power for a nearly exhaustive sample of democracies that have had popularly elected presidents. In a few instances, two lines are needed for a given case because the president's powers are different according to the type of legislation in question. In such cases only the aspects of presidential power that differ are shown separately, with the main line being simply an average of the two lower scores. We now turn to graphing these regime's scores in order to visualize how powerful different presidents are in different dimensions.

POWERS: LEGISLATIVE VERSUS NONLEGISLATIVE

Figure 8.1 graphs the strength of the presidents across all the cases in two dimensions. Thus the very strongest presidents in both dimensions would be found in the upper right region, while presidents with no power in either dimension would be at the origin (0,0). Most of the systems commonly understood to be presidential are located on the vertical line running at 12 on the dimension of nonlegislative power. These systems are thus all identical in the extent of authority they give to the president over the government and the assembly: All have exclusive authority over the cabinet and none may dissolve the congress. These systems differ only on the dimension of presidential legislative powers, but there is a very wide range of variation on this dimension. Two systems are located farther to the right – Chile 1989 and Paraguay – owing to the additional power granted to the president, who may dissolve the congress. To the immediate left of this group are those presidential systems in which the assembly must confirm cabinet appointments. All those farther left provide for censure, including the several cases of premier-presidentialism. We shall see later another way to visualize these cases that clarifies the distinction between presidential and premier-presidential regimes. For now, we attempt just to assess an overall measure of presidential power, as located in a two-dimensional space.

We have divided the space of Figure 8.1 into six regions, numbered counterclockwise from the upper right. Region I consists of the very power-

Table 8.2. Powers of popularly elected presidents by country

| Country | Pack. Veto | Part. Veto | Decree | Excl. Intro. | Budg. Power | Refer. | TOT. | Cab. Form. | Cab. Dism. | Cen-sure | Disso-lution | TOT. |
|---|---|---|---|---|---|---|---|---|---|---|---|---|
| Argentina | | | | | | | | | | | | |
| current | 2 | 0 | 0 | 0 | 0 | 0 | 2 | 4 | 4 | 4 | 0 | 12 |
| proposal | 2 | 0 | 0 | 0 | 0 | 0 | 2 | 1 | 2 | 0 | 4 | 7 |
| Austria | 0 | 0 | 0 | 0 | 0 | 0 | 0 | 1 | 0 | 0 | 4 | 5 |
| Bolivia | 2 | 0 | 0 | 0 | 0 | 0 | 2 | 4 | 4 | 4 | 0 | 12 |
| Brazil | | | | | | | | | | | | |
| 1946 | 2 | 3 | 0 | 1 | 1 | 0 | 7 | 4 | 4 | 4 | 0 | 12 |
| 1988 | 1 | 2 | 4 | 1 | 1 | 0 | 9 | 4 | 4 | 4 | 0 | 12 |
| Bulgaria | 0 | 0 | 0 | 0 | 0 | 0 | 0 | 0 | 0 | 0 | 0 | 0 |
| Chile | | | | | | | | | | | | |
| 1891 | 2 | 3 | 1 | 1 | 1 | 0 | 8 | 4 | 4 | 0 | 0 | 8 |
| 1925 | 2 | 3 | 1 | 1 | 1 | 0 | 8 | 4 | 4 | 4 | 0 | 12 |
| 1969 | 2 | 4 | 1 | 2 | 1 | 2 | 12 | 4 | 4 | 4 | 0 | 12 |
| 1989 | 2 | 0 | 0 | 1 | 2 | 0 | 5 | 4 | 4 | 4 | 3 | 15 |
| Colombia | | | | | | | | | | | | |
| pre-1991 | 1.5 | 2.5 | 2 | 1 | 1 | 0 | 8 | 4 | 4 | 4 | 0 | 12 |
| (expend.) | 2 | 3 | | | | | | | | | | |
| (other) | 1 | 2 | | | | | | | | | | |
| 1991 | 1 | 2 | 1 | 0 | 1 | 0 | 5 | 4 | 4 | 0 | 0 | 8 |
| Costa Rica | 1 | 0 | 0 | 0 | 0 | 0 | 1 | 4 | 4 | 4 | 0 | 12 |
| (budget) | 0 | | | | | | | | | | | |
| (other) | 2 | | | | | | | | | | | |
| Cuba 1940 | 2 | 0 | 0 | 0 | 0 | 0 | 2 | 4 | 4 | 3 | 0 | 11 |
| Dominican Republic | 2 | 0 | 0 | 0 | 0 | 0 | 2 | 4 | 4 | 4 | 0 | 12 |
| Ecuador | 1.5 | 1.5 | 1 | 0 | 0 | 2 | 6 | 4 | 4 | 0 | 0 | 8 |
| (budget) | 0 | 0 | | | | | | | | | | |
| (other) | 3 | 3 | | | | | | | | | | |
| El Salvador | 2 | 0 | 1 | 0 | 0 | 0 | 3 | 4 | 4 | 4 | 0 | 12 |
| Finland | 0 | 0 | 0 | 0 | 0 | 0 | 0 | 4 | 0 | 0 | 4 | 8 |
| France | 0 | 0 | 1 | 0 | 0 | 0 | 1 | 1 | 0 | 0 | 3 | 4 |
| Germany (Weimar) | 0 | 0 | 2 | 0 | 0 | 2 | 4 | 4 | 4 | 0 | 4 | 12 |
| Guatemala | 2 | 0 | 0 | 0 | 0 | 2 | 4 | 4 | 4 | 4 | 0 | 12 |
| Haiti | 0 | 0 | 0 | 0 | 0 | 0 | 0 | 0 | 0 | 0 | 0 | 0 |
| Honduras | 2 | 0 | 0 | 0 | 0 | 0 | 2 | 4 | 4 | 4 | 0 | 12 |
| Iceland | 0 | 0 | 1 | 0 | 0 | 2 | 3 | 4 | 0 | 0 | 4 | 8 |
| Ireland | 0 | 0 | 0 | 0 | 0 | 0 | 0 | 0 | 0 | 0 | 0 | 0 |
| Korea | | | | | | | | | | | | |
| 1948 | 1 | 0 | 1 | 0 | 0 | 0 | 2 | 4 | 4 | 0 | 0 | 8 |
| 1962 | 2 | 0 | 1 | 0 | 3 | 0 | 6 | 4 | 4 | 4 | 0 | 12 |
| 1987 | 2 | 0 | 1 | 0 | 3 | 0 | 6 | 1 | 4 | 4 | 0 | 9 |
| Mexico | 2 | 3 | 0 | 0 | 0 | 0 | 5 | 4 | 4 | 4 | 0 | 12 |
| Namibia | 2 | 0 | 0 | 0 | 0 | 0 | 2 | 4 | 4 | 0 | 2 | 10 |
| Nicaragua | 1 | 2 | 0 | 0 | 0 | 0 | 3 | 4 | 4 | 4 | 0 | 12 |
| Nigeria | 2 | 0 | 0 | 0 | 0 | 0 | 2 | 3 | 4 | 4 | 0 | 11 |
| Panama | 2 | 3 | 0 | 0 | 0 | 0 | 5 | 4 | 4 | 4 | 0 | 12 |
| Paraguay | 2 | 2 | 2 | 0 | 0 | 0 | 6 | 4 | 4 | 4 | 4 | 16 |
| Peru | 0 | 0 | 0 | 0 | 0 | 0 | 0 | 4 | 4 | 0 | 1 | 9 |
| Philippines | 2 | 3 | 0 | 0 | 0 | 0 | 5 | 3 | 4 | 4 | 0 | 11 |
| Portugal | | | | | | | | | | | | |
| 1976 | 4 | 0 | 0 | 0 | 0 | 0 | 4 | 1 | 4 | 0 | 4 | 9 |
| 1982 | 1.5 | 0 | 0 | 0 | 0 | 0 | 1.5 | 1 | 2 | 0 | 3 | 6 |
| (for. pol.) | 2 | | | | | | | | | | | |
| (other) | 1 | | | | | | | | | | | |
| Romania | 0 | 0 | 0 | 0 | 0 | 2 | 2 | 1 | 0 | 0 | 1 | 2 |
| Sri Lanka | 0 | 0 | 0 | 0 | 0 | 4 | 4 | 4 | 4 | 0 | 4 | 12 |
| United States | 2 | 0 | 0 | 0 | 0 | 0 | 2 | 3 | 4 | 4 | 0 | 11 |
| Uruguay | 1 | 1 | 0 | 2 | 2 | 0 | 6 | 4 | 4 | 2 | 1 | 11 |
| Venezuela | 0 | 0 | 0 | 0 | 0 | 0 | 0 | 4 | 4 | 4 | 0 | 12 |

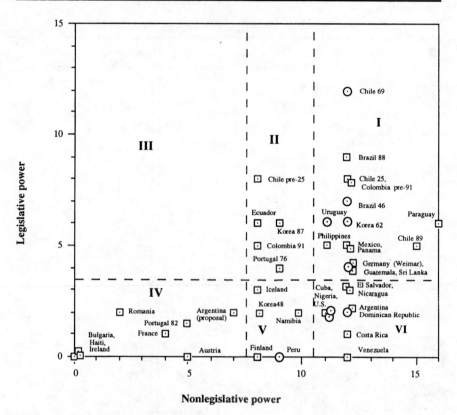

Figure 8.1. Powers of popularly elected presidents (democratic regimes that have broken down indicated by circles)

ful presidents. Presidencies in Region I have great powers in both dimensions. Region II comprises presidents with great legislative powers, but whose powers outside the legislative process are somewhat weaker. Region III is empty, reflecting the lack of any logical reason to give great legislative powers to a president whose power over the composition of governments is even weaker than those in Region II. Region IV, in the lower left of Figure 8.1, contains our weakest presidents in both dimensions. Almost all of the premier-presidential regimes are located here. Region V also includes premier-presidential systems, as well as other systems with moderately powerful presidents. Finally, Region VI includes only presidential systems with relatively weak legislative powers but great powers over government formation.

If we consider the performance of the regimes in Figure 8.1, we find reason to believe that the more powerful presidencies are also the more problematic. First let us remove from consideration those cases that are

Table 8.3. *Frequency of democratic failure, grouped by regions in Figure 8.1*

| Region of Figure 8.1 | Number of cases | Number of breakdowns | Percentage of breakdowns |
|---|---|---|---|
| I | 12 | 6 | 50 |
| II | 3 | 0 | 0 |
| III | 0 | 0 | 0 |
| IV | 4 | 0 | 0 |
| V | 4 | 1 | 25 |
| VI | 9 | 3 | 25 |

*Note*: Nondemocratic systems and constitutions under which a full electoral cycle had not been completed as of 1990 are excluded.

clearly nondemocratic, or have been nondemocratic for most of their existence. This criterion eliminates Mexico and Paraguay, which happen to be among the Region I very powerful presidencies, lending support to our suggestion in Chapter 3 that there might be an affinity between very strong presidencies and authoritarianism. By the criterion of nondemocracy, we should also eliminate Sri Lanka, since elections were suspended for a long period during emergency rule and civil strife. Other cases to be set aside in order to investigate the link between presidential powers and democratic performance are those too new to evaluate: Brazil 1988, Bulgaria, Colombia 1991, Haiti, Korea 1987, Namibia, Panama, and Romania, as well as the mere proposal made for Argentina. This leaves us with thirty-two cases, which are grouped by region in the manner shown in Table 8.3.

Although the sample is too small to make any claims of statistical significance, six of the ten breakdowns have occurred in the region we have suspected would be most problematic: very strong presidencies (Region I). Fully half of these cases have suffered breakdowns at some point. We thus have reason to be concerned (absent constitutional revision) about the future viability of democracy in three countries. In the 1980s, Brazil and the Philippines have adopted constitutions with powers at least as strong as in the earlier, failed constitutions. Chile has adopted a new constitution that, while weakening legislative powers compared to the earlier period, expands nonlegislative powers.

Regions II and V of Figure 8.1, which contain the "confused" cases of shared presidential-parliamentary authority over cabinets, also include several cases of dubious democratic performance, although only one breakdown. (Two more such regimes, the Weimar Republic and Sri Lanka, are found in Region I.) Besides Peru, where a breakdown occurred, the Chilean parliamentary republic and Portugal 1976 both engendered discontent that resulted in significant constitutional revision, strengthening overall presidential powers in Chile and weakening them in Portugal. Finally, among this group is Ecuador, arguably the Latin American case with the most aggravated presidential–congressional relations in the 1980s (Conaghan 1989).

We are left with two regions. One, Region IV contains three premier-presidential systems and no breakdowns.[2] The other, Region VI, contains the presidential systems with relatively weak presidential legislative powers. Of the nine cases, two (Argentina and Nigeria) have suffered breakdowns at some time. Cuba's ambiguous system (see Chapter 6) is also found here. We also observe that the longest-lived presidential systems – all scoring 11 or 12 on the dimension of nonlegislative power – may be found at the low end of the scale of presidential legislative powers. These cases include:

| | |
|---|---|
| Costa Rica | United States |
| Dominican Republic | Venezuela |

These are the four of the five longest-lived presidential democracies in the world (the other is Colombia, where presidential powers recently were reduced in both dimensions). If there really is a link, then there are reasons to be optimistic about several fledgling presidential democracies that rank low on presidential legislative powers. Regimes such as those of Argentina and El Salvador, for example, have weathered severe crises that have not been allowed to become clashes between the two elected branches of government over constitutional powers, in part because the assembly is clearly the dominant branch.

### SEPARATION OF SURVIVAL AND PRESIDENTIAL CABINET POWER: DEVELOPING A COMPREHENSIVE TYPOLOGY OF REGIMES

We next consider the relation between presidential authority over the cabinet and the extent to which the survival of executive and assembly powers are separate, themes discussed in Chapter 6. Legislative powers do not enter into the consideration at all. We are concerned here with the nature of the regime and the power of the president over its officials. As noted in Chapter 2, these are the dimensions on which the various types of regime diverge. Considering these dimensions will allow us to develop a comprehensive typology of regimes. The value of this typology is not simply in providing cells into which empirical regimes may be placed, but, more fundamentally, in letting us perceive what has not previously been an obvious point to scholars or regime designers: Any given democratic regime involves some shading on the degree to which powers rest only in the

2 This lack of breakdowns among the premier-presidential systems provides support for Lijphart and Rogowski's (1991) suggestion that such regimes may be especially well equipped to manage political cleavages.

assembly or in an official elected outside the assembly (a president). We still have ideal types and definitions, as presented in Chapter 2, but we also have many intermediate types. This is an important finding because it makes clear that the basic types (presidential and parliamentary and, for that matter, premier-presidential) are not based on incompatible principles but rather on mixtures of elements, such as separate survival of powers or assembly sovereignty over cabinets, that may be applied in varying degrees to come up with different regime constellations.

In developing this typology, a regime's score on Presidential Cabinet Authority is the sum of the scores on Cabinet Formation and Cabinet Dismissal from Table 8.2. The other dimension takes into consideration Censure and Dissolution. For the latter score on this dimension, however, it is necessary to reverse the scoring order from that used in Table 8.2, for here we are not measuring dissolution as an indicator of presidential power, but rather as an indicator of the degree to which the assembly's survival is separated from the president. Where a president has the power to dissolve the assembly, the latter's survival is not separate, hence the score of such a regime is lowered on that dimension.

Figure 8.2 shows how the cases fit in these two dimensions. The groups defined above as being near the two extreme corners, (0,0) and (8,8), thus encompass those regimes in which the definition of authority and survival are clearest: premier-presidential and presidential, respectively. At the far upper right are the "pure" presidential systems, with maximum separation of survival and maximum presidential control over the cabinet. As we move away from this corner but remain close to it, a regime still exhibits the characteristics of presidentialism, as with the systems that are slightly lower on the dimension of authority over the cabinet: Nigeria, the Philippines, and the United States. Moving to the left we find several regimes that begin to deviate from the basic principles of separation of powers that define presidentialism. These regimes include Chile 1989, Cuba 1940, and Uruguay, which, while not "pure" types, resemble presidential systems more than any other type that we have identified.

At the lower left are the premier-presidential systems. In the far lower left corner (at 0,0), where we have no empirical cases, would be a system in which the premier, whose authority stemmed only from the parliamentary majority, was constitutionally dominant over the president. Nevertheless, since there would be no separation of survival in such a system, the president could dissolve the assembly. In this hypothetical system, the only way presidents could hope to have any say in the composition of the cabinet would be to use their power of dissolution. At times this could work for the president, with the voters returning a majority to the president's liking; at other times it might not work. Thus the compatibility of president and premier (and the cabinet headed by the latter) would depend entirely on what cabinet could gain the assent of the assembly. This feature of such a

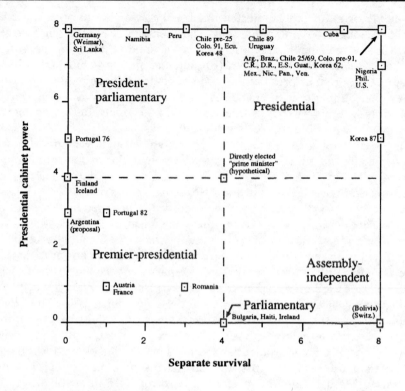

Figure 8.2. Separate survival and presidential cabinet power: a comprehensive typology of democratic regime types

system justifies placing the title of the executive who depends on parliamentary confidence ahead of that of the popularly elected official: premier-presidential. As we move away from the lower left, either the president gains increasing authority over the composition of the cabinet (upward movement) or the president's powers of dissolution are restricted, at least to some degree (rightward movement).

There is also a considerable cluster of cases near the upper left of the figure. Regimes in this area have divided authority over the cabinet as well as a lack of separate survival of powers. The extreme point is represented by Weimar Germany and Sri Lanka: no separation of survival plus presidential authority to appoint members of cabinets (subject to censure) as well as full authority to dismiss ministers. Because of the greater role of the president in these regimes than in premier-presidentialism, and the likelihood that the premier (if any) would be unable to serve as a viable head of government, we have suggested that these regimes be identified as "president-parliamentary," reflecting their lack of clarity on the question of who wields authority over the government. Some cases, such as the new constitution of Colombia and the Chilean parliamentary republic, are intermediate cases between the presidential and president-parliamentary types.

The group of regimes we have identified as president-parliamentary can be regarded as troubled, or even confused, as each has suffered from regime crises and each has broken down at some time or been re-formed to make it conform to one of the pure types, either presidentialism or premier-presidentialism. For instance, Chile's parliamentary republic was transformed into a presidential system after a pair of presidential coups in 1925, and Portugal was transformed toward the premier-presidential type by an assembly-sponsored constitutional amendment in 1982. While this group consists of several cases and thus constitutes an identifiable regime type that has proven attractive to some regime designers, most recently to delegates to Colombia's and Namibia's[3] constituent assemblies, we suggest that it is a type best avoided.

Now let us consider the lower right, for the final "pure" type that is suggested by the two dimensions of Figure 8.2. Literally understood, such a regime would be one in which there was maximum separation of survival of powers – neither censure nor dissolution – but no presidential role in the composition of the cabinet. Such a regime has never existed, to our knowledge, with a popularly elected president. However, the scenario just described comes close to fitting a regime such as that of Switzerland, in which the entire cabinet is chosen by the assembly but is not responsible thereto. Bolivia would be similarly situated (unless a presidential candidate's slate were to win a majority of the popular vote), even though the assembly formally elects only the president, who then chooses the rest of the executive. The dependence of the president, and therefore ultimately the whole executive, on selection by the assembly – but for a *fixed* term – implies assembly primacy in the origin of the executive to an extent that nearly approximates that of Switzerland. Therefore these regimes could be placed in this cell and called assembly-independent regimes, in order to identify both what institution has control over the origin of executive power, and the separation of survival.[4]

3 As we have discussed, Namibia's constitution contains one provision that may make for somewhat less contentious presidential-assembly relations than in cases like Weimar or Sri Lanka: dissolution in Namibia requires a new presidential election.

4 Because the terms of comparison literally require a popularly elected president, and there is much room in the lower right of Figure 8.2 for intermediate cases, is there any basis to imagine a hypothetical regime in which a president would have some (limited) powers over the composition of the government but there would be separation between the survival of assembly and executive powers? Imagine a popularly elected president who could propose a cabinet to the assembly, which would then have to ratify (or reject) the proposal. Once

A few regimes appear as borderline between the main categories. We have already referred to those, such as the new constitution of Colombia, that are basically president-parliamentary but tending more toward presidentialism because of the lack of a power of dissolution. Finland and Iceland appear to be intermediate regimes between president-parliamentary and premier-presidential types. While this placement is somewhat surprising, it results from the provision in both constitutions that the president alone appoints all ministers.[5] This feature, combined with the provision that only the assembly may remove ministers, gives the president at least marginally greater influence over cabinet composition, as we argued in Chapter 6. As a result, greater instability of cabinets is a possibility, although, as Finland demonstrates, this need not be regime-threatening, as is the combination of features that characterizes the Weimar Republic or Sri Lanka. If Finland and Iceland represent cases that deviate from an ideal type of premier-presidentialism by granting the president marginally greater power over cabinets, Korea's 1987 constitution represents a deviation from presidentialism that grants the president marginally less power over cabinets. It does so by providing that only the premier is directly appointed by the president, subject to confirmation by the assembly. The premier then appoints all other ministers. All ministers, including the premier, may be removed by the president but are not subject to censure, thus accounting for this regime's placement on the far right-hand axis. As discussed in Chapter 6, this design makes the president's ability to get his or her preferred cabinet dependent entirely on how good an agent the premier proves to be, but the president retains the key powers of initiative in the process.

*Parliamentary regimes.* Another small cluster of intermediate cases in Figure 8.2 turns out to be identical to one of the most basic regimes types: parliamentarism. Literally, as with assembly-independent regimes, parliamentary regimes are off this figure unless there also happens to be a popularly elected president. However, in the same sense that assembly-independent regimes can be accommodated conceptually within the dimensions of whether or not authority over the cabinet rests within a separately elected constitutional power, so can parliamentary regimes. Such regimes feature assembly censure of the executive, but no popularly elected president with authority either over the government or to dissolve parliament. Thus, parliamentary regimes have a score of 4 on separate survival and 0 on presidential authority

ratified, however, the government would not be subject to parliamentary confidence, nor could the president dismiss the ministers. (Of course, if the president could dissolve the assembly, the regime would be located to the left side of the lower-right cell.)

5 Recall that our definition of premier-presidentialism requires only that the president have some powers, but that those powers not include unrestricted authority to dismiss ministers or cabinets that enjoy parliamentary confidence.

over the cabinet. Such cases in Figure 8.2 are Bulgaria, Haiti, and Ireland. In none of these constitutions does the president have any constitutional authority, rendering these cases effectively parliamentary. If we ignore the question of whether or not there is a popularly elected president in a parliamentary system on the grounds that such a president would be utterly feckless anyway, then all parliamentary systems are located at the point (4,0) on our graph, along with Bulgaria, Haiti,[6] and Ireland.

Another intermediate type of regime is represented by the case of Lebanon, which was discussed briefly in Chapter 5. Lebanon and similar regimes that have existed at one time or another in Indonesia, Kenya (before 1969), Turkey, and elsewhere, have an executive chosen entirely by the assembly, but part of that executive depends on parliamentary confidence while another part of it serves a fixed term that is, under some constitutions, longer than that of parliament. If the fixed-term part of the executive is more than just a ceremonial head of state, the regime's score on the horizontal axis of Figure 8.2 is somewhat greater than 4 but less than 8. (It still scores 0 on the vertical axis, given the lack of a popularly elected president with authority over the cabinet.) Some of these assembly-selected presidents have initiative in cabinet formation, the power to dissolve the assembly, a veto on legislation, or some combination of these and other powers. As with assembly-independent regimes, the "president" in this regime format remains an agent of the parliament, but a more independent one than a purely parliamentary executive, given the lack of a vote of no-confidence. If the agent is eligible for reappointment, there should be little slack between the wishes of the parliamentary majority and the actions of the agent, since the agent can anticipate the possibility of being denied reappointment. In some of these regimes, however, the president cannot be reappointed and is thus potentially truly independent. Still, given the mechanism of parliamentary confidence binding a part (usually the more important part) of the executive to the assembly on an ongoing basis, these regimes, while not strictly parliamentary, are closer to that type than to any other.

*A possible alternative regime: the directly elected "prime minister."* A question that might arise is whether or not there is any conceivable regime

6 One interpretation of the military coup that ousted Haitian president Jean Bertrand Aristide in September 1991 is that the president, while enormously popular, had failed to win a majority in either house of the parliament and therefore was powerless. He proceeded to use his popularity to incite mob action against the parliament, compelling it to accept a pro-Aristide prime minister that the president had no constitutional authority to impose. The military subsequently removed the president on the not entirely unfounded grounds that he was acting unconstitutionally. The Haitian experience suggests that a president should not have *zero* constitutional powers, even at the same time that several other cases that we have studied have led us to the conclusion that presidential powers should be quite limited in the constitution.

design that would be placed at or near the center of Figure 8.2, where we have no empirical cases. While not the only possible configuration that would place a regime at the center of the figure, there is an important alternative regime type that has been proposed by reformers in countries such as Israel (Libai et al. 1990), Italy (Barbera 1990), and the Netherlands (Lijphart 1984). Such proposals are typically referred to as featuring the direct election of the "prime minister," and Barbera calls his proposal "neo-parliamentary"; however, the elected head of government would be a president by our definition. The proposals consist of the concurrent election of the head of government (whom we shall call a prime minister, in keeping with the terminology of the proposals) and the assembly. The prime minister would be permitted to dissolve the assembly, but then she or he would have to stand concurrently for reelection. Similarly, the assembly could censure the prime minister or the entire government, but then it would have to stand for reelection along with the prime minister. Thus, on separation of survival, we would score a 4, that is, 2 on each aspect, as the powers of censure and dissolution are both restricted by requiring the new election of the power that initiated the process. The placement on the vertical dimension would depend upon the specific process by which members of the government other than its elected head would be appointed and dismissed. The Israeli proposal would require the elected prime minister to present her or his government to the assembly for investiture, thus suggesting a score of 3 on (President's) Cabinet Authority. The proposal would also allow the prime minister to dismiss ministers at will, leading to a combined score on this dimension of 7. Because of the possibility that, especially in a multiparty context, the prime minister and the assembly majority might not always be entirely compatible, it might be advisable to weaken the prime minister's power of dismissal. Otherwise some of the same kinds of conflicts that befall the president-parliamentary regimes could result, although the means of breaking deadlock would be more symmetrical, given the assembly's ability to oust the "president." Some restrictions – for example, by number of dismissals or how long a minister who enjoys parliamentary confidence must be allowed to serve before being dismissed by the prime minister – would reduce the overall score to a 5. If the prime minister's power of dismissal were made "constructive" (akin to the constructive vote of no-confidence) by requiring that the prime minister present for the assembly's approval an alternative candidate for the minister that she or he wants to replace, then the regime would score 4 on both dimensions, with neither elected body being more powerful than the other. We would thus have the "ultimate" compromise between the principle of parliamentary sovereignty over the composition of cabinets and that of placing governmental authority in the hands of an extra-parliamentary offical. Even without the suggested restrictions on the power of the directly elected prime minister, such a regime is indeed a compromise regime. Thus it is not surprising that it would be developed as an alternative in some countries where there is dissatisfaction with existing parliamentarism. Perhaps what should be surprising is that there are no empirical cases, as of 1991.

Our examination of the dimensions of presidential power suggests the regimes with great presidential legislative powers are problematic, as are those in which authority over cabinets is shared between assembly and president. These issues need to be addressed in turn. On matters of legislation, we suggest that relatively strong assemblies should be associated with more stable and effective government relative to strong presidencies because assemblies serve as arenas for the perpetual fine-tuning of conflicts. An assembly represents the diversity of a polity far better than an executive dependent on the president's whims is likely to do. Because of the diverse forces represented in an assembly, such a body has the potential for encompassing divergent viewpoints and striking compromises on them. The dual democratic legitimacies decried by critics of presidentialism – the claim that no democratic principle exists to resolve conflicts over who better can claim to represent the "will" of the electorate – are minimized to the extent that an assembly is accorded a more powerful role in legislation than is the president. Thus presidentialism with a strong congress indeed does afford a democratic principle for the regulation of interbranch conflicts; that principle is that the assembly prevails, subject to a need for compromise with the president. The relatively weaker presidents (those of Costa Rica and the United States, for example) cannot use decree legislative authority to break a "logjam" in congress, as many presidents can do with perfect legality. Thus, a fundamental conclusion is that the criticisms of presidential regimes should not be put forward as if all presidencies were created equal; rather, these criticisms apply with greatest force to strong presidents.

On the matter of authority over cabinets, again the shared control that we said typifies the president-parliamentary type goes right to the heart of the concern of many with dual democratic legitimacies. If there is no "democratic principle" that defines who fills cabinet posts, one of the most basic elements to any democracy, then conflicts of a very basic nature are likely. Are the ministers the president's ministers, or are they the assembly's? In some regimes the answer is both. In either a premier-presidential regime or a presidential regime, on the other hand, the primacy of one branch over the other is clear. Both types make for a cabinet subject (whether exclusively or primarily) to one branch or the other even when the branches are controlled by different political tendencies. This does not prevent conflict, but it is not as clearly guaranteed to generate conflict as is the president-parliamentary type. Democratic institutions are supposed to be conflict regulators, not conflict generators. Either giving great legislative powers to the most majoritarian component (the presidency) of a regime meant to be consensual, or granting shared authority over the composition of the cabinet, is a potentially dangerous arrangement. Finally, we saw in this chapter that actual regimes, as well as a promising proposal for a directly elected "prime minister," entail varying combinations on two dimensions – separation of survival of executive and assembly, and presidential power over cabinets. In the next chapters we shall see how presidential powers interact with the means of electing the assembly and president.

# 9

# Electoral dynamics: efficiency and inefficiency

In this and the following three chapters we discuss institutional variations related specifically to elections. The way in which the checks and balances of presidentialism or the relations between president and cabinet in premier-presidentialism play themselves out depends in part on how likely it is that the president confronts an assembly that does not reliably conform to the president's will on legislation. As we shall see, such factors as the method of electing the president and assembly and the relative timing of elections to the two branches are crucial factors in affecting the number of competitors. Thus we must return to the issues with which we started this book and which constitute one of its major themes: the ways in which the processes of electing representatives and of executive formation interact. Here we deal with electoral dynamics, by which we mean the ways in which the practices used for electing the assembly interact with the form and powers of the executive to shape the functioning of democratic regimes. This chapter concerns itself primarily with presidential systems, while the following three deal with both presidential and premier-presidential regimes.

We begin this chapter by reconsidering the tension between representation based on parochial interests versus that which articulates national policy perspectives. We develop an archetype of a presidential system in which the two forms of representation coexist. In so doing, we are drawn to a novel conclusion: that regimes that maximize the articulation of local particularism in congressional elections tend to be associated with very powerful presidencies. We develop a theoretical consideration of why this would be so, then contrast these regimes with those that entail weaker presidents, concluding that the latter regimes are more conducive to the articulation of national policy alternatives, especially when elections to the two branches are concurrent. Thus we build in this chapter on the concerns of the previous one on presidential powers, while introducing new concerns about the organization of elections for president and assembly.

## PAROCHIALISM VERSUS NATIONAL POLICY

There is a certain tension inherent in presidential systems, since the legislative assembly and the executive have separate origin and survival. On the one hand, unlike parliamentarism, presidentialism has a directly elected national executive. This allows, at least in theory, the voters to confer a mandate upon a particular political force to govern the country for a specified period of time. At the same time, the assembly can represent diversity without compromising the survival of the executive. Recall from Chapter 1 that we have identified two basic forms of representation: that based on local particularism and that based on group interests and national policy preferences. The two are not mutually exclusive, but rather opposite ends of a continuum, with real systems exhibiting some mix of these two ideal types. Recall further that we indicated that there is a trade-off between representativeness and efficiency, but that the trade-off is theoretically less acute under presidentialism than under parliamentarism. We shall sketch a bit more here what we touched on in Chapter 1, the origin of policy-related voting in Britain. We do so mainly to provide a contrast to how the process of executive formation affects local representation under presidentialism and in order to define an "archetype" of presidentialism.

### The articulation of national policy in parliamentary systems

How are parochial interests transcended in the process of forming an executive, thereby permitting national policy to be formed and approved despite the narrowness of regional representatives' concerns? In a parliamentary system, the primary mechanism is the requirement that some group of those narrow-minded district representatives must come together and sustain a government in office. Thus developed party organization in the parliament. Although the degree to which the process is completed varies empirically across cases, the theoretical process of transcending district-level parochialism implies the following, drawn from Gary Cox's the *Efficient Secret,* in which the emergence of parties in the British case is examined.

Once the practice of the government's dependence on the confidence of the parliamentary majority became established in Britain, backbench members saw the progressive erosion of their powers of legislative initiative. The cabinet leadership more and more monopolized the agenda. As this process continued, members of parliament lost most of their ability to curry voter support in their districts by means of attention to purely local concerns and the provision of specific benefits.

If members' time for attending to parochial concerns is curtailed – and if pursuing such concerns might imperil one's own government – then candidates in the districts must differentiate themselves on the basis of what the policies are or would be of a government formed by the party to which they belong rather than on servicing their constituencies. That is, rather than seek to promise to deliver goods, candidates begin to identify with a package of national policies (presumably always being careful to explain what benefits said policies will provide to one's district). The process just described, then, is one in which parliamentarians, rather than continuing to be narrow-minded so as to reflect only the needs of their parochial districts, begin to act collectively. This collective action is manifested in the development of more programmatic, nationally oriented parties and a policy-oriented electorate (Cox 1987). With voters having to choose from among only one candidate from each of two (or more) parties, rather than from competing members in each party (as had been the case in many British districts before the Reform Acts of the mid-nineteenth century), the competition became categorical: one party/cabinet or the other, rather than competition over the provision of specific benefits to supporters. As this process plays out, an "efficient secret" has emerged: The party now has a "brand name" by which to identify itself to the voters.

The process just discussed has been inhibited in those parliamentary democracies in which the electoral system affords voters a choice of candidates *within* parties. The interaction of executive form with the electoral system is seen very clearly in Japan, where the ruling Liberal Democratic Party, in order to maximize its majorities, not only needs the party program that goes along with parliamentary confidence, but also must provide "pork" to its rank and file to cultivate support groups within the districts. In this way, the LDP – like similar parties elsewhere – is able to ensure the loyalty of core groups of voters to particular members of the Diet without having a situation in which intraparty competition dilutes the overall representation of the party, as would happen if members of the party competed with one another on the basis of policy programs. The result, relative to the United Kingdom, is *inefficiency:* The success of LDP members in securing a large portion of the total vote on non-policy grounds limits the potential for voters to designate alternative policy programs, a defining criterion for electoral efficiency. Moreover, the electoral system also encourages inefficiencies in budgetary allocations. For example, according to McCubbins and Rosenbluth (1992), around 30 percent of the Japanese budget goes to particularistic allocations (public works, subsidies, etc.), while a comparable figure for either the United Kingdom or the United States would be about half that. Such "inefficiency" may be expected, *ceteris paribus,* in any electoral system with intraparty competition,[1] where such means of cultivating votes become relatively more important compared to voting on broader policy options than in systems that do not afford intraparty choice.

If we are correct that parliamentarism without intraparty preference voting (as in the United Kingdom) encourages national outlook on the part of local representatives, then we expect presidentialism to create a very

---

1 We refer here to any electoral system in which the criterion determining the order in which candidates get elected is how many personal votes they have amassed. Other electoral systems, including those of Belgium and the Netherlands, allow voters to express votes for candidates within lists, but the party leadership's rank order of candidates on the list is the dominant criterion in determining election.

different electoral dynamic. This should be so especially with a congressional electoral system requiring intraparty competition. Members of congress need not submerge their district interests beneath a national focus in order to maintain an executive in office. Also, control over the agenda of the assembly is not the imperative for the executive that it is in a parliamentary system. To the extent that the assembly itself takes on an important policymaking role, the necessity of acting collectively will pull our parochial representatives in the general direction of national focus. However, even if this process occurs in a presidential system's assembly – and it may not – there is no theoretical reason to believe that it must take place in some sort of harmony with the national policy being debated and chosen in the presidential election. Moreover, where the electoral system favors the distribution of "pork," the absence of collective responsibility for the government may (theoretically) render the process of budgetary allocation even more inefficient than in parliamentary Japan.[2]

### The articulation of national policy in presidential systems

Having reviewed the process by which local interests are transcended within parties in parliamentary systems and institutional arrangements that favor particularistic allocations, we turn more directly to the question of presidential systems. It is self-evident that the election of the president favors the articulation of national concerns, at least if there either is no regionally elected electoral college or if campaigns for electors to such an electoral college are conducted as if they were campaigns for president directly. Indeed, that the process of choosing electors in two presidential systems with electoral colleges – Argentina and the United States – should have developed rather early into a nationwide campaign for the single office of the presidency is testimony to the nationalizing tendencies of elections for a national executive. As Cox (1987:143) suggests, it was a mistake of the U.S. Founding Fathers "to believe that voters would entrust a decision to others which they could make themselves." If the office to be elected is constitutionally disposed to be the representative of the "whole nation," then candidates and parties have strong incentives to conduct

2 While we should expect a theoretical and empirical link between electoral and budgetary inefficiency, the case of electoral efficiency is less clear. The ability of voters to make a categorical (efficient) choice does not guarantee budgetary efficiency. It is conceivable that electoral efficiency might simply consist of voters choosing which group of spoils they prefer, as indeed was the case for the pre–civil service United States. The difference is that, without intraparty competition, spoils are under leadership control to a greater extent than in systems with intraparty competition. Reform away from inefficient economic and bureaucratic policies should be more difficult when the electoral system itself is inefficient, in the sense used here. See Geddes (1991) for a similar argument. This relation between relative electoral efficiency and efficiency (in the economic sense) of policy outcomes is a highly promising area for future research.

campaigns for that office on the basis of national concerns. This observation applies when there is an electoral college as much as when there is a direct popular vote, as candidates to be delegates to the electoral college have only one thing to offer voters: their voting intentions for president.

Thus we find, for the election of the national executive, the emergence of electoral efficiency in the form of the articulation of policy options. Cox applies the term to elections for members of parliament in the British case, quoting Bagehot's very same analogy of the House of Commons to the U.S. electoral college: "The main function of the House of Commons is [as] an electoral chamber; it is the assembly which chooses our President" (quoted in Cox 1987:143). Efficiency in voters' ability to designate a policy direction in the national executive, then, stems from their voting for either an executive directly or an assembly that functions mainly as a means of translating voter preferences into the formation of an executive. This element of efficiency we should expect to exist in a typical presidential system.

### Preservation of local representation in presidential systems

Where presidential systems may be likely to fail the test of efficiency is in that other branch that is also elected. The assembly need not be chosen with an eye to the national executive or national policy direction preferred by the plurality of voters, especially when the electoral rules favor the cultivation by candidates of particularistic support groups. The separation of powers does not by itself guarantee linkage between the executive and assembly either in elections or in the functioning of these institutions between elections. In particular, when elections for president and for congress occur at separate times, congressional campaigns are more likely to focus primarily upon local issues, or, to take the other form of representation discussed in Chapter 1, on narrow ideological or partisan interests.

While a calendar of elections that entails separation of campaigns is especially likely to reduce the salience of national issues in congressional races, the process that retards nationalization of congressional campaigns is inherent in the institutional basis of presidentialism. The separation of powers that characterizes a presidential system means that candidates for congressional seats need not tie their fortunes to a national policy position in order to be elected. Where this process inhibiting nationalization of congressional campaigns has been transcended, we should expect most often to find closed party-list systems, which enhance the value of the party label in elections by not requiring members of a party to compete against one another for personal votes and by giving party leadership the ability to reward its most loyal rank-and-file members by reserving for them the list ranks most certain to secure election.

The inherent separation of campaigns has been a source of frustration for advocates of reform in the United States who have decried the localism that so dominates congressional campaigns and the "errand boy" functions performed by members of Congress (e.g., Stedman 1968; Robinson 1985; Sundquist 1986). Many of these would-be reformers, whose arguments are predicated on their own presumption that national issues should dominate congressional as well as presidential elections, advocate abolishing midterm elections. They reason, with good cause, that the salience of national issues is diminished in midterm elections by the lack of a national office being elected simultaneously. For many of these critics, however, even eliminating midterm elections would be insufficient to accomplish their stated goals, and they advocate other reforms to make parties more "responsible" to a national platform (see Ranney 1962 for a review). Some even go so far as to recommend doing away with separate elections altogether, by requiring a "team ticket," as in Bolivia and Uruguay and some elections in the Dominican Republic, such that voters could not split their votes between presidential and congressional candidates of opposing parties (see Robinson 1985:177–79).[3] These frustrations over the different constituencies of the Congress and executive in the U.S. presidential system stem from the inherent tension of presidentialism between national and particularistic representation.

The tension in presidentialism, stemming from the separation of powers and separation of campaigns, may be a source of frustration for reformers who value the national focus that presidential elections can give to the polity and disdain the "obstructionist" role of the particularistic congress. Yet these same frustrations also point to a key advantage of the separation of powers and functions. If one values or at least recognizes a conditional utility to an electoral system that is designed to facilitate the expression of the interests of localities in the legislative process, presidentialism is more likely to serve the goal than is parliamentarism.

In a parliamentary system, one must choose between a national policy focus in elections and parties or else localism. Either one gets an efficient secret, in which politics is focused on party-centered national policy goals, but some of the benefits of locally oriented politics are lost. Or one maintains the advantages of politics based on provision of local services, but parties are weak, lacking national focus. Then governing becomes highly problematic, as with the famous *trasformismo* in Italy or the French Third and Fourth Republics, as well as several failed parliamentary systems in less developed countries (e.g., Burma and Nepal in the 1960s).

Where parliamentary systems have become fully developed, the existence of the institution of the vote of no-confidence has mandated an imposition of discipline. This party discipline in an archetypal parliamentary system (such

3 Curiously, few advocates of reform have argued in favor of a party-list electoral system, which would serve the reformers' desired end of more nationally focused parties without touching the basic separation of powers. Duverger (1984) and Amy (forthcoming) are exceptions to the general neglect of list PR as an alternative for the United States.

as the United Kingdom, New Zealand, or Norway, for example) is sure to be far stronger than in a typical presidential system's assembly, barring other mechanisms, such as a closed party list, by which party leaders exert discipline over their rank and file. Even if the assembly of a presidential system takes on an important policymaking function, as in the United States, the parties can afford more deviations from the party line than can parliamentary parties. If the party that has a majority in the congress also holds the presidency, there is no danger of losing the executive if individual members are allowed to continue to pursue their own districts' interests. If the party with the congressional majority does not hold the presidency, it cannot hope to displace the executive, but it can continue to offer opposition to the existing executive. Either way, it can afford more slack within the ranks than can a parliamentary party. Indeed, this affording of greater intraparty slack and articulation of local interests is a potential strength of presidential systems, even if it does cause frustrations for those seeking to carry out reformist policies on a national scale. It can allow for more accurate representation of constituent interests in the assembly (see Powell 1989).

## AN ARCHETYPAL PRESIDENTIAL SYSTEM

We shall now propose an ideal type of system based on a separation of powers. The system in question is archetypal in that it would allow, to the greatest extent feasible, both branches to do what they were defined in Chapter 1 as doing best. We must caution that by "archetypal" we are not proposing the most desirable system. Indeed, we shall argue that the archetype is not the most desirable form of presidentialism; moreover, its commonness as a form of presidentialism – and a frequently failed form – has given presidentialism *as a regime type* a "bad name." Our purpose is more limited than endorsing a particular regime type, however: We are merely articulating a conceptual construct.

The assembly in such a system would be highly representative, but the executive would be based upon a broad set of national goals endorsed by a majority (or nearly so) of the voting population, hence electorally efficient. To maximize these ends, presidential and congressional elections would always be conducted at different times and therefore on their own terms. If the basis of particularism in the assembly were localism, parties in congressional campaigns would not even have to operate on a national scale. Their purpose, after all, would be primarily to provide vehicles for the allocation of patronage or to give structure to local issues in locally run campaigns for congressional seats.[4] Come time for a presidential election, however, vari-

---

4 All of these seats, in order to meet the criterion of local representation would be allocated in districts. This should not, however, be taken to imply necessarily *single*-seat districts; indeed, as we have suggested, representation of local interests is maximized by systems that afford intraparty competition, meaning (small) multi-seat districts.

ous parties would coalesce to present two major candidacies for the presidency, offering voters a choice (an efficient choice indeed) for the direction of national policy over the next term.

The sketch just provided of an archetypal presidential system closely resembles Chile under the constitution of 1925. There are also strong similarities to the Brazilian constitution of 1946 and to Colombia from 1886 until 1991 (with the possible exception of the National Front period). However, as we shall see farther into this chapter, electoral reforms in Chile beginning in 1958 and, especially, a constitutional reform in 1970 changed that system considerably, moving it out of the category of the archetype. During the earlier period, congressional particularism was indeed high and based on local project- and patronage-oriented concerns. As a result of electoral and constitutional reforms intended to increase the efficiency of the system, the congress was transformed toward the other type of assembly discussed in Chapter 1: a body representing ideological and partisan differences that transcended many of the previously more prominent local matters. Simultaneously, as we saw in Chapter 8, the powers of the presidency were further increased. Once these transformations occurred, the system became so polarized that a constitutional crisis eventually led to a military dictatorship. Thus, Chile demonstrates both how a regime based on rather inefficient congressional elections can function as a stable democracy and how *not* to reform a system if one hopes to make it at once efficient and stable. To foreshadow a conclusion of this chapter's study, let us indicate that the more promising means of increasing efficiency rest in enhancing the strength of party leadership while simultaneously *decreasing* the strength of the presidency.

### PARTY STRENGTH AND PRESIDENTIAL STRENGTH

We shall now look more closely at the connection between form of representation – as determined by the electoral system – and strength of presidents. The Chilean experience is discussed here at some length because it suggests that an archetype of presidentialism – extreme separation of congressional and executive constituencies – is most viable when the congress is highly local in its own constitution. However, Chile and other cases suggest that this kind of congress also generates pressures to delegate great constitutional powers to the presidency. This process may plant in the regime the seeds of its own destruction, especially once national "reformist" policy options come to be articulated. And recall that, owing to the nature of presidential elections, the articulation of such options is easier at that level, enhancing the prospects of interbranch conflict. Articulation of reformist options also becomes easier in congressional elections to the extent that party organizations are strengthened, thus decreasing the salience of particularistic campaigning. Should the assembly itself then come to be divided by ideological cleavages, presidentialism may be poorly equipped to handle the stress, especially if the president is accorded significant legislative powers. For now, let us observe that several cases of multiparty presidentialism, including Chile and Brazil,[5] as well as other cases, such as Colombia, the Philippines, and Uruguay, in which local particularism prevails, have also been among the systems with the most powerful presidents. Perhaps, therefore, these systems were designed precisely with the idea that a president with strong legislative powers was necessary to provide some efficiency and continuity to policy output. We shall develop this point further below.

We, along with Mainwaring (1992a), have wondered why the fact that Chile remained a stable multiparty presidential system for so long has gone unnoticed in the comparative literature. Still more remarkable is that Chile so closely resembled the archetype of a presidential system in which the electoral constituency of the congress is predominantly local and parochial while the executive is electorally connected to broader national coalitions. Before proceeding with a more detailed examination of the Chilean case, let us consider the relationship more generally between presidential strength and fractionalized party systems, including multiparty systems such as those of Brazil and Chile, as well as others that provide considerable autonomy to local rank and file.

We propose to develop a rough indicator of the strength of parties according to the constitutional and electoral rules that influence party leadership's control over local activists and elected officials. We shall consider five aspects of party strength. The first is control over nominations. Does the national party leadership determine who may run under the party name, or are there laws and constitutional provisions that decentralize the decisions on nominations? The second aspect is whether or not the party leadership controls the order in which candidates are elected by means of a list-rank order. The third aspect is whether votes for one candidate (or factional list within the party) help increase the votes and therefore seats won by the party as a whole by means of some procedure for pooling votes. Fourth, we shall ask whether there is internal party competition simultaneous with interparty competition. Fifth, how great are the barriers imposed by the district magnitude to forming new parties (or new intraparty lists)? As shown in Table 9.1, we score each of several countries as either lacking an aspect of party leadership strength (0), possessing it (+), or possessing it to a great degree (++). Each "+" will count as a point, leading to a maximum of 10 points for any party system. The lower the total score, the more decentralized the party system is and therefore the more the parties are under the control of local rank-and-file candidates and campaign workers, or *caciques*.

5 We could add the case of Ecuador but, as we have seen, it is not a true presidential regime, given the provision for censure. Still, the president has significant powers and much of the logic of the present argument should apply.

Table 9.1. *Strength of party leadership over rank and file in presidential democracies*

| Country | Control nominations? | Control order of election? | Pool of votes? | Lack internal competition? | Entry barriers | Score |
|---|---|---|---|---|---|---|
| Argentina | + | ++ | ++ | ++ | 0 | 7 |
| Brazil | 0 | 0 | + | 0 | 0 | 1 |
| Chile |  |  |  |  |  |  |
| (pre-1958) | 0 | 0 | + | 0 | + | 2 |
| (post-1958) | ++ | 0 | + | 0 | + | 4 |
| Colombia | 0 | 0 | 0 | 0 | + | 1 |
| Costa Rica | ++ | ++ | ++ | ++ | + | 9 |
| Dominican Republic | ++ | ++ | ++ | ++ | + | 9 |
| Ecuador | ++ | ++ | ++ | ++ | 0 | 8 |
| El Salvador | ++ | ++ | ++ | ++ | ++ | 10 |
| Nicaragua | ++ | ++ | ++ | ++ | 0 | 8 |
| Philippines | 0 | 0 | 0 | ++ | ++ | 4 |
| Uruguay | + | + | ++ | 0 | + | 5 |
| United States | 0 | 0 | 0 | ++ | ++ | 4 |
| Venezuela | ++ | ++ | ++ | ++ | 0 | 8 |

We consider here primarily those presidential systems with a fairly long record of democratic governance at some point in the twentieth century, as well as some others for which data on electoral systems were available, for a total of fourteen cases. Some of our rankings may require some explanation. The closed-list systems (Argentina, Costa Rica, and Venezuela) all provide leadership with control over nominations, but in Argentina there is some evidence (McDonald and Ruhl 1989) that this is weakened by state-level party organizations within the federal system. In Brazil a law known as the *candidato nato* makes it possible for any candidate once elected to a post by that party to continue to have a place on the party's future lists for that office regardless of the desires of the party leadership (Mainwaring 1991); thus we score this case as not granting the party control over nominations. For Chile, the electoral rules before and after a reform in 1958 must be scored differently. In 1958, a center-left coalition enhanced the meaning of the party label in the name of efficiency (Valenzuela 1989b), while before 1958 the rules more closely resembled those of Brazil. Control over order of election is generally straightforward, being granted by closed lists but not by open lists (and being irrelevant when $M=1$), but is weakened when there are multiple lists within the party. In such cases, whether there is any effective institutionally determined control or not depends on whether the party can control the use of the party name by the factions in the first place. Colombia's parties lack such control, while Uruguay's have it. Barriers to entry depend largely on district magnitude, and we have scored magnitudes of 4 or less as high barriers, magnitudes of 10 or more as low, and intermediate cases as moderate (+).

We now shall compare our indicator of party leadership strength to our indicator of presidential legislative powers (from Table 8.1). While we must

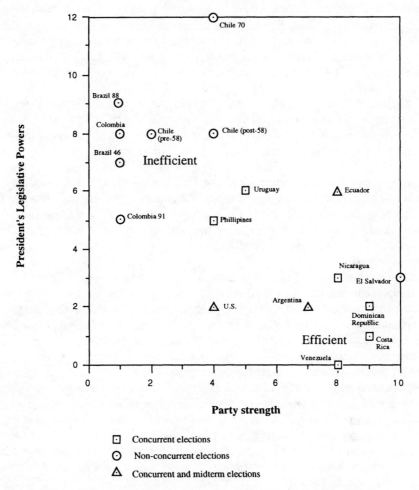

Figure 9.1. Party strength and president's legislative powers

be careful about drawing conclusions from such a small number of cases, Figure 9.1 suggests a striking relationship. We have seventeen cases – the fourteen different electoral systems from Table 9.1, plus three additional cases created by revised constitutions applied with identical electoral systems in Brazil, Chile, and Colombia. Most of the cases cluster in one of two groups: Those with strong presidents and weak parties constitute one group, while those with weak presidents and strong parties constitute another cluster. The latter group includes the three presidential systems that would have to be considered among the most successful as democracies: Costa Rica, the Dominican Republic and Venezuela. In the upper-left quadrant of Figure 9.1, we find that all the regimes except Colombia and the new regime of Brazil have suffered a breakdown, although two, Chile and Uruguay, were democratic for more than two thirds of the twentieth century. The graph also shows by different symbols some characteristics of the electoral cycle each country employs – whether or not congressional elections run concurrently with presidential elections. The importance of this variable will become apparent as we develop the arguments of this and the following chapters.

Most of the cases in Figure 9.1 fall close to an imaginary axis running from the upper left to the lower right. Two cases are obvious outliers. Of the long-term effective democracies, the United States is our clearest outlier, having relatively weak parties along with a president whose legislative powers are weak. Ecuador, a highly troubled democracy and not strictly a presidential system, anyway, lies alone among cases with presidents and parties that are both strong.[6] Colombia's new regime, also not a genuine presidential system, has weak presidential legislative powers compared to other cases with such weak parties. As we shall see, the axis runs from the inefficient presidential regimes (upper left) to the efficient ones (lower right).

Besides observing that strong presidents and weak parties appear to go together, can we draw any theoretical link that explains *why* these phenomena constitute a distinct cluster of presidential regimes? We shall suggest that, indeed, the designers of this group of regimes created strong presidencies precisely to serve certain interests. Given that this group also includes some conspicuous failures and problematic regimes, any theoretical construct that accounts for their existence may also allow us to address how presidential regimes can function more satisfactorily. Before proceeding with a theoretical argument, however, there are some other observations that are especially pertinent to the Chilean approximation of the archetype. These observations concern the number of parties, for the Chilean party system was most fragmented at precisely the time that it was least prone to crises, which was also the time that the regime was most responsive to local particularistic interests.

*The number of parties.* A look at the number of parties in Chile, in addition to their relative decentralization as organizations, will shed further light on the functioning of the archetype as well as its unraveling in Chile. We shall

6 This contradicts Conaghan (1989), who argues that Ecuadorian parties are "loose." In the sense that it is easy to form new parties (low barriers to entry) and that the majority runoff rule for presidential elections does not impose the incentives for broad coalitions that plurality election does (see Chapter 10), she is right. However, members' ability to be elected depends on their ranking in *closed lists,* controlled by party leadership. Thus the appearance of weak parties is dependent entirely on institutions favoring a fragmented multiparty system, not on the rules for allocating seats within parties, as in, for example, Brazil and Colombia. It is perhaps also possible that the provision for censure encourages a proliferation of parties because politicians can form parties as vehicles for achieving ministerial positions.

look to the "effective" number of parties, by which we mean a weighted measure that expresses the degree of fractionalization of a party system in terms of how many "significant" parties there are.[7] The use of this indicator is justified because it is the closest that we can come to expressing, with a simple number, both electoral efficiency and representativeness. Because efficiency is closely linked to the choice of competing policy options and therefore to identifiability, it follows that as the effective number of parties approaches two, we are approximating an efficient choice.[8] At higher values of $N$, it is likely that the party system is more representative (and clearly tends to be less efficient). The correlation between higher $N$ and greater representativeness is not perfect – there might be only two important political tendencies to be represented, as Riker (1982b) argued for Austria, or maybe a low $N$ disguises myriad intraparty factions from which voters may choose, as in Colombia and Uruguay. The use of any simple indicator conceals some information and reveals other. Still, we maintain that $N$ does a reasonably good job of capturing the trade-off between electoral efficiency and representativeness.

Chile's effective number of parties based upon votes ($N_v$) is displayed over time in Table 9.2, along with the same measure for presidential candidates. The values of $N$ in congressional elections were at their highest when the congress was most heavily based on local brokering of projects and other constituent services, as explained by Valenzuela (1989b). Many of these parties elected members in only one or two provinces, reflecting the regional basis of Chilean politics at the time, but there were few single-party regions. For the period from 1932 until 1957 the median $N_v$ was 6.9, an exceptionally high figure cross-nationally (Taagepera and Shugart 1989) and one that implies little obvious connection between the vote and legislative coalition building. There was an extreme peak, at $N_v = 11.8$, in 1953, when the "anti-politics" candidate, Carlos Ibáñez, had recently been elected, but the effective number of parties was in excess of 6 for this whole period. For the later elections (1961–73) before the military takeover, the median $N$ is 4.9. In the last election, months before the coup in 1973, it was 2.1. One puzzle here is that Chile's constitutional system did not face any crises that threatened its existence when it had an extremely high number of parties, but experienced a bloody overthrow as the culmination of a

---

7 The effective number of parties, $N$, presented by Laakso and Taagepera (1979), is a "self-weighted" measure of the number of significant parties in the system. Rather than apply arbitrary cutoffs below which a party is not considered a "party" for purposes of counting or some other arbitrary method of assigning weights, $N$ allows parties to weight themselves by simply squaring the fractional share (whether seats or votes) for each party. These squares are summed, and the reciprocal of the sum yields $N$. See Taagepera and Shugart (1989:259–60) for a brief methodological discussion.
8 If there is a pure two party system, $N$ will be less than 2.0 unless the two parties have equal vote (or seat) shares. If there are two major parties, but also some smaller ones, $N$ will be greater than 2.0, perhaps around 2.5 or 3.0.

Table 9.2. *Effective number of parties contesting congressional elections ($N_v$) and effective number of presidential candidates ($N_p$), Chile, 1931–1973*

| Date | $N_v$ | $N_p$ |
|------|------|------|
| 1931 |      | 1.9  |
| 1932 |      | 2.7  |
| 1933 | 10.6 |      |
| 1937 | 6.9  |      |
| 1938 |      | 2.0  |
| 1941 | 7.7  |      |
| 1942 |      | 1.9  |
| 1945 | 6.5  |      |
| 1946 |      | 3.1  |
| 1949 | 7.4  |      |
| 1952 |      | 2.9  |
| 1953 | 11.8 |      |
| 1957 | 7.4  |      |
| 1958 |      | 4.0  |
| 1961 | 6.4  |      |
| 1964 |      | 2.1  |
| 1965 | 4.3  |      |
| 1969 | 4.9  |      |
| 1970 |      | 3.0  |
| 1973 | 2.1  |      |

period of a steadily consolidating party system, implying a failure just as the regime – or at least its congressional election process – was becoming efficient. Indeed, this puzzle is problematic for arguments such as those of Linz (1987) and Mainwaring (1992a) that presidentialism and multipartism are inherently incompatible. Another puzzle is that presidential elections from 1931 until 1970 show a strikingly different side of Chile's party system.

In three of the first four presidential elections of the period, coalitions were structured behind two principal candidates, as reflected in values of *N* of 2.0 or less. The parties thereby offered voters the clear choice of two competing alternative executives. This feature accords with the archetype of presidentialism and with efficiency in the channeling of voters' expressed preferences into executive formation. In only one of the next five presidential elections, that of 1964, did a two-candidate race occur again. The divergent direction of Chile's party systems – simultaneous consolidation in assembly elections and increasing fragmentation of executive elections – may be seen in Figure 9.2.

Three of the two-candidate races occurred at precisely the same time that the party system for congressional elections was most highly fragmented: in 1931, 1938, and 1942. For the congressional elections closest in time to these presidential elections, the lowest value of *N* was 6.9 in 1937. Yet this extreme fragmentation of the party system did not prevent the structuring of national coalitions capable of generating majority electoral support be-

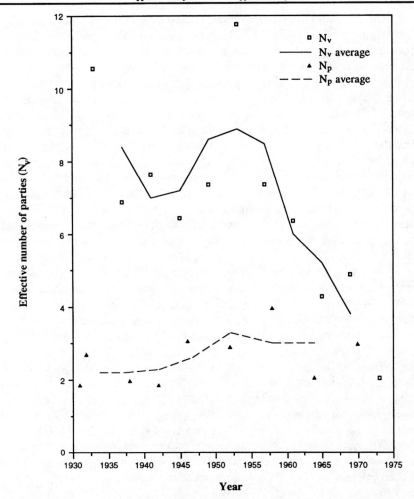

Figure 9.2. Effective number of parties contesting congressional elections ($N_v$) and effective number of presidential candidates ($N_p$), Chile, 1931–1973

hind an executive. Even in the one election in which there were several candidates, in 1932, one candidate brought together a coalition sufficient to garner a majority of votes.

*Majority-building in presidential elections.* It was not until 1946 that Chile experienced its first true multiparty presidential election under the 1925 constitution. The candidate who won the plurality of the popular vote, Gabriel González, had 40.2%, while the next two candidates, both of the right, had 29.8% and 27.4%. This was thus the first election in which the Chamber of Deputies would have the final say over who would become

president. The chamber ratified the electorate's plurality, voting for González by a vote of 138 to 46 (Urzua 1986:66–8). Thus was institutionalized the
precedent, followed in future cases when there was no winner of a popular
majority, of choosing the plurality candidate. This respect for the plurality
winner was aided by (and probably depended on) the usual practice of the
parties' having put together a broad preelectoral coalition that could not be
beaten in congress by any new postelection coalition. This preelection
coalition-building resulted from the desire of parties to support a winning
candidate for an office that had substantial power over legislation. Until
the presidential elections of 1958 and 1970, parties usually did structure
broad and decisive coalitions before the presidential election; that of 1946
was actually one of the less broad coalitions, but still one candidate led the
rest of the field by a considerable margin.

In the next presidential election, 1952, while no candidate won a majority, Carlos Ibáñez came close, at 46.8%, and did so by offering a national
vision of sorts, if a highly negative one. He was the "outsider," campaigning against the established parties. Despite his anti-party stance, the congress, while dominated by members of those same parties, selected Ibáñez
without incident. Thus the plurality principle was again upheld; it would
have been hard for parties to buck the bandwagon that had ensued behind
Ibáñez even though constitutionally they could have chosen the runner-up.

*Inefficiency in assembly elections.* During the period just reviewed, in
which the number of parties was at its highest, congressional politics was at
its most local. Electoral lists in districts were regularly drawn up for expressly local purposes, rather than for the purpose of providing voters with
a set of ideologically coherent policy priorities at the national level. Members of diverse parties, as well as local notables running as "independents"
would structure preelectoral pacts in which a vote for any of them helped
all their partners. After 1958, voters voted directly for a candidate within a
party list.

Valenzuela (1978, 1989a, 1989b), in various writings on Chile, has stressed
how that extreme localism and personal brokering of services rendered by
those elected coexisted with parties that were often highly polarized on
*national* issues. Parties thus were Janus-faced: highly personalistic in elections, highly combative in worldview. Indeed, one might say that the local
particularism was the "glue" that held together an otherwise polarized party
system. Despite the possible ideological gulf between them, members of a
particular locale's congressional delegation frequently came together across
party lines for the purpose of rendering services to their constituents. While
most presidential elections until 1958 were rather efficient in offering at least
one candidate who could articulate a national vision via a broad coalition,
congressional elections were conducted on entirely different kinds of campaigns. As we shall see, it was when congressional elections also began to be

conducted primarily around support or opposition to the national coalition and the more ideologically driven policy proposals offered at that level, that the system began to become unglued.

We thus might call the success of the Chilean system an approximation of the archetypal presidential system before the late 1950s the "inefficient secret." The secret was that the very inefficiency prevailing in the assembly accommodated both logrolling and polarization without threatening the stability of the system, while broader coalitions, sometimes even ones that were policy-based, formed for presidential elections. Congressional elections during the period in question (about 1930 until the late 1950s) were highly local, centering on district-specific and even citizen-specific benefits, what we know as "pork barrel," patronage, and casework. However, the existence of presidential elections, and especially the early emergence of a plurality character to those elections, meant that parties would need to present a broader focus in those elections. Thus the extreme localism of congressional elections did not inhibit substantial policy innovation in the case of the Popular Front, which was a majority coalition of the middle-class Radical Party and leftists contemporary to, and bearing much substantive resemblance to, the U.S. New Deal. We shall see shortly what changed to undercut the inefficient secret of Chile's presidential regime, but first let us see if any other systems have been characterized by this inefficient secret.

*Other examples of the inefficient secret.* We can identify some other cases that could be considered examples of an inefficient secret, although each has a considerably more powerful president, and this skewing of the balance can be linked to considerably less adequate functioning of these systems. Brazil from 1946 until the military takeover in 1964 bears some similarity to Chile. The new regime in Brazil since 1988 is similar in many respects. Colombia was another example of inefficient presidentialism.

The congressional electoral system in Brazil is one based on personal voting within parties. Indeed, according to the rating system used in Table 9.1. Brazilian party leadership is weaker than its Chilean counterpart. Members of congress pay special attention to bringing pork barrel benefits back to their districts (or "bailiwicks" within their districts) in order to cultivate a personal electoral following (Ames 1987). Brazilian parties are extremely uncohesive, because the electoral system contains several provisions that undermine party leadership in addition to simple candidate voting (Mainwaring 1991). We should like to emphasize another reason, not mentioned by either Ames or Mainwaring, why party building is hampered: the strength of a presidency that rendered the congress less effective as a national policymaking institution than its Chilean counterpart. Just as much as the electoral rules themselves, as we shall show, these constitutional rules inhibiting party development were products of a congressional rank and file that wanted weak parties.

As the rules of the policymaking game are skewed in favor of the executive, congress is left with little role beyond providing for its regionally based constituents. Mainwaring characterizes Brazilian presidents at mid-century as "circumventing" congress (Mainwaring 1992b), and he and Ames emphasize the greater importance of pork and patronage rather than policy debate in congressional elections. We are confident that the relative strengths of the two country's presidencies, coupled with their electoral systems, account for the regimes' divergent party systems and policy processes.

Colombia, especially before the 1991 constitutional reform, is another case of a congress heavily based on localism, and with a very powerful presidency (see Figure 8.1). Additionally, the party system, while generally consisting of only two major parties, had been highly factionalized, mainly along regional and personalistic lines. Splits and crises within the traditional Liberal and Conservative parties were every bit as critical as interparty disputes in leading to the breakdown of Colombia's oligarchical democracy in the 1940s. While intraparty splits are no longer viewed as a threat to a democratic regime (Hartlyn 1987), the electoral system has continued to reflect a legacy of regionalism and personalism by allowing factions of each party to compete with one another. The progression of institutional changes over time in Colombia demonstrates the importance of both the electoral system and the constitutional allocation of powers in facilitating or hindering the articulation of national policy goals.

In the 1930s the presidency had not yet been granted by congressional majorities the sweeping legislative decree powers and primacy in economic affairs that were parts of later constitutional reforms. Nor had the leaders of the principal factions yet lost control over congressional nominations, as happened when interparty competition was banned under the National Front regime. Thus in the 1930s, the Colombian Liberal party was able to carry out fundamental social reform in the so-called Revolution on the March (Dix 1967). By the 1980s, however, Colombian parties were generally regarded as almost completely feckless in addressing national policy challenges (Archer and Chernick 1988). Electoral lists for congress were not drawn up with policy options in mind so much as to garner personal votes on behalf of local vote brokers (Archer 1989, Shugart 1992a). The predictable result of a personalistic and faction-ridden congress coupled with a president holding dominant lawmaking powers was a congress ill-equipped to deal with fundamental challenges facing the country. As in Brazil, only perhaps more so, members of congress were reduced to being little more than lobbyists for the projects and patronage that enabled them to continue to deliver votes in congressional elections. The congress, through the electoral system, was structured so as to provide benefits on a particularistic, geographic basis. Power to address broader interests was ceded to the presidency, but congress retained important negative powers with which (until 1990) it was able to check "reformist" tendencies in the executive (cf. Archer and Chernick

1988). It was because of this preference of Colombia's rank-and-file congress members for a constitutional structure that permitted them to service their clienteles that an ironic situation had developed by 1990: an executive-sponsored constitutional revision to weaken the executive's power over legislation (cf. Shugart and Fernandez 1991). The explicit goal, only partially achieved, was to make the system more efficient so that the congress and executive alike could address serious policy challenges confronting the country. In short, Colombia as of 1990 perhaps had no longer an inefficient secret, but simply an inefficient regime.

*The U.S. case.* The United States comes to mind as a case with some similarities to the extreme electoral separation of the two elected branches. However, we saw that the United States occupies a distinctly different region of Figure 9.1. Does this accord with the regime's actual performance? In the United States, voting based on local interests contributes to the frequency with which opposing parties control congress and the presidency (Jacobson 1990), despite the fact that half of the congressional elections are held concurrently with the presidential elections. The safety of incumbency has also been explained by the ability of members to cultivate a "personal vote" (Cain, Ferejohn, and Fiorina, 1987), hence shielding themselves from national policy swings.

In this limited sense, the United States might appear to resemble the inefficient secret. However, there are important distinctions between the United States and the other cases discussed in this section. One is that, while congressional candidates are afforded considerable latitude by the congressional party leadership to tailor their messages to their constituents, the vote for Congress is still categoric by party: either a Democrat or a Republican.[9] Thus the salience of pork need not be as great as in intraparty preference electoral systems. A second critical difference is the lesser powers of the president over legislation than in those other cases. These two features, of course, account for the regime's placement in Figure 9.1. As a result, while we lack an easy way to scale it, policy voting in congressional elections is surely higher (hence less inefficient) in the United States than in Brazil, mid-century Chile, or Colombia.

While the U.S. Congress has generally maintained a frequently maligned tendency to deal with local services even at the expense of an articulation of a national policy perspective in congressional campaigns (for a review, see Cain et al., 1987), Cox and McCubbins (1992) have offered a convincing counterargument to those who would sound the death knell for American parties as organizations that structure policy debate at the national level. Nevertheless, even the case for the strength of parties acknowledges the

9 Primary elections do not significantly undercut this efficiency, since in all but a few states, voters are permitted in primaries to select candidates only within one party; unlike in the other cases examined here, the intraparty choice is not simultaneous to the interparty race.

importance of local pork in maintaining personalistic loyalties between congresspersons and their constituents, and the fact that party organizations in the United States have traditionally been strongest at the state and even local levels, all indicators of relative inefficiency. National policy issues remain less important in elections to the representative assembly in the United States than in many other countries' assemblies, particularly Britain's, and less important also than in U.S. presidential elections.

Our conclusions about the United States, then, are that despite their considerable local tendency, U.S. parties are able to attend to policy matters in elections to a greater extent than in the more inefficient cases primarily because of the electoral system and limited presidential powers. If a congress has preeminent legislative power, parties cannot afford excessive slack in discipline and inefficiency and still carry on with legislation. Because the electoral system reduces the salience of pork in campaigns, compared to the systems of Brazil, Chile, and Colombia, parties in the United States do not need to distribute particularistic benefits to regional politicians to the same great extent as in those other systems.

## LOCALLY BASED PARTY SYSTEMS: WHY SUCH POWERFUL PRESIDENCIES?

Now we have seen that presidentialism and electoral systems interact to shape the party system, but why is there a tendency for locally based party systems and strong presidencies to be associated? Here we argue that the answer lies in the origins of the regimes themselves. The Brazilian (1988) and Colombian (1886) systems were devised by congresses or similarly elected constituent assemblies, while the Chilean regime represented the culmination of a political tug-of-war between president and congress that had even resulted in a civil war in 1891. Thus it is not surprising that all have afforded great opportunities for representatives to attend to their local constituents. What is perhaps more paradoxical is that, as we have observed, these very same systems have tended also to have very strong presidents. Yet this is what is suggested by Figure 9.1, above. Why would these assemblies have approved constitutions allocating major budgetary, legislative, and even "emergency" decree powers to an institution outside the congress?

The model that follows is an abstraction derived from a theoretical consideration of two of the most extreme cases of strong presidents and weak parties: the regimes of Brazil after military rule and the Colombian system as it operated through most of the twentieth century. Later we suggest modifications that help account for variations in some of the inefficient systems, including the earlier Brazilian democratic regime and Chile. At first, our discussion applies to the class of inefficient regimes more generally, as all contain certain similarities in structure and origin.

Let us start from a very basic assumption. What do members want? We assume that they want to further their careers as politicians. To do so, they want to be able to bring benefits back to their regions in order that they might amass still greater political capital. The institutional arrangement that emerges is one permitting these representatives at once to free themselves and to bind themselves: to *free themselves* of direct involvement with broader national policy matters by creating a central, accountable agent to handle such matters without impinging on their ability to attend to constituent needs, and *to bind themselves* against excessive spending that could undermine the system itself. Let us now develop this idea further, first by asking the counterfactual: What if these systems had been parliamentary?

### *Freedom to service constituencies*

Under a parliamentary system, with its vote of confidence and the possibility of dissolution, these representatives would have been inevitably drawn into forming and supporting cabinets responsible for national policy. As we have discussed, in a parliamentary system, the only institution disposed to design and implement national policy is the cabinet. The responsibility of the cabinet to parliament makes parliament itself responsible for policy. Then either party whips become critical in sustaining governments in office through enforcing party discipline (e.g. Britain), or else the executive itself becomes unstable through frequent votes of no-confidence (e.g., Italy's *trasformismo*).

The very separation of powers afforded by a presidential system, on the other hand, allowed these regionally based vote brokers, often tied to big landowners on whom election to congress depended, to delegate national policy responsibilities to an executive such that they would not bind themselves to a particular set of policies that could impinge upon the local bosses' autonomy. We do not imply by this that congress simply abdicated policymaking because its members did not care about these matters or preferred to leave the "tough questions" to someone else. Instead, in a manner similar to that described by Kiewiet and McCubbins (1991) for the United States, we see a congressional majority delegating to achieve certain goals. As we have stated, when the method of election is one that places overwhelming importance on providing services to constituents because of factional competition, a paramount goal of majorities will be to obtain the resources to protect members' personal followings. Thus, members of this majority may advance their careers through keeping constituents' needs addressed, while a central agent, the president, can be charged with and held accountable for policymaking. As we saw in Chapter 7's discussion of delegation, congressional majorities retain ways to ensure that these presidential powers are used within acceptable limits, through the ability to cut expenditure requests, pass ordinary legislation, or even reform the constitution itself. The congress can do so without having either to sacrifice autonomy in the assembly or else to surrender the advantages of having a single identifiable agent for general policy, as would be the case in a parliamentary form of government.

Even if the foregoing characterization is correct, one might wonder, why a *separately elected* presidency? Perhaps the assembly-independent form of government discussed in Chapter 8 would be more appropriate for such politicians, since it would create an executive more dependent for its origin on the congress than a directly elected president, but would still avoid the vote of no-confidence and the resulting party whips (or cabinet instability). Indeed, some of the early Latin American constitutions did provide for approximations of such regimes, if we include an executive elected by an electoral college composed of other elected officials (and therefore controlled by the local politicians in question) to be more appropriately characterized as an assembly rather than a presidential regime. Also, as we have seen, the Bolivian system remains as a legacy of this type of executive selection process.[10] In Chile, too, the constitution provided for congressional ratification of alliances stemming from electoral success in prior, locally contested elections. Even where presidents came to be separately elected and not subject to congressional ratification, as in Colombia in 1910 (Gibson 1948), the electoral process often remained one in which the local elites and their followers rather than the state retained control over the distribution of ballots, as indeed was the case in Brazil in the 1950s and in Colombia until the election of 1990. Where regional authorities and party workers control even presidential elections, the emergence of efficiency is retarded at this level nearly as much as in locally contested congressional elections. Our argument is that this was exactly the intention of those who designed, developed, and sustained these regimes.

Most of these cases also employed nonconcurrent electoral cycles. Given that nonconcurrent elections afford greater independence of locally based politicians from presidential coalitions (see Chapter 10), we should expect these politicians to prefer such an electoral cycle. Indeed, in Brazil's constitution of 1946 elections for congress were initially concurrent, but the congressional majority shifted to separate dates after 1950. In Colombia, too, before the National Front, congressional elections were regularly held nonconcurrently. During the National Front, they were held with the presidential election, while from 1974 until 1990, they again were held before the congressional election.

### Binding congressional majorities

We have now discussed several ways in which the creation of the presidency, and a powerful one at that, served to free congressional majorities

---

10 A difference in Bolivia is that, since the 1952 revolution, Bolivia's electoral system has featured closed lists (Gamarra 1987).

to attend to constituent interests on which their electoral success depended. Now it is worth considering ways in which this institutional arrangement served to bind the congress. The creation of a powerful presidency would keep spending from going out of control. Servicing constituencies through the allocation of budgetary resources that provide subsidies, protection, jobs, and other specific benefits is an expensive undertaking. Left unchecked, such a process could easily kill the goose that laid the golden egg. Thus the goose is protected by creating an institution that exercises powers such as limiting the maximum expenditure for particular items or for the whole budget and a partial veto. We argue that this institutional arrangement offers the congressional majority a credibly enforceable commitment to some degree of fiscal restraint.

When a president possesses a partial veto, the ability of congress members to logroll *within congress* is undercut. Instead, their ability to do so depends on having ties directly to the president, who allows pork on the basis of transactions with congressional coalitions. Thus the locus of logrolling shifts much more decisively toward the president than it does in systems in which the president lacks a partial veto. The restrictions on increasing the president's proposed expenditures work much the same way. Since members continued to work within an electoral system that encouraged them to cultivate personal followings, the institutional incentives were for them to be be little more than lobbyists for regional particularistic interests, which, we argue, was what they intended for themselves to be.

It could be objected that fiscal restraint is a public good, so why would members go along with it? In short, what are the incentives for obeying? What levers exist? Most important is that the ability to provide the private goods on which election depends is itself dependent on deals struck with the president, because the partial veto gives the president the ability to set limits to expenditures on particular items.

### Origins of the inefficient systems

If this account of why some presidential regimes exhibit both a congress elected along clientelistic lines and an executive with great legislative strength is correct, then there should be levers by which the congress would retain ultimate authority even over such a strong executive, as well as ways by which congressional interests would ensure the continuation of their electoral perquisites. Otherwise we indeed would have examples of abdicated authority – and we are arguing that this is not the case. Since Brazil (1988) and Colombia (1886) are two of the strongest presidencies that we have seen, aside from the three-year-long experience in Chile after 1970, these are the two that should correspond most closely to the theoretical discussion of this section. After considering these cases, we return to the Chilean case.

Both the Brazilian constitution of 1988 and the Colombia of 1886 (and to a lesser extent, as we shall see, Brazil's of 1946) were products of constituent assemblies whose representation ran along regional, clientelistic lines. Thus both constitutions should be expected to represent the interests of these regional authorities as they were portrayed above: freeing congress members to service their constituents rather than deal with broader policy concerns, and binding themselves from spending extremes. If this is so, wherever there are extraordinary powers in the hands of the executive we should expect some countervailing check by the congress to make sure that the executive does not wield this power in ways that threaten regional interests. If the strong president is the guardian of the system, who guards the guard himself? What mechanisms exist to bind the president, in other words, to use the powers responsibly? The first is in the electoral system. Because members of the same party compete against one another as well as against other parties to provide constituent services, and because the president still needs legislative majorities to use the powers effectively, the president's ability to have such support depends on being able to get preferred congress members elected. The low barriers to election (given some minimal access to funds)[11] and especially the cultivation of clienteles in both countries mean that the president's ability to see one preferred member or factional group elected in some district instead of another, depends on providing budgetary resources to benefit that member's or faction's constituents. With so little central leadership control in either case over the specific members who are elected, the presidency, despite all its great strength, is dependent for congressional majorities on who has the vote-delivering ability. Vote-delivering ability, in turn, is greatly enhanced by having central budgetary resources. The result is a considerable degree of mutual dependency (cf. Shugart and Fernandez 1991). With such a decentralized congress one's ability to get access to funds by dealing wholly within the congressional labyrinth would be low, but by making deals with a powerful central figure, one's prospects for getting funds are improved. For the president, such deals are essential for getting legislative support, hence funds are likely to be directed where they have the greatest electoral payoff.

We have been speaking of the need for legislative support. But why is this critical for such a strong president? One major reason is that ordinary legislation passes by *simple majority*. This, of course, is hardly unusual;[12] what is unusual in these two cases is that a veto may be overridden by a majority of the congressional membership, rather than by an extraordinary

11 In Colombia, members each had a small share of the national budget (known as *auxilios parlamentarios*) to spend in their districts as they saw fit. Hartlyn (1987:99) refers to these funds appropriately as "pork-barrel funds."
12 The first ten years of the National Front were an exception, during which legislation required a two-thirds vote for passage.

(for example, two-thirds) majority. Thus the congressional majority is sovereign over legislation, subject to the president's ability to delete congressional amendments through the exercise of the partial veto. Only during the Liberal "Revolution on the March" in the late 1930s was a veto requiring an extraordinary majority to override enacted in Colombia, and then only on expenditure bills (see Gibson 1948:403). In the earlier Brazilian regime, which contained strong legacies of the populist Vargas movement (Mainwaring 1992b), there likewise was an extraordinary majority to override vetoes. In both instances, the existence of nationally focused parties or movements that controlled the presidency at the time led to the adoption of stronger veto authority, which, as a way to enforce consensus, could weaken the sway in congress of clientelistic majorities in favor of the more national oriented (often populist) presidential coalition. When clientelistic majorities prevailed, as in Colombia as well as Brazil after military rule, vetoes were weaker, being easier for the congress to override.[13] The great presidential powers that were provided were in areas other than ordinary legislation, including budgeting.

In the inefficient systems, budgetary powers are, to varying degrees, important. The ability of the congress in both countries to reduce the amounts allocated in the president's budget to particular items also is a meaningful weapon for congress, even if congress does not have the authority to expand the overall budget. By the threat of reducing items that the president wants, the congress can keep the president from using even his decree powers rampantly. The members of the congressional majority retain the means to hurt the president in areas important to him, even while simultaneously retaining the limit on their own ability to increase items (or overall spending) as a means to bind themselves. Finally, prohibiting the reelection of the president would prevent this official, once in office, from developing a popular constituency with which he could turn around and campaign against the "wasteful" spending by which the congress members serviced their constituents.

Perhaps the clincher for this theory of a congress ultimately able to get what its constituents want out of a strong presidency is congress's own sovereignty over the constitution. In neither case (nor in Chile and many other presidential systems) is the constitutional amendment process even remotely as cumbersome as in the United States. Congress retains the authority to reform these constitutions. In Colombia, as well as under the Brazilian constitution of 1946, congress could do so by *absolute majorities*

13 Other differences in the two Brazilian regimes relate to elections. Under the 1946 constitution, elections at first were concurrent, meaning they were more likely to be contested around national (at the time, populist) policy concerns. Moreover, in 1945 the electoral rules favored the largest party. Subsequently, including the new regime, elections have been nonconcurrent and electoral rules have favored fragmentation. See Mainwaring (1991, 1992b).

of the whole membership in two consecutive sessions. It thus would take time, but it would not take an extraordinary (for example, two-thirds) majority. A president would thus have to exercise some degree of caution when contemplating making law by decree: congress could amend away these powers if they were abused; theoretically, it could even amend away the presidential institution itself or at least bind the executive to congress more closely, perhaps by instituting censure of cabinet members. Our point is not that there were not any agency losses as a result of this substantial delegation of powers to the executive (see Chapter 7). Rather, our point is that the benefits of delegation discussed here for these congressional politicians must not have exceeded the cost entailed in agency loss, or else reforms to the process would be anticipated. The calculation that costs had outweighed benefits would have been most likely had a reformist or "outsider" become president and attempted to use his powers to the detriment of the congressional interests. Such a result did obtain in Brazil in 1961, as we discuss below.[14]

If the constitution that granted legislative faculties to presidents was left easily reformed by congress, the electoral law in Colombia on which the whole system depended was put beyond the reach of mere majorities. The electoral law required a two-thirds majority to reform under the 1886 constitution. Thus we have powerful testimony to what was more important to the designers of this constitution. The strong presidency was little more than "rules" by which to achieve congressional desires, and the strength could be modified at relatively low cost if necessary; the electoral law, on which their ability to service constituents and be free of party discipline ultimately depended, was made more difficult to change.

In Brazil, as well, despite having a federal system that might have encouraged a constitutional amending process similar to that of the United States, reforms to the basic institutions are relatively easy to make. The majority required in the 1988 constitution is three-fifths of each house, making the barrier higher than in Colombia or the previous Brazilian democracy, but lower than in many systems. There was one very prominent precedent for the use of this amending capability to curtail the powers of a president in whom much of the congressional politicians did not trust. In 1961, in response to the ascension to the presidency of Vice-President João Goulart upon the resignation of Jânio Quadros, congress passed an amendment creating cabinet responsibility before the congress and weakening the veto override from two-thirds to three-fifths. Moreover, in future constitutional terms, the president would have been elected by congress, had the system survived. Such a reform underscores the potential for a congress to check

14 An ultimate irony of the Colombian case is that when such a reformist president did win office, he used his State of Siege powers to invoke a constitutional reform process that sought to replace the system with a more efficient one. See, in addition to the brief discussion below, Shugart (1992a) and Shugart and Fernandez (1991).

even a president who is constitutionally very strong, or eliminate the independent executive altogether – provided, of course, that the constitution has left it relatively easy for congress to do so.

How does the story just told about congressional wishes in Colombia and Brazil apply to the case that we have suggested so typifies the presidential archetype? The Chilean regime before 1970 featured a congress at least marginally more capable of addressing national policy matters and a correspondingly more ideological party system that represented more diverse interests than in Colombia and Brazil. This implies that regional interests, which might have favored the highly inefficient type of regime seen in those other two countries, either were not present or were forced to compromise with other interests. Either way, they were weaker and the resulting constitutional structure placed less legislative burden on the presidency, making it more of the veto gate that it is in "classic" separation of powers theory, rather than the "supreme legislator" (Vásquez Carrizosa 1979) for national policy. The origin of the Chilean constitutions through 1970 was much less based in congress or regionally controlled constituent assemblies than was so in Colombia or Brazil, particularly in 1988.

The historical antecedent of the constitution that was in effect in Chile through the major reforms of 1970 may be found in a presidential commission after a brief civil war in the 1830s (Sigler, Blaustein, and Flanz 1981). This constitution granted the president an *absolute* veto but not the extensive legislative decree or budgetary powers that were to typify the constitutions of Colombia and Brazil. The absolute veto was reduced to one requiring a two-thirds override when congressionally supported forces defeated those of the president in the civil war of 1891, ushering in the so-called parliamentary republic. The constitution of 1925 resulted from a military-presidential intervention against congressional control over cabinets in the previous periods, but did not alter the basic legislative powers of presidents from what they had been since 1891. The irony, then, is that in Chile, greater presidential control over the constitution drafting in 1925 (with the legacy of the 1831 document) resulted by 1925 in a president with stronger package vetoes but significantly weaker budget and decree powers. This is not so surprising however, as long as it is recognized that the legislative powers other than the package veto are presidential faculties more desired by the regional interests represented in the assembly itself. Thus, where the constitution originated in a process that already checked the ambitions of these (typically landowning) congressional interests, as with the mid-eighteenth-century military leaders in Chile and Vargas in Brazil, those institutional features most favorable to them were attenuated. The result was that the Chilean Congress became a highly dynamic legislature. Those of Brazil after military rule and Colombia, on the other hand, did not, as the regionally based politicians were better positioned to craft a regime that would serve their interests.

### EFFICIENT PRESIDENTIALISM: STRONG PARTIES AND WEAK PRESIDENTS

We have been discussing a cluster of presidential regimes in which congressional elections are or were conducted mainly around the provision of locally targeted expenditures promised and delivered by candidates and congress members who have considerable autonomy from national leadership, a form of politics we have branded as inefficient. While we have been careful to point out important distinctions between Brazil and Colombia, on the one hand, and Chile, on the other, all of these regimes are differentiated in Figure 9.1 from another cluster. In the lower right of that figure, we find a series of regimes in which party control over local rank and file means that individual candidates and members of congress cannot outbid one another in providing benefits because their ability to be elected depends on the collective performance of the party rather than on their own ability to generate resources. We have branded this form of politics as efficient. We shall focus here on one case, Venezuela, that is almost the opposite extreme of the Brazilian and Colombian cases.

The method of electing the assembly is fundamental to understanding why Venezuela and some similar systems do not resemble the archetypal form of presidentialism. The Venezuelan Congress is not elected with localities as the basis of representation, as was Chile's during the period of the inefficient secret, or as is that of the United States. Instead it is elected from closed party lists,[15] in which voters select only a party and are not permitted to select a specific candidate within the party. Since being placed sufficiently high on the party list is the key to being elected, central party leaders are tremendously powerful (Coppedge 1988).

While election of the congress from closed party lists might make the articulation of preeminently local concerns more difficult than the election of the congress on the basis of individuals and what they can bring to their constituents, such an electoral system might be expected to make possible the other form of constituent representation discussed in Chapter 1: that of ideological or partisan interest. Yet in Venezuela since the early 1970s, there have been two main parties, thus limiting the degree of diversity that can be represented while enhancing electoral efficiency. Each major party

---

15 Regional multi-seat districts are used, but several features of the electoral system in use from 1958 to 1988 sharply limited the opportunity for the articulation of local interests. Most prominent among these was the totally closed-list format, meaning that individual candidates lacked the incentive to cultivate a personal vote. A vote for the list was a vote for everyone on the list, with the order – and thus the electability – of candidates predetermined by the leadership. Additionally, the concurrence of these elections with the national presidential election and the existence of nationwide seats to compensate minority parties for district-level deviations have further restricted localism. Reforms enacted after the 1988 elections are expected to increase the articulation of local interests, although perhaps only marginally. See Shugart 1992a.

is formed around a principal competitor for the presidency. As we shall see in Chapter 10 and 11, when presidential and congressional elections are concurrent, as they are in Venezuela, a party system dominated by two major parties is the norm, provided that the president is elected by plurality. But for the first three elections under the new regime founded in 1958, there was a multiparty system. The functioning of the Venezuelan system, in which the president's legislative powers are far weaker than in Chile, Brazil, or Colombia, shows how the strength of the presidency, the electoral system, and the electoral cycle work together to impact the degree of efficiency of the system.

### Venezuela's transitional multiparty system

In Venezuela, the presidency was originally consciously devalued by the leader of the parties as part of a political pact to ensure the stability of the young democracy. The idea was that if one party could gain sole control over a powerful office, the others would likely fail to respect the new rules of political contestation. In the system designed, the president lacks a veto, making the congress superior in terms of legislation (see Chapter 7).

The practice of Venezuelan democracy up to 1968 permitted multi-partism to flourish in the 1963 and 1968 elections, but a two-party format subsequently emerged. Among all the elections for plurality presidencies and concurrently elected PR congresses for which we have data, there are strikingly few in which the number of "serious" presidential contenders exceeds two.[16] Only three cases clearly stand out thereby as exceptions to the rule: the Dominican Republic in 1990 and Venezuela in 1963 and 1968. Such elections are certainly aberrant,[17] but the case of the Venezuelan multiparty elections deserves some further comment.

From 1958, the date of the founding of the Venezuelan democratic regime and of its first elections, until the inauguration of the president elected in 1968, Venezuela was governed by coalitions. The Pact of Punto Fijo, in which the principles of elite conciliation were laid down, provided that the winter of the 1958 presidential election would share power with other parties *regardless of who won*. While the parties could not agree on a common presidential candidate, neither was there any incentive for the opposition to the major party (Acción Democrática) to coalesce, given the limited stakes of the presidential election. Indeed, the president was meant to be *above politics* (Coppedge 1992), and with the congressional elections serving to determine the rough makeup of coalition cabinets, the incentives were much more in the direction of fragmentation than consolidation.

While some parties left and others joined coalitions between 1958 and

16 A party system with two big parties, each around 40% of the votes, plus one or two secondary parties will have a value of $N$ around 2.9.
17 Their occasional occurrence is explained in Appendix A.

1968, the formal practice of coalition government continued until the first non-AD victory in 1968 (with only 29% of the vote) confirmed that alternation was possible and led to the end of the practice of formal executive coalitions. President Rafael Caldera exercised his constitutional prerogative to choose the ministers he wanted and governed with single-party cabinets despite his narrow plurality. Thereafter, the party system consolidated into the two-party dominant system seen after 1973.

### Efficiency and representativeness in Venezuela

Before the two-party dominant system emerged, Venezuela had a highly representative congress but inefficient executive elections, owing to multi-partism. With no majority party (or even a near-majority party) in 1963 and 1968, the ability of voters to identify and endorse a package of executive policy options was very weak.

Once the party system coalesced around two major parties that offered meaningful competition for the presidency, identifiability increased. Thus the system became more efficient, but only to the extent that the president's party could command majorities in the assembly, since the president lacks formal legislative powers. On the other hand, if the president's party is merely the plurality party, but the major opposition party can coalesce with minor parties to control the assembly, the policy option endorsed in the presidential election may be rendered feckless. At times such a coalition has formed to "gang up" on the president and to legislate over his head. Having a congress composed of representatives who have been elected principally on presidential candidates' coattails and are not disposed to compromise individually, plus a president without a veto, is not a recipe for either faithful representation or smooth executive–congressional relations. What it does is make for an unusually majoritarian form of presidentialism, since the presidential check on congressional majorities is minimal. By being majoritarian and having such strong party discipline, this system bears considerable resemblance to the efficient secret of Britain, but with an important exception: the possibility that a president and the congressional majorities might be incompatible.[18]

Many Venezuelans have been widely critical of their system for its concentration of power in the party leadership, even coining the term "party-ocracy" (Coppedge 1988; see also Shugart 1992a). Yet, despite these criticisms, it remains true that this regime and two others that share with it the same region of Figure 9.1 (Costa Rica and the Dominican Republic, both of which have slightly stronger presidents) are among the most stable and

18 It has never happened that one party held the presidency while another held a majority of the congress. As mentioned above, however, there have been times when a coalition of parties in opposition to the president has legislated over the objections of the president.

crisis-free examples of presidentialism. Let us consider why that might be the case and whether we can generalize from the experience.

### Origins of efficient presidentialism

Our preceding discussion of the cases that combine strong presidents and weak parties led us to the conclusion that such a combination was desired by the very politicians who designed and maintained those regimes. Perhaps a similar story can be told about the regimes that combine comparatively weak presidents and strong parties. We theorized that the inefficient regimes had their origin in regionally based constituent assemblies that brought together politicians who sought a system that would allow them to continue to provide constituent services to their regions. The efficient regimes, on the other hand, have had their origin in revolutions or civil-military coups that detroyed traditional dictatorships and brought to power rather cohesive, reformist, and nationally oriented leaderships. In Venezuela, the Acción Democrática took power in a conspiracy with part of the military in 1945 and again in 1958 – this time in a pact with other parties. The AD was originally Leninist in its internal structure. More significant is what AD was not: It was not a collection of regional politicians. It was a social-democratic party of intellectuals and advocates for the urban middle class and the peasantry (Martz 1966). Similar origins typify the parties that dominated the constitution writing in Costa Rica after Jose Figueres's insurrection, the Dominican Republic after the fall of the dictator Rafael Trujillo, and Nicaragua after the Sandinista insurrection. But why would the particular combination of strong parties and weak presidents emerge?

Each system just mentioned has used closed party lists, which is hardly surprising when the leadership is in as commanding a position as in a post-insurrectionary period. Rather than permit local rank and file to contest elections and demand resources independently of the leaders' agenda, the party leadership could ensure control over its activists even after the initiation of competitive elections by means of control over lists of candidates. Logically, it also follows that party leaders who expected to be able ordinarily to dominate their rank and file, and who were relatively unconcerned with servicing particularistic geographic interests, would have less need to delegate legislative and budgetary powers to an external agent. The coordination and binding of members, which we discussed with reference to the Brazilian and Colombian cases, could be accomplished through leadership control over electability instead of through extraordinary legislative powers in the hands of a president. But that is not the full story; by maintaining an assembly more powerful than the president, the party (or parties) could ensure its continued viability as a policy-making body rather than risk becoming marginalized by a powerful president. Yet each of these founding parties, or revolutionary movements, was identified with a particular dominant leader. Thus it is not terribly surprising that they should create a presidency to allow that leader a fairly autonomous position from which to exercise limited executive power. We discussed in Chapter 5 the variations of presidential reelection; here we need only recall that these efficient regimes include the Dominican Republic and Nicaragua, two of the three Latin American systems that do not restrict presidential reelection.

The result of this process of a regime emerging from a reformist party's hold on power rather than from regionally based politicians is an institutional system that permits efficient voting on the basis of competing parties and encourages the nationalization of politics. It does so especially if congressional and presidential elections run concurrently and plurality rule is used for the presidency, as in Costa Rica, the Dominican Republic, Nicaragua, and Venezuela. In placing such a premium on national policy instead of local and more particularistic interests, the regime does not conform to the archetype we identified earlier. Indeed, it is the excessive deviation from the archetype – too little constituent responsiveness – that has led to calls for electoral reform in Venezuela to reduce the grip of leadership.

### *An optimal presidentialism?*

While our primary purpose in this book is not to prescribe a particular configuration of variables as being best according to some universal set of criteria, we do from time to time find that some ways of organizing a polity are preferable to others. If efficiency in the translation of voter preferences as expressed in elections into actual policy outcome is desirable, but we do not want to go to the extremes of Venezuelan-style partyocracy, we can find from the preceding discussion possible means of achieving such goals. It is reasonable to conclude that there might be potential institutional designs that grant only minimal legislative powers (greater than 0 but no more than 3) to the president while retaining considerable but not overwhelming leadership control over parties (perhaps what we would score in the range of 5 or 6) and that such a system would be efficient, but not to the utter exclusion of regional articulation.

What is questionable, however, is how such a regime would be brought about politically, given that powerful interests whose assent would be needed would likely exercise their vetoes to prevent reform. In the case of Venezuela, the well-esconced leaderships of the two dominant parties had much to lose if they were to weaken their influence over congressional candidacies. As a result, while the reformed congressional electoral system, passed for the 1993 elections, creates single-member districts for about half the seats and thus raises the potential for more constituent responsiveness, the remaining seats will continue to be elected from closed lists (Shugart 1992a). It remains to be seen, of course, what the effects of this system will be on enhancing representativeness within the parties. The experience does suggest the difficulty of bringing forth a potentially "optimal" configuration of variables already suggested. The Colombian constituent assembly of 1991, in which both national-reformist and regional interests obtained representation in a single nationwide district, might have suggested a process out of which a more efficient regime could emerge. However, the weight of the local interests that constitute the traditional parties proved too strong for dramatic changes to result (Shugart and Fernandez 1991; Shugart 1992a). Thus, what the Colombian experience of 1991 does is confirm again that constituent assemblies, as in 1886 in Colombia and 1988 in Brazil, are reflective of the interests of a majority. In an already particularistic political system, that majority, if elected through an essentially unchanged electoral system, is likely to want to maintain weak parties and a strong presidency.

We can relate one experience in which a reformist party emerged *within* an inefficient system and sought to bring about increased efficiency in a way that only increased conflict. We thus return to the Chilean case and its demise, for that case is yet further confirmation for one of our more general points: Powerful presidencies are problematic for the stability of presidential regimes. The quest for efficiency, where desired, should lead reformers toward a combination like that suggested as "optimal," at least by reducing presidential powers rather than enhancing executive faculties.

### THE DEMISE OF THE INEFFICIENT SECRET IN CHILE

Changes made in Chile in the final years before 1973 demonstrate that the inefficiency of congressional elections combined with moderately strong presidential legislative powers were the secret to that regime's previous success. The first of these changes that began to undermine the inefficient secret concerned the electoral laws. In 1958 a center-left coalition abolished joint electoral lists in an effort to eliminate the "corrupt" practice of structuring pacts among candidates of different parties at the local level for mutual electoral benefit. Valenzuela (1989b:182) says that "while this reform succeeded in making pre-election arrangements less 'political,' it also eliminated an important tool for cross-party bargaining." This reform coincided with the period in which an ideological Christian Democratic party was emerging alongside the already ideological left and the increasingly defensive conservative parties. It was inspired by a desire for efficiency, but undermined the basis for accommodation that, while certainly inefficient, was the glue of an otherwise polarized political system. The resulting regime was well off the axis that runs between efficient and inefficient regimes in Figure 9.1, foreshadowing its difficult combination of a strong presidency and parties increasingly attuned to national rather than mainly local concerns.

But it was the constitutional reform of 1970 that went farthest in under-mining the consensual basis of Chile's presidential system, placing the regime in a category all its own: exceptionally strong president and moder-ately strong parties. A constitutional amendment secured by the Christian Democratic administration of Eduardo Frei with support from the right required that no amendments could be attached to a bill unless they were directly germane to the bill itself. This was tantamount to enhancing the president's partial veto, especially because only the president could initiate many items of expenditure. The partial veto, even with an extraordinary majority override, allows congress to engage in attaching amendments to bills in order to secure passage, but delegates to the president the authority to decide which logrolls will be accepted. While, as we noted above, this means that much logrolling is transferred from congress to congressional–presidential negotiations, it at least permits such trade-offs to be made. If congress cannot make amendments that are not relevant to the main bill,[19] then the space for logrolling is not simply reduced and transferred to a new arena, as with a partial veto; it is eliminated. Thus a process begun in 1958 accelerated: The role of legislative bargaining across parties was being sharply reduced throughout this period.

These reforms, cases of political engineering designed to "rationalize" both local-level electoral politics and national policymaking, led to incipi-ent efficiency in congressional elections. That is, congressional elections came to be statements on preferred national policy direction. But to func-tion with a true efficient secret, elections for seats in the assembly would have to have been capable of determining the direction of the executive or at least the policy output of the policial process. However, by 1970 the presidency has been granted such great legislative powers as to characterize the regime by the most dominant of presidencies, as seen in Figure 8.1. Thus congressional elections took on far less import in the actual making of policy, making conflicts less manageable, as the effect was to place ever greater weight on the presidency. By doing so, Chilean politicians had made losing the presidency all the more costly to any of the three principal ideological blocs in the Chilean party system. It was during this period, therefore, that coalition building for that national executive became more complicated. The paradoxical result, then, was that reforms enacted in the name of efficiency for the polity as a whole utterly failed. As shown in Figure 9.2, only in the last congressional election were voters afforded an

19 The amendment also created a five-member Constitutional Court, three of whose mem-bers were appointed by the president, subject to assembly confirmation, and eligible for reappointment at the end of a fixed four-year term (shorter than the president's term by two years). Two other members were appointed by the Supreme Court from among its own members. Among the new court's functions was to pass judgment on whether bills were confined to one subject. Note that the new court's composition was such as to make it rather responsive to presidential preferences.

efficient choice – months before the coup that removed a constitutionally powerful president who represented the policy preferences of the losers of that congressional election.

### *Presidential elections: to coalesce or not to coalesce?*

We have seen that, despite a very high number of parties, in the age of the inefficient secret parties normally coalesced sufficiently before presidential elections to offer competing national candidates capable of obtaining a majority (or close to it) of the votes. However, as congressional elections came to be more policy-oriented, only one of the three presidential elections offered a two-way race. Two others were won by candidates receiving less than 37% of the vote.

The results of the one two-candidate race suggest the costs of coalition building when parties and ideological blocs are sharply defined and polarized. For even if a president is elected thanks to a cross-bloc pact made before the election, the president himself or herself still must come from one of the blocs. With such high stakes in holding the presidency, simply helping elect a president via a preelection coalition may not be sufficient. Indeed, if the stakes are sufficiently high, it may even become irrational to forge cross-bloc coalitions. The dilemma, of course, is that by failing to form a coalition, one bloc's or party's "greater evil" may be elected in a close three-way race. But in a polarized environment with a dominant presidency, even the probability of the greater evil among one's opponents might not be as evil as the certainty of losing the presidency to *any* other political tendency. Thus the dilemma: The more that coalitions are needed, given ideological cleavages needing to be bridged, the more irrational it may be to form them.[20] The Chilean presidential election of 1964, placed in the context of the preceding and following elections, serves to illustrate this point.

In 1964 the Christian Democratic candidate, Eduardo Frei, received the support of the Conservative and Liberal parties, which did not present candidates of their own. While the Radicals ran their own candidate, he endorsed Frei prior to the election, as all nonsocialists coalesced to block Salvador Allende, the candidate of a leftist coalition. Thus voters were presented with a clear choice, socialism or no, conforming once again to the archetype of efficiency in the selection of the executive. However, the costs were apparent in the aftermath. The winner of the election himself represented an ideological option, and, having had a majority election, Frei interpreted his victory as a mandate for Christian Democracy. In an event unprecedented for any party in Chile, the Christian Democrats won a

---

20 For reasons developed in Appendix A, this dilemma may be especially acute under three-bloc competition, as in Chile.

majority of seats in a congressional election held shortly after Frei's inauguration. Frei and his party then pursued a *partido único* (single party) strategy, shunning the traditional multipartisan logrolling that had long been the system's "glue." Each step in reducing the role of logrolling and increasing the powers of the executive raised the stakes of elections, both presidential (to determine who would have these prerogatives) and congressional (to determine whether the congress would be disposed to exercise even its increasingly feeble checks on the president).

The coalition's formation in 1964, while demonstrating the costs of turning over the head of a coalition to a single representative, especially an ideological one, was a response to the perceived dangers of not forming such a coalition in the presence of ideological polarization. In 1958, Arturo Alessandri won the presidency narrowly against Allende. At 31.6%, this was the smallest plurality ever in Chile's presidential elections. Allende received 28.9%. Thus the inability of the parties to forge a common front on either the left or the right resulted in a narrowly endorsed executive. Alessandri's presidency was less risky to the established system than either of the next two, which represented ideological alternatives to the traditional politics. Indeed, the "nightmare" that the traditional parties and the Christian Democrats were lucky to escape in 1958 and coalesced to avert in 1964, became reality in 1970, when a socialist executive was elected with 36.6% of the vote in a three-way race.

## Efficiency and the rationality of conflict

What had happened to the Chilean archetype as the reforms took effect, concurrent with the emergence of new ideological forces (most particularly the Christian Democrats, but also extremism on the left)? From the standpoint of parties as well as of individual legislators, it now became rational to dispute elections to congress on the basis of support or opposition to the national goals being articulated in the presidential coalition. For parties it was rational because the ability of party blocs in congress to exact concessions through legislative logrolling was being diminished. The goals at the level of locally conducted congressional elections instead would have to be to facilitate or stymie the president's ability to enact his own goals.

For individual legislators, it was now rational to stress national-level and ideological conflicts to a greater extent than before simply because there was little else to offer in exchange for votes. With the constitutional reforms cutting congressional involvement in budgetary trade-offs and the ability to engage in locally targeted spending, the payoff for stressing particularistic concerns in elections was likewise diminished. The nationalization of politics was occurring apace in the 1960s and 1970s, and with it electoral efficiency was increasing. Indeed, in the 1973 midterm elections for congress, which preceded the coup by only three months, for the first time all of the parties coalesced into two blocs supporting and opposing the presidential coalition. Thus a congressional election, as presidential elections had been earlier, became a great national vote on two general visions of the direction for Chilean society.

Chile might have been experiencing an incipient two-bloc party system replacing what had long been a party system divided into three "camps." Each party maintained its separate ballot identity even in 1973, so we can not speak of a two-*party* system, but the parties presented themselves in two broad and sharply opposed coalitions: for socialism or for capitalism. Thus, for the first time in modern Chilean history, a congressional election had provided as efficient a choice as an ideal presidential election. Indeed, the 1973 congressional election fits the ideal of efficiency better than had the presidential election in which Allende became president. Allende had been endorsed by only 36% of the electorate, while his supporters received 44% in 1973 in what was essentially a two-way race (the main opposition received 52%).

To be truly efficient, the 1973 election would have to have been capable of reorienting national policy. Alas, with a president opposed to the congressional majority, holding vastly superior legislative powers, and with three years remaining in his term, the midterm election could only intensify polarization and stalemate. What Chile needed in 1973, given that Allende would remain the constitutional president whatever happened in the elections, was not a great national "referendum" on two competing sociopolitical visions. That would await the 1976 presidential election. What Chile needed was an institutional way to resolve a deadlock that had reached insurmountable proportions. Lacking an effective arena of compromise or a constitutional "exit" from the crisis, the formerly stable but now chronically polarized Chilean democracy was destroyed by a military intervention (to which the Christian Democrats lent initial support) and ensuing dictatorship. Thus were prevented any further referenda on policy direction for more than fifteen years.

The Chilean experience suggests some conclusions about presidential systems, each of which will be elaborated on in subsequent chapters. First, the Chilean system was archetypal only in the sense that the logic of separation of powers suggests entirely separate constituencies for the two branches. Second, multiparty presidentialism is likely to encounter difficulties if the basis of these parties is ideological rather than localistic and if the presidency is very powerful. After the electoral reform of 1958, localistic interests were undercut. Chile's nonsynchronized terms further compounded the strains on the regime, as they meant that some presidents (e.g., Frei) had the opportunity to increase their bloc's share of the seats. At other times (e.g., Allende in 1973) the president's coalition could suffer a rather decisive defeat, yet the president remained in office. Then, with a powerful president in full control of the executive, there is a serious risk of deadlock.

As already suggested, the more promising way to bring about efficiency instead of the way that was attempted in Chile is to weaken the legislative powers of the presidency while making parties more nationally focused. The Chilean Christian Democrats, along with the conservative parties, could have sought such a reform when the deadlock of the Allende years reached crisis proportions. After all, this was the coalition – and, until 1973, the congress emanating from the same election – that had passed the 1970 reform enhancing presidential powers.[21] Instead, these parties preferred a military coup, which they expected would right the ship and return power to them (Valenzuela 1978). It may be hoped that after the experience of dictatorship in countries such as Brazil, Chile, and the Philippines, future attempts to address inefficiencies or deadlock will take the approach of constitutional reform to weaken presidents' powers over legislation (as well as to strengthen parties), rather than regime breakdown.

CONCLUSIONS: INTERACTION OF THE
LEGISLATIVE POWERS AND THE METHODS OF
ELECTING THE TWO BRANCHES

The contrast of the Chilean and Venezuelan systems, on which we have based much of this chapter's discussion, suggests that the methods of electing the congress – the electoral system itself, as well as the relative timing of elections to the two branches – are important to whether or not the branches are consistent in their outlook. While consistency in outlook implies a violation of the presidential archetype, an important dilemma of presidential democracy presents itself: How can we ensure either that there is harmony between the branches or else that, when the branches differ, there are institutional mechanisms for reaching compromise in order to avert interbranch crises? If the presidency and congress are controlled by different parties or blocs, how can the efficiency of presidential elections be maintained without giving the president such powers as to render the congress ineffective as a legislature? Such are the choices of constitutional design for presidential systems.

The Venezuelan system at first seems to suggest one answer to this question: Endow the congress with a national focus by making party and national (rather than local) policy the basis of its own election. The purest way to do this would be to make the congress, like the president, elected

21 It is, of course, also the congress that selected Allende instead of the traditional conservative (and ex-president) Alessandri, since the popular vote was not decisive. Because the Christian Democrats, whose candidate placed third, and the right had been engaged for years by 1970 in a battle for hegemony over the nonsocialist portion of the electorate, the Christian Democrats ironically considered a rightist presidency as worse for their political interests than the alternative of a socialist executive to which they could – and did – lead the principal congressional and electoral opposition.

from a single, nationwide, constituency. No presidential system has ever gone to this extreme,[22] but one, Nicaragua in 1984, has done the functional equivalent, using districts but allocating seats left over after district allocation on a nationwide basis (Taagepera and Shugart 1989).[23]

A presidential system in which the congress would be elected from one national constituency is far from the inefficient secret of the Chilean case at mid-century. It also would violate much of what Madison saw as the advantage of the separation of powers – the encouragement of checks on one branch by the other by having different branches respond to different constituencies. The same can be said for the Venezuelan and other similar systems, in which, as a result of the party lists and concurrence of presidential and congressional elections, the parties that provide the principal competition in congressional elections are primarily vehicles for expressing the coattails of the presidential candidates.

Denying the president constitutionally granted legislative powers, as in Venezuela, obviates much of the advantage of presidentialism, as originally intended. In such a system the policy options endorsed in congressional elections are sure to be translated into policy output. Of course, if president and congress are of different political makeup, presidential elections are then rendered inefficient, because the one office that is responsible to the whole nation is unable to implement or credibly bargain on behalf of a policy program. In Venezuela, efficiency has prevailed only because the electoral system (party lists) and the concurrence of elections have generally meant that the president's party has also been the largest party in congress. Still, the greater success of Venezuela (and Costa Rica) relative to Brazil, Chile, and Colombia, suggests the following combination of institutional features may be most conducive to effective presidentialism:

- A president elected by plurality, having limited legislative powers. (We suggest a veto that requires more than a simple majority to override.)
- A party-list electoral system (but not with such tremendous control by leadership over elections as that of Venezuela through 1988).
- Concurrent elections, or, at least, synchronized terms such that there are no midterm elections as there were in Chile.

We elaborate on these themes in the next chapters, considering especially variations on the method of presidential election and going into much greater depth on the subject of the consequences of different electoral cycles.

22 At least two Latin American presidential systems, Ecuador and Guatemala, use a rather halfhearted way of providing some members of the congress with a nationwide constituency by allowing voters to cast both a ballot for district representative and one for the national district, with seats in local and national districts allocated separately.

23 In Nicaragua, the congress was so elected in 1984 concurrently with the president, but this electoral system was changed before the 1990 election. Namibia uses a nationwide PR allocation and concurrent elections but it is a president-parliamentary regime.

# 10

# Electoral rules and the party system

In Chapter 9, we noted that Chile for many years combined a multiparty congress and, ordinarily, two-candidate competition for the presidency. In this chapter we generalize this observation with analysis of electoral rules. Students of electoral systems have long noted that plurality elections in one-seat districts tend to polarize electoral choices around two principal contestants, while systems of proportional representation are generally associated with multiparty systems. This chapter considers the implications of different electoral rules for party systems in presidential democracies. We have indicated already (in Chapter 2) that presidentialism does not by definition require that there be only a one-seat executive; however, the prevailing practice is to use districts of magnitude one ($M=1$) for the presidency. A district of $M=1$ requires that the electoral system be some form of plurality or majority. Empirically plurality rule is more common, although majority runoff systems have been widely adopted among newer democracies since around 1980 in Latin America, and 1989 in Europe and Africa.

As indicated in Chapter 9, systems of proportional representation, in which the district magnitude must by definition be greater than one ($M > 1$), are typical for assemblies even in presidential and premier-presidential systems. Before presenting empirical data on the effects of these electoral systems, we should review the most widely discussed statement on this matter, known as "Duverger's law" or "Duverger's rule."

## DUVERGER'S RULE AND THE NUMBER OF PARTIES

When Riker (1982b) wanted to demonstrate that political science had a history of cumulation of knowledge like the "hard" sciences, he turned to the set of reformulations known as Duverger's law. Although Riker identified formulations prior to Duverger's own, it is Duverger (1951, 1954) who normally gets the credit for having made questions about the influence of electoral rules on party systems a major concern of political science. Through repeated reformulations, a pair of propositions known as Duverger's law and Duverger's hypothesis and collectively referred to herein as *Duverger's rule,* have emerged. We shall briefly trace the origin of these propositions, which may be stated thus:

1. One-seat districts with plurality rule tend to reduce the number of parties to two (*law*); and
2. multi-seat districts with proportional representation tend to be associated with more than two parties (*hypothesis*).

The wording here is close to that employed in two recent discussions of the Duverger effects, Taagepera and Grofman (1985) and Taagepara and Shugart (1989).[1] Recently Duverger has emphasized that he never meant to imply that proportional electoral systems inevitably *produce* multiparty systems, but he still indicates that there is a "multiplying effect" of PR that manifests itself mainly in a proliferation of very small parties. National and social factors are more important, he says; electoral rules act "usually only as an accelerator or a brake" (Duverger 1986:73). This less forceful (perhaps even too weak) wording of the "multiplying" effects of PR, as opposed to the reductive effects of one-seat plurality, is what for Riker justified the use of the term Duverger's *hypothesis,* as distinct from the law.

The usual understanding of Duverger's rule has suffered from a narrowness of scope in the sense that studies of electoral systems have tended to assume implicitly that the only institutions that mattered were electoral rules for assemblies, taken in isolation from other institutions. Such isolation of the assembly from the process of executive formation may distort our understanding of the number of parties even in parliamentary systems; it especially is certain to do so in the case of presidential systems. Particularly when presidential and congressional elections are held at the same time, the presidential election imposes a single-seat nationwide district over the assembly districts. If the president is elected by plurality, the presidential election falls under Duverger's law, which suggests a reduction in the number of parties to two. The congressional election, if it is held in multi-seat districts using proportional representation (PR), suggests the possibility of a multiparty system, according to Duverger's hypothesis. As we shall see, the outcome may go either way, depending to a considerable degree on the relative timing of congressional elections with respect to presidential elections. Thus this chapter and the next one develop the notion that two variables are critical in shaping the nature of the party system: *electoral rules* (particularly district magnitude) and *electoral cycles.*

District magnitude is the decisive feature in electoral rules (Rae 1967; Sartori 1968; Taagepera and Shugart 1989). District magnitude, $M$, has

1 The two sources just cited add a clause to the hypothesis suggesting that the correlation of multipartism with $M > 1$ is conditioned on there being political issues sufficiently numerous to provide a basis for such parties. We no longer see this qualifier as necessary, as the "exceptions" no longer seem so exceptional. For example, Austria's party system has been dominated by two parties despite PR; yet Austria's effective magnitude before 1970 was very low. Thus, while one might have expected around three parties instead of almost exactly two, a low number of parties despite PR should not be seen as deviant when $M$ is very low. Since 1970, when effective $M$ was significantly increased (Taagepera and Shugart 1989), the dominance of the two big parties has been weakening, making Austria fairly consistent with Duverger's hypothesis.

been recognized at least since Hogan (1945) as the most important factor in proportionality. Since *dis*proportionality is what Duverger hypothesized to be the factor that would induce underrepresented parties to go out of business, the number of parties in a district must bear some relation to district magnitude.[2]

More recent quantitative analysis has looked at the relation between the number of parties and the number of seats across the whole range of observed district magnitudes. Taagepera and Shugart (1989) have done this using mainly nationwide data, while Shugart (1988) and Taagepera and Shugart (1992a, b) analyzed district-level data both within and across nations.

The other principal variable that we shall explore is the electoral cycle, simply meaning the timing of elections to the two branches, executive and assembly, in relation to one another. In some systems we find that all members of the assembly are elected at the same time as the president, that is, concurrently. Other systems employ terms of different length for the two branches and do not let election dates for president and congress coincide. We simply call such an electoral cycle nonconcurrent.

Do these and other institutional features of presidential and premier-presidential democracy make a difference? How do their effects compare with results of parliamentary democracies? Since one of our primary concerns in analyzing representative democracies is with the degree of representativeness, which in turn may be expected to be fairly closely related to the number of parties, we begin in this chapter with a survey of the relation between different institutional designs and the "effective" number of parties. We then proceed to a more systematic examination of data on the assembly party system that conforms to various electoral cycles. Chapter 11 then will seek to develop models of the number of parties in presidential systems, drawing upon earlier studies that concerned themselves principally with parliamentary systems.

### METHOD OF PRESIDENTIAL ELECTION

The first matter of institutional choice with which we concern ourselves is how to elect the president. One basic breakdown, mentioned already in Chapter 1, is between those systems in which there is an electoral college and those in which the voters vote directly for presidential candidates.

2 This means not that the particular type of allocation formula (such as simple quota or any of the various "highest average" formulas) does not matter, but that the relative emphasis on allocation formula versus district magnitude has all too often been reversed. Especially among reformers and designers of electoral systems, allocation rules have often attracted far more attention than they deserve, given their more limited impact on proportionality and the number of parties, compared to district magnitude. With $M = 1$, as we shall see, the precise electoral rule (plurality versus majority, for example) does indeed make an appreciable difference. In general, formula matters more with low $M$, less as $M$ increases.

However, in the modern era there is a more important distinction: between those direct elections that are by plurality and those that are by majority runoff, plus those in which the popular vote is not necessarily decisive. As we shall see, electoral methods in the latter category may function as if they were plurality, unless partisan (as opposed to presidential-candidate) voting is the primary criterion.

### Plurality rule

In several presidential systems the president is elected by plurality, in which the winner is simply the candidate with the most votes (sometimes referred to as the relative majority). Among the countries in which plurality is used to elect the president are the Dominican Republic, Nicaragua, the Philippines, and Venezuela. The average share of votes for the winner in straightforward plurality elections is 49.7%, and for the runner-up it is 34.9%, as seen in Table 10.1. Thus plurality elections have a tendency toward building two large blocs that together encompass around 85% of the vote, on average. Such a finding is consistent with Duverger's law. The following two features must then be taken as characteristic of plurality presidential elections:

1. the tendency for the formation of a broad coalition behind the front-runner;
2. the tendency to coalesce the opposition behind one principal challenger.

In Costa Rica, the constitution prescribes a runoff in the event that no candidate obtains 40% of the popular vote. We shall, however, consider this system to be effectively plurality, for two reasons. First, no runoff has ever been required. Second, the incentive to build a coalition large enough to surpass 40% is not so different from the incentive to build a coalition that is simply the largest, as in straight plurality, for reasons developed below. That this is so may be seen in Table 10.1, in which the shares of the vote for the first and second candidates are displayed for several presidential election formats. We shall have more to say about this 40% rule and its implications later on.

In Costa Rica the results look like pure plurality, or perhaps even stronger on the two tendencies of plurality just mentioned. The median vote share in Costa Rica is actually 50.3%, while that of the runner-up is itself more than 40%. As discussed in Appendix A, the 40% provision may be seen as a threshold that must be attained for a first-round victory. Pure plurality sets no threshold, meaning victory to the largest vote-winner, regardless of the actual percentage obtained. As the threshold is raised, so are the costs of failing to coalesce, unless the threshold is raised so high as to encourage many "spoiler" candidacies in order to influence the runoff. As we shall see next, the 50% threshold – the majority runoff system – is an example of a threshold too high to induce coalescence in most cases.

*Majority rule*

Most of the remaining presidential and premier-presidential systems use majority elections in two rounds; if no candidate receives a majority of votes (in some systems, a majority of all votes cast, including null or blank ballots), a second round is held to determine the winner.[3] Table 10.1 shows that the average share of votes for the candidate placing first in the preliminary round is 39.5%, about 10% lower than for plurality systems, including the Costa Rican variant. The second-place candidate, on average, falls considerably farther behind the first finisher (in the first round), with only 25.1%. More than 35% of the vote, on average, is divided among other candidates. Thus majority runoff can actually *discourage* coalescence of the opposing forces, even though only a single seat is at stake. These forces instead run separately with the intention of either (1) placing second in order to make the runoff themselves and thus attract the support of others who failed, or (2) enhancing their own bargaining position with one of the two candidates in the runoff, perhaps exchanging support for policy or office concessions. With the lower threshold, either the same leading candidate who, on average, receives just under 40%, or else another candidate, would be likely to win in the first round. The more attainable 40% threshold, for example, would ordinarily give supporters of potential minor candidates the incentive to join with a larger coalition rather than seek to influence an expected runoff.

*Nondecisive popular vote*

Some other systems, including those of Chile (before 1973), Argentina, and the United States, function much like plurality in their encouragement of large coalitions. However, each of these systems uses a different method in which the popular vote is mediated through an electoral college or the congress, at least in the absence of a decisive majority of the popular vote. We also shall see that one case, Finland, has an electoral college that is elected on a partisan basis rather than on a candidate basis. In that system, much as in the Bolivian case discussed in Chapter 4, we do not see coalescence behind two front-runners.

*Congressional ratification.* In the system of presidential election in Chile before 1973, as discussed in Chapter 5, the congress chose the president in the event that no candidate received a majority of popular votes. However,

---

3 There are two exceptions to this rule. The presidents of Sri Lanka and Ireland are elected by a method in which voters may rank the candidates on the ballot. If there is no majority of first preferences, second (and, if necessary, later) preferences are added, until a candidate obtains a majority of votes. The rule is usually called the "alternative vote" and is identical to the single transferable vote in one-seat districts.

Table 10.1. Median percentage of votes for two highest-finishing candidates in presidential elections, according to different electoral methods (first round in case of majority system)

| Country and time period* | Number of elections | % votes 1st | % votes 2nd |
|---|---|---|---|
| **Pure plurality** | | | |
| Brazil (1945-60) | 4 | 48.5 | 31.6 |
| Colombia (1930, 1942-46, 1974-90) | 8 | 47.4 | 34.2 |
| Dominican Republic (1962, 1982, 1990) | 3 | 46.5 | 33.9 |
| Nicaragua (1990) | 1 | 54.7 | 40.8 |
| Philippines (1946-69) | 7 | 55.0 | 39.5 |
| Venezuela (1958-88) | 7 | 49.2 | 34.6 |
| Mean of all plurality elections | 30 | 49.7 | 34.9 |
| **Effective plurality** | | | |
| Runoff if less than 40% plurality | | | |
| Costa Rica (1953-86) | 9 | 50.3 | 41.2 |
| **Majority (two rounds)** | | | |
| Brazil (1989) | 1 | 31.5 | 17.7 |
| Chile (1989) | 1 | 51.5 | 26.1 |
| Ecuador (1978-88) | 3 | 28.7 | 23.9 |
| France (1965-88) | 5 | 36.1 | 29.4 |
| Peru (1980-90) | 3 | 45.4 | 24.7 |
| Poland (1990) | 1 | 40.0 | 23.1 |
| Portugal (1976-86) | 3 | 56.4 | 25.4 |
| Mean of all majority elections | 17 | 39.5 | 25.1 |
| **Nondecisive popular vote** | | | |
| Congressional selection if no popular majority | | | |
| Chile (1931-70) | 9 | 50.5 | 34.8 |
| Electoral College | | | |
| Argentina (1983, 1989) | 2 | 50.6 | 36.9 |
| United States (1824-1988) | 42 | 51.6 | 43.3 |

* Excluded are elections that were boycotted by a potentially significant political force and those for which presidential and assembly votes were fused (straight-ticket).

in most elections, coalitions had been successfully structured before the election such that one candidate received a majority or very close to it. When congress entered the selection process, it was constitutionally bound to make its choice from among the top two contenders. The median shares of those two candidates were 50.5% and 34.8% (Table 10.1), hardly different from the pure plurality cases.

*Electoral college.* In two presidential systems there is an electoral college that functions more or less like plurality: Argentina and the United States. These institutions were expressly designed to be nondeliberative – indeed, the U.S. electoral college does not actually even meet as a body. In the United States if there is no candidate obtaining a majority of electors at the first count, the decision goes to the House of Representatives. If this were the usual occurrence, the United States might be institutionally similar to either Bolivia or Chile, except that the U.S. House votes for president on the basis of one vote for each state's delegation. However, the allocation of electors by plurality rule in each state (and therefore in multi-seat districts, which with list plurality are especially favorable to bigness), and the emergence of political parties as vehicles for electing presidents has meant that the United States has functioned effectively as plurality throughout nearly all of its history, encouraging broad coalitions that, on average, have garnered 51.6% for the front-runner and 43.3% for the runner-up.[4] In Argentina, similarly, if there is no majority of the popular vote, the decision rests with an electoral college that is chosen concurrently with the presidential race and represents the states of the Argentine federation. There, too, winning candidates have thus far won majorities of the popular vote.

*The Finnish case.* The Finnish case demonstrates that an electoral college can be designed in such a way as to make presidential elections more closely resemble the assembly selection method of systems like Bolivia's rather than popular presidential elections. Finland, a premier-presidential system, had not used truly popular elections for president until 1988. Instead, voters voted for parties (or more precisely, for one candidate within a party list) by a means similar to that used to elect the parliament. This system gave priority to parties. Besides having an electoral system based on parties, the Finnish electoral college differs from those of the United States and Argentina in that it is deliberative, taking multiple ballots when there is no majority on the first count. Additionally, before 1988, electors and parties did not necessarily pledge themselves to a particular presidential

---

4 There are some potential problems with the U.S. electoral college that could diminish its plurality character. The best known is the possibility that the electoral college might reverse the plurality verdict of the popular vote. However, the cause of this, which has happened only twice, lies in the state-by-state nature of the counting of electoral pluralities. Taking pluralities on this basis, and weighting them by states' populations, is hardly inconsistent with U.S. federalism and thus does not contradict the plurality character of the overall system. Potentially more serious, but within the realm of the theoretical, are the possibilities of sufficient "faithless electors" to overturn the popular vote, the lack of a mandate in federal law for either "faithful" electors or their allocation by plurality rule (it is the choice of the states), and the possibility of victory by unpledged electors in some states in order to force the brokering of an election in the House of Representatives, sitting as a second electoral college in which each state has only one vote. See Stedman (1968) and Peirce and Longley (1981).

candidate; now they must do so (Mackie and Rose 1991:109). The procedure, established in 1925, was a compromise between those who favored parliamentary selection of the president (as in the present-day systems of Greece and Israel) and those who favored a direct, popular election. Given its party-centered character, it was not much different from election in parliament; presidential candidates ordinarily did not even tour the country and campaign, according to Markku Suksi (personal communication). Even so, the restriction of the body chosen in these elections to the sole function of selecting a president did encourage electoral outcomes that differed somewhat from the normal pattern in Finnish parliamentary elections. Parties could still perform better if identified with a popular candidate, in order to be in a position to "deliver" a sizable share of votes to the eventual winner. This process of a party's being electorally rewarded for having a popular candidate may be demonstrated by the last election under this format, that of 1982. In that election, the Social Democrats received 43% of the vote when Mauno Koivisto was their candidate, even though this party's share of the vote in parliamentary elections has normally been less than 30%.

In 1988, there was a modification of the Finnish system. In that election voters cast a vote directly for a presidential candidate in addition to the party vote. The law provides that if no candidate receives a majority of personal votes, the electoral college will make the decision. In 1988, Koivisto received 47.9% of the personal votes, even though his Social Democratic party received only 39.3% in the concurrent contest for electors. (Three other parties endorsing Koivisto combined for 7.3%.) The electoral college ratified the electorate's plurality choice. With this new personal vote, Koivisto thus ran ahead of his own party in the concurrent party vote and even farther ahead of the party's showing in the previous parliamentary elections (24.1% in 1987). Thus the election took on one basic characteristic of plurality: the formation of a broad following behind a candidate in order to ensure a first place finish, although the opposition remained fragmented, resembling more the field of majority runoff systems.

## Which method to use?

We find the plurality rule appealing because it is more likely than majority runoff to give voters an efficient choice between the candidates of two broad coalitions. That this is so is supported by the data in Table 10.1. Majority elections, on the other hand, may discourage long-term consolidation of a party system. They may even encourage fragmentation. The appeal of majority runoff to recent constitution designers has been enhanced by its results in France, where a fragmented and multidimensional party system under the Fourth Republic rather quickly was transformed into stable two-bloc (left–right) competition after the initiation of presidential elections by majority runoff in 1965 under the Fifth Republic. Let us consider the experience of France and whether or not it might be generalizable.

*Two-bloc competition in France.* One should be careful about generalizing from the French experience. In France the two-bloc format of the party system has been aided by the use of majority runoff not only in presidential elections but also in elections for the assembly (except in 1986). Additionally, it has been aided by premier-presidentialism. Neither factor is present in many systems elsewhere, especially in Latin America, where majority runoff has recently been adopted for presidential elections.

The use of the majority runoff for French assembly as well as presidential elections aided the development of the two-bloc system because it allowed parties to make cross-district deals between rounds. Parties have been encouraged to withdraw candidates from some districts and support the candidates of other parties in exchange for reciprocal deals in other districts. Obviously this king of bargaining is not feasible where only one seat is at stake in the election, as with a presidential race. In many other cases, proportional representation is used for assembly elections, eliminating the French incentive for alliance formation.

The two-bloc system in France has been further aided by premier-presidentialism. Since the cabinet in France is dependent on the confidence of a majority of the assembly and not on the president, alliances are important in order to sustain a government or a credible governing alternative. Where the cabinet serves at the pleasure of the president and cannot be removed and reconstituted by the parliamentary majority through a vote of no-confidence, parties contesting congressional seats are not compelled to offer a formula for putting together an executive.

For these reasons, the majority runoff presidential electoral rule alone should not be viewed as being conducive to stable two-bloc competition. We shall leave aside the question of whether presidential systems in Latin America and elsewhere should adopt majority runoff for their assemblies as well as for president in an effort to institutionalize a two-bloc party system. One wonders whether party leaders in those systems would be willing to sustain the substantial deviations from proportionality that the system has entailed in France.[5] We wish to caution that *both* majority runoff assembly elections and premier-presidentialism have been crucial to the pattern of competition in France.

*Proliferation of candidates under majority runoff.* Peru is an example of a party system in which the use of majority runoff for presidential elections may be blamed for a proliferation of candidates. What had been a two-bloc

5 One of the newer systems in the Americas has adopted majority runoff for assembly as well as for president, albeit a constitutionally powerless president: Haiti.

party system before military intervention in 1968[6] led to two consecutive presidential elections in the 1980s that were won by first-round majorities of valid votes cast. However, by 1990 the majority runoff rules encouraged two "outsiders" to enter the first round as challengers to the established party system. With a decisive plurality election, such proliferation would have been far less likely. An "outsider" like Alberto Fujimori, the eventual winner, could not have appeared as a viable candidate under plurality rule. Fujimori's strategy centered around scoring an upset *second-place* finish in the first round in order to appear as a second-round alternative to the acknowledged front-runner, Mario Vargas Llosa, also an "outsider" to the established party system (albeit one who, unlike Fujimori, had forged a pact before the first round with some of the established parties).[7]

A similar first-round story may be told about the 1990 presidential election in Poland. A virtual unknown, Stanislaw Tyminski, finished a surprising second, with 23.1%, to Lech Walesa's 40.0%. As with Fujimori, Tyminski's strategy for winning centered around scoring an upset second place in the first round and then combining the anti-Walesa vote in order to win in the second round. Walesa, however, won an overwhelming victory in the runoff. With a plurality election, it is nearly inconceivable that Tyminski could have been anything but a fringe also-ran, while Walesa would likely have won with a bare majority (or perhaps slightly less than an absolute majority) instead of the large "mandate" he could claim on the basis of the second round.

*Majority runoff and efficiency.* If we desire presidential elections for their ability to allow voters to identify the most likely governing options being presented to them in the initial round and make an efficient choice, then majority runoff rules are less desirable than plurality rule. The basic weakness of the majority format is that its outcome depends on first-round contingencies. The principal contingency is the number of candidates encouraged to run in the first round by the fact that the first round is not decisive. Many such candidates would not run in the event of a plurality election, or would receive fewer votes if they did. The formation of a

6 The electoral system for president under the 1933 constitution was that the popular vote would be decisive if the leading candidate won at least one third of the vote. Otherwise the congress, elected concurrently, would choose the president from among the top three contenders.

7 See Cameron (1991) for a discussion of Vargas Llosa's "blackmailing" of his partisan allies by threatening to run his presidential campaign as an independent. The threats to resign from the alliance that Cameron describes would not have been so credible had the presidential election not been a majority runoff system. Because majority runoff opens up the possibility that a candidate finishing second initially can then go on to win, Vargas Llosa was able credibly to point to the possibility that he could win without a preelection coalition with established parties. Indeed, that is precisely how the election was won, but not by Vargas Llosa!

widely endorsed executive, and one with a sizable bloc of congressional supporters, may be compromised if many candidates enter the field in hopes of forcing one of the two who pass to the second round to make a deal in exchange for support.

The distinction between plurality and majority concerns in part the level at which strategic bargaining occurs. Some strategic bargaining is desirable when a single seat is being filled, in order to maximize the ability of voters to identify the alternative potential executives. To maximize their chances of victory, party leaders contesting a plurality presidential election in a multiparty environment must seek to build coalitions *before* the election. In most cases this means that the principal contenders will be two relatively moderate candidates. On the other hand, because majority runoff leaves much of the bargaining among parties to the period between rounds, the efficiency of presidential elections is reduced.

With majority runoff, some candidates will enter primarily to force a second round, as with Fujimori and Tyminski. That is, parties under this electoral method specialize (Schlesinger and Schlesinger 1991). Some seek mainly first-choice votes, while others seek to win as second-choice candidates. If the largest party (or most popular candidate) also is widely disliked, such a candidate may be defeated in a second round by whatever candidate finishes second. The most striking example of this effect was in Portugal in 1986, when Diego Freitas do Amaral won 46.6% to Mario Soares's 25.4% (the next candidate had 20.9%). Despite his wide and nearly decisive first-round margin, Freitas lost the runoff, 51.2% to 48.8%. Thus the outcome of majority runoff elections may frequently hinge upon which candidate is capable of beating out other contenders for the second slot and on whether or not this candidate can form alliances with defeated candidates between rounds. Unless the second-place candidate in a typically divided field can be predicted reliably beforehand, identifiability and efficiency suffer, compared to a plurality race in which parties have the incentive to offer voters broader preelection coalitions.

*A compromise: the double complement rule.* In making a case for plurality, however, we also understand that the results of Table 10.1 show tendencies, not absolutes. It is the occasional president endorsed by less than 40% of the electorate in direct plurality elections that stirs fears in those who have opted recently for majority runoff rules instead of plurality. One such occasion might be a regime's last, as in Chile, although one should not exaggerate the danger; several regimes have survived such presidencies. If one wants to avoid the second stage of an electoral college,[8] the Costa

8 Perhaps because of their inherent risks of reversing the nationwide plurality choice of the electorate, electoral colleges enjoy few favorable mentions nowadays. Other than Argentina, which reestablished its electoral college with the return to democracy in 1983, we know of no new regime in the twentieth century that has adopted such a format since Finland in 1925.

Rican rule looks like a very good compromise. The 40% threshold may be likened to a "safety valve," encouraging broad coalitions, like plurality, but with a built-in mechanism that prevents a winner with very limited endorsement in a multicandidate race.

Given the successful experience in Costa Rica, it is thus surprising that other systems have not incorporated such a rule. The 40% provision is often advocated by those in the United States who wish to abolish the electoral college (Peirce and Longley 1981). Generally, however, the preference in revised electoral procedures – principally in the new democracies of Latin America[9] – has been for a runoff in the event that no candidate obtains more than 50% of the vote. As we saw in Table 10.1, majority formats, while appearing to prevent their designers' fears of narrowly endorsed presidencies like Allende's, actually result in considerably lower average shares in the first round for eventual winners owing to a greater number of initial competitors. In Appendix A we discuss the dynamics of coalition building under plurality and why 40% emerges as a compromise between straight plurality and majority.

The 40% rule does have one potential drawback, however: A winner could still emerge from a very closely fought contest with a questionable mandate, for example, with 45% against a runner-up with 44%. Perhaps there might be a better compromise that is halfway between plurality and majority runoff. The derivation of such a rule is shown briefly here. An extended discussion may be found in Shugart and Taagepera (1992). The condition that defines plurality rule is that the vote share of the leading party ($v_1$) must be greater than the vote share of the second largest party ($v_2$):

$$v_1 > v_2,$$

while the first-round condition that defines majority runoff is:

$$v_1 > 50\%.$$

The arithmetic average of the two conditions is

$$v_1 > (\tfrac{1}{2})v_2 + 25\%.$$

We can rearrange this criterion and express it in terms of each party's difference from majority. We then have a *double complement rule*, which requires the following:

9 The trend toward majority runoff is particularly noticeable among cases of *redemocrati-zation*. In their returns to competitive elections since around 1980, the following countries have adopted majority runoff: Brazil, Chile, Ecuador, El Salvador, Guatemala, and Peru. Most previously used plurality or required congressional confirmation in the event of no electoral majority. In Finland, too, majority runoff rules are under consideration, while most of the new systems with directly elected presidents in East Europe and Africa have similarly opted for majority runoff.

$$50\% - v_2 > 2\,(50\% - v_1).$$

This rule thus stipulates that *the front-runner wins at the first round if the shortfall of the runner-up from a majority of votes is more than double the leading candidate's shortfall from a majority.* If the front-runner does not meet this requirement (or win a first-round majority), then there is a runoff between the top two contenders. We find this rule appealing for its simplicity and its discouragement of fragmentation.[10] We suspect that the double complement rule would be appropriate for most situations, except perhaps for electing a unitary presidency in polities that are characterized by significant ethnic or other ascriptive cleavages. For such societies, one rule that has been attempted, although it is very complex, is the rule of concurrent pluralities used in Nigeria.

*Concurrent pluralities and the problem of plural societies.* There is one final variant of plurality rule that encourages the construction of broad coalitions before a presidential election. A presidency may be filled by a system in which pluralities must be won concurrently in several regions of the country rather than in the country as a whole. The U.S. electoral college is effectively a variant of this form, since to be elected without recourse to the House of Representatives, a candidate must win pluralities in states that amount to a majority of total number of electoral votes. Since the electoral college overrepresents small states compared to a nationwide direct election, the accumulation of pluralities in a series of relatively smaller states is one way to win the presidency.

Another form of concurrent pluralities has been used in Nigeria. The winner must win a nationwide plurality plus at least 25% of the vote in no fewer than two-third of the states, which were themselves drawn mainly along ethnic lines. If no candidate met this requirement, a second election would take place between the one with the overall plurality and the one among the remaining candidates with the most votes in the highest number of states (Nigerian constitution, Article 126). In this way the designers intended to ensure the election as president someone who could win broad appeal across ethnic groups. In this task, according to Horowitz (1990), "they succeeded." The complexities of this rule and the possibility that no candidate would meet its criteria (in which case a new round of voting must begin, with new candidates) leave us skeptical about its viability. Indeed, in his discussion of the desirability of presidentialism for South Africa, Horo-

10 Since the rule is derived as an average of plurality and majority criteria, we might expect the vote shares of the typical two leading candidates also to be averages of the plurality and majority cases: 44.6% and 30.4%. If so, this would suggest that a runoff would be needed about half the time, rather than in nearly all elections, as is the case with majority runoff. Moreover, the figures suggest that if a runoff were needed, ordinarily the two candidates squaring off would be considerably farther ahead of the rest of the field than is often the case under majority runoff.

witz (1991) advocates the Irish and Sri Lankan alternative vote rather than the Nigerian concurrent pluralities. While we sympathize with Horowitz's claim that a presidency, given a proper method of election, can be an appropriate conflict-regulating institution for an ethnically divided society, we are not convinced of the utility of either alternative vote or concurrent pluralities. The alternative vote is not in practice much different from plurality (see Lijphart 1991), while the rule of concurrent pluralities may be unwieldy, whatever its intellectual merits. For these reasons, we prefer for plural societies the two-person or three-person collegial presidency that we proposed in Chapter 5, with the double complement rule being used to determine the winning ticket.

### THE NUMBER OF COMPETITORS

We have seen in Table 10.1 some variation among electoral methods in the vote shares of the two largest presidential contenders. How is the method connected to the number of contenders? Table 10.2 shows the effective number of presidential candidates ($N_p$) by country, grouped according to general categories of plurality and majority, as well as subcategories concerning the rules and timing of assembly elections. The table also shows the effective number of parties in assembly elections ($N_v$). For presidential candidates the dividing line between plurality and majority is clear, but of even more interest for our purposes are the differences within plurality countries.

Among the empirical configurations we find three major categories: (1) those in which the president is elected by plurality and the assembly by proportional representation in multi-seat ($M>1$) districts; (2) those in which the president and congress are both elected by plurality; and (3) those in which the president is elected by majority. Each group may also be further subdivided according to electoral cycle. In the third category, only France uses majority runoff for the assembly as well as for president, while the others use PR.[11] Because both majority runoff and PR are methods associated with multiparty systems (Duverger 1954), this distinction will not concern us. Indeed, of greatest interest are the countries that use both plurality and PR, as these are employing contradictory electoral systems, one that (as confirmed in Table 10.2) is associated with bipartism and one that is associated with multipartism.

*Plurality and PR.* In this first category, the variable that most clearly separates our cases is the electoral cycle. Table 10.2 breaks down these cases by those in which there are concurrent elections and those in which elections are all nonconcurrent.

11 France itself used PR in 1986.

Table 10.2. *Median effective number of presidential candidates* ($N_p$) *and median effective number of parties obtaining votes in congressional elections* ($N_v$), *according to different institutional formats*

| Country | $N_p$ | $N_v$ |
|---|---|---|
| **Regimes using (effective) plurality for president** | | |
| Assembly PR, concurrent | | |
| Argentina | 2.6 | 3.0 |
| midterm | -- | 3.2 |
| Brazil (1945-50) | 2.5 | 3.4* |
| Costa Rica | 2.2 | 2.6 |
| Dominican Republic | 2.7 | 2.9 |
| Nicaragua | 2.2 | 2.2 |
| Venezuela | 2.6 | 3.4 |
| Mean of all (excluding midterm elections) | 2.5 | 3.1 |
| | | |
| Assembly PR, all nonconcurrent | | |
| Brazil (1955-62) | 2.7 | 4.5* |
| Chile (1933-73) | 2.7 | 6.9 |
| Colombia | 2.7 | 2.1 |
| Mean of all | 2.7 | 5.0 |
| | | |
| Assembly plurality, concurrent | | |
| Philippines | 2.0 | 2.1 |
| United States | 2.1 | 2.1 |
| **Regimes using majority for president** | | |
| Assembly concurrent with first round | | |
| Chile (1989) | 2.6 | 2.6 |
| Ecuador | 5.0 | 7.4 |
| midterm | -- | 10.8 |
| Peru | 3.4 | 3.4 |
| Mean of all (excluding midterm elections) | 4.1 | 5.8 |
| | | |
| Assembly nonconcurrent | | |
| Brazil (1989-90) | 5.3 | 8.7* |
| France | 4.0 | 4.8 |
| Portugal | 2.3 | 4.0 |
| Mean of all | 3.5 | 4.3 |

*Seat-winning parties; figures for votes (which would be higher) were unobtainable.

When PR congressional elections are *concurrent* with the plurality presidential election, average $N_p = 2.5$, while average $N_v = 3.1$. The typical assembly party system for these cases has two parties sharing at least 75% of the vote, with the third largest party having about 5% to 10%. The range of national values for $N_v$ is 2.2 to 3.4. Not surprisingly, when we consider the effects of magnitude, *M*, this range is considerably greater than that seen for $N_p$, for which $M$ is always 1. Venezuela has the highest $N_v$[12] and is also the case with the highest effective $M$, owing to a provision that makes representation for very small parties quite easy. A party needs only about 0.55% of the nationwide votes, regardless of whether or not it wins any district-level seats (Taagepera and Shugart 1989:269; Shugart 1992a).[13]

The one case that uses midterm in addition to concurrent elections, Argentina, does not differ in any observable way from the others, in which only concurrent elections are used for the congress. Apparently, despite the holding of some elections at a different time, the holding of others along with the presidential is sufficient to induce the maintenance of the two-party dominance. However, this remains a new regime, and the number of parties has been showing a tendency to grow throughout the period (from 2.6 in 1983 to 3.4 in 1989), raising the possibility that the existence of two midterm elections for every concurrent one could enhance the prospects for smaller parties.

When elections are *nonconcurrent,* average $N_p = 2.7$ and average $N_v = 5.0$. For Brazil (before 1964) and Chile (before 1973), the gap between $N_p$ and $N_v$ is enormous, as the holding of congressional elections apart from presidential elections encouraged parties to run independently of presidents' parties. As noted in Chapter 9 in our discussion of archetypal presidentialism, the nonconcurrent format allows party systems for the two branches that are almost entirely different from one another.

Brazil changed its electoral cycle during the democratic regime that existed between 1945 and 1964. The first two elections, 1945 and 1950, were concurrent presidential-congressional elections. Thereafter, elections to the two branches ran nonconcurrently. In both periods, Brazil conforms to the norm for the appropriate category. In 1945 especially, the two candidates and their parties dominated the field. In 1950, the fragmentation of the party system that we have discussed began to assert itself. Perhaps

---

12 However, the value of $N_v$ is deceptively high. Besides including two unusually fragmented elections (1963 and 1968, which were addressed in Chapter 9), it also fails to indicate the degree to which two parties have dominated since 1973, as numerous very small parties push up the value of $N$. Consider this tabulation of vote shares for Acción Democrática (AD), the Christian Democratic COPEI, and the socialist MAS in Venezuela, 1973–88:

| | 1973 Pres. | 1973 Cong. | 1978 Pres. | 1978 Cong. | 1983 Pres. | 1983 Cong. | 1988 Pres. | 1988 Cong. |
|---|---|---|---|---|---|---|---|---|
| AD | 48.6 | 44.4 | 43.4 | 38.5 | 55.3 | 50.0 | 52.9 | 43.3 |
| COPEI | 35.2 | 30.2 | 45.3 | 38.6 | 32.6 | 28.7 | 40.4 | 31.1 |
| MAS | 3.7 | 5.3 | 4.7 | 6.0 | 3.4 | 5.7 | 2.7 | 10.2 |
| $N_v$ | | 3.4 | | 3.1 | | 3.0 | | 3.4 |

13 Taagepera and Shugart (1989:269) estimate Venezuela's effective magnitude to be 27, which is simply the geometric average of the extreme values: $M = 90$ for the very small parties, owing to the low threshold, and $M = 8$ on average in the districts where typically only the three largest parties win seats. The other PR systems in Table 10.2 are all in the range of 7 to 10, lacking the complicated minority-party provisions of Venezuela.

because this was desirable to the locally based politicians, they subsequently moved their congressional elections to different dates from the presidential and the fragmentation of the congressional party system increased substantially. At the presidential level, however, only in the 1955 election did the front-runner fail to draw as much as 48%, while the median shares for all presidential elections in this period are typical for plurality elections more generally, as we see in both Table 10.1 and Table 10.2.

Colombia is the only case for which, counterintuitively, $N_p > N_v$. This is explicable by the unusual electoral system used in Colombia, where factions of parties or individual candidates can present their own lists without necessarily having been endorsed by the party leadership and with no pooling of votes among lists (see Shugart 1992a). One or both of Colombia's parties have frequently presented more than one presidential candidate each in certain elections, thus $N_p$ is significantly greater than 2.0. In congressional elections, on the other hand, the same factions and more are counted with Liberals or Conservatives, hence low $N_v$. If we used factions rather than parties as the units of analysis, assembly $N$ for Colombia would be in the same range as for Brazil, or quite possibly higher.

These findings confirm empirically what was sketched out in Chapter 9, that holding congressional elections on their own terms allows such elections to represent diversity that is bound to be subsumed under broader coalitions – for assembly as well as president – when the elections are at the same time. More empirical data as well as theoretical justification for the observed patterns will be presented in Chapter 11.

*Plurality for both branches.* We have two cases in which both president and congress are elected by plurality in one-seat districts. In both the Philippines and the United States, the values of assembly $N$ are lower than in any of the cases using PR for their assemblies. Indeed, in the United States, at both presidential and congressional levels, $N = 2.1$, while for the Philippines the figures are $N_p = 2.0$ and $N_v = 2.1$. These two cases are thus the purest two-party systems that we observe. Over time these two countries have had practically no important third parties or presidential candidates, so high are the barriers that plurality rule imposes to minor parties. At least where PR is used, a third party can hope to win some seats on its own; such a party may then also run its own presidential candidate, thus raising $N_p$ as well as $N_v$.

The reason for the virtual absence of third parties stems from more than the simple barriers imposed by $M = 1$ and plurality, however. After all, regionally based third parties could compete for (and win) seats in some districts. The two-party configuration stems as well from an electoral system that facilitates members' cultivation of ties with local constituents rather than dependence on party (Cain et al., 1987), as would be the case if list PR were used or if the system were parliamentary. Because there is no vote of confidence in a presidential system, parties do not need to control who is elected under the party label. Because there is also no party list, given one-seat districts, parties can afford to accommodate some diversity that in either a parliamentary system or a party-list electoral system would be expressed by multiple parties (cf. Epstein 1967).

Presidentialism and concurrent $M = 1$ elections allow congressional candidates to enjoy two advantages simultaneously: identification with a national presidential candidate, and the freedom to pursue local particularism. Such parties should, obviously, be very diffuse and internally diverse, as well as involved to a great degree in the provision of constituent services. Such a characterization clearly fits the parties of both the United States and the Philippines.[14]

*Majority systems.* When the president is elected by majority runoff, there is not much obvious difference between concurrent and nonconcurrent electoral cycles in terms of the number of parties. The majority runoff exhibits considerably less consolidation of forces behind presidential candidates (Table 10.1), meaning that there is a multiparty system already at the presidential level.

In systems in which there is an assembly election concurrent with the first round of the presidential election,[15] the combination of PR (especially with high $M$) and the majority presidential election might encourage party leaders to present presidential candidates with the primary aim of attracting votes to their congressional slates. By doing so they could enhance their bargaining leverage with the candidates who will square off in the second round. When there is the expectation that there will be a second round and many slates enter the first round, there is a slim likelihood that the eventual winner of the presidential election will have a majority in congress. Thus the concurrence of a (high-magnitude) PR congressional election and majority presidential first-round election might encourage considerable fragmentation, as the experiences of Ecuador and Peru (especially in 1990) both suggest.[16]

14 Such a characterization also fits our other party system that is closest to being "pure" two-party: Colombia.
15 In Ecuador, the first congressional election (1979) was concurrent with the second round of the presidential election. Since then, however, congressional elections have been concurrent with the first round. There was no obvious difference in fragmentation in that first congressional election, although if such a practice were made permanent, we might expect less fragmentation over time.
16 In Ecuador, this fragmentation at the presidential level is much exacerbated because the electoral law prohibits a party from maintaining its own congressional list while simultaneously entering into an electoral coalition with another party behind a common presidential candidate (Conaghan 1989). Even without such a law, however, the incentive for unlikely winners might be to maximize their congressional representation for the sake of presenting the eventual presidential winner with a fait accompli something like the follow-

Peru's highly fragmented presidential election in 1990 ($N = 4.4$) followed previous elections that had been much less fragmented. As already suggested, the majority runoff encouraged this fractionalization of a party system once characterized by at most three important partisan blocs (APRA, ex-president Belaunde Terry's AP, and, after 1978, the left). In Ecuador, there is no obvious trend either toward or away from fragmentation. The Ecuadoran party system is extremely fragmented to start, but as shown in Table 10.2, it is even more fragmented in midterm elections ($N_v = 10.8$) than in those assembly elections that are concurrent with the presidential first round ($N_v = 7.4$). Thus in Ecuador, which (unlike Peru) started out with extreme fragmentation, the concurrence of the presidential election induces some consolidation, despite majority runoff. However, this consolidation is both feeble, owing to the majority system, and temporary, since there is always a midterm election two years away.

Among our cases, there is one in which there was consolidation of potentially competitive forces, in spite of the majority presidential election; it was also the one case in which a very low district magnitude was used for the congressional election that was concurrent with the presidential first round. In Chile in 1989, the center and left presented a common candidate who won in the first round. Why did they form a preelection pact, as we would expect with *plurality,* when one of the two would have been certain of advancing to the runoff in which it could have counted on the other anti-Pinochet candidate's supporters? The key rests in the low $M$ for the congress. With $M = 2$ and party lists (but with voters choosing a candidate within a list), the center and left could be assured of sufficient votes combined to win both seats in many districts. Had they run separately, in many of those same districts only one tendency, *either* a centrist *or* a leftist, might have won, with the other seat going to the right (Brager 1990). Running together, they could pool their congressional votes in order to maximize their representation. Thus, *low* congressional magnitude with a party-list allocation rule concurrent with the first round of a majority presidential election discourages the fragmentation that is otherwise encouraged by majority runoff.[17]

## CONCLUSION

We have seen empirically the effect on the party system associated with different electoral rules. Our first observation was that plurality election of

ing: "You'll have to deal with us once you're elected, so make a pact with us before the second round." Bolivia, where the "second round" is in the congress and among the top *three* candidates, thereby even further encourages fragmentation of the concurrently elected legislative slates (all the more so given that ticket-splitting is prohibited). In Bolivia, $N_p = N_v = 5$, approximately.

17 The new Chilean system may, at the discretion of a president exercising dissolution powers, have nonconcurrent elections as well.

the president tends to induce the formation of two blocs to contest the presidency, while majority elections are often considerably more fragmented. Even when there is a single large party under majority runoff, the opposition tends to be more fragmented than when plurality rule is used. Thus we have argued that the goal of gaining a broad, popularly endorsed, coalition behind a potential executive is better served by plurality rule than by majority runoff rule. Ironically, the plurality method is more likely to produce victory by a genuine electoral majority than is the method of majority runoff. The majority-endorsed candidate who must eventually emerge from a second round in a two-round majority system may have been endorsed in the first round by far less than a majority of voters and often less than a third. A candidate's ability to win the second round is largely contingent on which two happened to survive the first round. Thus first-round contingencies are especially important to determining who wins the second round. A key contingency is the number of candidates running, which tends to be quite high.

We admit a strong preference for election of the president by a method other than majority runoff. Almost any other method that we have discussed and that has been in use in some country or countries – plurality, a U.S.-style electoral college, the Costa Rican 40% rule, or the Nigerian concurrent pluralities – is more conducive to the forging by parties of preelection coalitions broad enough to approach closely, if not reach, an absolute majority. We find especially appealing the double complement rule. As a variant of plurality, it would encourage broad preelection coalitions, but it does not carry the risk of very narrowly endorsed plurality winners. The avoidance of such winners, as has occurred in some cases (Chile in 1970 being the most famous), is the purpose behind the recent move toward majority runoff rules in many countries. But the double complement rule has the further advantage of not encouraging the fragmentation of the field of competitors. For now, however, plurality rule remains the most common method for electing presidents. In the next chapter we discuss and analyze in more detail the effects of combining plurality rule for the presidency with PR for congress. We see no reason to doubt that the general conclusions derived there would apply just as robustly to any system that employed the variant of plurality we have called the "double complement rule."

# 11

# Electoral cycles and the party system

As mentioned in Chapter 10, most studies of the relationship between votes and seats have not taken into account the possibility that presidential and parliamentary systems might differ on the relations being investigated. Indeed, most have been based overwhelmingly, if not exclusively, on data from parliamentary systems. The empirical results of Chapter 10 suggest that presidential systems might make a difference in two ways. The first, and most obvious, is that, unlike parliamentary systems, presidential systems have separate elections for two separate agents of the electorate. The second, which flows directly from the first, is that these elections need not be at the same time; we have seen that the timing of elections, the electoral cycle, makes a difference in the number of parties. If the number of parties varies, so perhaps do such outcomes as the extent and quality of representation and the stability and effectiveness of the system. If concurrent elections by PR are employed along with plurality for the president, those wishing to articulate minority viewpoints might find themselves forced either to join a large presidential contender's party or else suffer electorally as a third party. Then, perhaps, the degree to which the system represents diversity may be undercut. On the other hand, if nonconcurrent elections are used, presidents might find they rarely have majorities in the congress.

## ROLE OF ASSEMBLIES AND THE NUMBER OF PARTIES

A principal theme of this book has been that assemblies do not exist in institutional isolation within their political systems. Instead they are elected either to form an executive (the cabinet in a parliamentary system) or to coexist with an executive (the president in a presidential system) or both (premier-presidentialism). This fundamental difference in the means of constituting the executive can be expected to affect the number of parties in the assembly inasmuch as the purpose of the assembly differs according to the type of executive.

Where the only means that voters and, during electoral campaigns, party leaders have to influence the composition of the executive is through parliamentary elections, the decision on whether or not to vote for or even to run candidates is affected by calculations on government formation. This is the process discussed in Chapter 9, and it is tied to the "efficient secret" (Cox 1987). As a result, even a party that has little chance of winning in a given district may present a candidate, or list of candidates, in that district in order to institutionalize itself in the voters' minds as a potential future government or partner in a governing coalition. Such a party, by perhaps playing a spoiler role, also serves a "blackmail" (Sartori 1976) purpose against parties in parliament.

In a presidential system, on the other hand, the election of the assembly need not bear any relation to the choice of the executive. Separation of powers carries with it separation of elections. This basic feature of presidential systems has been invoked to explain why congressmen in the United States spend so much time courting personal followings in their own districts in contrast to the United Kingdom, where qualities and skills of the candidate are found to have much less effect on the likelihood of election (Cain et al. 1987). In a parliamentary system like the United Kingdom's, voters select a party for policy purposes (Cox 1987). In a presidential system, on the other hand, the selection of a candidate or party for congress can be motivated differently from that for a preferred executive. Even so, we have noted (Table 10.2) that, despite the formal separation of elections and powers that define presidentialism, when plurality presidential and PR congressional elections occur at the same time, two major parties emerge.

In disentangling this issue let us take the case of $M = 1$ and plurality for the assembly races. If the system is parliamentary, the ability to offer a long-run collective alternative government and perhaps force a hung parliament is an incentive for third parties to run and for voters to cast "protest" votes for such parties, even in districts where their chances of victory are slim or nil. In a presidential system, the advantages of a few districts won by a minor party are not such an incentive when said party cannot play any meaningful role in selecting (or subsequently voting no confidence in) the executive. This reasoning accounts for why the U.K. and other parliamentary systems with $M = 1$ have multiparty races for MPs even if two parties are more important than the others ($N_v = 2.3$, according to Table 11.1), while the United States and the Philippines have almost *perfect* two-party systems ($N = 2.1$, according to Table 10.2).

Increase $M$ with PR and what happens? The incentive for multipartism grows. It was already higher in parliamentary systems even at $M = 1$, as Table 11.1 shows. Now, given higher $M$, even in presidential systems, the "prize" available to minor parties increases in value. Rather than, at best, a small number of token seats and lots of defeats with no ability to play a role in executive formation, a minor party in a presidential system with *PR* congressional elections has the opportunity of winning a proportional share of seats and thus institutionalizing itself. If elections are concurrent and the

Table 11.1. Effective number of parties in parliamentary systems, according to effective magnitude

| Effective magnitude (M) | Effective number of parties ($N_v$) |
|---|---|
| 1 | 2.3 |
| 2 - 5 | 2.7 |
| > 5 | 3.7 |

*Source*: Taagepera and Shugart (1989).

rule for the president is plurality, then unless a very large number of voters split their tickets, a basically bipolar system results; but an institutionalized presence of minor parties leads to the potential for coalition formation *before* future presidential elections. And, assuming that the congress has even minimal lawmaking powers, even a small share of seats won via PR might allow a minor party to induce the president to negotiate for legislative support. Thus the effective number of parties in the congressional elections of presidential systems with concurrent elections is higher (3.1 on average, according to Table 10.2) when $M$ is high than when $M = 1$, but not as high as in parliamentary systems that use large-magnitude PR. Note that Table 11.1 shows that, with parliamentarism and large $M$, average $N_v = 3.7$.

In considering the interaction of executive form, assembly $M$, and the electoral cycle, the basic combinations of institutional variables can be arrayed as in Table 11.2.

The institutional package that will concern us in greater detail in the next section of this chapter, plurality president elected concurrently with a PR ($M > 1$) congress, thus occupies an intermediate position. So does that which has provided much of our contrast and for which the phrase "efficient secret" was developed, the British-style parliamentary system with $M = 1$. As discussed, the British system occupies an intermediate position because, with parliamentary elections serving as the basis for choosing an executive, parties seeking to provide an alternative to the major parties will tend to run in many districts even outside of their own regions of strength. Examples of such parties are the Liberal Party and the Social Democrats in Britain, the Social Credit Party in New Zealand, and the Canadian New Democratic Party.

The presidential systems that are intermediate are encountered here because of the simultaneous action of the Duverger effects tending in both directions: the plurality presidency pushing the number of competitors toward two, and the PR congress pushing the number of parties upward. We have seen that the presidential effect does push the effective number of

Table 11.2. *Type of assembly party system and associated institutional arrangements*

| Type of assembly party system | Associated institutional arrangements and examples |
|---|---|
| Multiparty | Parliamentary with $M>1$ (Continental Europe) <br> Plurality president with nonconcurrent $M>1$ congress (Chile pre-1973) <br> Majority president (Ecuador, Peru) |
| Two-party, but with minor parties | Parliamentary with $M=1$ (New Zealand, U.K.) <br> Plurality president with concurrent $M>1$ congress (Costa Rica, Venezuela) |
| Almost pure two-party | Plurality president with $M=1$ congress (Philippines, U.S.) |

parties in the congressional elections down from what is observed in parliamentary systems when $M > 1$. A model to be shown in the next section suggests that there is also some effect the other way, pushing up the number of presidential contenders. Let us consider this type of electoral cycle.

### CONCURRENT ELECTIONS: NUMBER OF PARTIES

We have seen that the institutional design of plurality presidency and concurrent assembly by PR tends to support two major parties, plus some minor parties. Thus far our discussion of this association between a particular configuration of institutions and a type of party system has been primarily empirical. In this section we turn to a theoretical discussion of this particular type of presidential regime, placing it in the context of parliamentary regimes.[1]

1 In contrasting this type of system with parliamentary regimes, we shall also be effectively contrasting it with those presidential systems that use only nonconcurrent elections or elect their presidents by majority runoff. As we have seen, these latter systems tend to behave more like large-$M$ parliamentary systems in the sense that they are associated with multipartism. We must add, however, that $N$ for such presidential systems tends to exceed by a considerable degree $N$ for parliamentary systems using comparable magnitude. While the institution of parliamentary confidence is seen to increase $N$ at low $M$, at higher values of $M$, the desire of parties in parliamentary systems to be able to present themselves as viable governing parties must temper the increase in $N$. This finding relates directly to the theoretical argument about inefficiency in regionally based party systems: These politicians would have lost much of their ability to service local interests had parliamentarism been adopted, since some fusion of diaparate parties would have been encouraged. Thus at high $M$, presidential systems using nonconcurrent elections or majority runoff rules have higher values of $N$ than parliamentary systems.

(This discussion of the "presidential difference" requires the use of mathematics, but for the sake of less mathematically inclined readers, we have left the more complex matters out of this chapter. Readers who want to see how the model presented herein was derived, as well as more in-depth discussion of its implications, should refer to Appendix B. Others may ignore that appendix without loss of continuity.)

### Theory of the number of parties

The model for the number of parties in presidential systems is part of a broader family of models of the relationship between district magnitude and number of parties. The model starts with the most simple assumptions about the relationship between assembly $M$ and seat-winning parties, then adds necessary complexity to take account of multiple districts. Only then is it possible to estimate the effects of presidentialism on the basic relationship. The agreement to empirical data, as we shall see, is quite good, considering the several steps involved.

The first step, suggested originally by Taagepera (1989), is to estimate a mathematical relationship between the number of seats available in a district ($M$) and the number of parties that can win those seats, which is designated by $p_s$, the number of actual (not effective) parties winning at least one seat each. Taagepera suggested that the relationship, in the absence of other information, might be expected to be the geometric average of 1 and $M$; i.e.,

$$p_s = M^{.5}.$$

Shugart (1988) tested this expression and others derived from it against empirical data from several systems and found that the data tended to agree with the estimate. Taagepera and Shugart (1992a) made further adjustments to the reasoning, indicating that such a simple model could apply only in the simplest district. Such a simple district would be the only district in the political system, such that the politics of other districts, perhaps with a smaller or greater $M$ or different political cleavages, could not "contaminate" the effects of $M$ in our "test" district. Fortunately there are such systems in which this simplest of individual districts exists: those in which seats are allocated in a single nationwide district, as in Israel and the Netherlands. For such districts, the above equation provides an excellent fit to empirical data (Taagepera and Shugart 1992a).

We are confronted with a question as to why the relationship should take this form. Why would party leaders and candidates assemble their lists and campaigns, and why would voters distribute their votes, in such a way that this relationship between $p$ and $M$ would prevail, on average, instead of some other. To begin untangling this question, let us start by considering the range of possible outcomes. In a district of $M$ seats, obviously there are clear boundaries to the range of outcomes. On the one hand, one party may win all the seats, in which case $p = 1 = M^0$. On the other hand, each seat may be won by a different party, in which case $p = M = M^1$. We seek a value, $k$, for the general equation $p = M^k$, in which $0 < k < 1$. But why should $k = .5$? Obviously $k = .5$ means that it is simply the average of the extreme cases, implying a normal distribution. However, this assumes that both extremes are equally likely, or equally unlikely, to occur. Is this justified?

Assume the simplest of parties and allocation procedures in the simplest of districts with a value of $M$ considerably greater than 1. We shall not concern ourselves with the precise allocation rule – what kind of quota or divisor is used to allocate seats to parties – as long as it is some form of PR. We should, however, assume a closed-list form of PR, as this will allow the model to depend only on parties and not on intraparty vote competition. Thus the determinants of whether a candidate wins a seat are simply the interaction of some number of parties within a district of $M$ seats taken in isolation from any other districts and from the process of executive formation. Candidates in this model are assumed only to seek a seat in the district for its own sake. They do not care about executive formation or policy debates. What would we expect an aspirant for such office to do?

If policy and executive formation did not matter, candidates could group together on a list of $M$ candidates that would maximize each aspirant's chance of winning. In other words, they would strive to form a list capable of winning all $M$ seats, giving us $p = 1$.

But what if there are more than $M$ aspiring candidates? If there are, what happens to the candidate who would merely be ranked by this unique party as candidate number $M + 1$? His chances of winning would be zero, until some future election when a member higher on the list died or retired. So he or she would do just as well to form his or her own list and seek to win without the dominant party. As soon as this is done, the certainty of winning for the candidate ranked in position $M$ on the dominant party's list is diminished. The party may still win all $M$ seats or it may now win only $M - 1$ seats. Candidate $M$ now has to weigh the expectation of winning on the dominant list versus the possibility of winning by joining with the candidate who defected from the $M + 1$ position. Alternatively, candidate number $M$ might also present his or her own list. Each time someone makes such a calculation in favor of defecting, the exponent in the equation $p = M^k$ increases from zero and toward one. If all candidates except the one in the number one list position defect, we have $p = M^1$. The point is, therefore, that as long as there are more than $M$ aspirants, one list that wins all seats is not expected to be an equilibrium, except possibly at the lowest values of $M$ and, of course, when $M = 1$. Someone who is left out of the first $M$ list positions will set up a rival list, thereby inducing defections from the dominant list.

But why start with the assumption that $M$ aspirants initially seek to form one list? We need not. Let us try starting with the assumption that each aspirant presents his or her own list. The seats now go to the first $M$ vote winners in what becomes a system of the Japanese single-nontransferable-vote variant of plurality. We would then have $p = M^1$, or as many "parties" winning seats as there are seats to be won.

But given the option of forming lists in a PR system, candidates who expect to fall lower than $M$ in the voters' rankings may calculate they are better off joining with a candidate likely to finish higher. Any such candidate thus joins a list of a candidate who is more resourceful, more charismatic, or otherwise more likely to secure the election of the candidate whose chances of winning independently are not as great. Again, as long as there are more than $M$ aspirants, an extreme value of $p$, in this case $p = M$, is out of equilibrium. Some aspirant will always seek to run in tandem with some other, in order to increase her or his own chances of election. Such an arrangement should in turn be desirable to the stronger candidates, by making other politicians dependent on them. That is, by "sharing" their electoral strength, they can increase their influence in the assembly. They are, in effect, avoiding "wasting" their excess electoral strength.

If either extreme is equally unlikely, the pulls toward separate candidacies, on the one hand, and toward unity, on the other, must converge in the center, unless we assume that one pull is stronger than the other. Lacking any reason to assume a greater pull from either end, the exponent on $M$ for this simplest of all isolated districts would be the average of 0 and 1: $p = M^{.5}$.

The reasoning thus far has assumed no political issues, no executive, and no other districts. Deviations from the norm, represented by $p = M^{.5}$, must be accounted for by any one or combination of these additional factors. Taagepera and Shugart (1992a) account for one: the existence of other districts in most systems. Their means of doing so are reviewed briefly in Appendix B. Here we concern ourselves with the effects of one particular form of executive formation, the election of a president (with $M = 1$ and plurality) at the same time as the election of members to fill assembly seats (with $M > 1$ and PR).

Once again, the complexities of this mathematical exercise are developed in Appendix B. If $p = M^{.5}$ is the model for a basic district and provides a reasonable fit to data drawn from *parliamentary* systems, as it does (Shugart 1988), what exponent would be appropriate for the assembly of a presidential system? Recall that our concern here is with systems in which president and congress are elected concurrently. Therefore the congressional election is occurring at the same time as another election for which $p$ must be 1, or $p = M^0$.

What if there could be no ticket-splitting and the assembly and executive were of equal importance electorally? Then our estimate should be an average value between the exponent .5 (for assembly) and 0 (for president). This would predict an exponent of .25, or a fourth-root relationship.

However, voters need not cast a single ballot, so the effects of the presidential election on the congressional (and vice versa) must be tempered. Taking averages again (lacking a basis on which to make some other procedural assumption), we get the following estimate for $p$ for the congress of such a system:

$$p = M^{.375} = M^{\frac{3}{8}}.$$

This relationship is tested in Figure 11.1 for data from three presidential systems that meet the criteria: concurrent elections, president elected by plurality, and congress by (closed-list) PR. These countries are Costa Rica, the Dominican Republic, and Venezuela. The figure shows a good agreement with data. The agreement is improved by the equation that takes into account the effects of multiple districts (instead of assuming an isolated district). That equation is represented by the dashed curve in Figure 11.1, and its derivation and form are shown in Appendix B.

*The effective number of congressional parties.* By a procedure elaborated upon in Appendix B, it is possible to move from this expression of the number of *actual* seat-winning parties to the number of *effective* parties winning seats. This relationship, which also gives a very good fit to data, is derived and presented in Appendix B. Here we shall show only the final step, an expression of the relationship between $M$ and the effective number of electoral (vote-winning) parties $(N_v)$. This relationship is shown in Figure 11.2. The equation for the curve derived from the theoretical model is

$$N_v = 1.5M^{.21}.$$

Also shown in the figure is a dashed curve conforming to the model's prediction for parliamentary systems, $N_v = 2M^{.25}$. The derivation of this expression and the data that confirm its validity are provided in Taagepera and Shugart (1992b), and a brief overview may be found in Appendix B.

We discuss in Appendix B the degree of fit of the equation above to the data in the figure. Recall that this expression is meant to be a theoretical statement; it was *not* derived through empirical curve-fitting, as would be a regression of $N_v$ against $M$. That this equation should express the right tendency in the data relative to the parliamentary data set gives us cause to believe in the validity of the general theoretical reasoning.

*The effective number of presidential contenders.* The expression for the effective number of presidential contenders in concurrent elections according to congressional district magnitude is derived in Appendix B and is

$$N_p = 1.68M^{.09}.$$

This expression tells us that minor parties fare slightly better in larger-magnitude districts than in smaller ones, not only for congressional

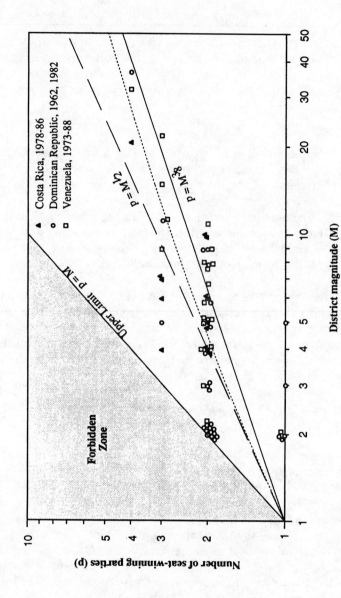

Figure 11.1. District magnitude and number of seat-winning parties, Costa Rica, Dominican Republic, and Venezuela

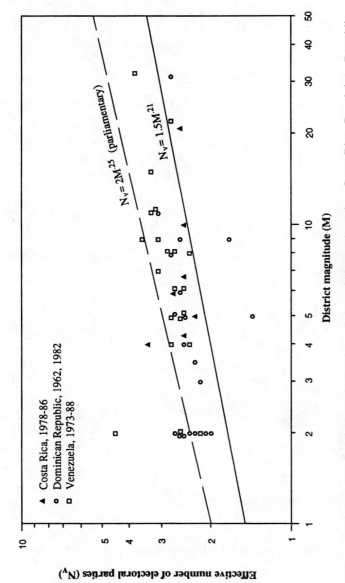

Figure 11.2. District magnitude and effective number of electoral parties, Costa Rica, Dominican Republic, and Venezuela

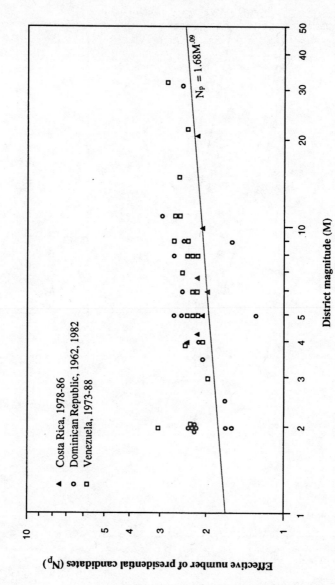

Figure 11.3. District magnitude and effective number of presidential candidates, Costa Rica, Dominican Republic, and Venezuela

elections but also for presidential. They do so despite plurality rule for the presidency and despite the clear dominance of the two biggest parties, as indicated in Figure 11.3.

CONCURRENT ELECTIONS: POLITICAL STRATEGIES

Appendix B develops a theoretical model of the number of parties in presidential systems with concurrent elections. That model is a macrostructural model that concerns itself with systemic-level variables. How do the systemic level independent variables (electoral rules) lead to the party system dependent variable? Can we suggest ways in which electoral rules affect the behavior of individual political actors – party leaders and voters? The following section is an attempt to consider how rational actors' goals and strategies, within a given institutional context, lead to observed outcomes. The microlevel explanation below produces results consistent with the macrolevel explanation of the preceding section and Appendix B.

*Major parties and concurrent elections*

We have noted that it is possible, given the mix of plurality and PR in many presidential systems, to have two-candidate competition for the presidency but multiparty competition for congress. Yet, in systems employing this mix of electoral rules, such a configuration of competition has been observed primarily in systems using only nonconcurrent elections (Chile before 1973 and Brazil in the 1950s). A qualified exception is Costa Rica until the 1970s, where a coalition of conservative parties maintained separate congressional identity even while running a common presidential candidate at each election. More recently, however, even Costa Rica has conformed to the two-party dominant format in congressional as well as presidential elections. Why do parties not more commonly take advantage of the mixed electoral rules and maximize their individual organizational interests by maintaining separate ballot identities, as they do when all elections are nonconcurrent?

To approach an explanation, we have to look at the incentives of individual members of parties within the bloc endorsing a particular presidential candidate, as well as at the voters. First, let us assume that most politicians are motivated both by power seeking (winning office or the spoils of office) and by policy goals. This means, especially in a presidential system, that they seek to maximize their chances of being in a team that wins the executive.

Moreover, the great visibility of the presidential candidate in the race suggests that voters are likely to focus on the candidate's own party as the vehicle by which to endorse their preferred presidential bloc congressionally as well as in the executive. The Costa Rican experience confirms the strength of these coattails, as even when there was an explicit coalition, the presidential candidate's own party significantly outpolled the other parties in the coalition, even beating those parties that had been important in earlier periods.[2] Thus, rational office-seeking politicians – whether or not they also have important policy goals – would be better off being on the president's common slate of proponents in the congressional race. A candidate might be expected to prefer the near certainty of being elected on such a common slate, with the list position being negotiated before the election, over the risk of being overlooked on a separate list as a result of the president's coattails.[3]

   This discussion has considered why a presidential candidate's *party* would dominate over other possible parties supporting that same candidate, and is borne out by electoral dynamics in the Costa Rican case. But why wouldn't parties seek to endorse a common candidate who did not have his or her own party? After all, nonparty heads of government are far more common in presidential systems than in parliamentary ones (Blondel and Suárez 1981). Aside from the difficulty of convincing presidential candidates to have separate congressional slates supporting them – an irrational situation for them because it muddles the message of their own campaign and proposals for government – there is a straightforward problem of campaign dynamics. How can leaders of separate parties maintain the necessary unity to elect a president, if at the congressional level they are busy pointing out to voters why they should support this slate over those others? Such a multiple-slate approach is likely to undermine the common themes and sense of purpose – and hence the efficiency – of the whole campaign. Thus, even Violeta Chamorro, although unaffiliated with any party in her successful bid for the Nicaraguan presidency in 1990, had a common "UNO" slate behind her. This common slate was crafted even though there were clear centrist, rightist, and even leftist tendencies within the anti-

2 When the Unión Nacional candidate was the standard bearer for the conservative parties in 1958, its congressional slate received 19.2%, compared to 6.1% in the previous (1953) election. In 1962, when it did not have the conservatives' presidential candidate, its congressional vote declined to 12.8%. In that election the presidential candidate was from the Partido Republicano, whose slates for congress obtained 32.5%, compared to 20.1% in 1958. In 1966, without a presidential candidate, the party's only surviving independent faction obtained only 0.4%.

3 This observation can also account for why, especially in Venezuela with its easily cleared threshold for minority party representation, only very small parties tend to participate separately for congress while endorsing a major party presidential candidate. Individual political entrepreneurs who can place themselves number one on their own lists can stand a chance of getting elected in a high-magnitude (or, in Venezuela, nationwide) district. However, if one is going to be farther down on some list, it is better to be number eight in a twenty-five-seat district (for example) on the list for a presidential contender's party that, as the unified expression of the presidential candidate's supporters, might win 40% of the vote, than it is to be number four on a secondary supporting party that might not even win 15%.

Sandinista front. The common slate was a collective solution to what otherwise would have been a highly individualistic congressional campaign. Closed lists made it even more collective, eliminating any rationality of pointing out differences among members of the coalition – until after the election of course. Conveniently for the opposition, as it turned out, the Sandinista's electoral law already mandated closed-list PR.

### Voters: Why so little ticket-splitting?

The models and empirical data suggest that there is indeed some ticket-splitting in the concurrent elections format. Yet there is not enough to make for a parliamentary-style multiparty system even when a high magnitude is used. Why not? Surely most of the answer has already been provided. Most politicians want to enhance both their office-seeking and their policymaking potential. To do so means lining up behind a party capable of winning the executive, that is, the presidency. Thus there is a substantial gap in size between those two parties that contest the presidency and the remaining parties that do not seriously do so, at least in the present election. This means there are not many options for voters besides the two big parties.

Another institutional reason reinforces straight-ticket voting by the great majority of voters in the systems under consideration: the list form of PR. Especially with the closed list, but presumably with most variants of open list, the party can present itself as a team.[4] Given the concurrence of the congressional election with the presidential, voters are likely to perceive that voting for the president's party is a means of confirming the endorsement given to the presidential candidate against his or her opponent. Voting for third parties might increase the probability that the party representing the team opposed to one's preferred president will be able to stymie the president. Therefore, most voters who really prefer that presidential candidate are also likely to endorse her or his team.[5]

4 Some variants of open list clearly undercut this "team" tendency, as in Colombia and Brazil. The multiple list system used in Colombia makes that country's elections at least as candidate-centered as in the United States. Thus, we may be able to point to an institutional reason why Colombia's two parties remain so dominant: the combination of plurality-presidentialism with a congressional electoral system that emphasizes personal over policy-oriented voting, as in the United States. The Brazilian form, which is combined with numerous ancillary features that weaken partisan identity, is an exception (Mainwaring 1991). Even if this electoral system in Brazil were used concurrently with a plurality presidential election, it might remain as individualistic as in the United States, where ticket-splitting is indeed high. Less extreme forms of open-list systems should be somewhere in the middle range. Currently no presidential system has had long experience with concurrent elections and an open list variant of PR, although Venezuelan voters beginning in 1993 will have one-seat districts for half the seats. Such a format should weaken the virtual "team ticket" nature of parties found under presidentialism and closed lists. See Shugart (1992a).

5 This assumes, of course, that voters want the same things from their representatives at both levels, president and congress. Jacobson (1990) has recently suggested that this may not be

## The interaction of presidential and congressional elections

The reasoning, presented above and in Appendix B, that leads to expressions for both congressional and presidential parties suggests that the concurrence of elections for an assembly using $M > 1$ and PR with an executive using $M = 1$ and plurality leads to a two-way "contamination." The effective number of parties winning votes (and seats) for the congress tends to be lower at a given magnitude than what we find both theoretically and empirically is the case among parliamentary systems. Thus, even though high $M$ could accommodate many more effective parties, the plurality presidential election dampens the number of parties. The above equation that showed that $N_p$ rises with $M$ tells us that the congressional election also contaminates the presidential election with more effective parties than would be expected in the absence of the congressional election.

We do see evidence of some ticket-splitting, yet its extent is limited for the reasons suggested above. Minor parties do exist, however, because of PR, and even though they do not expect to win the presidency, they may nonetheless present presidential candidates. They may do so in part to present a long-run alternative political force that, they hope, may win the presidency at some future election. However, such long-run goals need not be present to encourage "third" parties to present candidates for the presidency. It is likely that a party would expect that its ability to maximize its potential congressional representation would be aided by having a full slate, including a presidential candidate, in order to attract attention and votes. At the end of this chapter, the special dilemma of third parties in concurrent elections is contrasted with their position in nonconcurrent elections.

How does this idea of "two-way contamination" in concurrent elections compare to other institutional formats? We, of course, do have cases of elections for assemblies where there is no popular election – concurrent or otherwise – for an executive. These are the parliamentary systems, although one theme in this book is that we can never completely divorce an election for an assembly from the executive-formation process. Indeed, we have seen that parliamentarism does affect the number of parties by encouraging parties to act as potential "spoilers" or alternative governments in $M = 1$ countries and to seek to enter coalition cabinets when $M > 1$. There are two regimes that come close to divorcing the concurrent presidential

so in the United States; enough voters regularly split their tickets to make divided control the rule, despite concurrent elections. The critical difference in the U.S., compared to other presidential systems discussed in this chapter, is the lack of a party list, meaning that party leadership controls the election of members far less than in, say, Venezuela. Under U.S. circumstances, candidates tailor their messages to maximum effect for the districts, a fact that Jacobson acknowledges even while emphasizing that party matters far more than is allowed by those who have decried an "incumbency advantage" based upon constituent servicing and campaign finance imbalance.

election from voting for the assembly; it is not surprising that they are cases of exceptionally weak presidents. One such case is Bolivia, where, as discussed in preceding chapters, the congress makes the ultimate selection of the chief executive in a way that takes this case outside the class of presidential regimes. In Venezuela through the 1968 election, an interparty pact mandated power-sharing cabinets and a president intended to be above politics. In both these cases, $N_v$ exceeded five. However, as soon as a president in Venezuela chose to govern with a single-party cabinet – as he was constitutionally permitted to do – Venezuela developed a two-party system. This process was described in more detail in Chapter 9.

In considering cases where the interaction of executive and assembly elections is weakened, we obviously cannot find the logical opposite of the above cases, which would be an election for executive in which there is no assembly – again, concurrent or otherwise. The desire of minor parties to contest presidential elections, even though they have no chance of winning, in order to attract support to a congressional slate is potentially present in any presidential system in which $M$ for the congress is greater than $M$ for the presidency. However, the contamination effect described here is weaker when the presidential elections are nonconcurrent.

### *"Contamination" in concurrent versus nonconcurrent formats*

Indeed, there is some support for the notion that the effective number of presidential candidates is more likely to be as low as 2.0 when the congressional election is nonconcurrent and the contamination effect of minor parties from a concurrent congressional election is thus absent. In the data presented in Chapter 10, we have fifteen nonconcurrent elections by (effective) plurality rule; four of those, or 27%, had $N_p$ of 2.0 or less. We have twenty-five concurrent presidential-congressional elections; four of those, or only 16%, had such low $N_p$.[6] We thus have a bit of an irony: The greater frequency of low values of effective number of presidential contenders is found in precisely those cases in which the effective number of congressional parties tends to be highest. Nonconcurrent elections are best able to support separate party systems, mutliparty for congress and two-party for president, as we suggested in Chapter 9 would be the case for an archetype of presidentialism. Concurrent elections, on the other hand, bring about a dampening of the number of parties in congress and, simultaneously, a

6 Recall, however, that the average effective number of presidential candidates was observed to be higher under nonconcurrent elections (2.7) than under concurrent elections (2.5). The reason is that while fewer presidential elections in the cases of Brazil and Chile had the pattern of several minor parties that occurs regularly under concurrent elections (hence average $N$ of 2.5), some had $N$ of 3 or higher. In other words, the range of $N$ values observed under nonconcurrent elections is greater, given the greater frequency of elections with three principal candidates, resulting from the occasional failure of party leaders in a multiparty system to coalesce for presidential elections.

slight increase in the number of presidential candidates. In so doing, concurrent elections run some risk of lessening the ability of elections to both branches to perform their functions best, as defined at the outset of this book. The congress, despite PR, may be less representative, while there may be additional presidential competitors, despite plurality.[7] Still, concurrent elections seem to strike a balance between efficiency and representativeness and are certainly superior in providing efficiency compared to a system with all off-cycle congressional elections.

## NONCONCURRENT ELECTORAL CYCLES

The preceding section, concerning concurrent elections, concluded with observations about the interaction of elections to congress and president. In cases of nonconcurrent elections it is feasible that there might be little or no interaction. Such an expectation would be consistent with the archetype of a presidential system that was presented in Chapter 9, in which the principle of separation of powers is carried to the logical end of separation of campaigns and party systems in presidential and congressional elections. Such extreme separation could prevail only to the extent that congressional elections were not conducted as referenda on the coalition or party controlling the presidency at the time of the congressional election. As we shall see, nonconcurrent elections often do appear to serve the function of referenda. Therefore, with this format, too, there is an interaction between presidential and congressional elections. How this interaction works depends to a great degree on matters of electoral timing more specific than the simple dichotomy between concurrent and nonconcurrent elections. We must also consider honeymoon, counterhoneymoon, and midterm elections.

*Honeymoon elections.* We define any election that occurs within one year of the president's inauguration to be a honeymoon election. Such elections tend to be particularly beneficial electorally to the newly elected president's party. A few regimes, including especially premier-presidential regimes, allow a honeymoon election at the discretion of the president. Thus, François Mitterrand twice dissolved parliament immediately after his own election to call a honeymoon election. The new Chilean constitution gives the president a similar prerogative.

---

7 At an extreme, this process might make the presidential election less efficient, since the votes being cast for minor presidential contenders would cut into the share of the larger parties. However, in the cases seen in Table 10.1, the normal vote shares of the two largest parties are about 50% and 35%. The case with the highest magnitude favoring small parties is Venezuela; yet the nationwide vote shares for the two major presidential contenders do not tend to be on the low side in Venezuela. The equation just given, expressing $N_p$ in terms of $M$, implies that with extremely high magnitude – and in the absence of smaller regional districts as exist in Venezuela – these shares would drop appreciably; if so, we have further reason to use the double complement rule we discussed in Chaper 10.

*Counterhoneymoon elections.* If honeymoon elections are those that occur within one year after the president's inauguration, it follows that an election that occurs within the year before the presidential elections would be a counterhoneymoon one. Such elections might be used by parties to provide information on electoral trends that they can use in upcoming negotiations over the formation of coalitions before presidential elections. This was certainly the case in Chile (Valenzuela 1989a), and in Colombia, although in the latter instance the effect works mainly on internal party factions that present separate congressional lists (Hartlyn 1987). We shall have little to say about this form in this chapter, because of its limited empirical scope. However, we shall return, in Chapter 12, to counterhoneymoon elections in our discussion of the role of electoral cycles in designing constitutions.

*Midterm elections.* Any election that does not occur within a year before a presidential election or within a year after a new president has taken office will be considered a "midterm" election. Thus some midterm elections do not occur at precisely the middle of the president's term, although in many countries they do. The United States and Ecuador, for example, have half their congressional elections concurrent with presidential elections and half at the exact midpoint between presidential elections. Argentina has concurrent elections and two midterm elections in each six-year presidential term, one about two years after the presidential elections, the other two more years on. Some countries, including Chile before 1973, France, and El Salvador, may have assembly elections at varying points in the presidential term, owing to terms for the two branches that are of different length.

*Mixed cycles.* Many systems have been quite haphazard in the occurrence of elections of these various types. Nonsynchronized terms in some cases have meant that some presidents experience a honeymoon election while others do not. Some coalition-building negotiations in advance of presidential elections have been informed by parties' fates in counterhoneymoon elections, while others have not. Our own view is that any of these formats may be valid for maximizing particular political goals, but that consistency from one presidential term to the next is desirable, in order not to treat different presidents differently owing to a "luck of the draw." We return to these political issues in Chapter 12, after we have completed our empirical observations. Our empirical investigation of nonconcurrent elections continues now with Chile, a case that especially demonstrates the consequences of haphazard electoral timing.

### The Chilean experience

Presidential elections in Chile before the coup of 1973 were held every six years. Elections for the congress were held every four years. All municipal councils nationwide were also elected on a separate cycle, originally every three years, later at four-year intervals. Never did elections to two or more types of office coincide.

There was a honeymoon election in most presidential terms, but not always for the congress. Some were for municipal councils. Furthermore, Chile's varied election calendar meant that, in addition to the honeymoon elections, either a congressional or municipal election would occur at mid-term and that some kind of election would occur near the end of the president's term (a counterhoneymoon). Thus, Chile offers an especially rich environment for examining the impact of the timing of elections. Municipal elections in Chile may be treated as equivalent to congressional elections for our purposes, since they were contested on essentially the same terms as the congressional elections. Before the emergence of "nationalized" politics, localism prevailed in both congressional and municipal elections. Later on, municipal elections became sort of "referenda" on the ideological and partisan forces that disputed all other elections in Chile.[8] Also, for municipal and congressional elections nearly identical forms of PR were used.

For Chile, Table 11.3 shows the percentage of votes obtained by the president's party or coalition of parties in each presidential term for an entire electoral cycle: the last election before the president was elected and the three elections that would be held before this president completed his term. The corresponding figure for the president himself is also shown. This figure is not directly comparable to the congressional and municipal data because it is partly dependent on the number of candidates running and is a true personal vote, not a party vote. It is especially not comparable for the height of the period of the inefficient secret (particularly in the 1930s and 1940s), when majority or near-majority presidential coalitions were common and were clearly separate from congressional lists.

Indeed, before the emergence of nationalized politics in legislative races, presidential elections had less effect on congressional support of the president's party or coalition than in the 1960s and 1970s. There are two exceptions to this observation. The first is the Popular Front, a time of unprecedented reformism and labor organization, sponsored by the administration of President Cerda (1938–42). Unfortunately, we lack data for the honeymoon municipal election of 1939. What we can see is that the leftist and Radical portion of the electorate grew from 1937 to 1941. In the other presidential terms, the usual pattern was for supporters of the president to experience a decline in support by the end of the president's term. Such declines are especially evident in the terms of Ibáñez and Frei, all the more so because those presidents experienced major surges in support in their honeymoons.

8 Indeed, even elections in schools and private associations were contested on partisan lines (Valenzuela 1989b).

Table 11.3. Percentage of votes for parties supporting president during each term, Chile, 1938–1973

| | Cerda 1938-42 (Socialist, Radical, Communist) | Rios 1942-46 (Radical, Socialist, Falange) | Ibañez 1952-58 (Agrarian Labor, "Ibañistas") | Alessandri 1958-64 (Conservative, Liberal) | Frei 1964-70 (Christian Democrat) | Allende 1970-73 (Popular Unity) |
|---|---|---|---|---|---|---|
| **Base** (prior to Presidential election) | 34.1 (1937) | 51.8 (1941) | 13.1 (1949) | 33.3 (1957) | 22.0 (1963) | 43.9 (1969) |
| **Presidential election** | 50.5 | 56.0 | 46.6 | 31.2 | 56.1 | 36.6 |
| **Honeymoon** | NA | NA | 45.4 (1953) | none | 42.3 (1965) | 48.6 (1971) |
| **Midterm or later** | 54.7 (1941) | 45.0 (1945) | 7.9 (1957) | 31.4 (1961) | 35.6 (1967) 29.8 (1969) | 44.0 (1973) |

*Note*: The presidential term running from 1946 to 1952 is omitted because the Communists, who had supported the president's election, were subsequently proscribed.

*Source*: Urzua (1986).

Using the last election of the preceding presidential term as a base, the mean increase in votes for the president's supporters in the honeymoon election was very large, 19.1%. In those same terms the percentage of votes going to the party or parties supporting the president fell at the midterm election by an average of 16.2% from its honeymoon peak. As Table 11.3 shows, the percentage of votes for the relevant party or parties fell back to a level close to or even below its base point by the end of the president's term in the cases of Rios, Alessandri, Ibáñez, Frei, and Allende. If we include the Cerda administration in our calculations, the average net change from the base election to the midterm is +3.4%, but without that administration, the figure is −0.1%. So we could say that, excepting the period of rapid social transformation and mobilization of the Popular Front, Chile's pattern was for there to be, on average, no long-term change in the representation of the several partisan blocs as a result of electing a president. Electing a president would mean a temporary surge (+19% on average) if there were a honeymoon election in the given term, but over the longer run, normal political trends reasserted themselves.

*The special effects of honeymoon elections.* We now turn specifically to honeymoon elections. Such elections, as we have already noted, tend to be beneficial to the largest party or coalition from the presidential election, but at whose expense? Here we shall see that it is the second largest party that suffers the greatest losses. Another finding is that the third largest party also gains in honeymoon elections. The explanation for this is that if the usual tendency is for plurality presidential elections to polarize around two major contenders, then some of the votes that go to one of the two largest parties in the presidential election must have come from those who would vote for smaller parties in elections for which PR is used. The presidency, because of the single-seat district, imposes a restraint on third parties when plurality rule is used. A nonconcurrent congressional or municipal election with multi-seat districts releases this restraint (cf. Shugart 1988). The effect presumably could apply to fourth or lower-placed parties, but in the party systems under examination here, parties ranking below third either do not exist in the presidential election or are so small that the effect is negligible.

Chile represents a "paradigmatic" case because of its multiparty system and frequent elections, some of which were honeymoon. We can even inspect the effects of honeymoon elections on two different party configurations. The presidential elections studied are 1964, when only two major candidates ran, and 1970, when there were three major contenders because of a failure of party leaders to coalesce before the election. In 1964 the coalescence of the center and right restrained voting for the Radical Party's candidate such that the vote shares of the top (and only) three contenders were:

| | |
|---|---|
| Eduardo Frei | 56.1% |
| Salvador Allende | 38.9% |
| Julio Durán | 5.0% |

Many voters who usually would have voted for the Radical candidate, Durán, instead voted for one of the two probable winners, Frei or Allende, presumably most for Frei. The Radicals were the only one of Chile's traditional center-right parties (including the Liberals and Conservatives) not to join the candidacy of Frei, the Christian Democrat, in order to block the leftist Allende. The result was that many Radical voters deserted Durán in the polarized campaign between Allende and Frei.

In the honeymoon congressional election of 1965, Frei's Christian Democratic party gained significantly over its level in the previous congressional election, as shown in Table 11.3. However, because this party was only one of the parties backing Frei, Frei's vote share cannot be attributed to the Christian Democrats alone (as discussed in Chapter 9).

When we look at the other parties, we really see the differential effects of the (effectively) plurality presidential election, in which there were only two "serious" contenders, and the PR honeymoon congressional election. The supporters of the runner-up Allende, the Communists and Socialists, received a combined 22.7% in 1965, down from their 39% in the presidential election. On the other hand, Durán's radicals rebounded substantially. While the party could only muster 5% in the polarized contest in the presidential election, it managed 13.3% in 1965. We could even say that the traditional Conservative and Liberal parties enjoyed the most spectacular honeymoon surge of all, from 0% in 1964, when they presented no candidate of their own, to 12.5% in 1965.

The situation was rather different in 1970. The constitutional ineligibility of Frei for reelection and the by-election successes of some right-wing candidates late in Frei's term encouraged the Conservatives and Liberals, now united in a new National Party, to go it alone (see Valenzuela 1978). The Christian Democrats, emboldened by Frei's absolute majority in 1964, refused to endorse a right-wing candidate, and Allende ran again, this time with backing from a declining Radical party. Thus, with all three ideological blocs presenting their own candidates and no cross-bloc endorsements, each of the three candidates was perceived as having a real chance at obtaining a plurality. Given the expectation, already discussed, that the Chilean congress would confirm as president the candidate with the popular plurality, only slightly more than 33% of the votes would be needed to elect the president. The actual results were:

| | |
|---|---|
| Allende (Left) | 36.6% |
| Alessandri (Right) | 35.2% |
| Tomic (Christian Democrat) | 28.1% |

What happened in the 1971 honeymoon election? Allende's leftist supporters experienced a honeymoon surge to nearly half the vote in the ensuing municipal election (see Table 11.3), while the runner-up National Party declined to 18%. The third-place Christian Democrats also declined, but only slightly, winning 26% of the vote.

It is interesting to compare Allende's administration to the previous one in Chile that was committed to major social transformation, the Popular Front of Cerda. That Allende's supporters could obtain close to half the vote in 1971 after Allende's having been endorsed by only 36% may appear to represent a significant boost in support for Allende and perhaps for socialism. However, the comparison to the previous election before Allende's own reveals one of the smallest honeymoon surges shown in Table 11.3. Perhaps such a small surge is not surprising, given that Allende's election was made possible only by the split in the nonsocialist forces in 1970. A combined Christian Democratic and rightist candidate would surely have made 1970 a virtual replay of 1964.

We have now seen how nonconcurrent elections in Chile allowed for fluctuating strengths for parties in a multiparty system. The reason why there was no consolidation of the party system around the supporters of the major presidential contenders was that in each Chilean presidential term there were subsequent elections in which parties could test their strengths independently. Later elections in Chile allowed parties outside the president's coalition to reassert themselves in elections that used proportional representation and thus had no bipolarizing tendencies. Valenzuela (1989a) has observed that the frequent elections encouraged parties even within the president's original coalition to distance themselves from the president. Thus the electoral cycle in which there were honeymoon, midterm, and counterhoneymoon elections allowed parties to demonstrate their potential worth as future coalition partners in subsequent presidential contests. The resulting fluctuations might even mask an underlying stability in voter opinion, as Prothro and Chapparo (1974) argue was so in Chile between 1952 and 1973.

### Honeymoon elections in Venezuela's revised electoral cycle

From 1958 to 1973, Venezuelan municipal elections as well as congressional elections were held concurrently with the presidential election.[9] In recent electoral cycles, however, separate municipal elections have been held within the president's honeymoon period. This reform provides a valuable test of the effects of honeymoon elections. Do the patterns observed in

9 Elections for all offices except president were fused, meaning there was no ticket-splitting at these levels. Through 1988, this continued to be true for congress, senate, and state assemblies. For an analysis of the effects of these fused elections, see Shugart 1985.

Table 11.4. Percentage of votes for three largest parties in concurrent and honeymoon elections, Venezuela, 1978–1984

| Party | Pres. | Congress (concurrent) | Municipal (honeymoon) | Difference, concurrent to honeymoon |
|---|---|---|---|---|
| | 1978 | 1978 | 1979 | |
| AD | 43.4 | 38.5 | 30.2 | -8.3 |
| COPEI | 45.3 | 38.6 | 49.1 | +9.4 |
| IU* | 9.0 | 14.5 | 16.3 | +1.8 |
| | 1983 | 1983 | 1984 | |
| AD | 55.3 | 50.0 | 52.6 | +2.6 |
| COPEI | 32.6 | 28.7 | 21.7 | -7.0 |
| MAS | 3.4 | 5.7 | 7.2 | +1.5 |

*Party abbreviations*: AD, Acción Democrática (Democratic Action); COPEI, Christian Democrats; IU, Izquierda Unida (United Left); MAS, Movimiento a Socialismo (Movement to Socialism).

* Common list in the 1979 elections. For 1978 the component parties, the most important of which was MAS, ran separately. The figures listed are the sums for the member parties.

*Source*: Official documents of the Consejo Supremo Electoral, Caracas.

Chile hold in a country that had been previously unaccustomed to such elections?

Table 11.4 shows the percent of votes obtained by the three largest parties in the Venezuelan 1978–9 and 1983–4 electoral cycles.[10] Following the Chilean example, we should expect to see in 1979 and 1984 a surge in votes for the president's party in the municipal elections. In 1979 the new president's party, COPEI, received 49.1%, a surge of 9.4% from the congressional election (which was held concurrently with the presidential elections). The 1.8% increase in votes for the combined left also is consistent with results in Chile. Without a presidential contest to polarize the campaign, minor parties fare better, just as the separate elections in Chile helped support a multiparty system there.

In 1984–5 the party that won the presidency, Acción Democrática, had its share of votes increase 2.6% from the congressional to the municipal election and the left increased its share slightly. The AD vote in 1984 was actually less than what the party's presidential candidate had received in 1983. This

10 For the 1989 elections, an analysis is more problematic because for the first time in Venezuela, mayors and governors were directly elected along with municipal councilors. Thus regional coalitions emerged for the first time since the crystallization of the two-party-dominant system in 1973. With localism playing a significant role in the 1989 elections – a phenomenon not observed in 1979 and 1984 any more than in the concurrent elections – comparisons of the 1988 presidential-congressional and 1989 regional elections are difficult. See Shugart 1992a.

Table 11.5. *Percentage of votes for party or parties supporting president in systems using majority runoff for president*

| | El Salvador | France | | |
| | Duarte (Christian Democrat) | Mitterrand I (Socialist) | (Socialist/ Communist) | Mitterrand II (Socialist) |
|---|---|---|---|---|
| **Base** | 40.2 (1982) | 22.6 (1976) | 43.2 (1978) | 31.2 (1986) |
| **President** | 43.4 (1984) | 25.8 (1981) | 41.1 (1981) | 34.1 (1988) |
| **Honeymoon** | 52.4 (1985) | 37.5 (1981) | 53.7 (1981) | 37.5 (1988) |
| **Midterm** | 35.1 (1988) | 31.2 (1986) | 41.0 (1986) | — |

may seem anomalous, but it is not inconsistent with the combined effects of concurrent and honeymoon elections. We expect that with plurality being used for the presidency, a major party presidential candidate will receive a higher vote share than its congressional slates. In the honeymoon election, AD did gain again over its share in the previous election for which plurality was not used (the congress), consistent with expectations. This result is similar to that seen in Chile in 1964–5. Frei's Christian Democrats gained in regard to the previous PR congressional election, while the party's candidate ran far above the party's own usual share in the presidential race because plurality had led to a two-bloc configuration.

### Honeymoons after a majority presidential election

For systems using majority runoff and honeymoon elections, we have few cases, but those cases fully support the results seen with plurality presidential elections, as shown in Table 11.5. Thus in the premier-presidential system of France, as well as the presidential system in El Salvador, the supporters of the president gain in honeymoon elections and lose in later elections. Whether the president was elected by plurality or majority thus does not affect the basic tendency of honeymoon elections. Some of these gains, and particularly that of the French Socialists in 1981, are especially great.

After François Mitterrand was elected president in 1981 with 25.6% of the first-round votes, his party's share of the votes for assembly increased to 37.5% in the honeymoon election. It had been only 22.6% in the assembly election before the presidential election. If we include the Communists' votes, Mitterrand's electoral coalition achieved an absolute majority of votes in the honeymoon election, despite previously having been in the low 40s, a level to which the coalition would return at the midterm. The pattern for José Napoleon Duarte's Christian Democrats in El Salvador is very similar.

These examples, as well as that of Chile in 1970–1, suggest that where the presidential election is contested by multiple candidates, the honeymoon surge is the greatest. Or, viewed from a slightly different perspective, the honeymoon surge after a two-candidate presidential election might be said to have a lower "ceiling." The reason is that the election of a president from among only two "serious" choices, as is usual in plurality elections, means that some voters who normally support other parties in congressional (or municipal) elections have contributed to the winning margin in the presidential elections. Many if not most of these voters might be expected to return to these parties in the next nonpresidential election.

To sum up the effects of honeymoon elections, we can say that the following tendencies are observed:

- The president's party gains over its share in the previous nonpresidential election;
- if the presidential election was itself a multicandidate affair (including the first round of a majority runoff election), the president's party may gain even over its own presidential candidate's showing;
- the vote share of the party whose candidate was the runner-up in the presidential election declines;
- third parties regain their strength after having been suppressed in the case of a two-candidate presidential race.

### *Long-term consequences of nonconcurrent election cycles*

A question that might present itself at this point is whether there were any long-term effects on the party system made possible by the election of a president from a particular party. To investigate this question, we have computed ratios that indicate the fluctuating vote shares for the parties supporting presidents over time. These data are presented in Table 11.6, while the raw data come from Tables 11.3 and 11.5. Obviously for this exercise we can use only those presidential terms in which there were both a honeymoon and a midterm election. Each ratio was computed by using as the denominator the percent of votes won by the president's own party or

Table 11.6. Ratios of votes in honeymoon and midterm election to votes before presidential election, president's own party and whole coalition

(Base = 1.00 for vote share in last election prior to presidential election)

| President | Honeymoon | Midterm |
|---|---|---|
| **Ibañez** | | |
| Party | — | — |
| Coalition | 1.44 | 0.60 |
| | | |
| **Frei** | | |
| Party | 1.92 | 1.62 |
| Coalition | 1.05 | 0.96 |
| | | |
| **Allende** | | |
| Party | 1.86 | 1.53 |
| Coalition | 1.11 | 1.00 |
| | | |
| **Duarte** | | |
| Party | 1.30 | 0.87 |
| Coalition | — | — |
| | | |
| **Mitterrand** | | |
| Party | 1.66 | 1.38 |
| Coalition | 1.24 | 0.95 |

coalition in the last election before the presidential election. What Table 11.6 makes clear is that, in the cases where it is possible to identify both a particular party of the president and a coalition contributing to his election, the honeymoon gains by the president's own party are greater than for the coalition as a whole. Additionally, in the three cases for which we can identify both a single party and a coalition (Frei, Allende, and Mitterrand's first term), the president's party remained larger at the midterm than at the base-point (although smaller than at the honeymoon). In each case, however, the total coalition's support at the midterm returned to no more than the level at which it had been before the president's election.

The overall effect is depicted graphically in Figure 11.4. Here are presented medians of the ratios from Table 11.6, but with the support of the coalition additionally expressed as a ratio to the presidential party's base-point support. The complete picture, shown in the figure, is that the election of a president in a multiparty system leads to a realignment *within* the bloc of parties supporting the president, but does not aid the overall coalition. Thus, for example, the Socialists in both Chile and France benefited electorally from having held the presidency, but they did so primarily at the expense of their own coalition partners (Communists and Radicals in Chile, Communists in France). Put another way, and in terms reflective of a point we made in Chapter 9, it is costly not to hold the presidency, as partners in the coalition are unable to reap the rewards of – and indeed they suffer the costs of – incumbency. It is these incumbency costs – being in the presidential coalition but not having the presidency oneself – that make coalition formation in multiparty presidential systems difficult and now and then lead to multicandidate presidential contests under the format of nonconcurrent elections even in systems in which the president is elected by plurality.

## MINOR PARTIES AND ELECTORAL CYCLES

The foregoing discussions of both concurrent and nonconcurrent elections suggest that the electoral cycle employed makes quite a difference in whether minor parties are able to achieve much representation. Such parties are considerably "more minor" under concurrent elections (assuming a plurality presidency, of course) than under nonconcurrent, including honeymoon, elections. We conclude our overview of the effects of electoral cycles by considering the institutional context in which leaders and (potential) voters of such parties must operate. We shall speak in terms of the payoffs and strategies for such actors, drawing upon the literature concerning party behavior (see Strom 1990). We shall assume that payoffs can come in the form of officeholding and policy. At times the two forms of payoff may conflict, as when a party's policy preferences are long-term and thus lead it to adopt a platform that does not make the winning of many assembly seats a viable course for the party in the short run. For the purpose of this discussion, we shall assume rather efficient (policy-oriented) voting. Such voting is, as discussed in Chapter 9, hindered to the extent that voting for congress takes place on a particularistic and personalistic basis, rather than on the basis of party platforms.

In a *concurrent election* format in which the president is elected by plurality and the congress by PR, what are the payoffs and strategies for a party that is not a serious presidential contender, owing to its relatively small

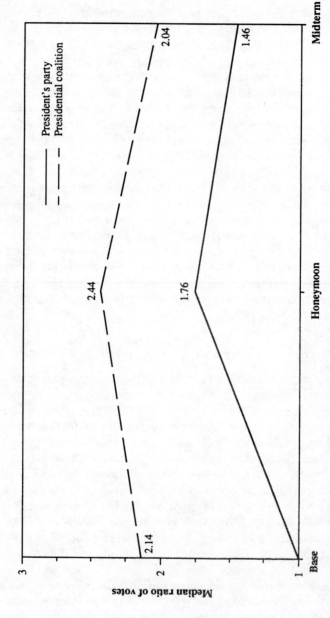

Figure 11.4. Median ratio of votes for president's party and coalition in honeymoon and midterm elections to votes for president's party in last election before presidential election (base = 1.00)

following? In the presidential race, there can be no immediate office pay-off, because by definition the party is too small to win. In the congressional races, there is such a payoff, as PR will allow it to win some share of seats approximating its share of votes.

What about policy payoffs? In the short run, policy requires the ability to win office, although not necessarily executive office. There is likely to be some uncertainty about the short-term payoffs. If one of the major parties does not win a majority of seats, the third party may play a critical role in forming legislative majorities and may thus obtain some portion of its policy agenda. If the president's party does win a majority in the assembly, there may be few opportunities for minor-party influence over policy, especially if closed lists are used.

On the presidential side, the short-term policy payoffs are as certain as the office payoffs, as both are zero if the party cannot win the presidency. However, the long-run payoff is that the party may hope one day to be part of a presidential coalition. A party may not appear to be a serious contender for national power if it does not present a presidential candidate. It is hard to say, "Here is what we would do if the people entrusted us with the presidency," while running only a congressional slate. It is especially difficult given the different purposes of the two branches, and the more immediate and perhaps more mundane concerns of voters that congressional candidates must frequently address in lieu of grand policy options.

Because of the greater uncertainty regarding elections years hence, the long-run payoffs of one day influencing policy via the executive are sure to be discounted, compared to the short-term benefits of winning congressional seats. The certainties in the short run are that the party will win some seats in the congressional races and that one of the two big parties will win the presidency. Thus, rationally, many voters who like the minor party's program will split their tickets. And party leaders may even encourage this to some extent, or at least remain indifferent to it.

The short-term cost is that by running and voting for a presidential candidate, the minor party and its followers risk tipping the presidential race to their less preferred option among the two serious presidential contenders.[11] Thus there are rational motivations that predict that a minor

11 Thus, ticket-splitting should be greatest when the race between the two big contenders is expected to be close. In a close race, the short-term costs of not taking sides in the presidential race are greater (assuming that the party's leaders and voters are not perfectly indifferent to the choice between the big two). Additionally, given an expectation of closeness, the potential payoff of holding the congressional balance of power is great. However, while a close contest between the big two should depress the voting for president by those who favor the minor party, closeness may make it more difficult for the minor party to draw votes from marginal supporters in the congressional race. It is possible in ordinary elections that some voters whose choice of general policy direction is best articulated by a big party might cast a vote for the minor party for congress (perhaps to express a

party will win presidential votes, even when it has no hope of winning the presidency, and that there will be ticket-splitting. However, based on the two-party dominance that prevails in the congressional election and the theoretical reasoning regarding ticket-splitting that we have offered, it appears that ticket-splitting is practiced more by voters who prefer minor parties but want to cast an effective vote for president, than it is by voters whose first preference is for a major party presidential candidate. If the latter form of ticket-splitting were more common, third parties should perform better in the congressional election. Third parties' fates in concurrent elections are thus more determined by the constraint of a plurality presidential election than they are by the opportunities of a PR congressional election.

In honeymoon elections (or midterm elections in systems without concurrent elections), we notice that "third" parties perform better than in concurrent elections. This was observed both cross-nationally (Brazil and Chile compared to Venezuela and Costa Rica) and within one country where both concurrent and honeymoon elections have been held (Venezuela). Why should we observe this pattern? For some voters who supported the runner-up in the presidential election but who are not committed followers of that party, the third party may be attractive as a way to continue one's vote against the president while not backing a perceived loser. There could even be a policy motivation. The likelihood that the president might cooperate in congress with leaders of the party of his or her defeated opponent may be lower than the possibility of cooperation with the third party, which is less threatening. Such voters may perceive an opportunity to provide a more plausible check on the president by voting for a party other than the second-largest party.

For minor party *leaders,* honeymoon or midterm elections offer a way out of a conundrum presented by the concurrent election format. In concurrent elections, if they seek to maximize their forward-looking policy payoffs by emphasizing national policy differences with the big parties, they may lose votes for congress. After all, we are speaking of a party whose fundamental policy alternatives must not be appealing to great numbers of people, given that it is a small party. So the party also seeks to maximize its congressional vote. How does it do that? To some degree, its candidates may seek to address more local, mundane, and immediate concerns of voters in their regions. The party is thus caught trying to do two things at once: provide a long-run policy alternative in a race it cannot immediately

more qualified endorsement, or for reasons of local particularism). But in a close race, these same voters may prefer not to risk that their preferred party fails to control congress and thus may not vote for the minor party. Only with ballot-by-ballot analysis (to count actual split ballots) and by survey research (to find out what party voters really feel closest to, as done for Spain by Gunther 1989) could we really disentangle this issue.

win, and appeal to a constituency in races it can win and has won in the past.[12]

In a nonconcurrent election, the party can focus its resources solely on winning congressional seats and speak to voters in terms of what it can do for them *now*. Much of that will concern mundane items, but policy themes need not be excluded. In a honeymoon election, once the congressional election takes place, it will already be known who is president (and for how long) and what that individual's policy commitments are. The third party can promise either cooperation or vigorous opposition, whichever is likely to maximize its votes and influence. If it gains sufficient congressional representation, it can then seek to win accommodation from the president. In a counter-honeymoon election, the minor party can seek to demonstrate its value as a coalition partner for the upcoming presidential election. These observations recall those of Chapter 9 that nonconcurrent elections let the campaign for assembly take place on its own terms. While the presidential outcome influences a honeymoon election, such an election is at least not overshadowed by a simultaneous presidential contest. For the minor party with its mixed and sometimes contradictory short-run and long-run goals, taking the assembly contest out of the immediate influence of a presidential race that it cannot win lightens its load and reduces its contradictions.

## CONCLUSIONS

We have seen that there are special problems raised by the combination of presidentialism and proportional representation, yet most presidential systems have elected their congresses by PR. The original presidentialism, that of the United States, and its one former colony, the Philippines, are the only two presidential democracies to have used plurality rule for their congressional elections for a long period of time.[13] It is important to realize that a format that combines plurality and PR, as do most presidential and premier-presidential systems, may not be the best way to maximize both of the goals that we suspect (there apparently being no "Framers' Memoirs" on this topic) were in the minds of those who opted for such a format:

- a broadly representative congress for which parties can run without the need to form coalitions first (hence PR);

12  We refer here to the addressing of constituent interests by the party as a whole, since we are assuming closed lists, which do not allow particular candidates to cultivate votes independently. Many electoral systems are somewhere in the middle of this implied continuum between highly candidate-centered voting (Brazil, Colombia) and party-centered voting (Venezuela), as suggested by Table 9.1.

13  Nigeria also has used this combination in its brief democratic experience. Mexico, which may be in a transition to democracy, also uses this combination, but not in a pure form, as there are seats reserved for minority parties that do not win in single-seat districts.

- an executive under the control of one party and endorsed by a majority (hence presidentialism, and more particularly, plurality elections whenever there was a dominant political force at the time of adoption of the rule).[14]

Not surprisingly, if we seek to maximize these goals at once, we are likely to fall short. We may even get at times the reverse of these goals. For example, when concurrent elections are used, we may not get a faithful representation in the congress, owing to the powerful incentives of minority political tendencies to join with one of the presidential contenders' parties. Yet because PR encourages a multiparty system, some presidents under plurality rule may be endorsed by considerably less than a majority. Ironically, however, majority runoff, the institutional fix frequently chosen to redress this problem, tends to increase fragmentation rather than to induce consensus. Worse, it makes lack of presidential–congressional harmony highly likely, as do nonconcurrent electoral cycles.

We next take up the question of "engineering" electoral cycles, suggesting alternative institutional designs that may do a better job at serving goals such as those just mentioned. These alternatives involve being cognizant of how the choice of a presidential or premier-presidential regime interacts with the electoral cycle to maximize particular political goals.

14 Where no one party dominates the initial rule-making and each of several parties perceives a likelihood of winning sole control over the executive, majority runoff may be a more likely result, as in Ecuador and Peru, and the recent constituent assembly in Colombia. Or, if plurality is chosen, nonconcurrent election cycles would be expected in order to enhance parties' independence vis-à-vis the executive. These situations would also seem most likely to produce restrictions on reelection, in order to ensure alternation. We are inspired to undertake these suggestions by Geddes (1990), but we recognize a need for further work on the question of political origins of institutions.

# 12

# Electoral cycles and compatibility between president and assembly

We have seen how presidentialism permits a nationally endorsed executive while still allowing the representation of minority or regional interests to be expressed through the assembly. We have also seen that premier-presidentialism entrusts presidents, with their electoral mandate, to form a government, but only if the government can hold the confidence of the assembly. There are, of course, no guarantees that the president's party or coalition must hold a majority of seats. This chapter will consider electoral cycles in presidential and premier-presidential regimes and how they may effect patterns of governance. The longest-lived premier-presidential regimes (e.g., France and Finland) have had their elections and terms for president and parliament on wholly different cycles, as have some presidential systems (e.g., Chile before 1973 and the current regime of Korea). Presidents in such systems are elected for longer terms than are parliaments, although in most of the premier-presidential systems the president has the option to dissolve parliament and call new elections. In France, the president also may shorten his own mandate and call a new presidential election. Even when such options exist, an important characteristic of actual premier-presidential regimes is that there is no constitutionally prescribed harmony in the timing of elections and therefore terms, despite the importance that electoral cycles were shown in Chapter 10 to have. Under the nonconcurrent cycles and varying-length terms used in these systems, some assemblies are likely to be elected in the president's honeymoon and others at midterm or late in the term. Even if a newly elected president possesses and uses the power to dissolve parliament and should happen to achieve a majority to his or her liking in new (honeymoon) assembly elections, having terms of different length still means that this president's mandate outlasts that of the assembly (and the government that may be responsible to it). Compatibility may not always be necessary or even desired. But we caution that the polar opposite of compatibility, cohabitation between a president and premier who are one another's principal political opponents, or "divided control" between president and congress, may be problematic in many settings. In a presidential system, we suspect, incompatibility between coalitions and parties holding the executive and assembly may be even more a problem, as presidentialism offers less clear-cut mechanisms for resolving such differences. We take up later in this chapter potential scenarios in which incompatibility might be acceptable or even preferred in *premier-presidential* systems. First, let us consider the logic of compatibility and electoral cycles likely to produce it.

## QUASI-PRESIDENTIALIST ELECTORAL FORMATS

If the presidential election is to be efficient in terms of leading to actual policy output akin to what was endorsed in the presidential election, there should be some institutional means of making likely that president and assembly will be at least roughly compatible in their partisan persuasion. Otherwise the attempts of the president to pursue a legislative program are likely to be checked by an opposition-controlled assembly and, in a premier-presidential system, also by the cabinet itself. We thus would want to avoid cohabitation or divided control.

We shall refer here to "quasi-presidentialist" electoral formats. The defining characteristic of such formats is that the presidential election exerts a strong "pull" on the assembly elections – the phenomenon that we discussed at length in Chapters 10 and 11. The reason for this presidential pull is traced to the electoral cycle. Thus quasi-presidentialist formats would have either concurrent or honeymoon elections for the assembly as well as terms for president and assembly that are synchronized. Such formats make likely an assembly majority (and the cabinet, if it is responsible to the assembly) in harmony with the partisan alternative endorsed in the presidential election. Midterm elections might seem desirable in order to provide some check on the presidential majority. However, given the demonstrated tendency of midterm or later elections to result in defeats for the presidential coalition, such elections are likely to counteract the effect of the quasi-presidentialist format, and we do not recommend them for most circumstances. As seen in France in 1986–8, the presidential majority might suffer a midterm electoral defeat even when the president herself or himself proves capable of subsequently being reelected.

In a later section, we suggest an alternative, to be called "quasi-parliamentarist," in which the assembly election does not concur with or follow upon the presidential election, and so is not subject to the presidential "pull." In most quasi-parliamentary formats incompatibility is thus more likely. Nevertheless we can envision a format in which it can be made less likely, without giving temporal precedence to the presidential election, as is done in the quasi-presidentialist formats. We shall also discuss systems that employ hybrids of these two basic formats.

Whatever the electoral cycle employed, we reiterate that the president should be elected by plurality or the double complement rule that we discussed in Chapter 10. Throughout the following discussion, when we refer to presidential elections, we mean one of these methods, unless othewise indicated. In this manner we can approximate the ideal that the executive power should be formed out of a broadly endorsed electoral program.

### Concurrent elections

If the elections were concurrent, we would expect two major parties, but the party winning the presidency would not necessarily have a majority of seats in the assembly, especially if a high magnitude were used for assembly elections. This has been the pattern in the presidential regimes of Venezuela and Costa Rica. Because we have already discussed this format in considerable detail with regard to presidential systems (Chapter 11), let us consider the implications of concurrent elections under premier-presidentialism.

With the concurrent elections, the ordinary result would be that the president could appoint a member of his or her own party as premier. No doubt that government would sometimes be a majority government, but at other times it would be either a minority cabinet or a coalition. Is this advantageous? We have sought, in suggesting this as a possible institutional design, to create both the ability of the voters to designate a general policy direction and to have minority viewpoints represented meaningfully. The first criterion may be met by the electoral method used to elect the president. As for the second criterion, minority views must be taken into account in forming governments whenever the president's own party is short of a majority in the assembly.

One actual regime that comes close to the model just broached, in some aspects, is that of Namibia.[1] Under the Namibian constitution of 1990, the president and assembly are elected at the same time, with the president appointing a premier and cabinet that are subject to parliamentary confidence. There are important aspects in which the actual Namibian system deviates from our proposal, however. The first concerns presidential powers. The president as well as the assembly may dismiss cabinet ministers, and there is also a presidential veto. As suggested earlier, the lack of ultimate authority by one or the other elected branch over the cabinet is often problematic, and the veto means that even a government controlled by the president's opposition can not be sovereign over legislation. Another deviation from our suggested regime design is that the Namibian constitution specifically requires that a majority system be employed for

1 Haiti's 1990 elections were concurrent. However, if the regime stabilizes, concurrent elections will occur at most only every twenty years, since the constitution provides for five-year presidential terms and four-year assembly terms (and is silent about concurrence in years when both types of election occur). Romania's 1991 premier-presidential constitution mandates four-year terms for both president and assembly.

the election of the president. If the party formed out of the former guerrilla movement, the South-West Africa People's Organization (SWAPO), remains dominant (it won 57% of the vote in 1989), this provision will be unimportant. Indeed, the majority election may make it more difficult for other parties to present a common alternative than if the electoral method were plurality, especially given a district magnitude for the assembly that is very high (72). Moreover, the concurrence of parliamentary elections with what would be merely the first round of a majority runoff presidential election could lead to a degree of party fragmentation resembling that seen in a country such as Peru or Ecuador (Chapter 10). If this is the case, and SWAPO ceases to be a majority party, then the system could foment conflict between the president and assembly over cabinet composition. We thus could have incompatibility despite concurrent assembly elections because of the majority runoff election of the president.

The election of the president by majority runoff, as in Namibia, coupled with the importance of the assembly in forming the government might very well inhibit the consolidation of an alternative party (or bloc) to compete against SWAPO. Without this consolidation, the presidential election would fall short of our ideal of efficiency. Is there also such a risk even with plurality, as long as the assembly plays such a role? It could be argued that parliamentary confidence in a premier-presidential regime would inhibit the consolidation of parties around two major contenders, despite the concurrent election and the use of plurality for president. Indeed, we have seen one presidential system with a plurality presidency in which there was a period of clear assembly supremacy: Venezuela before 1968.

If the source of the multiparty system in Venezuela through 1968 was indeed the power that party leaders gave congressional elections to determine the membership in government coalitions, as suggested in Chapter 11, on what basis can we argue that a premier-presidential regime would not result in the same? That the Venezuelan congressional elections should have come to be dominated by two parties despite the superior constitutional position of the assembly over legislation is testimony to the power of the pull toward bipartism exerted by the plurality presidency, once parties have focused on winning this office as their major objective.[2] In a premier-presidential regime, too, given the president's power to propose a premier, the presidential campaign would be likely to bring about two-bloc dominance of the concurrent assembly election, although important third parties might be expected to hold the key to coalition making. While assembly representation takes on great importance here, as it does in basic parliamentarism, the contestation of the presidential election and the concurrent assembly election around themes of national policy significance would pro-

2 As discussed in Chapter 10, this was not effectively the parties' goal in the earliest years of the Venezuelan regime, when an interparty power-sharing pact had weakened the role of the presidency and made being in "opposition" less costly.

vide powerful incentives for most political actors to line up with a coalition capable of winning the presidency.

*Possible disadvantages of the concurrent cycles.* The system of concurrent elections would tend to maximize the effects of the normally two-party presidential competition on the congressional representation. What if we do not desire this dominance of two, probably catchall, parties in the assembly, but still want the presidential coalition and the assembly majority to be ordinarily in consonance? As we saw in Chapter 11, in nonconcurrent elections we would anticipate a greater presence for (larger) "third" parties than with the format of concurrent elections. Such parties, by finding it easier to maintain their separate identity as significant parties, might be in a better position to influence the structuring of future presidential coalitions, even if at some given moment they are outside the government.

### Honeymoon elections

Data presented in Chapter 11 showed that honeymoon elections are more likely than other electoral cycles to produce an assembly majority for the just-elected president. At times this may even be a very large majority, with the second-largest party (as determined by the presidential runner-up) falling well behind. This pattern is seen most clearly in Venezuela's 1979 and 1984 honeymoon elections for municipalities that were elected on the same party-list basis as the concurrent congressional elections. These honeymoon contests produced a surge in support for the newly elected president's party. In the case of the premier-presidential regime in France, François Mitterrand obtained a majority in 1981 and thus could appoint a Socialist premier, thanks to the honeymoon election. In 1988, in another honeymoon election following his own reelection, Mitterrand was again able to obtain a government consistent with what he proposed to the electorate. Calling for an "opening to the center," Mitterrand was able to appoint a minority Socialist government dependent for support on centrist tendencies that had supported him instead of the Gaullist candidate in the second round of the presidential election (and the cabinet occasionally relied upon the support of Communists, who also had supported Mitterrand in the runoff).

This experience illustrates how a honeymoon election might preserve sufficient third-party strength to provide alternatives to the president's party. However, it should be remembered that majorities for the president's party frequently do result from honeymoon elections, thus meaning that the alternatives preserved by this format may be future-oriented, while governance will tend to be majoritarian. Unlike the concurrent format, however, in which the third party's representation may be very limited, the honeymoon format is likely, as shown in Chapter 11, to reduce the gap between second and third parties, thereby potentially anticipating a future coalition to oust the (currently) dominant party.

### QUASI-PARLIAMENTARIST FORMATS

The previous discussion considered electoral cycles likely to give the president an assembly majority influenced by the voters' choice for president. Whether concurrent or honeymoon elections are used, both formats have in common a potentially dominant role in legislation and cabinet-formation for the newly elected president's party. In some other settings, it might be desirable to give primacy to the parties and their ability to garner votes in assembly elections without the overwhelming importance of the presidential election. To weaken the presidential effect on assembly elections in this way implies using either counterhoneymoon or midterm elections. Counterhoneymoon elections may preserve the advantages of presidential–assembly compatibility without making assembly elections overshadowed by presidential elections; midterm elections, on the other hand, are almost certain to limit the prospects for compatibility.

### *Likely compatibility preserved: counterhoneymoon elections*

An election held as a counterhoneymoon is one that closely precedes a presidential election. In the institutional pattern to be discussed here, the terms of the president and assembly are synchronized, but the elections themselves are on separate dates.

Suppose that there were a counterhoneymoon election, perhaps with rather large $M$ for the assembly. The presidential election then would follow soon afterward, within a few months, as was formerly the case in Colombia. With more efficient congressional elections than in Colombia and without Colombia's factionally based electoral system, a multiparty system would be likely. However, given the use of plurality or the double complement rule to elect the president, parties might anticipate an advantage in lining up behind two basic blocs to elect the president. Assembly elections might be said in such a format to function as almost a "primary" for the presidential election (much as they have often done in Colombia for the various internal factions of the two traditional parties). It is even possible that such a format might produce two rather large blocs among the parties contesting the congressional elections, thus serving a function similar to that of the first round of *majority* presidential elections in France. However, even if the party system did not exhibit the French two-bloc pattern, but instead featured two large parties plus a third one needed to achieve a majority, this institutional package would have potential advantages over either a two-round majority presidential election or a pure parliamentary system.

Unlike a two-round majority system when there are three or more blocs, the eventual (second-round) presidential victor would not be so dependent on first-round contingencies such as the precise number of candidates and which ones happened to finish first and second in the preliminary round. Instead, there would be time for negotiations leading to the presentation of two principal presidential candidates *after* the voters had been given the chance to express partisan preferences in a nonpresidential election. The advantage over parliamentarism is that these negotiations among the parties would still have to be ratified by the electorate in the presidential election, unlike the products of coalition-making negotiations in parliamentary systems. There would thus be an electoral check on the parties' coalition-building negotiations that would take place after the assembly elections.

The format of counterhoneymoon elections is called quasi-parliamentarist because of the primacy of the assembly election and parties represented in the assembly. The direction of the interaction in this format is principally from assembly election to presidential, rather than vice versa, as in a quasi-presidentialist format. Primacy is also accorded to parties and assembly elections in those regimes that employ midterm elections. The difference between systems using counterhoneymoon elections and those that would employ exclusively midterm elections is the diminished likelihood of presidential-assembly compatibility.

### Midterm elections

As already suggested, midterm elections go the farthest in weakening the impact of presidential elections over elections to the assembly. Also, compared to counterhoneymoon elections, midterm elections are less likely to produce a coalition that will be presented to voters in the following presidential election. Midterm elections, then, are conducted "on their own terms" to the fullest extent possible. Moreover, we have seen in Chapter 11 that the fortunes of the president's party tend to fade in midterm elections. Thus we would expect a premier-presidential regime after a midterm election to be premier-dominated rather than president-dominated, while an opposition-controlled congress would typify a presidential regime.

Most actual presidential or premier-presidential regimes that have employed midterm elections have been inconsistent. Presidents in such regimes have sometimes governed with assemblies elected under the influence of their own presidential elections (e.g., Mitterrand 1981–6, Frei 1965–9, and Duarte 1985–8) and at other times with an assembly elected apart from the influence of the presidential election (Mitterrand 1986–8, Allende 1970–3). In Argentina, Ecuador, and the United States, every president governs with both types of assembly, given a frequency of congressional elections that is half (or in Argentina, one-third) the length of the presidential term.

If we want to ensure that the minimization of the presidential effect applies to every assembly election, all such elections must be midterm. There is some question, however, about the value of having a *politically important* presidency if an assembly elected at around the midterm were the body entrusted with forming a cabinet, as in a premier-presidential regime. And in a presidential system, the efficiency of the presidential election is severely compromised when the president is almost sure to lose legislative support after the midterm. For this reason we dismiss midterm elections in (pure) presidential systems as being undesirable. We maintain that where the electoral cycle makes a regime disposed to cost the president the likelihood of a majority, there should be an institutional means of reconstituting the government. Because only premier-presidential regimes afford such means, the remainder of this discussion will be devoted only to premier-presidential systems.

If we are to reconcile the conflicting mandates expressed through off-cycle elections to the two branches that express different policy directions for the political system, it follows that the president's powers should be sharply circumscribed. Such a president's role would consist mainly of being the one who designates which party leader shall seek out coalitional prospects within the assembly. A regime of this type with off-cycle elections does not seem to us to be particularly viable where there is a clear government–opposition format to the party system, that is, where there are two parties or at least two blocs. However, if there is a multipolar party system in which it is quite feasible that the president's party would be a part of most governments, this presidential role could add a degree of accountability and efficiency absent from most multiparty parliamentary systems. Indeed, a premier-presidential regime with such a format would allow the regime to function the way the designers of the French constitution expected their system would function, but seldom has: with shifting majorities (Pierce 1990).

It is the above-mentioned presidential role that, in our interpretation, has been accorded presidents in the premier-presidential regimes of Finland and Portugal (since 1982). In the French case, on the other hand, the two-bloc nature of the party system at least through Mitterrand's first term has made for a pattern of cabinets either basically compatible with the president, or else diametrically opposed to him (as in 1986–8). Because the longer-lived premier-presidential regimes have employed midterm elections, and therefore at least phases of quasi-parliamentarism, let us briefly consider the implications of this format in Finland and France.

*Finland.* The Finnish experience, particularly during the presidency of Urho Kekkonen, gives us a taste of the role of a president in a premier-presidential regime in which there is neither a two-bloc division of the party system nor an expectation of presidential–cabinet compatibility. However,

Finland also cannot be considered a case of cohabitation, since by that term we mean a president whose party is shut out of the cabinet owing to an assembly controlled by the president's opposition. Kekkonen was associated with the Center (originally called Agrarian) Party, even though he frequently secured the endorsement of most other major parties as well. During the presidency of Kekkonen the Center Party was in government for all but 12% of the time (based on data in Strom 1990). Since Mauno Koivisto became president, his Social Democrats have been in government all the time from his election in 1982 until mid-1990. While both presidents' parties have regularly been in government, and thus cohabitation has not been the norm, coalition partners have frequently shifted, such that average cabinet durability during the period has been just over twelve months (Strom 1990:251–2).

The role of the presidency in Finland thus might be seen as a primarily regulative or arbitral one. This is especially visible during the period in which Kekkonen was supported by all major parties. In as complex and fractionalized a party system as Finland's, the parties have, in effect, ceded authority over government formation to the president. To comprehend why they would do so requires an understanding of both the difficulties of coalition building in Finland and the peculiar institutional position of the Finnish president.

Not only have changes of government been more frequent than in most Western parliamentary systems, but also the government-formation process has been to only a very slim degree informed by elections. Strom's identifiability rating for Finland is zero, meaning that voters are never able to discern and choose from among alternative cabinet possibilities before a parliamentary election. In this context, a president fills a need for a figure to take responsibility for arbitrating among parties. Under Kekkonen, parties regularly delegated to the president initiative in the formation of coalitions, effectively giving him powers of confidence over the government that are not formally part of the constitution.

In pure parliamentary systems, when there is no clear choice stemming from elections as to which party should make the first formation attempt, the role of designating a *formateur* (or proto-premier) falls occasionally to a monarch or speaker of the house, but more often to a president. The difference in Finland is that this president is chosen through an electoral process, rather than by the parties directly in parliament (perhaps with an extraordinary majority), as are the presidents of Greece and Israel, for example.

The Finnish procedure, at least up to 1988, made presidents inherently more dependent on parties than any procedure short of simple selection in parliament. An electoral college in which voters vote for party along the same format as in parliamentary elections, and in which brokered presidential elections are at least theoretically possible, gives parties primacy. (We might even speak of "quasi-parliamentarist" *presidential* elections.) Using this institutional arrangement, parties are able to ensure that no president who had even limited powers of designation would be unresponsive to them. Moreover, the lack of limit on reelection has meant that the president remains accountable at the end of the term to the parties through the next election for delegates to the electoral college. Multiparty endorsement, with resulting extraordinary majorities, coupled with the party-list format of presidential elections thus has given the parties control over the president to a degree approximating that of many pure parliamentary systems. If, in the post-Kekkonen era, presidential competition returns, there may emerge a degree of presidential accountability to the electorate that was lacking during Kekkonen's long rule. The recent steps toward giving the president some personal electoral connection to the electorate (see Chapter 10) should hasten this process. If so, greater electoral efficiency may emerge in the process of choosing who shall choose – meaning that voters might be presented with differing alternative themes that the president, once elected, would attempt to have reflected in the interparty government-formation process. Not surprisingly, however, this potential for more popularly accountable presidents has also ushered in a constitutional debate in which parties may seek to curtail the president's formal powers further and impose limits on reelection.[3]

*France.* Given the two-bloc nature of the French party system before Mitterrand and through (at least) his first term, it is somewhat of a surprise that cohabitation did not occur earlier. Closely fought elections in 1973 and 1978 nearly produced assembly majorities that would have represented the exact opposite governmental preference from that of the president.

Indeed, were it not for the constitutional right of the French president to dissolve parliament, François Mitterrand in 1981 would have been required to appoint a premier acceptable to a conservative-dominated assembly that had been elected in 1978.[4] There would not have been an assembly election until 1983. We cannot predict what kind of majority would have been returned in that election, but it might not have been socialist. The only socialist governments to date in the French Fifth Republic have resulted from an institutional structure that permits or even encourages an impact of presidential elections on assembly elections by permitting the president to call a honeymoon election, as happened in 1981 and 1988.

3 Markku Suksi (in personal communication) indicates that in the 1988 election, which used a ballot with presidential candidates' names for the first time, candidates toured the country to court voters, a practice not ordinarily seen in previous Finnish presidential election years. On the reform debate, we rely on Berglund and Worlund (1990) and personal communication with Sten Berglund.

4 This, of course, ignores previous dissolutions as well as shortened presidential terms that indeed had already altered the electoral calendar from the basic "7–5" plan (seven-year presidential terms and five-year assembly terms) with which the Fifth Republic began.

In 1986, such a division of the executive against itself finally occurred, and its relatively smooth functioning has been attributed to a series of contingencies that add up to a best-case scenario for cohabitation in a bipolar party system (Pierce 1990). However, the old left–right divide may be be declining in significance, given the virtual demise of the Communist Party, Mitterrand's "opening to the center," and the rise of an extreme right, which may force future conservative presidents to look leftward for coalition partners, to avoid depending on extremists for an assembly majority. If so, shifting coalitions may become the norm and, as such, coalitions might come to depend on party bargaining positions more than on "automatic" majorities for one potential government or the other, as with the two-bloc party system. In such phases, the electoral format and pattern of government formation would resemble what we have called "quasi-parliamentarist." If, however, presidents retain the constitutional right of dissolution during the honeymoon,[5] there will also continue to be potential five-year phases of quasi-presidentialist governance. In this sense of phases alternating between quasi-presidentialist and quasi-parliamentarist formats, France approximates a final type: the "true" hybrid.

### HYBRID FORMATS

Finally, there is a possible electoral format for a premier-presidential regime that combines features of both quasi-presidentialist and quasi-parliamentarist formats. Indeed, the French case during Mitterrand's first term exhibited this mix of qualities. The pattern in the years of Mitterrand may become standard practice in France, with presidents dissolving the assembly in order to call a honeymoon election in which they can maximize their own support, then losing their advantage after a midterm election. This means that cohabitation is likely to become commonplace and, we agree with Pierce (1990), it might not always take place under such favorable circumstances as it did in 1986–8. There are alternatives to the particular institutional design of France that might nonetheless allow us to maintain advantages of both quasi-presidentialist and quasi-parliamentarist formats.

Duverger (1980) called premier-presidentialism (or, for him, "semipresi-

---

5 The possibility that parties in a post-bipolar party system might seek a constitutional restriction on the president's prerogatives of honeymoon dissolutions can not be ruled out. In Finland, with the expectation that presidential elections will become more competitive and personalized for reasons that we have discussed, and with proposals for abolishing the electoral college outright, some parties are advocating that the president's powers of dissolution also be abolished (personal communication with Sten Berglund). Such a stance by parties would be quite consistent with the quasi-parliamentarist format, especially as party control over presidential selection would be curtailed. Of course, unless the terms of president and assembly are also modified so as to be synchronized, honeymoon elections would still occur in some (but not all) presidential terms.

dentialism") a hybrid form of government. We have argued that the pattern of president–cabinet relations associated with premier-presidential regimes depends to a great degree on the electoral cycle. The electoral cycle strongly influences a polity's pattern of governance, meaning the degree of checks imposed upon the government, the likelihood of single-party versus coalition cabinets, and the probability that the cabinet will be politically compatible with the president. For these reasons we have argued that the choice of electoral cycle should be made carefully.

There is one pattern we have yet to discuss: A premier-presidential regime with an electoral cycle that places some elections in the temporal context of the presidential elections and others at midterms would be a true hybrid because some cabinets would be formed out of assemblies elected under the influence of the presidential "pull," while others would not. This pattern is indeed the best description of the current French regime. We have suggested that there may be certain advantages to ensuring that all cabinets result from *either* quasi-presidentialist or quasi-parliamentarist electoral formats; however, this does not mean that true hybrid designs should be ruled out. As always, it depends on the goals sought.

What is the primary potential advantage of such a hybrid design? Perhaps its best feature is the opportunity to provide a "mid-course correction" on the president's cabinet. Because the support of the president's party nearly always declines at midterm (see Chapter 11), the quasi-parliamentarist coalition to be structured after the midterm election might have to bring in different partners, in accordance with new voter preferences expressed in the composition of the renewed parliament. Would this design not make periods of cohabitation, as in France in 1986–8, highly probable? Our answer is that it depends on the precise electoral cycle used and on the parliamentary electoral system.

Before proceeding to these considerations in the context of the hybrid premier-presidentialism, we should point out that we do not, in the first instance, intend to condemn cohabitation universally. We do, however, caution that its relatively smooth experience in France might not be the norm. If presidents have grown accustomed to having cabinets compatible with them politically, and then suddenly must submit to a cabinet from across a sharp ideological divide, the experience of cohabitation might be less happy.

Assuming that in many instances it would be preferable to keep the president's party in the cabinet after the midterm election, but have the cabinet shift from single-party to a coalition or from one coalition to another, an appropriate hybrid format can be designed. First of all, we should rule out concurrent elections, as this cycle is likely to produce a party system dominated by two parties. In such a party system, the midterm is likely to see a shift of electoral support to the one principal opposition party, ushering in cohabitation with confrontation. Second, we should require that such a system use proportional representation, so that a small shift in votes at midterm would not be exaggerated into a large swing in seats that would depose the president's party from the cabinet. It was exactly such a motivation that led the French Socialists to change the electoral system from majority runoff to PR in advance of the 1986 midterm election. Had the majority runoff been maintained, the Socialists' decline and the right's gains could have produced a very large majority opposed to the president instead of the razor-thin one that resulted. For our purposes, though, what is more interesting is what would have been the coalition possibilities had PR been used in 1981 as well.

The French Socialist vote in 1986 was 31.2%, a not so dramatic decline from their vote share in 1981, which was 37.5%. The majority runoff system used in the 1981 parliamentary election translated that vote share into 59% of the seats. Suppose a PR system had been in use in 1981. The percent of seats would have been around 40%, making a minority cabinet of the president's party feasible. If not a minority cabinet, Mitterrand either would have been forced to rely openly on Communist support[6] – their support was indeed critical to his own election – or else to form a center-left government (centrist votes, too, were necessary in his own runoff victory).

At the midterm, the decline of the Socialists would have seemed less dramatic. Given dissension within the right-wing bloc, particularly with both Raymond Barre and Jacques Chirac seeking to be the next president, a center-left cabinet might have remained a viable possibility. This is particularly so since the less majoritarian climate fostered by an institutionalized PR system would have been in place for the whole period. Indeed, whether taking the form of formal participation in the cabinet or not, centrist support would in all probability have been vital for enacting part of the government's program after 1981. This would have meant clearer differentiation of centrists from the (Gaullist) right and perhaps made viable a continuing role for the president's party after the midterm.

The point of this counterfactual exploration of the French case has simply been to demonstrate that a honeymoon-plus-midterm electoral cycle, using PR, could allow the president's party to remain in office, but with a midterm correction. But wherever such a system is implemented, its designers should bear in mind that cohabitation or even conflict would be a real possibility. Parties opposed to the president could always refuse to accept any premier and cabinet presented by the president that included the president's own party.

The hybrid format for a premier-presidential system is probably most viable in a three-bloc party system, in which the president might obtain a

---

6 Communists were brought into Mitterrand's first cabinet, but were not needed to maintain a majority and subsequently departed.

majority government in the honeymoon election and then accede to a coalition between his or her own party and the third-largest party after the midterm. In a two-bloc party system, there might not be a party of the opposition that would be willing to form a coalition with the president's party rather than with other opposition parties. However, part of the point of this discussion is that with PR and the electoral cycle suggested here, the French party system might already by 1981 have appeared three-bloc instead of two-bloc, and now all the more so, given the increasing marginalization of the Communist Party.[7]

### ELECTORAL FORMATS: CONCLUSIONS

The prospects of compatibility between president and assembly may be shaped by the electoral cycle used. We have spoken of compatibility not necessarily in the sense of the same party controlling the presidency and a majority of the assembly, but in the more minimal sense of not being a situation of either divided control or cohabitation. Divided control refers to a congress controlled by the opposition party or bloc of parties that form the principal opposition to the president. Cohabitation refers to a premier-presidential system in which the premier and president come from opposite partisan blocs. Either divided control or cohabitation raises the potential for conflicts in the form of competing democratic legitimacies, although the conflicts might be relatively less troublesome in a premier-presidential regime, in which the assembly has ultimate authority over the cabinet and the president lacks veto power. In a presidential regime there are no means to reconstitute the government and the president retains his or her veto against the new majority. Such occurrences can happen with any format, but are far more likely when midterm elections are employed than when all assembly elections are scheduled either as counterhoneymoon, concurrent, or honeymoon elections. For these reasons we are deeply suspicious of the compatibility of midterm elections with effective government, except for the specific scenarios we have considered here.

7 To minimize potential conflicts between a president seeking reelection and a premier perhaps also positioning himself for a run at the presidency, here might be an institutional design in which no (immediate) reelection would be desirable. If the president and premier were both presidential candidates, the third party that might be needed to augment the president's position in the assembly would have an incentive to join with the president's main opposition in order to provide differentiation for the upcoming campaign. With the president's ineligibility for immediate reelection, an anticipatory coalition for the next presidential election could be more easily formed, with the third party perhaps being able to influence the incumbent president's successor.

# 13

# Conclusions

This book has been devoted to the study of those democratic constitutional designs in which there are two agents of the electorate. The common ideal-typical parliamentary regimes have only one such agent, the assembly, which in Linz's expression, is "the only democratically legitimated institution" (Linz 1987:5).[1] Many other democratic regimes provide for two agents of the electorate, one of which is the assembly, while the other is a president with some power over the composition of governments or legislation, or both. Wherever the electorate has two agents, it becomes critical for the relative powers to be spelled out clearly in the constitution. We have seen a great range of powers provided in actual constitutions featuring popularly elected presidents.

In considering different constitutional designs, we have stressed that among the purposes of democratic institutions is to provide what Powell (1989) refers to as "citizen control" over representatives. Citizens may control their representatives through elections according to two basic models. The first provides that voters should have the ability to assess clear responsibility on the part of an incumbent government and either return it to power or toss it out in favor of an alternative government. Institutions that provide voters this form of control are deemed to provide electoral *efficiency*. A second basic model of citizen control assumes that voters should have a large menu of partisan choices from which to select, in order that nearly every voter has a party close to his or her ideal policy point. Institutions that provide voters this form of control are deemed *representative*.

The trade-off, which we introduced in Chapter 1, between efficiency and representativeness is that it is not possible to maximize both at once. If

1 As we have indicated, Linz's point does not apply equally to all parliamentary regimes, as some have an upper house that has policymaking powers. Where such an upper house has no power of confidence over the cabinet, dual democratic legitimacy may be said to exist, as the government and upper house remain under divided control. Such cases are few, including Canada, Germany, and Japan on certain types of legislation. In general, we do not regard two houses of parliament as being two agents of the electorate. Throughout this book, we have spoken of "assembly" in a way that refers to both houses whenever there is bicameralism.

voters are offered only two choices on election day – the ins or the outs – the choice is efficient, but many voters are bound to feel that they will go unrepresented or inadequately represented, whoever may win. On the other hand, if there are many viable choices on the ballot, the system will be very representative, but assessing responsibility and directing the preferred composition of the government by means of the vote becomes difficult. Hence, designers of constitutions must choose one ideal over the other or else balance the two in some way.

We have argued that parliamentary regimes force this choice very starkly, simply because there is only one agent. Our assertion is backed up by the work of Powell (1989), who finds that parliamentary systems that afford voters clear governmental accountability are low on representativeness. Examples include the United Kingdom and New Zealand. Those with particularly high scores on representativeness seldom afford clear governmental accountability. Examples are Belgium and Italy. Intriguingly, Powell also considers an intermediate model of citizen control, which he calls "government mandates." Such a constitutional design must combine features of the other models that are negatively correlated: party choices (a component of representativeness) and electoral decisiveness (a feature required to afford accountability). The implication is that such a regime would tend to have governments that were coalitions, in order that more than one party's policy views would be sure to be represented in the legislative process, but that there would still be a clear government–opposition divide, so that voters could assess responsibility and identify the alternative governmental choices. Powell (1989:121) finds that Greece scores highest on this model of citizen control. Some other parliamentary systems, such as Spain, Norway, and Sweden, provide a fair balance between permitting accountability and identifiability, on the one hand, and being fairly representative on the other. However, such a balance may be precarious: Greece in the late 1980s experienced two consecutive elections in which the two largest parties failed to achieve a majority but neither had a desirable coalition partner in the assembly.

Where there is only one agent of the electorate, as in a parliamentary system, the electoral function that lets citizens exercise control over the political process cannot maximize the ends of government responsibility and representativeness at once. If there are two agents, on the other hand, it may be feasible to maximize both through elections. In two-agent constitutional designs, how identifiability and representativeness are balanced in the final policy output depends on the ways in which presidential and assembly powers are balanced, shared, and checked. While the cabinet must be formed by the assembly when the latter is the only agent of the electorate, under any format in which there is a second agent, the cabinet may be derived in whole or in part from the agent whose election can more readily afford accountability and identifiability through elections: the president. Once constitutional designers have settled on a system with two agents of the electorate, the process of deciding on the exact shape of the regime has only begun. It is necessary subsequently to decide how cabinet appointments are to be made, how much legislative power the president shall have, and what electoral rules to use, including the critical question of the relative timing of elections of the two agents (the electoral cycle). Such have been the principal themes of this book.

Returning to *The Federalist Papers,* we were able to identify one principle around which regimes featuring two agents could be designed: maximizing separation of the origin and survival of the two branches of government. Following from this principle, we were able to construct a simple two-dimensional typology (Figures 2.1 and 8.2) that encompasses the major ways in which regimes with two agents differ: who has control over cabinets, and how separate is the survival of the two agents. Presidential regimes constitute the extreme in both dimensions, although they vary greatly in how they allocate legislative powers (Figure 8.1). If presidential regimes are one extreme type in the two dimensions identified, we found that the type we called premier-presidential approximates the other extreme. Parliamentary regimes are a special case in which the second agent, the president, either has no authority over governments (or legislation), as in Ireland, or else there is only the one agent. The exercise also allowed us to identify a cluster of regimes that exhibit limited or no separation of powers, yet provide the president great powers over governments and sometimes over legislation as well. This latter type, which we dubbed "president-parliamentary," has a dubious record of democratic stability and is represented by such cases as the German Weimar Republic, the Chilean "Parliamentary Republic," and the present regime of Peru.

Our remaining task is to assess the two major regime types to which we have devoted most of our attention in this book: presidentialism and premier-presidentialism. In doing so we discuss directions for further research.

### POWERS IN PRESIDENTIAL SYSTEMS: EMPIRICAL AND THEORETICAL CONSIDERATIONS

In Chapter 8 we provided estimates of the relative strengths of presidents in several constitutions that have featured popularly elected presidents. In Chapter 9 we gave a theoretical explanation for why some presidential regimes have featured far stronger legislative powers than others. Our work in these areas is certainly preliminary. Much remains to be done on the relative powers of presidents and assemblies. Let us consider some further implications of the balance of powers in (pure) presidential systems, after which we shall consider the implications of premier-presidential systems.

Empirically, we should hope to see studies of actual power relationships, preferably on specific policy matters, in individual countries and cross-nationally. Our empirical knowledge of the mechanisms of congressional oversight of presidencies and bureaucracies, of the effectiveness of presidential vetoes, and so on, has been poorly developed by political scientists. We suggest that researchers on specific countries follow the wave of recent studies on such matters in the United States. Examples of such studies include McCubbins and Schwartz (1984) on congressional oversight; Rohde and Simons (1985), Carter and Schap (1987), and Miller and Hammond (1989) on the role of vetoes in presidential–congressional relations; and Kiewiet and McCubbins (1991) on principal–agent relations in the budgetary process.

On the theoretical side, studies of power relationships are still in their infancy even with regard to the most studied of presidential systems, the United States (see Brams 1989, but, for reservations about the methodology, see also Petracca 1989). Such approaches could be usefully applied to the institutional contexts of various presidential systems, both real and hypothetical. By expanding the scope of possible constitutional balances of powers beyond the static example of the U.S., theoretical development might be enhanced.

A particular area in which more work should be done is the question of delegation versus abdication of authority. Many studies of presidential democracies, having reported minimal congressional oversight of the executive and frequent use of decrees, have assumed that congress was thereby playing a subservient role and ignoring what are its supposed constitutional prerogatives. On the United States, Cater (1964) and Ripley and Franklin (1980) represent this view, which Shepsle (1988) has called "The Textbook Congress." Works on Colombia (Archer and Chernick 1988) and Bolivia (Gamarra 1987), and Venezuela (Coppedge 1988), among others, have made similar observations. We should point out that a lack of explicit congressional action against an executive initiative does not necessarily indicate congressional abdication. It may even indicate nearly perfect correlation between congressional and executive desires or acquiescence by the congressional majority to a second-best outcome, or some other more subtle process. As Kiewiet and McCubbins (1991) advise, simply reporting a lack of explicit intervention by the congress is, by itself, nothing more than an unexplained observation that might conceal an institutional equilibrium.

It is possible that effective oversight and direction of executive acts by congress are rarer in many presidential democracies than in the United States. At the same time, our investigation in this book has made us cautious about such claims. Where oversight is less effective, it is often attributable to these systems' institutional designs, which are typically different from that of the U.S. Because the constitutional allocation of powers to executive and congress are different, so would their own equilibria be different. In particular, a congress is constrained in its ability to provide specific direction to policy and to oversee the policy implementation and regulatory acts of the executive to the extent that the presidency is constitutionally provided any of the following: superior budgetary authority, a partial veto, or wide-ranging decree powers. Several Latin American presidential democracies and the Philippines provide at least one of these legislative faculties to their presidents. One system, Colombia, provided all three in the constitution that was in effect until 1991. Still, limited congressional action contrary to executive actions does not indicate a lack of interbranch equilibrium, as defined by the system's own constitutionally mandated allocation of responsibilities and capabilities.

Having offered this caveat on the state of our specific knowledge about power relationships and equilibria among branches in presidential systems more generally, what do we know that could prove useful to those who would "craft democracies" (Di Palma 1990), and who would opt for presidentialism?

### Balance of assembly–presidential powers: consequences

Our analysis in this volume has suggested that some institutional choices are more conducive than others to democratic longevity, which is a crude, but useful, measure of such harder-to-define concepts as legitimacy and stability. For instance, we do not believe it is merely coincidental that the two Latin American countries that are, as of 1991, longest-lived and generally regarded as the "most" democratic, are also two with the most highly constrained presidential powers over legislation, both in times of "emergency" and in ordinary legislation (see the discussion in Chapter 8). Put another way, these two systems, Costa Rica and Venezuela, allow their congresses to be quite dominant. Similarly, in Chapter 9 our reasoning suggested that the decline and ultimate downfall of Chilean democracy likely followed the increased concentration of legislative and particularly fiscal powers in the presidency by more than mere coincidence.

### Electoral cycles and their relation to the balance of powers

In Chapters 9 through 12 we considered the importance of electoral cycles. We can draw useful conclusions about the interaction of presidential powers and the electoral cycle in presidential democracies by comparing two "paradigmatic" cases: Chile and Venezuela. In Chile, the existence of honeymoon elections made for a potentially destabilizing and temporary enhancement of the partisan strength of some presidents' parties, even though the presidents had been elected as part of much broader coalitions. Indeed, without the honeymoon congressional election of 1965, it is doubtful that President Frei could have obtained the constitutional amendments of 1970 that further enhanced presidential legislative powers. The large bloc of Christian Democrats, themselves a majority in one house, combined with a rightist coalition that itself expected to be able to win the presidency to adopt a plan to increase the presidency's powers.

The Chilean tragedy suggests that the electoral cycle might affect the salience of cross-branch checks, as does the Venezuelan case, too, but for different reasons. In Venezuela, congress has come to be dominated by two principal parties owing to the concurrence of elections to the two branches (and, of course, owing to the plurality election of the president). At times this has meant one-party government, rather than the more consensual form of government envisioned by the regime's founders. On other, but less frequent, occasions, the lack of an effective presidential veto in the context of a modified two-party system has shut out the president's party from legislative power entirely when the president's main opposition party and smaller parties have combined on certain legislative proposals to legislate over the president's head. A more typical pattern of legislative coalition-building in a country with Venezuela's combination of plurality presidency, congress elected concurrently by rather large-magnitude PR, and weak presidential legislative power is a party of the president holding less than a majority but able to enlist minor parties' support for particular legislative packages.

Both Venezuela and Chile therefore offer important lessons in the design of presidential systems. Assuming that the president is elected by plurality or some variant thereof, such as the double complement rule (see Chapter 10), so that either there is a two-party system or parties in a multiparty system are encouraged to forge broad agreements before the initial presentation of candidates to the electorate, the interaction of the electoral cycle and veto override procedures affects the balance of congressional–presidential powers.

With concurrent elections, the congressional election is likely to be a contest between two parties, with third parties faring somewhat better in congressional races than in the contest for the presidency, for reasons shown in Chapter 11.[2] There is thus an efficient choice, as we have defined that term. In such a context, especially if a high magnitude is used for the congressional electoral system, the president's party will be the largest but often short of a majority. How would the interaction of the resulting party system and president's legislative powers work out? An extraordinary-majority override of vetoes would allow the president to block legislation that entailed, in the president's view, too great a compromise with the minor parties needed to make the original legislative majority. Because the veto override would ordinarily require the participation of the principal

---

2 Again, we wish to emphasize that this supposition would not apply if a majority runoff system were used to elect the president. Then we would expect multipartism in both presidential and congressional elections.

opposition party, override ought to be rare. If, on the other hand, the veto override is a simple majority, minor parties have somewhat greater bargaining power because they can threaten to join forces in a legislative coalition with the principal opposition to the president. This possibility may actually preserve accountability *between elections* more than the extraordinary majority override does, as responsibility for every piece of legislation can be made clear and public. The president and his or her party at the next election will be seen to have been either for the bill or against it, thus preserving a distinction between government and opposition.

The simple majority override also makes the granting of temporary legislative decree powers less costly for the congress because a simple majority can prevent an effective veto of any bill rescinding such enabling legislation. However, it is also true that an extraordinary override on vetoes of ordinary legislation does not preclude a constitutional provision that decrees must be voted on by the congress, with a simple majority against them being sufficient to prevent their taking effect. We suggest that wherever a constitution is to provide for decree legislation, congressional action ought to be mandated, with a simple majority sufficient to "veto" the act.

In the multiparty context, the presidential election (if not by majority runoff) retains efficiency in electoral terms, but the congressional election may not. In this context, then, the president's retention of a more effective veto (requiring an extraordinary majority to override) can prevent legislation over the president's head from possibly becoming the normal state of affairs. Thus the combination of nonconcurrent elections (*without* honeymoon elections) and extraordinary majority override is an important inducement to compromise, for two reasons. First, the electoral cycle makes unlikely a majority or even near-majority for the president's party. Second, the extraordinary majority override of a veto virtually prevents the exclusion of the president from legislative coalitions.

In this light, Venezuela's choice in 1961 of a simple majority override is doubly ironic. In the first place, the presidency in that country was intended to be little more than an arbiter of multiparty coalitions expressed through a powerful congress. But the simple majority override fosters a strongly majoritarian bent in the Venezuelan legislative process. Second, the Venezuelan electoral cycle eventually proved more conducive to a party system dominated by two major parties rather than to multipartism. In the end, then, Latin America's most majoritarian – and one of its most stable – democracies developed largely unintentionally. A look at Venezuela's institutional format might have led to a prediction of these developments; its founding fathers most likely would not have foreseen the effects of their constitutional design.

Had Venezuela adopted a cycle with only midterm (or, perhaps, counterhoneymoon) elections, or had presidential elections been conducted under the majority runoff method, Venezuelan presidential elections could have become truly inefficient in terms of determining policy. Under such formats, multipartism would probably have been maintained and the president often would have lacked a majority in the congress. Since the congress is sovereign – able to legislate even over the president's objections – presidents would have had no legislative authority. Therefore, for a multiparty system, an extraordinary majority override is desirable as a means to ensure meaningful presidential participation in the legislative process. In the two-party context, the choice is less critical, but it still affects the kinds of coalitions that are likely to form, as well as the ability of the president to play a meaningful role in policymaking and to be held accountable at election time for that role.

## Political sources of presidential strength

In Chapter 9 we noted that several presidential regimes with great legislative powers also have featured highly decentralized parties with weak leadership control. We suggested that this was a deliberate delegation of powers by regional politicians whose major purpose in designing such regimes was to preserve their own autonomy to service their constituents. Features such as partial vetoes, presidential budgetary authority and decree powers, as well as nonsynchronized presidential and congressional terms, were institutional devices to achieve such separation not only of powers but of the electoral processes themselves. All of these institutional features are designs about which we have expressed skepticism.

Weaker presidencies tended to be associated with stronger parties as well as concurrent elections; the latter combination, which we have dubbed "efficient presidentialism," also has a stronger record of democratic success among presidential systems. We noted that attempts to enhance efficiency by *strengthening* presidential powers were of dubious value, as demonstrated by the decline and ultimate overthrow of Chilean democracy in the 1960s and 1970s.

The link between the gradual strengthening of the presidency in Chile and the deepening crisis of that regime calls attention not only to the role that the electoral cycle might play in affecting the balance of powers but also to the link between politicians' and parties' interests and the resulting institutional choices. Chile's constitutional reform of 1970 resulted from an expedient coalition of the then-governing centrist Christian Democrats and the rightist parties that expected to win the next election. The process by which Chile's constitution was revised suggests that Geddes's (1990) reasoning about the proclivity of parties or leaders who expect to be able to win presidential elections to therefore favor presidentialism could be modified to take account as well of parties' choosing how strong that office shall be. As Chile's once fragmented party system consolidated, it became easier to forge a coalition that sought to delegate even greater legislative powers in order to overcome inefficiency in the assembly that was a legacy of the regime's origins.

The sequence of events in Chile thus calls our attention to the undesirability of permitting constitutional revision to be carried out by even a two-thirds extraordinary majority of a congress that may be temporarily under the effective sway of one coalition. On matters as crucial to the success of presidentialism as the relative balance of powers, amendment or revision should have higher barriers.[3]

## PREMIER-PRESIDENTIALISM

We have also devoted considerable attention to potential benefits of premier-presidentialism, although we have endeavored to make clear that this regime type is not a mere halfway house between parliamentarism and presidentialism, as implied by the more common name, semipresidentialism, but a regime type unto itself (see Chapter 2).

We have also cautioned that the experiences of the two longest-lived premier-presidential regimes may not be an accurate guide to how such regimes would function more generally. In France for many years, presidents regularly had working majorities in the assembly and thus compatible cabinets, partly because of the electoral system used and partly because of the political polarization engendered by de Gaulle. The experience of cohabitation between 1986 and 1988, on the other hand, showed that when the president could not command a majority in the assembly, the premier would take over as the clear head of government. Yet, given the power of initiative in the process of appointing the premier, a situation of a president and assembly majority confronting one another from across a sharp political divide may provide a less happy experience than that seen in France in those years. Indeed, our theoretical model in Chapter 6 does not predict a prime ministerial appointee at the assembly's ideal point, even though this was the case in France. Thus we suggested in Chapter 12 ways to minimize the prospect of cohabitation in premier-presidential regimes. Indeed, where premier-presidentialism is perhaps most desirable is in precisely those systems in which there is no clear polarization of the party system. In such contexts the ability of the president to use powers of

3 In this book we have deliberately not devoted attention to amending procedures because our primary (though hardly sole) purpose has been to describe and analyze the consequences of actual or hypothetical constitutions once adopted rather than to delve into the constitutional design process itself. We might recommend, however, that mechanisms for constitutional revision require the assent of lower elected bodies even in nonfederal systems, or passage through commissions in which smaller parties are overrepresented. In some cases, simply raising the threshold for revisions affecting the balance of powers to 75% or so or requiring an intervening congressional election and then a second vote, might be sufficient to avoid the Chilean problem of fundamental constitutional revision based on short-term fluctuations in the partisan balance.

initiative to exploit the lack of a clear majority in the assembly (see the discussion in Chapter 6) is advantageous, in our view, because it brings enhanced efficiency to the process of government formation, compared to multiparty parliamentarism, while still retaining in the hands of the multiparty assembly ultimate sovereignty over the maintenance of reconstituting of cabinets.

Finland is a case in which the president has exercised a considerable degree of power in shaping governments. The generalizability of the Finnish case is, however, hampered by the long tenure of one particular president elected by a party-dominated electoral college, which made him in many ways an agent to whom parties delegated considerable authority. Kekkonen's presidency thus resembles some "presidents" chosen in parliaments of pure parliamentary systems (as in Israel and Italy) more than presidents of the other systems we have considered. We have expressed a preference for a president elected directly, so that the president is capable of functioning as the agent of the electorate, rather than of the parties.

Historically, premier-presidentialism and the less effective president-parliamentarism have emerged primarily as alternatives to parliamentarism. Examples include the several European countries that won their independence from the empires that were weakened or defeated in the early twentieth century, such as Austria, Finland, and Germany. Also in France, premier-presidentialism emerged as an alternative to a parliamentary regime that was regarded as a failure. The major alternative to presidentialism has tended to be president-parliamentarism. In Latin America, several countries, including Ecuador, Peru, and now Colombia, have had experience with such regimes. The experience has not been a happy one, in most cases.

As an option for existing presidential systems, especially those with multiparty systems, premier-presidentialism holds promise as a way to diminish the majoritarian tendencies of presidential executives. Because the prime minister and cabinet are subject to parliamentary confidence, they are more likely than in a pure presidential system to be of a different party than the president, when that party does not hold a majority of seats. By employing midterm elections, such a regime can also limit the extent of the presidential "pull" on assembly elections, and thus on the cabinet. Such a design is thus potentially more consensual, but, as indicated in Chapters 4 and 12, this device risks simply transforming presidential–congressional conflicts into presidential–cabinet conflicts. Thus careful attention should be paid to both the electoral cycle and to ensuring that the premier is able to take over as the real head of government and chief policymaker whenever the president loses his or her majority in the assembly.

We have devoted a great deal of attention to premier-presidentialism in this book, in part because it is relatively unfamiliar as a regime type but also because it shows considerable promise as an effective constitutional design. In the late 1980s and early 1990s, the design of such regimes certainly appears to be a growth industry, as premier-presidentialism is emerging as the regime of choice in much of Central and Eastern Europe and Africa, and has received favorable consideration in Latin America. In a few cases, however, what has emerged is not really premier-presidentialism but, rather, president-parliamentarism. Because of the dubious record of the latter type, we devoted much care to distinguishing between the two forms, mainly in Chapters 3, 4, and 6.

## PRESIDENTS AND DEMOCRATIZATION

As we noted in Chapter 3, the preponderance of recent academic writing on constitutional forms has stressed the superiority of parliamentarism over presidentialism, considering only a dichotomous classification of regimes, as unfortunately has been the case in most previous discussions. The enthusiasm among academics for parliamentary regimes has been most especially extended to newly democratic polities, for which presidentialism is said to have perils and dangers (Blondel and Suárez 1981; Linz 1987, 1990; Mainwaring 1989, 1992a; Di Palma 1990). Yet this academic preference has hardly been shared by most actual constitution writers or by the authors of this book. Is it possible that designers of constitutions for new democracies have legitimately recognized the advantages of the presidential and premier-presidential forms of government? Or are they simply following habit, particularly in the case of new democracies in countries that also have a prior history of presidentialism (Latin America)? Or, are constitution writers simply following their own self-interest, unable to resist the temptation stemming from their expectation of being able to hold the power of the presidency themselves (as Geddes 1990 suggests), even to the detriment of the broader interest of democratic stability?

As we conclude this book, we should like to suggest that the very possibility that actual constitution drafters may see their best self-interest served by presidentialism or premier-presidentialism may in itself be beneficial to the transition to democracy under certain conditions and as long as legislative powers are not skewed in the president's favor. We agree with Di Palma (1990) in his assessment that the fuzzy concept of "legitimacy" of a new democracy is best judged simply by whether or not the rules of the game achieve "behavioral compliance," but we disagree with his assessment that parliamentarism is almost universally superior to presidentialism for new democracies. There may be instances in which a compromise based on the establishment of a popularly elected president with some circumscribed political powers can be crucial to attaining that behavioral compliance and, therefore, to stabilizing a young democracy.

The advantages of parliamentarism for new democracies, according to its advocates, stem from that regime type's supposed superior ability to regulate conflict. Yet having a popularly elected president can offer potential advantages in conflict regulation. These advantages stem from the logic of presidential elections in giving voters identifiability over the choice of executive authority and even from the big-party bias inherent in presidential elections.

On identifiability, presidential elections, unlike parliamentary elections in nonmajoritarian systems, allow elites to present to voters alternative governments and allow voters to determine what are the possible executive options being placed before them. It might be countered that identifiability is thus a luxury that only a stable democracy can afford. Objectors might further argue that in a conflictual environment it is more important to make elections a "permissive" or "feeble"[4] reflection of diverse interests with executive power to be constituted afterward.[5] However, presumably the desire to prevent fragmentation means that extreme PR would not be adopted. Then the irony of adopting parliamentarism as a conflict-regulating procedure, as advocated by Di Palma and others, is that as district magnitude is reduced to limit fragmentation, the number of competitors is likewise reduced and so is the likelihood of broadly inclusive coalitions. As coalitions become less likely, so does the possibility of using parliamentarism's principal conflict-regulating device, the vote of no-confidence.

In a parliamentary system with single-party government or stable coalitions (a diverse group including Britain, Spain, and Norway, for example), the identifiability of elections is almost as great as it would be in a presidential system. But so are the fixed-term and single-party natures of the executive, for which presidentialism is criticized.[6]

Now let us alternatively consider those cases in which interests that must be protected in order to achieve assent to a constitution are so numerous that multiparty coalitions are nearly always necessary. In the multiparty parliamentary context, the resulting coalitions typically will not be clear

4 These terms to describe high-magnitude PR with a low threshold (if any) come from Lijphart (1984) and Sartori (1968), respectively.

5 This characterization, it might be noted, applies not only to parliamentary but also to assembly-independent systems in which the "president" is chosen by, but not responsible to, the assembly, as in Bolivia, El Salvador (1982–4), Lebanon, and Switzerland (see Chapter 5). These systems score at least as low on identifiability as any multiparty parliamentary system. The latter two do so especially, owing to their (unelected) collegial executives. Unlike multiparty parliamentarism, these systems' executive stability in the face of deep sociopolitical divisions could be held to make up for what they lack in identifiability. Moreover, Bolivia's constitutional design may have helped that country become one of the first Latin American democracies to successfully implement an austerity program, and El Salvador's can be credited with gaining the behavioral compliance of the extreme right despite violent polarization between right and left and the latter's abstention from the regime.

6 Of course, there remains the possibility of early elections even with a single-party parliamentary cabinet, but especially if that single party holds a majority of seats, the early election will occur only at a time calculated by the ruling party to be to its electoral advantage.

before elections. In such a setting, the relative inability of parties to present a meaningful picture of what they can hope to achieve – as opposed to what merely they will ask for – is an argument against parliamentarism. If there is a presidential election and the electoral formula is the double complement rule, moderation and conciliation in the choice of executive will be encouraged without compromising the representativeness of the assembly, which can be elected by PR, even a very feeble PR. As we discussed with regard to the Chilean system at mid-century, the improvements we offered in Chapter 5 for collegial presidencies, and the electoral formats discussed in Chapter 12, the ability of voters to identify a general direction in which they would like to orient policy and mutual guarantees against majoritarianism need not be incompatible goals of constitutional design.

Second, to the extent that new democratic rules are a result of a bargaining process involving established parties (such as those associated with an outgoing authoritarian regime or restricted democracy) or where democratization involves incorporating a potentially major party that was previously excluded, a "presidential compromise" may actually facilitate the striking of a bargain. While Di Palma (1990: 217–18) clearly disparages the compromise struck in Poland in 1989, the establishment of a presidency initially reserved for the outgoing dictator but subsequently to be an elective position could be seen as an ingenious form of conflict regulation. The Polish bargainers set aside a presidency to provide assurances to the defeated forces of the old regime while leaving primary legislative responsibility to a more democratically endowed parliament and a government responsible thereto.

The Namibian constitutional compromise of 1989 is also an example of a presidency having been chosen as a bargain between a strong party and several weak opponents. The dominant SWAPO received the presidency, but the assembly, over which SWAPO is more likely to lose sway in the short run than the presidency, has the power of no-confidence. While the regime is fundamentally president-parliamentary, the willingness of the president to exercise full presidential powers may be tempered by a provision that requires a new presidential election if the president chooses to dissolve the assembly.

Venezuela's constitution of 1961 represents an example of pure presidentialism as a product of accommodation among elites. The presidency had already been won by a major party, but a multiparty pact to share power was institutionalized through making the presidency an exceptionally weak institution in terms of legislation. Thus any of the various regime types with an elected president may emerge as a bargain that can protect the interests of nonmajority parties. Having an elected president does not doom the polity to zero-sum conflicts, competing legitimacies, false mandates, and exaggerated majoritarian tendencies, as has been charged by various critics. Any or all of these defects may occur, but are far less likely to do so if the regime is crafted so as to prevent dominance by the president and diminish the possibilities of clashes of powers.

Our intention is not to dispute Di Palma's basic point that parliamentarism may contain mechanisms that are conducive to conflict regulation. Rather, we wish to point out that presidentialism or premier-presidentialism *properly crafted* can exhibit conflict-dampening advantages of their own that should not be overlooked. In certain contexts, as when one party dominates such that it might be able to win control over the executive by itself under parliamentarism, a presidential or premier-presidential regime might even offer *better* opportunities for conflict regulation than would a parliamentary regime. The keys to crafting a system with a popularly elected executive properly for purposes of conflict regulation are:

1. A representative assembly elected by PR to ensure "fair" representation of diversity and endowed with:
   a. superior legislative powers relative to the executive, in the case of presidentialism, or
   b. the ability to censure and replace the cabinet, in the case of premier-presidentialism; and
2. A presidency elected in a way to encourage a broad preelection coalition and thus moderation and endowed with carefully circumscribed authorities, such as:
   a. a veto with more than simple-majority override, but only if the president is the constitutional head of government, or
   b. conditional power to dissolve the assembly and call new elections, but only if the regime is premier-presidential.

## CONCLUSIONS

Much of our discussion in this book has been about how to elect an executive, or an agent besides parliament with power over the composition of the executive, without sacrificing the advantages of the more consensual pattern of democratic governance that is implied by a multiparty system. It is for this reason that we have focused so much attention on the question of interactions between elections for assembly and the process of forming an executive. In conclusion, we have argued in this book that trade-offs are involved when one attempts to maximize the advantages of both an accountable and electorally identifiable executive as well as an assembly representative of the diversity of the society and polity. Systems with elected presidents, taken at face value, would appear not only to strike a balance between the two, but also to maximize both simultaneously. The reason is the existence of two agents of the electorate. However, as we have seen, having a separate executive and assembly requires careful attention to how the powers of the two overlap and check each other. The institutional choices that comprise variants on presidentialism and premier-presidentialism, as well as on the electoral rules and electoral cycle employed, may compromise considerably the advantages of one function or the other.

We have seldom identified a particular institutional feature as universally preferable to any alternative. Where we have a clear preference, we have been explicit on it. The basic preference that has guided us in this book has been that for accountability and identifiability in executive formation (which normally means an elected presidency) and for broadly representative assemblies (which normally means PR). Another has been our preference for a variant of plurality election of the president, most particularly the double complement rule, rather than majority runoff. Yet another has been our warning to stay away from president-parliamentary designs. Our primary purpose, however, has been not to prescribe but to make clear what the institutional choices and trade-offs are, given a set of goals that one might want to maximize. As Lijphart noted in the conclusion of his study of *Democracies* (1984), there are many ways to run a successful democracy. We hope we have successfully highlighted many more such ways, as well as some less successful ones.

# Electoral rules for one-seat districts and coalition-building incentives

We saw in Chapter 10 that in Costa Rica, the rule requiring a candidate to obtain at least 40% of the vote or else face a runoff has led to a pattern of competition almost identical to that seen in straight plurality presidential systems. The Costa Rican rule thus contrasts rather starkly with majority provisions, in which there is a runoff in the event that no candidate obtains at least 50% plus one of the votes. In such majority runoff systems, the vote shares of the first and second finishers in the first round tend to be considerably lower than in plurality rules, including the Costa Rican variant.

Is this outcome fortuitous, or is there something to the 40% rule that encourages broad preelection coalitions as does pure plurality? This question is worth investigating, especially given that there is only one case of a system using the 40% rule. Perhaps Costa Rica, where a runoff has never been required, is a special case because of its single well-organized mass party, the Party of National Liberation (PLN). Perhaps this party has a "natural" share of the vote that approximates 50% anyway. If so, it might ordinarily win elections (which it certainly does), and it could only lose to a united opposition – that is, one that could itself approach the magical 50% mark. Indeed, in six of the ten elections since 1958, the PLN has obtained an absolute majority. The lowest winning share of the vote in a Costa Rican presidential election since the 40% provision was adopted was just over 43% in 1974 (by the official candidate of a split PLN). An opposition candidate won in 1958 with about 45%. Is this tendency in Costa Rica to have large blocs inherent to the 40% rule or simply inherent to the Costa Rican political scene?

## CHOOSING A THRESHOLD

Let us suppose that all single-member district systems that employ a categorical ballot – meaning any that require voters to vote for one candidate, as opposed to ranking candidates by order of preference (Rae 1967) – can be placed upon a continuum according to the level of votes that the first finisher must surpass in order to be elected without necessitating a runoff. Let us call this level of vote the threshold, $T$, expressed as a percentage.

The useful range of values for *T* is effectively from nearly zero to 50% of all votes plus one vote. *T* = 0 would be operative in the imaginary situation in which a field of candidates all obtained no votes except for one who got a single vote or when all candidates obtained a single vote and the winner was chosen by lot. In either case, when applied to large national electorates, the winner would have a votes share tending toward zero. In more realistic scenarios (or tiny electorates), *T* = 0 simply conforms to an electoral rule that is silent about the share of votes needed to win; all that is thus required is for the winner to surpass the votes of his or her closest rival. *T* = 0, then, means straight plurality.

Clearly *T* = 50% + 1 refers to majority systems. The first-place finisher is not the winner of the office at stake unless he or she obtains an absolute majority, one vote more than half of all the votes cast (or valid votes cast) in the election. Seemingly this is as high as *T* would logically be set. Indeed, we know of no electoral law used among mass electorates in which a candidate for any office must obtain an extraordinary majority (say *T* = 60% or *T* = 66.7%). However, theoretically, such a value is possible; indeed, some parliamentary systems mandate *T* >> 50% for the election *within parliament* of their presidents. With such a small electorate (the size of the assembly) and the practicality of holding several ballots, having failed candidates withdraw and the opportunities for logrolling and trading of favors that operate within a parliamentary body with much greater facility than within mass electorates, such extraordinary majorities are feasible (if a bit unwieldy). For mass electorates, *T* = 50% + 1 is certainly the highest feasible value, simply because that value of *T* is sure to be met in the runoff if only two candidates are permitted to contest the second, decisive round, as is almost always the case.[1]

## WHY 40%?

We are still left with the question of why constitutional engineers might settle upon a 40% threshold. Besides its actual use in Costa Rica, the 40% rule has been proposed in the United States as a replacement for the existing electoral college. At least in the U.S. case, the motivation for the proposal appears to be twofold. First, of course, is the desire to avoid the possibility of the winner of the highest office having been endorsed very narrowly. Second, there is apparent recognition of what was demonstrated empirically in Chapter 10; when *T* = 50% + 1, the number of contestants grows.

1 Alternatively, *T* may be set at zero for the second round, as in the French National Assembly elections. (In the French case there is also a threshold on first-round votes that must be met before a candidate can participate in the runoff in which a plurality is sufficient. Occasionally rules have provided for *T* = 50% + 1 in each of two rounds, then dropped to plurality for a third round in the event the outcome had yet to be decided.)

Let us consider, then, that these two concerns are in the minds of certain constitutional engineers. We look for a value of $T$ that encourages two principal challengers for the presidential office. If we set $T$ as high as an absolute majority, the number of challengers is likely to exceed two, for two reasons. First, it appears difficult to obtain backing of an absolute majority; majority winners are empirically relatively rare in single-round presidential elections, partly because there is almost always some segment of the political leadership and electorate that prefers to run or support a certain nonwinner, either for purposes of protest or with the long-run goal of promoting an alternative for the future. Or, in the case of concurrent presidential and congressional elections, a minor party may present its own presidential candidate principally as a means to attract nationwide attention to its congressional slate, as discussed in Chapter 11.

Second, and stemming from the difficulty of obtaining an endorsement from an absolute majority, is that a threshold of 50% + 1 increases the expectations that the first election will not be decisive. If this is the expectation, then some leaders are bound to prefer the "blackmail" value of achieving their own voting bloc in the first round in hopes of exacting concessions from one of the first two finishers between rounds.

If the threshold is set too low, the number of candidates who might be seen as credible winners may at times exceed two. Ordinarily, the uncertainty of multicandidate competition is expected to induce alliance building. One can block one's "worst evil" by forming alliances with lesser evils. It is even possible that the more potential competitors there are, the *stronger* the incentive is to form a really broad coalition under plurality rule. This incentive would be further strengthened in situations in which there is one formidable incumbent foe that the fragmented opposition seeks to oust. Under plurality rule, such an opposition must unite if it is to win, given plurality rule, or else the incumbent might win even with considerably less than a majority. Ferdinand Marcos of the Philippines gambled and lost that his opposition could not bury its differences to present a unified front (under plurality rule) against him when he called his "snap" presidential election for 1986. Panama in 1989 and Nicaragua in 1990 are two other cases with plurality rule in which fragmented opposition forces abandoned their differences just long enough to agree on a common-front presidential candidate.[2]

However, our discussion in Chapter 9 on the case of Chile suggests a possible pitfall of plurality rule when there are three sharply defined blocs. If these three blocs are approximately of equal size, any one of the three can reasonably aspire to win. While one could say the same about all four

2 One prominent case stands as testimony to the irrationality of failing to coalesce in situations like those just discussed. In South Korea in 1987, President Rho Tae Woo gambled and won that his opposition could not present a united front. Rho won the election with 36% of the vote.

candidates in four-bloc competition, three-bloc competition may at times pose special problems for plurality rule. What is special about three-bloc politics? If there were four blocs, each having an expected vote within a narrow range around 25% and each having its own potential candidate, any two could coalesce and expect a majority or near majority. These expectations would tend to produce two candidates under plurality rule (and four under majority runoff rule).

However, with three blocs, each expecting around 33% of the vote, coalition building becomes more complicated if the ideological distance (or perhaps personal enmity among the candidates) is great. Any two together can expect to win 60% to 70% of the vote, far more than needed to win. For the bloc that contributed about half of such an extraordinary majority – but not the candidate – to the coalition, the expected spoils of office might be so low as to deter the formation of the coalition in the first place. This condition, in which three candidates could be a stable outcome despite plurality, would be expected to occur relatively rarely. When the expectation of winning and thus enjoying the whole spoils of office is high for all three, and being a mere junior partner in a coalition is not likely to produce great rewards (especially given the single-seat character of the presidential election), three-way races may result. Examples of such three-way races are Brazil in 1955, Chile in 1958 and 1970, and the Dominican Republic in 1990.

If we desire to select a value of $T$ that will prevent situations in which any one of three candidates might win, $T$ must be greater than 33%. But it must be less than 50% lest candidates' attention be focused on a probable runoff instead of the initial election. If the boundary conditions are thus 33% and 50%, either an arithmetic or a geometric mean will produce a value of around 41%. Thus 40% or a bit higher is a likely value of $T$ at which only two candidates will be perceived (and perceive themselves) as likely winners, but the first round will be perceived as likely to be decisive. As a round number, 40% has greater appeal than 41%, and this rounded value receives theoretical justification from the reasoning presented in this appendix.

The 40% rule does not, however, prevent a narrowly endorsed winner. It merely prevents one endorsed by less than 40% from becoming president without first clearing a second round. For this reason we have proposed in Chapter 10 a "double complement rule." This rule would have one of the desirable features of the 40% rule in that it would simultaneously safeguard the electoral process against the relatively rare case of fragmentation in ordinary plurality elections and the common case of fragmentation in the first round of majority runoff elections. The double complement rule has the additional advantage of safeguarding the process against an inherent possibility when the 40% rule is used: the chance of a very narrow winner, perhaps by a margin of 45% to 44%, with some third-party candidate whose supporters might prefer the runner-up over the front-runner.

The double complement rule, unlike the others mentioned in this appendix, expresses the threshold that must be achieved for victory not only in terms of the front-runner's share of votes but also in terms of the gap between that candidate's share of the votes and the vote share of the runner-up. The simple formula for determining whether a candidate has met the rule's requirement is given in the main text of Chapter 10.

A further appealing feature of the rule is that it has an almost self-enforcing elegance. While theoretically a candidate could win with 30% or a lower share of the vote, there is no reason to attach a minimum share (such as 35% or 40%) in addition to the provision of the double comple-ment rule. If the largest share won by any competitor were to be 30% and, further, that candidate were to have met the provision of the double com-plement rule, the runner-up could have no more than 10% of the vote. In such an imaginary field of competitors, there would have to be, in addition to the leader, at least seven candidates, each with no more than 10%. Such a field is highly unlikely, but were it to occur, the candidate who had won the 30% would almost appear to have a mandate (and would be a likely second-round winner anyway). By requiring a minimum winning margin, rather than a minimum winning share, the double complement rule guards against the greatest dangers of other methods: narrowly endorsed winners.

# Theoretical explanation for models predicting number of parties in presidential systems

Our task here is to achieve models for predicting the number of parties in a political system according to various institutional features. As mentioned in Chapter 10, the most important of these features has for some time now been recognized to be district magnitude, $M$. Additionally, according to the reasoning regarding Duverger's rule, also discussed near the beginning of Chapter 11, presidential systems might be expected to be different from parliamentary systems in their number of parties, for a given magnitude. That this should be so, at least for those presidential systems employing concurrent elections and plurality rule for the presidency, was foreshadowed by Table 10.2, in which nationwide values of effective number of parties ($N$) are given. Our task here is to go beyond the purely empirical observations of Chapter 10 and seek theoretical explanation.

This discussion builds upon Taagepera and Shugart (1992a, b), in which are developed general models of the relation between magnitude and number of parties. By general models, we mean models for the simplest of general cases, that is, primarily parliamentary systems. When we add to the PR assembly electoral system the complexity of a concurrently elected presidency using plurality rule, it is necessary to make further assumptions in the model. Some of this material has already been discussed in Chapter 11, but the discussion here is more technical.

## THEORY OF THE NUMBER OF PARTIES

The general model has its origins in theoretical work by Taagepera (1988, unpublished) which received empirical testing in Shugart (1988). Taagepera suggested the following reasoning behind the number of parties in a district. The number of parties winning seats in any given district – the actual, not effective, number – has a lower limit of 1 and an upper limit of $M$. In the absence of further information, and knowing these absolute limits, it is justifiable to take as an estimate the geometric average of these extreme values. The geometric average yields $p = (1 \times M)^{.5}$, or the square root of $M$.

As explained in Taagepera and Shugart (1992a), this is the expectation for a simple district. When, as in all but a few countries (such as Israel and the Netherlands), a country's electoral system consists of several districts, $p$ may be higher. A plausible reason for this is that the districts examined are not themselves self-contained but, rather, are subnational units within larger systems. Thus, parties that would be discouraged from competing in a single nationwide district of, for example, $M = 20$, might run in several separate districts of $M = 20$ within a larger country – even outside the parties' regions of normal seat-winning strength. Sometimes these parties win seats in such districts, producing an upward pressure on $p$.

For simple nationwide districts, $p = M^{.5}$ provides a good fit. But for districts within systems made up of several districts, $p > M^{.5}$, according to a factor that corrects for assembly size (Taagepera and Shugart 1992a), *provided that the system is parliamentary*. The general form for all these expressions is

$$p = M^k, \tag{B.1}$$

where $k$ is an exponent that depends on specific institutional features of the political system. If there is only one district and the system is parliamentary, $k = .5$, such that

$$p = M^{.5}. \tag{B.2}$$

If there are several districts in a parliamentary system, the value of $k$ must take account of the size of the national assembly of which any given district is one component:

$$k = 1/[q + (M/S)^{1/lnS}], \tag{B.3}$$

where $q$ is a factor that reduces $k$ to its basic value for a district when there is no nationwide effect to consider and $S$ is the total number of seats in the assembly. For parliamentary systems, in order to get back to $k = .5$, $q = 1$. (The derivation of this exponent is given in the appendix of Taagepera and Shugart 1992a). For the usual range of assembly sizes ($50 < S < 500$), the value of Equation B.3 changes little with $S$, for $M < 30$. For larger $M$, most cases are countries in which there is one single nationwide district, hence $S = M$. Since there is little effect of $S$, we can simplify the previous equation by introducing a median value of $S$. We then get

$$k = 1/[q + .37M^{.2}], \tag{B.4}$$

which is the exact value when $S = 148$, or around the median $S$ observed worldwide. The above considerations for values of $k$ assume parliamentary systems. Our next step then is to determine what $k$ is for presidential systems, or, more precisely, for presidential systems using plurality for the presidency and electing the congress concurrently.

## TESTING THE NUMBER OF PARTIES IN
## PRESIDENTIAL SYSTEMS

If the basic model for the general (parliamentary) case has as its starting point $k = .5$, what should be the starting point for the variant of presidential system considered here? For the number of seat-winning parties, perhaps we should think of the upper limit being the number in the general case, for which let us use the simpler expression $k = .5$, while the lower limit could be $k = 0$, the value that corresponds to $p = 1$ for the single-seat presidency being elected simultaneously.

Such reasoning would suggest an average of these values, such that $k = .25 = \frac{1}{4}$. However, this reasoning implicitly incorporates two further assumptions, which may not be valid. The first, valid in only a few cases, is that the votes for president and congress must be the same. In a few cases these elections are or have been so "fused." For such cases – for example, the Dominican Republic in 1966–74 – $k = \frac{1}{4}$ might apply, provided that the second implicit assumption is met. That assumption is that the two branches are equal in importance.

Now what if the elections for president and congress are not fused, as is usual? Let us hypothesize that, with $p = M^{1/4}$ as the base point for presidential systems (with plurality presidencies and $M > 1$ for the concurrently elected assembly), the value for the congress would tend upward from this point, toward the general expectation for (parliamentary) assemblies. To begin a process of predicting a value for *votes* for the presidency (again, $p$ is obviously 1), we might expect a useful prediction is one that tends down from $p = M^{1/4}$. We now have the following expressions, which are testable:

$$p_c = M^{3/8}, \text{ and} \tag{B.5}$$

$$p_p = M^{1/8}, \tag{B.6}$$

where $p_c$ is the number of seat-winning parties in a district for congress and $p_p$ is a fictitious "presidential seat-winning parties," which we will use to derive an expression for $N_v$. It might be useful to think of $p_p$ as the number of parties that would win seats in the congressional district were the presidential votes used to allocate assembly seats in that district (assuming, of course, that the votes would be unchanged if this took place).

The model for $p_c$ was tested in Figure 11.1. The largest cluster of points is indeed below what is found for $p$ in the general case (cf. Taagepera and Shugart 1992a). Figure 11.1 also shows an expression that curves upward from Equation B.5. This is an adjustment that takes into account that we are dealing (again, in all but a few cases) with several districts within a larger nation, rather than a single (nationwide) district. The form of the adjustment is precisely what is done for the general case in Taagepera and Shugart. For the upward curve, we use the value of $k$ in Equation B.4, with

$q$ set at 1.67, the value it must be if the expression is to reduce to $k = .25$ when $M = S$, as the simpler expression assumes.

The expression that fits better is the one adjusted for the effects of nationwide politics on individual districts. This is the the upward bowed curve shown in Figure 11.1. Thus the existence of several districts matters in the assembly of presidential systems to the same degree as in parliamentary systems, even though the values themselves are indeed lower, owing to the concurrence of a plurality presidential election. Another way of putting this result is that in presidential systems with the electoral format being considered here nationwide politics matters twice: once in the form of the presidential race and again in the form of nationwide politics for the assembly.

Before returning to the number of presidential parties, let us continue with the congress. Using a set of equations derived in Taagepera and Shugart (1992a,b), we can proceed to predictions of the relationship between *effective* parties and magnitude in the assemblies of presidential systems. Each equation is independent of the connection between $p$ and $M$. They predict an average relation between $p$ and the share of the largest party, and between this latter quantity and the effective number of parties.[1] Following the steps in Taagepera and Shugart, we get the following predicted expression for $N_s$:

$$N_s = M^{9/32} = M^{.28}. \tag{B.7}$$

The form of this equation is $N_s = M^{.75k}$, and is thus lower than the simplest expression derived in Taagepera and Shugart for parliamentary systems, which is $N_s = M^{3/8} = M^{.375}$. The expressions both for parliamentary and for presidential systems are empirically slightly too low for their respective data sets; this is because they do not incorporate the correction for national politics. The correction, defining $k$ as in Equation B.4, is shown as the upward curve in Figure B.1, along with Equation B.7.

A final step for the congressional party system is to derive a prediction for $N_v$. Again using equations derived by Taagepera and Shugart,[2] we get a prediction that is approximately

$$N_v = 1.5M^{.21}. \tag{B.8}$$

This is the lower line shown in Figure 11.3. For the data shown, this expression appears to be too low, although the slope is credible. Perhaps a better fit would be $N_v = 1.7M^{.21}$; however, we shall stick with the theoretically derived expression. Most of the data points are from Venezuela, which would be expected to have higher values of $N_v$. The reason for this is a provision for additional seats for "vanity parties" (Shugart 1988), allowing any party that accumulates about 0.55% of the votes nationwide to win

---

1 These equations, each of which is justified theoretically and tested empirically in Taagepera and Shugart, are $s_1 = p^{-.5}$, where $s_1$ is the share of seats for the largest party, and $N_s = s_1^{-1.5}$.
2 Here the equations are $v_1 = (s_1 M - 1)/(M - 1)$ and $N_v = v_1^{-1.5}$.

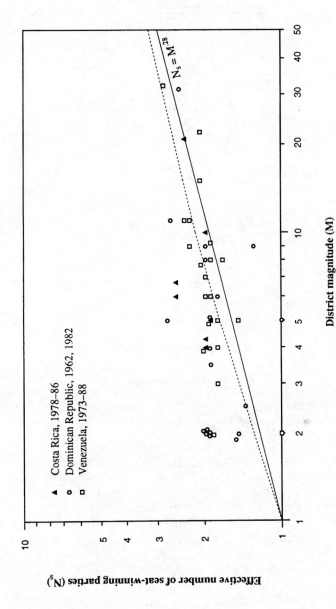

Figure B.1. District magnitude and effective number of seat-winning parties, Costa Rica, Dominican Republic, and Venezuela

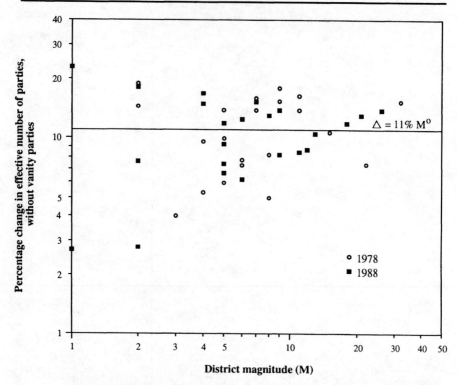

Figure B.2. District magnitude and percentage change in effective number of parties, without vanity parties, 1978 and 1988

a seat. Because the Venezuelan party system can be broken down into vanity parties, which compete only for nationwide seats, and all other parties, which compete for district-level seats, it is possible to remove their votes "experimentally" from the district-by-district totals.

Figure B.2 shows the percent difference in $N_v$ with and without vanity parties graphed against district magnitude. The figure shows that there is no relation between $M$ and the extent to which voters who prefer a vanity party cast a vote for such a party; because the only hope for these parties and their voters to win a seat is through the nationwide allocation, vanity parties' votes are not influenced by within-district factors. (Votes for those minor parties which *do* win district seats, such as those for Venezuela's third-largest party, MAS, are indeed influenced by $M$, as shown in Shugart 1988.)

Figure B.2 shows that the average difference in $N_v$ when vanity parties' votes are set aside is about 11%. The percent difference between Equation B.8, above, and what was identified as an empirical best fit (with intercept 1.7) is 11.8%. Our goal was to develop an expression for $N_v$ that would predict the likely number of parties in the congressional *districts* of presidential systems using concurrent elections and plurality rule for the presidency. When we remove the votes for parties in Venezuela that would certainly not compete without the extremely permissive provision for *nationwide* seats, we must declare our task quite successful indeed.

### Presidential parties

If we return to Equation B.6, we find an expression for the number of presidential parties, which we expect to be lower than the number of congressional parties. Equation B.6 obviously predicts only one seat-winning party, plus a fractional "party" even at very high magnitudes (when $M = 100$, $p_p = 1.8$). Recall that this is the actual (not effective) number of seat-winning parties that would be predicted if the votes that were cast for presidency were used to allocate $M$ seats within the district. It is apparent that following the procedures used in Taagepera and Shugart and briefly summarized above would predict unrealistically low values for $N$. A solution can be devised if we ask ourselves, what is the expected number of vote-winning parties ($p_v$) when the number of seat-winning parties is one (as it must be for an $M = 1$ presidential election)? The answer, of course, is two, as predicted by Duverger. Thus, for this simplest of all districts, which is $M = 1$ nationwide, let us use $p_v = 2p_p$. Substituting $p_v$ for $p$ in the equations of Taagepera and Shugart,[3] we get the following estimate for $N_p$, the effective number of presidential candidates:

$$N_p = 1.68M^{.09}. \qquad (B.9)$$

As with the expression for $N_v$, above, a better fit would be higher. Votes for vanity parties, unlike votes for parties that actually compete for district seats, are not significantly different for president than for congress; thus the same adjustment made for congressional $N$ could be made for presidential $N$. If this were made, the points for Venezuela would fall in line with the derived expression, which is expected to work for presidential systems in which all congressional seats are allocated in districts.

Equations B.8 and B.9 above suggest a curious aspect of concurrent elections in countries that use PR for their assemblies, the class of democracies for which they were developed. The prediction at $M = 1$ for the effective number of parties in the congressional election is actually lower (albeit not by much) than the prediction for the presidential election in that district, 1.5 to 1.7. Is this feasible? Perhaps it is, if we remember that the reason that there are multiple presidential candidates even though only two are "serious" is that there are many districts within the country with $M > 1$. In other words, once again we must incorporate an effect of national poli-

---

3 This means using $v_1 = p_v^{-.5}$ and, as before, $N_v = v_1^{-1.5}$.

tics in a district. If some voters' first choice is for one of these third parties, they may cast their protest votes for such parties' presidential candidates. At the same time, however, they may prefer to support a candidate with a chance of winning their own congressional district, for whatever advantages might accrue to the district from having its local member of congress. This suggests the possibility of some "reverse splitting" in the smallest districts (when $M = 2$ as well as when $M = 1$). Because the theoretical predictions are so close, they cannot be sorted out empirically; study would have to rest upon access to actual ballot papers to see the incidence of such reverse splits.[4] It is at least plausible, therefore, for the two curves to cross each other.

4 An alternative possibility is to use an assumption for congressional elections that is analogous to that used for presidential: that when $p_c < 2$, $p_v = 2p$. This would predict a flattening of the curve for $N_v$ at values of $M < 5$, such that $N_v = 1.7 = N_p$ when $M = 1$. Since the issue can not be disentangled empirically, owing to the small differences in the expressions' predictions, we will stay with the simpler equation presented in the text. It is possible, however, that the question of which expression is more pertinent might depend on the extent to which voters perceive advantages to casting an effective vote for a district representative. The more important the district is (in addition to the relative importance of the congress vis-à-vis the president), the greater would be the incentive for reverse splitting for those voters whose first preference, as expressed in their presidential vote, is for a minor party.

# Bibliography

Ames, Barry. 1987. *Political Survival in Latin America*. Berkeley: University of California Press.

Amy, Douglas. Forthcoming. *Real Elections*.

Anckar, Dag. 1984. "Presidential Elections in Finland: A Plea for Approval Voting." *Electoral Studies* 3:125–38.

Archer, Ronald P. 1989. "The Transition from Traditional to Broker Clientelism in Colombia: Political Stability and Social Unrest." Paper presented at the Annual Meeting of the Latin American Studies Association, Miami, Florida. December 4–6.

Archer, Ronald P., and Marc W. Chernick. 1988. "El Presidente frente a las Instituciones Nacionales." In *La Democracia en Blanco y Negro: Colombia en los Años Ochenta*. Bogotá: Fondo Editorial CEREC.

Argentina. 1987. Consejo para la Consolidacion de la Democracia, *Reforma Constitucional: Segundo dictamen del Consejo para la Consolidación de la Democracia*. Buenos Aires.

Arrow, Kenneth. 1951. *Social Choice and Individual Values*. New Haven, Conn.: Yale University Press.

Arter, David. 1981. "Kekkonen's Finland: Enlightened Despotism or Consensual Democracy?" *Western European Politics* 4:219–34.

Arter, David. 1985. "Government in Finland: A 'Semi-presidential System?" *Parliamentary Affairs* 38:472–95.

Asian–African Legal Consultative Committee (New Delhi), Secretariat. 1968. *Constitutions of Asian Countries*. Bombay: N. M. Trpathi Private Ltd.

Bagehot, Walter. 1966. *The English Constitution*. Ithaca, N.Y.: Cornell University Press.

Barbera, Augusto. 1990. "Un'alternativa neoparlamentare al presidenzialismo." *Democrazia e Diritto* 2.

Batlle y Ordoñez, José. 1911. "El P.E. Colegiado." In *El Día*. Montevideo, Uruguay.

Berglund, Sten, and Ingemar Wörlund. 1990. "The Impact of Electoral Reform: A Scandinavian Comparative Perspective." Paper prepared for presentation at the Western Political Science Association Annual Meeting, Newport Beach, California, March 22–4.

Birnbaum, Jeffrey H., and Allan S. Murray. 1987. *Showdown at Gucci Gulch: Lawmakers, Lobbyists, and the Unlikely Triumph of Tax Reform*. New York: Random House.

Blaustein, Albert P., and Gisbert H. Flanz, eds. 1971–present. *Constitutions of the Countries of the World*. Dobbs Ferry, N.Y.: Oceana Publications.

Blondel, Jean. 1984. "Dual Leadership in the Contemporary World: A Step Towards Executive and Regime Stability?" In *Comparative Government and Politics: Essays in Honour of S. E. Finer,* edited by Dennis Kavanagh and Gillian Peele. Boulder Colo.: Westview Press.

Blondel, Jean, and Waldino C. Suárez. 1981. "Las Limitaciones Institucionales del Sistema Presidencialista," *Criterio* (Buenos Aires), February 26, pp. 57–71.

Boyer, Yves. 1986. "French Foreign Policy: Alignment and Assertiveness." *The Washington Quarterly* 9:5–14.

Brager, Stephen. 1990. "The Chilean Elections of 1989: An Account, an Analysis, and a Forecast for the Future." Unpublished.

Brams, Stephen J. 1989. "Are the Two Houses of Congress Coequal?" In *The Federalist Papers and the New Institutionalism,* edited by Bernard Grofman and Donald Wittman. New York: Agathon Press.

Bruneau, Thomas C., and Alex Macleod. 1986. *Politics in Contemporary Portugal.* Boulder, Colo.: Lynne Rienner.

Cain, Bruce, John Ferejohn, and Morris Fiorina. 1987. *The Personal Vote.* Cambridge, Mass.: Harvard University Press.

Cain, Bruce E., and W. T. Jones. 1989. "Madison's Theory of Representation." In *The Federalist Papers and the New Institutionalism,* edited by Bernard Grofman and Donald Wittman. New York: Agathon Press.

Cameron, Maxwell. 1991. " 'Rational Resignations.' Coalition Building in Peru and the Philippines." *Comparative Political Studies.* Forthcoming.

Campbell, Angus, Phillip E. Converse, Warren E. Miller, and Donald E. Stokes. 1964. *The American Voter.* New York: Wiley.

Carey, John M. 1992. "Premier-Presidentialism: The Third Alternative?" In *Presidentialism and Democracy,* edited by Matthew S. Shugart and Scott Mainwaring. Forthcoming.

Carter, J. R., and D. Schap. 1987. "Executive Veto, Legislative Override, and Structure Induced Equilibrium." *Public Choice* 52:227–44.

Cater, Douglass. 1964. *Power in Washington.* New York: Random House.

Chappel, Henry W., and William R. Keech. 1989. "Electoral Institutions in the Federalist Papers: A Contemporary Perspective." In *The Federalist Papers and the New Institutionalism,* edited by Bernard Grofman and Donald Wittman. New York: Agathon Press.

Conaghan, Catherine. 1989. "Loose Parties, Floating Politicians, and Institutional Stress: Presidentialism in Ecuador, 1979–88." Paper presented to the Research Symposium, "Presidential or Parliamentary Democracy: Does It Make a Difference?," Georgetown University, Washington, D.C., May 14–16.

Conaghan, Catherine M., James M. Malloy, and Luis A. Abugattas. 1990. "Business and the Boys: The Origins of Neo-Liberalism in the Central Andes." *Latin American Research Review* 25:3–30.

Coppedge, Michael. 1988. *Strong Parties and Lame Ducks: A Study of the Quality and Stability of Venezuelan Democracy.* Ph.D. dissertation, Yale University.

Coppedge, Michael. 1992. "Venezuela: Democratic Despite Presidentialism." In *Presidential or Parliamentary Democracy: Does it Make a Difference?,* edited by Juan J. Linz and Arturo Valenzuela. Baltimore: Johns Hopkins University Press.

Cox, Gary. 1987. *The Efficient Secret.* New York: Cambridge University Press.

Cox, Gary, and Mathew McCubbins. 1992. *Parties and Committees in the House of Representatives.* Berkeley: University of California Press.

Craig, Ann L., and Wayne Cornelius. 1991. "Houses Divided: Parties and Political Reform in Mexico." In *Building Democratic Institutions: Parties and Party*

*Systems in Latin America,* edited by Scott Mainwaring and Timothy R. Scully. Forthcoming.

Cuba. 1940. *Constitución de la República de Cuba.* Havana, Cuba: Compañía Editoria de Libros y Folletos O'Reilly.

de Gaulle, Charles. 1969. "The Bayeux Manifesto." In *Politics in Europe,* edited by Arend Lijphart. Englewood Cliffs, N.J.: Prentice Hall.

Diamond, Larry, Juan J. Linz, and Seymour M. Lipset. 1989. *Democracy in Developing Countries.* 4 vols. Boulder, Colo.: Lynne Rienner.

DiBacco, Thomas V. 1977. *Presidential Power in Latin American Politics.* New York: Praeger.

Di Palma, Giuseppe. 1990. *To Craft Democracies.* Berkeley: University of California Press.

Dix, Robert H. 1967. *Colombia: The Political Dimensions of Change.* New Haven, Conn.: Yale University Press.

Dix, Robert H. 1980. "Consociational Democracy: The Case of Colombia." *Comparative Politics* 12:303–21.

Drake, Paul. 1978. *Socialism and Populism in Chile.* Urbana: University of Illinois Press.

Duverger, Maurice. 1951. *Les Partis Politiques.* Paris: Le Seuil.

Duverger, Maurice. 1954. *Political Parties: Their Organization and Activity in the Modern State,* translated by Barbara and Robert North. New York: Wiley.

Duverger, Maurice. 1980. "A New Political System Model: Semi-presidential Government." *European Journal of Political Research* 8:165–87.

Duverger, Maurice. 1984. "Which Is the Best Electoral System?" In *Choosing an Electoral System,* edited by Arend Lijphart and Bernard Grofman. New York: Praeger.

Duverger, Maurice. 1986. "Duverger's Law Thirty Years Later." In *Electoral Laws and Their Political Consequences,* edited by Bernard Grofman and Arend Lijphart. New York: Agathon Press.

Epstein, Leon. 1967. *Political Parties in Western Democracies.* New Brunswick, N.J.: Transaction Books.

Erikson, Robert. 1988. "The Puzzle of Midterm Loss." *Journal of Politics* 50:1011–29.

Ertekun, M. Necati Munir. 1984. *The Cyprus Dispute and the Birth of the Turkish Republic of Northern Cyprus.* Nicosia: K. Rustem.

Eulau, Heinz, and Kenneth Prewitt. 1973. *Labyrinths of Democracy.* Indianapolis: Bobbs-Merrill.

Evans de la Cuadra, Enrique. 1970. *Relación de la Constitución Política de la República de Chile.* Santiago: Editorial Jurídica de Chile.

*Federalist Papers, The.* 1961. (Alexander Hamilton, James Madison, and John Jay), edited by Clinton Rossiter. New York: New American Library.

Fiorina, Morris P. 1981. *Retrospective Voting in American National Elections.* New Haven, Conn.: Yale University Press.

Fiorina, Morris P. 1982. "Group Concentration and the Delegation of Legislative Authority." California Institute of Technology, Social Science Working Paper No. 112.

Ford, Henry James. 1898. *The Rise and Growth of American Politics: A Sketch of Constitutional Development.* New York: Macmillan.

Gamarra, Eduardo A. 1987. *Political Stability, Democratization, and the Bolivian National Congress.* Ph.D. dissertation, University of Pittsburgh.

Gamarra, Eduardo A. 1990. "Bolivia's Perestroika?" *Hemisphere* 2:16–19.

Gamarra, Eduardo A. 1992. "Hybrid-Presidentialism and Democratization: The Case of Bolivia." In *Presidentialism and Democracy,* edited by Scott Mainwaring and Matthew S. Shugart. Forthcoming.

García Laguardia, Jorge Mario, and Edmundo Vásquez Martínez. 1984. *Constitución y orden democrático.* Guatemala City: Editorial Universitaria de Guatemala.

Geddes, Barbara. 1990. "Democratic Institutions as a Bargain Among Self-Interested Politicians." Paper prepared for presentation at the Annual Meeting of the American Political Science Association, San Francisco.

Geddes, Barbara. 1991. "A Game Theoretic Model of Reform in Latin American Democracies." *American Political Science Review* 85:371–92.

Gibson, William M. 1948. *The Constitutions of Colombia.* Durham, N.C.: Duke University Press.

Gillespie, Charles G. 1989. "Presidential–Parliamentary Relations and the Problems of Democratic Stability: The Case of Uruguay." Unpublished.

González, Luís E. 1989. "Presidentialism, Party Systems and Democratic Stability: The Uruguayan Case." Unpublished.

Grofman, Bernard N. 1987. "Will the Real New Institutionalism Stand Up and Take a Bow." Unpublished.

Grofman, Bernard N. 1989. "The Federalist Papers and the New Institutionalism: An Overview." In *The Federalist Papers and the New Institutionalism,* edited by Bernard Grofman and Donald Wittman. New York: Agathon Press.

Gunther, Richard. 1989. "Electoral Laws, Party Systems, and Elites: The Case of Spain." *American Political Science Review* 83:835–58.

Halperin, S. William. 1963. *Germany Tried Democracy: A Political History of the Reich from 1918 to 1933.* Hamden, Conn.: Archon Books.

Hartlyn, Jonathan. 1987. *The Politics of Coalition Rule in Colombia.* New York: Cambridge University Press.

Hartlyn, Jonathan. 1989. "Presidentialism and Colombian Politics." Paper presented to the Research Symposium, "Presidential or Parliamentary Democracy: Does It Make a Difference?," Georgetown University, Washington, D.C., May 14–16.

Heise Gonzalez, Julio. 1974. *Historia de Chile: El período parlamentario, 1861–1925.* Santiago: Editoriales Andrés Bello.

Herman, Edward S., and Frank Brodhead. 1984. *Demonstration Elections.* Boston: South End Press.

Herman, Valentine, and John Pope. 1973. "Minority Governments in Western Democracies." *British Journal of Political Science* 3:191–212.

Hess, Stephen. 1988. *Organizing the Presidency.* Washington D.C.: Brookings Institution.

Hogan, James. 1945. *Elections and Representation.* Cork, Ireland: Cork University Press.

Horowitz, Donald. 1990. "Comparing Democratic Systems." *Journal of Democracy* 1:73–9.

Horowitz, Donald. 1991. *A Democratic South Africa? Constitutional Engineering in a Divided Society.* Berkeley: University of California Press.

Hucko, Elmar, ed. 1987. *The Democratic Tradition: Four German Constitutions.* New York: Berg/St. Martin's Press.

Huntington, Samuel. 1991. "Democracy's Third Wave." *Journal of Democracy* 2:12–34.

Jacobson, Gary C. 1990. *The Electoral Origins of Divided Government: Competition in U.S. House Elections, 1946–1988.* Boulder, Colo.: Westview Press.

Kaminsky, Elijah Ben-Zion. 1989. "The Executive: Stable Governments, Changeable Institutions." Paper delivered at the APSA Annual Meeting, September.

Karl, Terry L. 1986. "Petroleum and Political Pacts: The Transition to Democracy in Venezuela." In *Transitions from Authoritarian Rule: Latin America,* edited by Guillermo O'Donnell, Philippe C. Schmitter, and Laurence Whitehead. Baltimore: Johns Hopkins University Press.

Kelley, R. Lynn. 1977. "Venezuelan Constitutional Forms and Realities." In *Venezuela: The Democratic Experience,* edited by John D. Martz and David J. Myers. New York: Praeger.

Kelsen, Hans. 1945. *General Theory of Law and State,* Part 2. Cambridge: Harvard University Press.

Kernell, Samuel. 1977. "Presidential Popularity and Negative Voting: An Alternative Explanation of the Midterm Decline of the Presidential Party." *American Political Science Review* 71:44–66.

Kernell, Samuel. 1986. *Going Public: New Strategies of Presidential Leadership.* Washington D.C.: Congressional Quarterly Press.

Ketchman, Ralph, ed. 1986. *The Anti-Federalist Papers: and, The Constitutional Convention Debates.* New York: New American Library.

Kiewiet, Roderick, and Mathew McCubbins. 1985. "Appropriations Decisions as a Bilateral Bargaining Game Between President and Congress." *Legislative Studies Quarterly* 9:181–202.

Kiewiet, Roderick, and Mathew McCubbins. 1991. *The Logic of Delegation: Congressional Parties and the Appropriations Process.* Chicago: University of Chicago Press.

Kirchheimer, Otto. 1969. "Weimar – And What Then? An Analysis of a Constitution" (1930), and "Constitutional Reaction in 1932" (1932). In Otto Kirchheimer, *Politics, Law, and Social Change,* edited by Frederic S. Burin and Kurt L. Shell. New York: Columbia University Press.

Kyriakides, Stanley. 1968. *Cyprus: Constitutionalism and Crisis Government.* Philadelphia: University of Pennsylvania Press.

Laakso, Markku, and Rein Taagepera. 1979. "Effective Number of Parties: A Measure with Application to West Europe." *Comparative Political Studies* 12:3–27.

Lepsius, M. Ranier. 1978. "From Fragmented Party Democracy to Government by Emergency Decree and National Socialist Takeover: Germany." In *The Breakdown of Democratic Regimes,* edited by Juan J. Linz and Alfred Stepan. Baltimore: Johns Hopkins University Press.

Levine, Daniel H. 1973. *Conflict and Political Change in Venezuela.* Princeton N.J.: Princeton University Press.

Libai, David, Uriel Lynn, Amnon Rubinstein, and Yoash Tsiddon. 1991. *Changing The System of Government in Israel – Proposed Basic Law: The Government.* Jerusalem: The Jerusalem Center for Public Affairs and The Public Committee for a Constitution for Israel.

Lijphart, Arend. 1977. *Democracy in Plural Societies: A Comparative Exploration.* New Haven, Conn.: Yale University Press.

Lijphart, Arend. 1984. *Democracies: Patterns of Majoritarian and Consensus Government in Twenty-one Countries.* New Haven, Conn.: Yale University Press.

Lijphart, Arend. 1989. "Presidentialism and Majoritarian Democracy: Theoretical Observations." Paper presented to the Research Symposium, "Presidential or Parliamentary Democracy: Does It Make a Difference?," Georgetown University, Washington, D.C., May 14–16.

Lijphart, Arend. 1990a. "Six Lessons For Latin America." *Government and Opposition* 25:68–84.

Lijphart, Arend. 1990b. "The Political Consequences of Electoral Laws, 1945–85." *American Political Science Review* 84:481–96.

Lijphart, Arend. 1991. "The Alternative Vote: A Realistic Alternative for South Africa?" *Politikon: The South African Journal of Political Science.* Forthcoming.

Lijphart, Arend, and Ronald Rogowski. 1991. "Separation of Powers and the Management of Political Cleavages." In *Political Institutions and their Consequences,* edited by Kent Weaver and Bert Rockman. Washington, D.C.: Brookings Institution.

Linz, Juan J. 1978. "Crisis, Breakdown and Reequilibration." In *The Breakdown of Democratic Regimes,* edited by Juan J. Linz and Alfred Stepan. Baltimore: Johns Hopkins University Press.

Linz, Juan J. 1987. "Democracy, Presidential or Parliamentary: Does It Make a Difference?" Unpublished.

Linz, Juan J. 1990. "The Perils of Presidentialism." *Journal of Democracy* 1:51–69.

Linz, Juan J. and Alfred Stepan. 1978. *The Breakdown of Democratic Regimes.* Baltimore: Johns Hopkins University Press.

Linz, Juan J., and Arturo Valenzuela, eds. 1992. *Presidential or Parliamentary Democracy: Does It Make a Difference?* Baltimore: Johns Hopkins University Press.

Lipset, Seymour M. 1990. "The Centrality of Political Culture." *Journal of Democracy* 1:80–3.

Loosemore, John, and Victor J. Hanby. 1971. "The Theoretical Limits of Maximum Distortion." *British Journal of Political Science* 1:467–77.

Lowi, Theodore J. 1979. *The End of Liberalism: The Second Republic of the United States.* New York: Norton.

Mackie, Thomas T., and Richard Rose. 1991. *The International Almanac of Electoral History,* 3rd ed. Washington, D.C.: Congressional Quarterly.

Mainwaring, Scott. 1989. "Presidentialism in Latin America: A Review Essay." *Latin American Reseach Review* 25:157–79.

Mainwaring, Scott. 1991. "Politicians, Parties, and Electoral Systems: Brazil in Comparative Perspective." *Comparative Politics,* [October]:21–43.

Mainwaring, Scott. 1992a. "Presidentialism, Multiparty Systems, and Democracy: The Difficult Equation." *Comparative Political Studies.* Forthcoming.

Mainwaring, Scott. 1992b. "Institutional Dilemmas of Multiparty Presidential Democracy: The Case of Brazil." In *Presidentialism and Democracy,* edited by Scott Mainwaring and Matthew S. Shugart. Forthcoming.

Malloy, James M., and Eduardo A. Gamarra. 1987. "The Transition to Democracy in Boliva. In *Authoritarians and Democrats: Regime Transition in Latin America,* edited by James M. Malloy and Mitchell A. Seligson. Pittsburgh: University of Pittsburgh Press.

March, James G., and Johan P. Olsen. 1984. "New Institutionalism: Organizational Factors in Political Life." *American Political Science Review* 78:734–49.

Marotta, Daniel. 1985. *El Uruguay y el Segundo Colegiado.* Montevideo: IDEAS.

Martz, John D. 1966. *Acción Democrática: Evolution of a Modern Political Party.* Princeton, N.J.: Princeton University Press.

McCoy, Terry L. 1971. "Congress, the President, and Political Instability in Peru." In *Latin American Legislatures: Their Role and Influence,* edited by Weston H. Agor. New York: Praeger.

McCubbins, Mathew, and Thomas Schwartz. 1984. "Congressional Oversight Overlooked: Police Patrols Versus Fire Alarms." *American Journal of Political Science* 28:165–79.

McCubbins, Mathew, and Frances Rosenbluth. 1992. "Electoral Structure and the Organization of Policymaking in Japan." Unpublished.

McDonald, Ronald H., and J. Mark Ruhl. 1989. *Party Politics and Elections in Latin America.* Boulder, Colo.: Westview Press.

McKelvey, Richard D. 1976. "Intransitivities in Multidimensional Voting Models: Some Implications for Agenda Control." *Journal of Economic Theory* 12:131, 472–82.

Miller, Gary J., and Thomas H. Hammond. 1989. "Stability and Efficiency in a Separation-of-Powers Constitutional System." In *The Federalist Papers and the New Institutionalism,* edited by Bernard Grofman and Donald Wittman. New York: Agathon Press.

Moe, Terry M. 1987. "An Assessment of the Positive Theory of 'Congressional Dominance.' " *Legislative Studies Quarterly* 12:475–520.

Moe, Terry M. 1989. "The Politics of Bureaucratic Structure." In *Can the Government Govern?,* edited by John E. Chubb and Paul Peterson. Washington, D.C.: Brookings Institution.

Montesquieu, Charles de Secondat, baron de. 1989. *The Spirit of the Laws.* New York: Cambridge University Press.

Needler, Martin. 1959. "The Theory of the Weimar Presidency." *The Review of Politics* 21:692–8.

Needler, Martin. 1965. "Cabinet Responsibility in a Presidential System: The Case of Peru." *Parliamentary Affairs* 18:156–61.

Neumann, Franz. 1942. *Behemoth: The Structure and Practice of National Socialism.* New York: Oxford University Press.

Neustadt, Richard E. 1960. *Presidential Power, the Politics of Leadership.* New York: Wiley.

Nogueira Alcala, Humberto. 1986a. *El régimen semipresidencial: Una nueva forma de gobierno democrático?* Santiago: Editorial Andante.

Nogueira Alcala, Humberto. 1986b. *Teoría y práctica democrática.* Santiago: Editorial Andante.

Nousiainen, Jaakko. 1988. "Bureaucratic Tradition, Semi-presidential Rule and Parliamentary Government: The Case of Finland." *European Journal of Political Research* 16:221–49.

Opello, Walter C. 1985. *"Portugal's Political Development.* Boulder, Colo.: Westview Press.

Opello, Walter C. 1986. "Portugal's Parliament: "An Organizational Analysis of Legislative Performance." *Legislative Studies Quarterly* 11:291–319.

Ordeshook, Peter. 1986. *Game Theory and Political Theory.* New York: Cambridge University Press.

Pak, Chi-Young. 1980. *Political Opposition in Korea, 1945–1960.* Seoul, Republic of Korea: Seoul University Press.

Pennock, Roland. 1979. *Democratic Political Theory.* Princeton, N.J.: Princeton University Press.

Perera, N. M. 1979. *Critical Analysis of the New Constitution of the Sri Lanka Government.* Colombo: V. S. Raja.

Petracca, Marc P. 1989. "The Distribution of Power in the Federal Government: Perspectives from *The Federalist Papers* – A Critique." In *The Federalist Papers and the New Institutionalism,* edited by Bernard Grofman and Donald Wittman. New York: Agathon Press.

Peirce, Neal R., and Lawrence D. Longley. 1981. *The People's President: The Electoral College in American History and the Direct Vote Alternative.* New Haven, Conn.: Yale University Press.

Pierce, Roy. 1990. "The Executive Divided Against Itself: France 1986–1988." Paper presented at the Annual Meeting of the American Political Science Association, San Francisco.

Pinoargote, Alfredo. 1982. *La república de papel.* Guayaquil, Ecuador: Artes Gráficas Senefelder.

Pitkin, Hannah. 1967. *The Concept of Representation.* Berkeley: University of California Press.

Polsby, Nelson. 1983. *Consequences of Party Reform.* New York: Oxford University Press.

Polyviou, Polyvios G. 1980. *Cyprus: Conflict and Negotiation, 1960–1980.* London: Duckworth.

Powell, G. Bingham, Jr. 1982. *Contemporary Democracies: Participation, Stability, and Violence.* Cambridge, Mass.: Harvard University Press.

Powell, G. Bingham, Jr. 1989. "Constitutional Design and Citizen Electoral Control." *Journal of Theoretical Politics* 1:107–30.

Prothro, James W., and Patricio E. Chapparo. 1974. "Public Opinion and the Movement of the Chilean Government to the Left, 1952–72." *Journal of Politics* 36:2–34.

Rae, Douglas W. 1967. *The Political Consequences of Electoral Laws.* New Haven, Conn.: Yale University Press.

Ranney, Austin. 1962. *The Doctrine of Responsible Party Government.* Urbana: University of Illinois Press.

Rasmussen, Eric. 1989. *Games and Information: An Introduction to Game Theory.* New York: Blackwell.

Riker, William H. 1967. *The Theory of Political Coalitions.* New Haven, Conn.: Yale University Press.

Riker, William H. 1982a. *Liberalism Against Populism: A Confrontation Between the Theory of Democracy and the Theory of Social Choice.* San Francisco: W. H. Freeman.

Riker, William H. 1982b. "The Two-Party System and Duverger's Law: An Essay on the History of Political Science." *American Political Science Review* 76:753–66.

Ripley, Randall, and Grace Franklin. 1980. *Congress, the Bureaucracy, and Public Policy.* Homewood, Ill.: Dorsey Press.

Robinson, Donald L., ed. 1985. *Reforming American Government.* Boulder, Colo.: Westview Press.

Rogowski, Ronald. 1990. "Comment on 'Separation of Powers and the Management of Political Cleavages' by Arend Lijphart" (draft). February.

Rohde, David, and Dennis Simons. 1985. "Presidential Vetoes and Congressional Responsibility." *American Journal of Political Science* 29:397–427.

Rose, Richard. 1988. "Presidents and Prime Ministers." *Society* 25:61–7.

Rustow, Dankwart. 1970. "Transitions to Democracy." *Comparative Politics* 2:337–63.

Sartori, Giovanni. 1968. "Political Development and Political Engineering." In vol. 17 of *Public Policy,* edited by J. D. Montgomery and A. O. Hirschman. Cambridge: Cambridge University Press.

Sartori, Giovanni. 1976. *Parties and Political Systems: A Framework for Analysis.* New York: Cambridge University Press.

Sartori, Giovanni. 1992. "Neither Presidentialism nor Parliamentarism." In *Presi-*

*dential or Parliamentary Democracy: Does It Make a Difference?*, edited by Juan J. Linz and Arturo Valenzuela. Baltimore: Johns Hopkins University Press.

Schap, David. 1986. "Executive Veto and Informational Strategy: A Structure-induced Equilibrium Analysis." *American Journal of Political Science* 30:755–70.

Schelling, Thomas C. 1960. *The Strategy of Conflict.* Cambridge, Mass.: Harvard University Press.

Schlesinger, Joseph A., and Mildred Schlesinger. 1991. "The Reaffirmation of a Multiparty System in France." *American Political Science Review* 84:1077–1101.

Scott, Robert E. 1973. "National Integration Problems and Military Regimes in Latin America." *Latin American Modernization Problems*, edited by Robert E. Scott. Chicago: University of Illinois Press.

Shepsle, Kenneth. 1988. "The Changing Textbook Congress: Equilibrium Congressional Institutions and Behavior." Center for American Political Studies Occasional Paper 88–31, Harvard University.

Shugart, Matthew. 1985. "The Two Effects of District Magnitude: Venezuela as a Crucial Experiment." *European Journal of Political Research* 13:353–64.

Shugart, Matthew S. 1988. *Duverger's Rule, District Magnitude, and Presidentialism.* Ph.D. dissertation, University of California, Irvine.

Shugart, Matthew S. 1989. "Electoral Cycles and the Party System in Presidential Democracies." Paper presented to the Research Symposium, "Presidential or Parliamentary Democracy: Does It Make a Difference?," Georgetown University, Washington, D.C., May 14–16.

Shugart, Matthew S. 1992a. "Leaders, Rank and File, and Constituents: Electoral Reform in Colombia and Venezuela." *Electoral Studies.* Forthcoming.

Shugart, Matthew S. 1992b. "Guerrillas and Elections: An Institutionalist Perspective on the Costs of Conflict and Competition." *International Studies Quarterly* 36:121–52.

Shugart, Matthew S., and Raul A. Fernandez. 1991. "Constitutional Reform and Economic Restructuring in Colombia." Paper presented at the Annual Meeting of the North American Association of Colombianists, Ibagué, Colombia, August.

Shugart, Matthew S., and Rein Taagepera. 1992. "Majority Versus Plurality Election of Presidents: A Proposal for a 'Double Complement Rule.' " Unpublished.

Sigler, Jay A., Albert Blaustein, and Gisbert H. Flanz. 1981. "Chile." In vol. 5 of *Constitutions of the Countries of the World,* edited by Albert Blaustein and Gisbert Flanz. Dobbs Ferry, N.Y.: Oceana Publications.

Stauffer, Robert B. 1970. "Congress in the Philippine Political System." *Legislatures in Developmental Perspective,* edited by Allan Kornberg and Lloyd D. Musolf. Durham, N.C.: Duke University Press.

Stauffer, Robert B. 1975. *The Philippine Congress: Causes of Structural Change.* Beverley Hills, Calif.: Sage.

Stedman, Murray S., Jr., ed. 1968. *Modernizing American Government: The Demands of Social Change.* Englewood Cliffs, N.J.: Prentice-Hall.

Stockman, David A. 1986. *The Triumph of Politics: How the Reagan Revolution Failed.* New York: Harper & Row.

Stokes, William S. 1949. "The Cuban Parliamentary System in Action, 1940–1947." *Journal of Politics* 11:335–64.

Strom, Kaare. 1986. "Deferred Gratification and Minority Governments in Scandinavia." *Legislative Studies Quarterly* 11:583–605.

Strom, Kaare. 1990. *Minority Government and Majority Rule*. New York: Cambridge University Press.

Suárez, Waldino Cleto. 1982. "El poder ejecutivo en América Latina: su capacidad operativa bajo régimenes presidencialistas de gobierno." *Revista de Estudios Políticos*, 29:109–44.

Suleiman, Ezra N. 1981. "Presidential Government in France." In *Presidents and Prime Ministers*, edited by Richard Rose and Ezra Suleiman. Washington D.C.: American Enterprise Institute.

Suleiman, Ezra N. 1986. "Toward the Disciplining of Parties and Legislators." In *Parliaments and Parliamentarians in Democratic Politics*, edited by Ezra Suleiman. New York: Holmes & Meier.

Suleiman, Ezra N. 1989. "French Presidentialism and Political Stability." Paper presented to the Research Symposium, "Presidential or Parliamentary Democracy: Does It Make a Difference?," Georgetown University, Washington, D.C., May 14–16.

Sundquist, James L. 1981. *The Decline and Resurgence of Congress*. Washington D.C.: Brookings Institution.

Sundquist, James L. 1986. *Constitutional Reform and Effective Government*. Washington D.C.: Brookings Institution.

Taagepera, Rein. 1989. "A Theory of the Number of Parties." Unpublished.

Taagepera, Rein, and Bernard Grofman. 1985. "Rethinking Duverger's Law: Predicting the Effective Number of Parties in Plurality and PR Systems – Parties Minus Issues Equals One." *European Journal of Political Research* 13:341–52.

Taagepera, Rein, and Matthew S. Shugart. 1989. *Seats and Votes: The Effects and Determinants of Electoral Systems*. New Haven, Conn.: Yale University Press.

Taagepera, Rein, and Matthew S. Shugart. 1992a. "Theory of the Number of Parliamentary Parties: A Quantitative Model of Duverger's Mechanical Effect." Unpublished.

Taagepera, Rein, and Matthew S. Shugart. 1992b. "Theory of the Number of Electoral Parties and Deviation from Proportional Representation." Unpublished.

Taylor, Philip. 1960. *Government and Politics in Uruguay*. New Orleans: Tulane University Press.

Therborn, Göran. 1979. "The Travail of Latin American Democracy." *New Left Review* 113:71–109.

Urzua Valenzuela, Germán. 1986. *História Política Electoral de Chile, 1931–1973*. Santiago: Universidad de Chile.

Valenzuela, Arturo. 1978. *The Breakdown of Democratic Regimes: Chile*. Vol. 4 of *The Breakdown of Democratic Regimes*, edited by Juan J. Linz and Alfred Stepan. Baltimore: Johns Hopkins University Press.

Valenzuela, Arturo. 1989a. "Party Politics and the Failure of Presidentialism in Chile: A Proposal for a Parliamentary Form of Government." Paper presented to the Research Symposium, "Presidential or Parliamentary Democracy: Does It Make a Difference?," Georgetown University, Washington, D.C., May 14–16.

Valenzuela, Arturo. 1989b. "Chile: Origins, Consolidation, and Breakdown of a Democratic Regime." In *Democracy in Developing Countries*, Vol 4: *Latin America*, edited by Larry Diamond, Juan J. Linz, and Seymour Martin Lipset. Boulder, Colo.: Lynne Rienner.

Valenzuela, Arturo, and Alexander Wilde. 1979. "Presidential Politics and the Decline of the Chilean Congress." In *Legislatures in Development: Dynamics of Change in New and Old States*, edited by Joel Smith and Lloyd Musolf. Durham: Duke University Press.

Vázquez Carrizosa, Alfredo. 1979. *El Poder Presidencial en Colombia.* Bogotá: Enrique Dobry, Editor.

Veloso Abueva, Jose, and Raul P. de Guzman, eds. 1969. *Foundations and Dynamics of Filipino Government and Politics.* Manila: Bookmark.

Verney, Douglas. 1959. *The Analysis of Political Systems.* London: Compton Printing Works.

Warnapala, W. A. Wiswa. 1980. "Sri Lanka's New Constitution." In *Asian Survey* 20:914–30.

Warnapala, W. A. Wiswa, and L. Dias Hewagama. 1983. *Recent Politics in Sri Lanka: The Presidential Election and the Referendum of 1982.* New Delhi: Navrang.

Weber, Max. 1968. "Parliament and Government in a Reconstructed Germany." In vol. 3 of *Economy and Society,* edited by Guenther Roth and Claus Wittich. New York: Bedminster Press.

Whitehead, Laurence. 1986. "Bolivia's Failed Democratization, 1977–80." In *Transitions from Authoritarian Rule: Latin America,* edited by Guillermo O'Donnell, Philippe C. Schmitter, and Laurence Whitehead. Baltimore: Johns Hopkins University Press.

Wilson, A. Jeyaratnam. 1979. *Politics in Sri Lanka: 1947–1979.* London: Macmillan.

Wood, David M. 1968. "Majority vs. Opposition in the French National Assembly, 1956–65: A Guttman Scale Analysis." *American Political Science Review* 62:88–109.

Zafrullah, H. M. 1981. *Sri Lanka's Hybrid Presidential and Parliamentary System.* Kuala Lumpur: University of Malaya Press.

# Index